The Kagerō Diary

Michigan Monographs in Japanese Studies
Number 19

Center for Japanese Studies
The University of Michigan

The Kagerō Diary

A Woman's Autobiographical Text from Tenth-Century Japan

Translated with an Introduction and Notes
by Sonja Arntzen

Center for Japanese Studies
The University of Michigan
Ann Arbor, 1997

Published by the Center for Japanese Studies, The University of Michigan, 108 Lane Hall, 204 S. State Street, Ann Arbor, MI 48109-1290

Library of Congress Cataloging in Publication Division

Michitsuna no Haha, ca. 935–995.
[Kagerō nikki. English]
The Kagerō diary : a woman's autobiographical text from tenth-century Japan / translated with an introduction and notes by Sonja Arntzen.
xv, 415 p. 23.5 cm. — (Michigan monograph series in Japanese studies ; no. 19)
Includes bibliographical references and index.
ISBN 0-939512-80-7 (cloth : alk. paper). — ISBN 0-939512-81-5 (paper : alk. paper)
1. Michitsuna no Haha—ca. 935–995—Diaries. 2. Authors, Japanese—Heian period, 794–1185—Diaries. I. Arntzen, Sonja, 1945– . II. Title. III. Series.
PL789.F8
895.6'813—dc21
[B] 97–15880
CIP

Jacket and cover illustration: *Tale of Genji Screen* (detail), Japanese, Edo period, early 17th century. One of a pair of six-panel screens, ink, colors, and gold on paper. Asian Art Museum of San Francisco, The Avery Brundage Collection (1991.65.1).

Jacket and cover design: Seiko Semones

This publication meets the ANSI/NISO Standards for Permanence of Paper for Publications and Documents in Libraries and Archives (Z39.48—1992).

Printed in the United States of America

Contents

Illustrations

All photos by the author, Sonja Arntzen.

Preface

The catalyst for the project to create a new translation of the *Kagerō Diary* came from my attending a conference at the University of Calgary in 1986, entitled, "The Effect of the Feminist Approach on Research Methodologies." That conference opened up new fields of vision for me. In a word, what I saw was the possibility in exploring difference. I began to read Virgina Woolf, starting with *A Room of One's Own,* and became intrigued with the question of whether there might be such a thing as a woman's voice, language, and syntax. If such a distinction could be drawn, then classical Japanese literature of the Heian period (794–1185), with its large number of foundational works by women, should be of great interest to the world. Moreover, when I was reading Woolf, I had an eerie sense that she was writing English in a style that had some affinity with the prose style shaped by classical Japanese women authors. At about the same time, I happened to hear the contemporary Canadian author, Daphne Marlatt, reading exceprts from her recently completed autobiographical novel, *Ana Historic,* and was even more struck by how the style of this author, who is very consciously exploring a woman's voice, resonated with what I knew of classical Japanese women's writing.

Further reading brought awareness of questions that were engaging feminist critics, such as the construction of women's "self" in literature and the link between women writers and the autobiographical mode. Here again, Japanese classical literature of the Heian period is fertile material for study since it contains many autobiographical texts by women. As I read through books examining the relation between women and autobiography, I wondered why, except for a chapter by Richard Bowring in Domna Stanton's *The Female Autograph,* the Japanese example was virtually unmentioned.

Intrigued to see whether the sense of similarity between the style of some modern feminist writers and that of Heian Japanese women would hold up under closer scrutiny, I decided to give a close reading to the original of one of the Heian women's diaries, and I picked the *Kagerō Diary* as a place to start. I had not liked the text when I had read it many years ago in English translation, mainly because I thought the author complained too much, but I was aware nonetheless how extraordinary a text it was for its candor and acuteness of psychological observation. It seemed "modern" even though that term is so difficult to define. Contact with the original validated my initial perception of the affinity in women's prose styles across language and time and revealed a text of great beauty and complexity. I realized then that while *The Gossamer Years*, Edward Seidensticker's deft and clear translation of *Kagerō nikki*, conveyed the content of the text, it gave little sense of the style, and perhaps the style was critical. In the style was the material of interest to those engaging in questions of the construction of the female self in literature, the issue of truth and fiction in autobiography, and the distinctiveness of woman's voice and language in literature. A new translation seemed essential.

I have broken with the long and distinguished tradition of translating the *kagerō* of the diary title as "gossamer." Arthur Waley began the tradition by entitling his partial translation of *Kagerō nikki* the "Gossamer Diary" when he appended it to the second volume of his translation of the *Tale of Genji* (*The Sacred Tree* [Boston: Houghton Mifflin, 1926]). Edward Seidensticker followed Waley's lead on the reasonable justification that Waley's "title makes up in poetic worth for what it lacks philologically" (*The Gossamer Years*, p. 8) Recently, Helen McCullough has followed suit with the "Gossamer Journal" as the title for her translation of book one included in her *Classical Japanese Prose: An Anthology* (Stanford University Press, 1990). So why do I now fly in the face of a tradition established by those in the field whom I revere? It is just that I want to retain the complexity of the double meaning of *kagerō*. It means both "mayfly" and "the shimmering of heat waves" and thus stands for both the ephemerality of a life and its insubstantiality. The only way to keep the double meaning was to keep the word in Japanese and explain the complexity with a note. Clearly I cannot resort to this strategy often. If I did, I might as well give up translating entirely and take up a mission instead to teach the rest of the world classical Japanese. In this one instance, however, I trust it may be allowed, and should a non-Japanese reader want to speak about the text to a Japanese person, at least the title will be mutually understood.

As I worked on this translation, my sense of whom I wanted to share the translation with grew beyond specialists in the field of classical Japanese literature and critics interested in women's writing to include my friends, relatives, neighbors, and anyone interested in Japanese culture or literature in general. This has had ramifications on the process of the translation. Feeling a musical orality in the original, I wanted to have the translation sound well when read aloud. Thus, even at the early stages, I have read passages aloud to anyone who would listen. Somehow, due to this process, it has become a translation, I am told, that with its long, run-on sentences looks a little formidable on the page but makes sense when read aloud. Someone at a recent conference where I presented some of the translation even suggested publishing the text with an accompanying tape of it being read. I have not done that, but if, from time to time, readers find that the line of thought in a passage seems hard to follow, I would recommend trying to read it aloud.

When I read passages to listeners, I found myself stopping here and there to supply information and interpretive comments as a way of opening up the listener's appreciation. One of my early listeners, Jane Munro, said, "You should model the notes after the way you are speaking to me right now. They should be a voice in conversation with the reader." This is what led to the current format of the work with the text on the right- and notes on the left-hand page. The reader will find that the text and the notes are two different worlds. The text unfolds in psychological time, slipping between past and present, moving by association from memory to thought to conversation. Emotional states are given more weight and attention than events. The text is disjunctive in the sense that the narrative is constantly being interrupted by poems, the quotation of voices of others, and the intrusion of the author's own thoughts as bits of interior conversation. The notes exist in a more solid, if ultimately equally illusory, world of linear time in which chonology is clarified and names and dates ground the reader. The notes flesh out events only alluded to in the text and provide background wherever possible for the figures the author mentions so fleetingly. Fragments in the text are knit together in the notes. The intention is for the reader's eye to be able to float across to the left, acquire some grounding, perhaps contemplate a little, and then slide back into the text. The presence of the notes makes the reading experience a little more disjunctive than if they were not there, but as I mentioned above, the *Kagerō Diary* can be perceived as already a disjunctive text, and thus breaking up the reading may even suit it.

A note about some technical matters is in order. Japanese names are given in Japanese order, that is, surname first. Except for the years mentioned in the notes and the introduction, dates are not converted to the Western calendar. So, for example, the designation "fifth month" refers to the month in the old lunar calendar. Since the lunar New Year generally began between our January twenty-fifth and February twenty-fifth, one gets the seasons right if one thinks of the Japanese months as about one month later than the number of the month would suggest. Thus, the fifth month is more like June.

Explanation is also needed for the romanization system used to transcribe the originals of the poems. Romanization of classical Japanese presents special problems because the sound values for certain graphs of the Japanese syllabary and pronunciation patterns in general have changed over time. The greatest sound change has happened in the *ha* line, that is, the five syllables はひふへほ for which the modern pronunciation is *ha, hi, fu, he, ho*. Furthermore, there seems to have been a distinction in classical Japanese between those voiced sounds derived from (again in their modern pronunciation) つ *tsu* and す *su*, which in modern kana usage are pronounced the same and generally rendered with a single graph, ず *zu*, but if one wanted to make the distinction, they would be better rendered as *dzu* and *zu*. With romanizing classical Japanese texts, one has three choices these days. The first one, which has been the conventional practice, is to transpose the classical text into a modern Japanese reading; so, for example, the word for the plant heart-vine, written in the classical language as あふひ *afuhi*, would be romanized in terms of the word's pronunciation in modern Japanese, *aoi*. The second is to use a romanization system based on the attempts of linguistic scholars to reconstruct the sound of Heian Japanese; thus, heart-vine becomes *aFuFi*, in which the capital *F* stands for a conjectural construct of an initial sound somewhere between *f* and *h*. The third method, which I first noticed in the works of Joshua Mostow, is to literally transcribe the graphs in terms of the sound values of the modern language as expressed in the Hepburn romanization system, which produces for heart-vine, *afuhi*. This struck me as a good if not perfect compromise solution to the problems of the first two methods, which I would summarize as follows. The first method creates the illusion that there is no difference in sound between the classical and the modern language. Moreover, the puns that are a critical part of Heian poetics are obscured. For example, the word for "love and longing" in the classical language, *omohi*, has embedded in it a pun on *hi* "fire," which is used to poignant effect in many poems. In the transposition to modern pronunciation, *omoi*, that pun is effaced. In the reconstruction method, where *omohi* becomes *omoFi*, the capital *F* signals an ultimately unknowable sound. Whenever I read *omoFi*, I find myself transposing it back to *omohi*, whereas having gotten used to reading *omohi*, I do not find myself transposing back to *omoi*. Recognizing that the *hi* sound I am using is not the sound used in the Heian period, I can still give voice to something that is different from modern Japanese. The third method, then, seems to offer recognition of difference and makes visible the puns based on older pronunciation without taking the romanization out of the realm of pronunciation. Accordingly, this is the romanization system that I have used to romanize the poems; the standard modern romanization is used for peoples names, terms, and so on in the introduction and notes. So, for example, the title of this work will be the *Kagerō Diary* as opposed to the *Kagerofu Diary,* which would be the historical spelling, and aside from the context of talking about usage in a particular poem, the plant, heartvine, will be cited as *aoi.*

The text I have followed for this translation is that of the *Nihon koten bungaku zenshū,* vol. 9 (Tokyo: Shōgakkan, 1973), with notes and commentary by Kimura Masanori and Imuta Tsunehisa. In abbreviation, since there will be frequent citation, these will become the *Zenshū* text and *Zenshū* commentators. There are no manuscripts for the *Kagerō Diary* that predate the seventeenth century, and it is generally lamented that all extant manuscripts are flawed by many lacunae and copyist's errors. The gaps, while regrettable, can simply be left as blanks. However, where the text is so corrupt as to be incomprehensible and the collation of texts does not resolve the problem, the various commentators over the years have suggested corrections, which come from their own interpretative framework. Where different opinions as to the emendation of texts result in alternate interpretations, my policy has been to follow the *Zenshū* interpretation unless I felt strongly that an alternate one was better. When I do follow an alternate interpretation, it will be noted.

My source for alternate interpretations came mainly from the monumental work by Uemura Etsuko, the *Kagerō nikki kaishaku taisei,* (Compendium of Interpretations of the Kagerō Diary). It contains all the pertinent interpretations for every line of the text starting from the work of Keichū, a seventeenth-century scholar, up to the most recent commentaries. including the joint commentary produced as a series of articles by Akiyama Ken, Kimura Masanori, and Uemura Etsuko over a nine-year period from 1962–71, which formed a kind of foundation for the work. Since there will be frequent citation of *Kagerō nikki kaishaku taisei* in the notes, it will be abbreviated to *Taisei*. Lastly, I consulted very closely the interpretive commentary to the *Kagerō Diary* provided by Sumiko Shinozuka in a series of short monthly aritcles, entitled *Kagerō nikki nōto* (Kagerō Diary Notes), over a fourteen-year period from 1977 to 1991 for the journal, *Keisei,* which is devoted to Japanese *tanka** poetry. Professor Shinozuka of Kyōritsu Women's University is a *tanka* poet herself as well as a scholar of classical and comparative literature. I found her interpretations most illuminating, and citations of her work will accordingly occur

**Tanka* is the thirty-one-syllable form of poetry that has a tradition going back to the eighth century in Japan. In the classical context, it is more often referred to as *waka*.

frequently. She has just recently compiled and edited her "Notes" into a single volume, *Kagerō nikki no kokoro to hyōgen* (Tokyo: Benseisha, 1995).

The *Kagerō nikki* text is sprinkled with allusions to poetry by other authors. Most of the allusions are to *Kokinshū*, which is available in many Japanese editions, but the poem numbers are the same in all editions. Therefore, I have cited *Kokinshū* poems by number alone. As for English translations of *Kokinshū* poems, I have generally used those of Laurel Rasplica Rodd (*Kokinshū* [Princeton University Press, 1984]). When no translation is noted, then the translation is my own. For allusions to poetry outside *Kokinshū*, when poems come from texts that are available in the the major collections of classical works like Iwanami's *Nihon koten bungaku taikei*, I have cited them in one of those collections. However, when the allusion is to a poem from a text for which no commonly available modern edition exists, such as the *Kokin rokujo*, I cited the *Zenshū* text of *Kagerō nikki*, which includes in its commentary all the original texts for alluded poems.

When one gets to the end of a project like this one, the sense of gratitude toward all those who have contributed to it is quite overwhelming. I will begin by thanking the Japan Foundation for the senior fellowship that enabled me to spend one full year working on this translation project with the guidance of Akiyama Ken on the beautiful campus of Tokyo Women's University. Professor Akiyama was unfailingly patient with my questions, so thorough and insightful in his answers, and ever generous with his time. Sumiko Shinozuka welcomed me as a kindred spirit, provided me with a compete set of copies of her articles for *Keisei*, and spent hours in coffee shops with me responding to questions and engaging in animated discussion. She also read the entire translation in draft form and gave valuable suggestions. Another scholar who was generous with his time and wisdom was Kondō Jun'ichirō of Hokkaidō University. Professor Kondō passed away suddenly in the autumn of 1995, and I am one of the many who miss him sorely. Then there are the generous souls who either read or listened to the manuscript at various stages and contributed many insights: Ann Altmann, Bob Amussen, Pamela Asquith, Valerie Arntzen, Rob Croach, Charmian Johnson, Maya Koizumi, Beverly Maize, Joshua Mostow, Jane Munro, Valerie McDonnel, Catherine Nelson-McDermott, Manjot Randhawa, Ingrid Takahashi, Rob and Marguerite Todd, and my daughter, Samara Van Nostrand. Several classes of students in my Classical Japanese Women's Literature course worked with drafts of the translation and helped shape its final form; I thank them all. Finally, I want to acknowledge my editor, Bruce Willoughby, who showed an early interest in this project and accepted right from the start the idea of placing the notes next to the text. With his patience and fine attention to detail, he has contributed enormously to the final form of this work. As the snow drifts down in this land where winter lasts forever, I am moved by how much I owe to others.

Sonja Arntzen
Edmonton, March 1997

Introduction
Reclaiming an Ancestress

"For we think back through our mothers if we are women."
Virginia Woolf, *A Room of One's Own*[1]

> It is just that in the course of living, lying down, getting up, dawn to dusk, when she looks at the odds and ends of the old tales, of which there are so many, they are just so much fantasy, that she thinks perhaps if she were to make a record of a life like her own, being really nobody, it might actually be novel, and could even serve to answer, should anyone ask, what is it like, the life of a woman married to a highly placed man, yet the events of the months and years gone by are vague, places where I have just left it at that are indeed many.

With these few lines of remarkable self-awareness, the author of this diary, a woman of a thousand years ago known to us only as Michitsuna's Mother (936–95?), declares her purpose in writing about her life. Her text is part of a corpus of distinguished literary texts by women in the Heian period (794–1185). The texts of this corpus, including *The Tale of Genji*, *Izumi Shikibu Diary*, *Murasaki Shikibu Diary*, *The Pillow Book of Sei Shōnagon,* and *Sarashina Diary*,[2] established the foundation for classical Japa-

1. Virginia Woolf, *A Room of One's Own* (London: Grafton Books, 1977), 72–73.
2. Edward Seidensticker, trans., *The Tale of Genji* (New York: Knopf, 1976), or the translation by Arthur Waley, *The Tale of Genji: A Novel in Six Parts by Lady Murasaki* (Boston: Houghton Mifflin, 1935); Edwin A. Cranston, trans., *The Izumi Shikibu Diary: A Romance of the Heian Court* (Cambridge: Harvard University Press, 1969), or the translation by Earl Miner in his *Japanese Poetic Diaries* (Berkeley: University of California Press, 1969); Richard Bowring, trans., *Murasaki Shikibu, Her Diary and Poetic Memoirs: A Translation and Study* (Princeton: Princeton University Press, 1982); Ivan Morris, trans., *The Pillow Book of Sei Shōnagon* (New York: Columbia University Press, 1967); Ivan Morris, trans., *As I Crossed a Bridge of Dreams: Recollections of a Woman in Eleventh Century Japan* [*Sarashina nikki*] (Harmondsworth, England: Penguin Books, 1971).

nese prose. That the writing of women played such an important role in the creation of a national literary tradition is certainly an anomaly in world literary history. *Kagerō Diary* is one of the first of these foundation texts by women and therefore deserves special interest as a pioneering work. Moreover, it is fascinating how relevant this text is to issues of women's writing in a contemporary global context.

Examined closely, there are many things in the diary's opening statement to catch the attention of someone attuned to contemporary literary discussions about the nature of autobiography and the possibility of a female voice in literature. One of the first things one notices is that the author sets out to record her own life as a sort of antiromance. She makes reference to all the old tales (in Japanese, *monogatari*) that "are just so much fantasy." The age this author lived in is now known as the age of *monogatari*, "tale" or "romance" literature.[3] Most of the *monogatari* extant from this period—with the great *Tale of Genji* at the top of the list—actually date from the generation after Michitsuna's Mother, that is, from about 1000 to the end of the twelfth century. However, reading back through later tales, it is evident that some of the tales Michitsuna's Mother likely had in mind were works in which men and women fell in love and lived happily ever after, whereas her own story as told in this diary could be subtitled, "I married the prince and we didn't live happily ever after." In that sense, she is writing about a "real" life.

It is noteworthy in the context of world literary history that this author should consider her life worth writing about at all. A woman's personal life, whether in fiction or writing of the self, does not become a topic worthy of attention in world literature elsewhere until very recently indeed. Her urge to record her life does not appear to stem from a perception that her life was extraordinary or that she played some important role in society. She describes herself both as "married to a highly placed man" and as "being really nobody." She was indeed a member of a small aristocracy; the narrowness of its parameters will become apparent as one reads this diary, if only because almost all the people she mentions are related to one another. Her husband belonged to the most powerful branch of the Fujiwara family and had a brilliant political career. She herself, however, came from the provincial governors' class, which had little social prestige. (More details about the provincial governors' class will be provided in the next section.) Moreover, if, as is generally supposed, she started setting down this account of her life around 971 when her marriage was approaching its crisis, she would have been acutely aware of the obscurity awaiting her after the dissolution of her marriage. Her life was undistin-

3. Akiyama Ken, *Ōchō joryū bungaku no sekai* (Tokyo: Tōkyō Daigaku Shuppankai, 1972), 209.

guished as she judged it by the standards of her own world, which makes her will to record it all the more remarkable.

It has been noted by more than one scholar of the text that the *Kagerō Diary*'s author contributed a realistic mode of writing to Japanese prose. Edward Seidensticker, who did the first complete English translation of the text, says of it, "It is the first attempt in Japanese literature . . . to capture on paper, without evasion or idealization, the elements of a real social situation."[4] However, in struggling to write against romance, she was nonetheless caught in it. Rachel Brownstein, in her study on the fascination of the heroine for women readers of the English novel, makes an observation that also casts light on the situation of the author of the *Kagerō Diary*:

> The history of both women and fiction has been influenced by the fact that the self has been identified, in novels, with the feminine. The idea of becoming a heroine marries the female protagonist to the marriage plot, and it marries the woman who reads to fiction.[5]

Fictional narrative in the *Kagerō Diary* author's period, extrapolating from later examples like *The Tale of Genji*, was just as concerned with the "marriage plot" or the "romance story" as the English novels of Jane Austen or the Brontë sisters. In addition to "romantic fiction," there was also a literary tradition of love poetry that married women to an imagined world of romance. That world of romance had a powerful pull for the *Kagerō Diary* author. Despite her apparent intention to write against that tradition, the episodes she chooses to narrate from her life are often those moments when her marriage lived up to the romantic ideal. The self the author constructed in this diary was inextricably mixed with the notion of a romantic heroine. Thus, this text too can be examined just as fruitfully as the novels of the grand tradition in English literature to provide insight into the question of "how the self and self-consciousness are mutually and problematically involved, and involved in literary forms and language."[6]

Another noteworthy aspect of the diarist's opening passage is that she equates writing about her life with writing about her marriage. Is it not fascinating that one of the earliest self-writings in the world by a woman should have a relationship at its core? Estelle Jelinek, in her study *The Tradition of Women's Autobiography from Antiquity to the Present*, states,

4. Edward Seidensticker, *The Gossamer Years: The Diary of a Noblewoman of Heian Japan* [*Kagerō Nikki*] (Rutland, VT: Charles E. Tuttle, 1964 [1985 reprint]), 14.

5. Rachel M. Brownstein, *Becoming a Heroine: Reading About Women in Novels* (London: Penguin Books, 1984), xvi.

6. Brownstein, *Becoming a Heroine*, xxi.

"the subjects that women write about are remarkably similar: family, close friends, domestic activities."[7] The *Kagerō Diary* supports her thesis. Here we have a record from a thousand years ago of a woman's domestic life as it is bound up in her relations with others. The principal relationship is with her husband, but her relationship with her son and the triangular relationship between the three of them is drawn in some detail as well. This diary can stand as a document of husband and wife relations. I suspect the reader will be amazed how much commonality exists between her marital relationship and contemporary ones, if only in the difficulty of communication between husband and wife.

The author mentions in the opening passage how "the events of the months and years gone by are vague," acknowledging the fallibility of memory and suggesting that all that is written in the text may not actually be as it happened. The psychological sophistication of this observation stands out. The recognition of the mutability of mental states and that memory distorts and invents are realizations of the modern age in the West. Another related perception underlying the opening passage is the awareness of the author's life as a story. She does not claim it for the truth; she says only that the diary of an ordinary life might be "novel." Note how she starts the opening passage by talking about herself in the third person as though she were a character in a tale and gradually shifts over to the first person perspective. This awareness of the fictiveness of her telling is borne out throughout the text by her preference in the original for a type of perfective verb ending associated with storytelling. Again, in Western literature it is a comparatively recent revelation that, since life as it occurs is formless in its plethora of experience, one has in some sense fictionalized one's life the moment one writes it down as a narrative. In this awareness as well, she seems strangely close to a modern Western perspective. It is almost as though she might agree with Paul Eakin that "autobiographical truth is not a fixed but an evolving content in an intricate process of self-discovery and self-creation, and, further, that the self that is the center of all autobiographical narrative is necessarily a fictive structure."[8]

If we attend to the style of this opening passage, we see a sentence that is both sinuous and disjunctive, something close to "stream of consciousness." Jelinek notes that in women's autobiography through the ages the prevalent style is "episodic and anecdotal, nonchronological and disjunctive."[9] It is intriguing that such characteristics should show up in a

7. Estelle C. Jelinek, *The Tradition of Women's Autobiography from Antiquity to the Present* (Boston: Twayne, 1986), xiii.

8. Paul John Eakin, *Fictions in Autobiography: Studies in the Art of Self-Invention* (Princeton: Princeton University Press, 1985), 3.

9. Jelinek, *The Tradition of Women's Autobiography*, xiii.

woman's text completely outside the Western tradition. I see this text as a pertinent document for the inquiry that Virginia Woolf initiated in *A Room of One's Own* about the possibility and nature of a "woman's sentence."[10] I do not raise this issue to take a position on whether there is an "essential" woman's style in writing. In my view, the question of whether there is such a thing can produce valuable discoveries without being taken to closure.

By signaling the aspects of this text that resonate with lively debates going on in modern literary circles about autobiography and the nature of feminine difference in literary style, I emphasize the relevance and accessibility of the *Kagerō Diary* for modern Western readers. However, there are other aspects of this text that distance it. It remains a voice from a very different time and culture, and we need to imaginatively reconstruct the author's historical and linguistic context in order to hear that voice. The remaining chapters of the introduction will provide that context, but there is one necessary and overarching piece of information that a modern English reader needs to respond to the text, namely, that the text comes out of a discourse of sorrow. We do not often reflect upon the fact that we are all caught in the discourse of our time and place. We grow unconsciously into what it is possible to think and say within our culture, our gender, and from our position in the world. The wrapper of language we live in shifts with time, since new modes of thought and language are constantly being invented. Moreover, we are not in a single unitary envelope of discourse, but rather various overlapping discourses. For more than a century, part of a discourse shared by most modern Western readers entails a positive stance vis-à-vis the world. I would suggest that, particularly when we read accounts of people's "real" lives, we are unconsciously looking for the success of their struggle, how they took command of their own minds and lives. Furthermore, we have very little patience for people complaining. People should not complain, they should do something about their lives. From a perspective like that, this diary may look like one long self-indulgent whine.

However, the world did not occur that way to the author and others of her age. One of the dominant discourses of her age was Buddhism, which starts from the premise, "Life is suffering." To come to an intimate knowledge of suffering so that one is no longer fooled by the pleasures of the world is part of the process of enlightenment. That basic conception of life was modulated through a Japanese literary tradition of *mono no aware*, sometimes translated as the "ahness of things" because *aware* etymologically is onomatopoeia for a sigh. We are most often moved

10. Woolf, *A Room of One's Own*, 72–73.

to sigh by sadness, so *aware* is clearly used in some contexts to mean "sadness." The *mono no* is problematic: it can mean simply "of things," so another translation for *mono no aware* is "the sadness of things." However, *mono* has embedded in it a sense of the supernatural, the mysterious power in things, as in the phrase *mono no ke,* literally, "the spirit of things," but meaning "spirit possession." This aspect of the phrase communicates a sense of awe with respect to the world, encompassing nature and humanity. Thus the phrase *mono no aware* takes its place among a legion of aesthetic terms in Japanese literature and art that resist precise definition but convey a wealth of connotation. *Aware*, at least for the purposes of appreciating this diary, may be understood as a fine-tuned sensitivity to the transience of things, an awareness that things are most precious just when their loss is imminent. This sensitivity was requisite for participating in another one of the most powerful discourses of the age, poetry. Love is a principal subject for poetry in the Japanese tradition, and the tone of expression in love poetry is almost exclusively that of yearning or lamentation—the burning longing to be with the lover, and lamentation if desire is denied or when the "thrill is gone."

The use here of a blues lyric is deliberate. The possible analogy with the blues opened up my own appreciation of the entire genre of Heian poetry, and this diary in particular. For its fans, at least, the blues produces joy; its particular alchemy is to turn pain into pleasure. Part of this transformation rests in the power of expression for expression's sake. Pain expressed is pain released. In terms of an art form, it is the artistry of the expression that contributes the pleasure. If one imagines removing the music and the timbre of the singer's voice from a blues song and paraphrasing its lyrics, one would be left with repetitive whining and grating complaint. That is what I felt we had so far in translations of the *Kagerō Diary*. We had the content of her complaining but not its style, not the artistry of its expression.

There is a further complexity to this. Given that the literary discourse of her time was designed for the expression of sorrow, even if she should want to convey the joy in her marriage, it might have to be channeled through the discourse of sorrow. I am indebted for this revelation to conversations with two Japanese scholars, Akiyama Ken and Kondō Jun'ichirō. On separate occasions, both scholars expressed the same view to me that an underlying message in the diary, particularly in book one, was the author's pride in the splendor of her marriage. This view shifted my perception of the diary a hundred and eighty degrees. There was no room in the discourse of the age to say: "See how much he loved me. He came to visit me every night. It was noticeable when he did not visit for even one day." Or, "Look what fine poems he wrote for me; see what a hold I had over him." Or, "We had been married for fourteen years or more and he still felt moved to come all the way to meet me at Uji when I was returning from a trip." Judged by the standards of the time, her marriage was an excellent one. Moreover, one wonders why a text that apparently heaps so much criticism on the powerful head of the Fujiwara clan would have been allowed to survive. There is a distinct possibility that far from being disgruntled by her account of their marriage, her husband may have taken pride in it. He did not have time to compile his own poetry anthology, so she did it for him and his prowess in poetry was recorded for posterity.[11]

Intriguing and revealing as such perceptions are, the litany of sorrow and the delineation of depression in this text cannot all be understood as a paradoxical affirmation of the success of her marriage. This diary is also a record of the death of her marriage and her struggle to find a reason for living once it was no longer possible to exchange poetry with her husband. She was an artist; to write poetry was an important reason for living. Although nowhere does the author state it explicitly, she writes herself to freedom through this record. When one of my Japanese colleagues heard that I was going to study this text and that my inspiration for embarking on the project was related to feminism, she cautioned me not to characterize the author of the diary as an oppressed woman or the diary itself as a record of protest against unjust treatment at the hands of men.[12] Her reason for objecting to such an approach was that it was anachronistic. It projected the attitudes and perception of our time and culture onto a text from a totally different milieu. She went on to say, however, that she felt the text should be looked upon as a kind of therapy for the author. I wondered, was not "therapy" a concept from our own time and culture? Yet I agreed with her. The process of writing the diary seems to have given the author some distance from her situation. She writes herself into some sort of freedom, which for her was the possibility of living without her husband. The Japanese scholar Shinozuka Sumiko has explored the interpretation of the *Kagerō Diary* as a kind of therapy for the author.[13] In explicating a passage where Michitsuna's Mother regains her health after having written down her feelings in a letter to be opened

11. I am indebted for this insight to an article by Joshua Mostow, "The Amorous Statesman and the Poetess: The Politics of Autobiography and the Kagerō Nikki," *Japan Forum* 4.2 (October 1992): 305–15.

12. The *Kagerō Diary* has already been characterized in this manner by someone who would not perhaps welcome the label of "feminist." In his preface to *The Gossamer Years*, Seidensticker says that "the diary is in a sense her protest against the marriage system of her time, and her exposition of the thesis that men are beasts" (8–9).

13. Shinozuka Sumiko, *Kagerō nikki no kokoro to hyōgen* (Tokyo: Benseisha, 1995), 69–71.

should she die, Shinozuka even suggests that language itself was "the spring" Michitsuna's Mother used to bring herself back to health.[14] Perhaps it can even be said that, for the *Kagerō Diary* author, language was a means of creating a self with the power to live.

The issue of the relation between language and the construction of the self brings the discussion in a full circle back to the common ground between the *Kagerō Diary* and contemporary literary concerns. There has been a worldwide explosion in women's writing in this century, particularly in the last fifty years. There has also been a major effort by feminist scholars to reclaim writing by women in the past which has been abandoned or pushed to the margins of the literary heritage. All this is a worthy enterprise because when one scans the last two thousand years of human history, women's expression is conspicuous in its absence. It is within this enterprise that I claim the *Kagerō Diary* author as ancestress for us all in the writing of the self and commend her to your attention and reading pleasure.

Historical Context

The author of the *Kagerō Diary* lived in the middle of the Heian period, a period of relative peace and stability. There were no significant military threats to the authority of the imperial court from either within or outside the nation. The court had taken the decision in the early Heian period to cease official communication with China, thus effectively isolating the country from the rest of Asia. The aristocratic society of the capital of Heian (present-day Kyoto) had turned inward and its members were only interested in what went on in the capital city. Within that society, women's society also had an insular quality.

Although the Heian world is a thousand years removed from the present, there is a surprisingly rich historical record from which to draw information. To begin with, there is the comprehensive *Sonpi bunmyaku*,[15] which gives genealogies and career records for virtually all male upper echelon aristocrats of the Heian period as well as some anecdotal material about prominent figures. Furthermore, several of the diaries in Chinese by men of the court are extant, and, while rather dry and short on personal revelations, they are good sources for the chronology, protocol, and names of participants for court ceremonies and other noteworthy events. By contrast, the fictional and autobiographical texts in Japanese, mainly of fe-

14. Ibid., 217.

15. *Sonpi bunmyaku*, vols. 58–60 in Kuroita Katsumi, ed., *Kokushi taikei*, 66 vols. (Tokyo: Yoshikawa Kobunkan, 1924–64). The *Sonpi bunmyaku* was compiled toward the end of the fourteenth century on the basis of a large number of earlier documents.

male authorship (the *Kagerō Diary* included), give a detailed picture of the personal side of life. Finally there are two lengthy histories written in the mid to late Heian period. One, the *Eiga monogatari*,[16] is by a woman, perhaps with additions from other women, and the other, the *Ōkagami*,[17] is written by a man. Both histories are in the Japanese language and include fictional elements, and both focus on the history of the Fujiwara family as it reaches its apogee in the career of Fujiwara Michinaga, who is incidentally the son by another wife of the husband of the *Kagerō Diary* author. The two texts are valuable documents for social and political history. With such a wealth of resources, the difficulty lies in choosing which material to relate. The following outline of the historical context of the diary will concentrate on the information that makes the accounts in the diary more comprehensible and will accordingly focus on social rather than political history.

Marriage and Familial Relations

Since the story of a marriage is at the core of this diary, let us start with Heian marriage customs.[18] The most salient and foreign feature of marriage at this period is that husband and wife did not normally live together, particularly in the early part of their marriage. Although the husband would often end up living in the house of the wife who had the most children once the children were of marriageable age, virtually all marriages began as "visiting" arrangements. The husband would visit the wife's home where she resided with her mother and extended maternal family. Moreover, polygyny was common for men, so a man might be involved in a visiting marriage with two or more households, as well as conducting casual liaisons on a sporadic basis. Sometimes, from a contemporary Western point of view, it is difficult to distinguish how in the Heian period formal marriage was much different from a casual liaison.

16. *Eiga monogatari*. Citations will be to the English translation by William H. McCullough and Helen Craig McCullough, *A Tale of Flowering Fortunes: Annals of Japanese Aristocratic Life in the Heian Period* (Stanford: Stanford University Press, 1980).
17. *Ōkagami*. Citations will generally be to the English translation by Helen Craig McCullough, *Ōkagami, The Great Mirror: Fujiwara Michinaga (966–1027) and His Times* (Princeton: Princeton University Press, 1980).
18. There is an excellent article on Heian marriage customs by William H. McCullough, "Marriage Institutions in the Heian Period," *Harvard Journal of Asiatic Studies* 27 (1967): 103–7. The succeeding account draws heavily on that article, but also incorporates observations from fictional and autobiographical texts of the period. A more recent article by Peter Nickerson, "The Meaning of Matrilocality: Kinship, Property, and Politics in the Mid-Heian Period," *Monumenta Nipponica* 48.4 (1993): 429–67, while relying on the same basic data as the McCullough article, has a more detailed analysis of the power relations involved in the Heian marriage institution.

Indeed, the very marriage ceremony itself appears to mimic secret affairs. For example, the meeting of the couple was preceded by the exchange of poetry in both marriages and affairs. Once the correspondence had reached a certain level of intimacy, the groom would visit the bride's house under the cover of night and sleep with her. In most cases, this would be the first time the couple would have met one another in person. Both the first and second night, the groom would leave before dawn as though it were a secret tryst. On the third night—it was his coming three nights in a row that actually constituted the wedding—he would stay until morning, at which point the parents would welcome him and he would eat special cakes with his new bride. One can imagine the humiliation for a young woman and her family if the groom only visited once or twice and never returned.

Often the first marriage for a young man would be arranged by his family to cement political alliances, but he would go courting for his other marriages. In the case of the *Kagerō Diary* author's marriage, it was a first marriage for her and a second marriage for him. The author registers annoyance that her husband did not come courting properly, which would have meant cultivating a connection with a female member of her household so that he could deliver love letters to her secretly (cf. p. 57). This would have been more like a secret affair and therefore more romantic. Instead her prospective husband went first to her father and seems to have pursued his objective in a casual way. Her husband was of a much higher status than the author's father and likely did not expect the father or the daughter to resist the proposal. Nonetheless, they performed a three- or four-month courtship through the medium of poetry. The author must have known of the existence of her husband's first wife who had already borne him a son, since much later she remarks that she had corresponded with the woman before (cf. p. 75), but she does not mention the first wife at all in the account of the beginning of her own marriage.

Views of marriage customs in the Heian period have been distorted by assuming that society actually followed the Yōrō legal code modeled after Chinese laws and instituted during the eighth century.[19] In that code, there was a clear hierarchy of first wife, second wife, and concubines. In reality, the situation in Heian Japan was much more fluid. There was a notion of "principal" wife, which was not always determined by order of marriage. It was the social status and material wealth of the wife's family that determined whether she would be considered the principal wife. If two wives were of roughly the same social status, as was the case with the *Kagerō Diary* author and her husband's first wife, then the

19. William McCullough, "Marriage Institutions in the Heian Period," 105–6.

wife's position would often come to depend on the number of children she had. As will be explained in more detail below in the section on Heian politics, children were political capital, so the more the better and the more powerful the wife's position.

Children were raised in the mother's home, which made the ties between the children and their maternal relatives much stronger than with their paternal relatives. Likewise the relations between siblings of the same mother were generally closer than those that shared only the same father. Given that polygyny was the common practice, most people had half siblings of one kind or another.

Aristocratic society within the capital was very small and closed, so that marriages among near relatives were common. Marital connection was only forbidden between parents and children, and brothers and sisters. This meant that cousins, uncles and nieces, aunts and nephews could and did marry. For example, in book three of the *Kagerō Diary*, the author adopts a daughter born from her husband's casual affair of several years before (cf. pp. 285–95). This adopted daughter comes to be courted by her husband's younger brother from a different mother. In contemporary Western terms, it would be like an uncle courting his niece. However, given the lack of close contact between families of different mothers, this younger brother actually seems very distant from his elder brother, never having seen either his sister-in-law or her adopted daughter, his niece. Indeed, his courting ends without his actually having seen either woman.

Women were not normally seen by any men other than their fathers, brothers of the same mother, husbands, and sons. Aristocratic women tried to be seen by as few people as possible. Even when they went outside, they generally traveled in curtained carriages. They held audiences from behind screens. For a woman, allowing oneself to be seen by a man was tantamount to inviting violation, and the literature of the period abounds in "peeping tom" scenes. The only aristocratic women exempt from keeping themselves hidden were women who served at court whose duties exposed them.

Economic Foundations

As mentioned above, women normally lived out their lives in the homes of their mothers. Residences within the capital were usually inherited along the female line, and this provided women with an independent economic base. If Virginia Woolf is right and the prerequisite for a woman becoming a writer is "money and a room of her own,"[20] then aristocratic women of

20. Woolf, *A Room of One's Own*, 6.

the Heian period had met that prerequisite. It might go a long way toward explaining why there was such a flowering of women's writing during the period.

The author of the *Kagerō Diary* shifts residences four times. She starts out in the house of her mother; after about eleven years of marriage she moves to a house apparently owned by her husband close to his official residence, then moves back to her maternal home, and finally to a house on the outskirts of the city owned by her father. At no time, however, is she exclusively dependent on her husband's resources, although a remark she drops here and there seems to indicate she expects him to contribute to the upkeep of her dwelling (cf. pp. 133–35). There is some indication in fictional texts of the period, like *The Tale of Genji,* that the husband contributed support in terms of building materials and workmen's labor to the houses of women recognized as wives. It is also evident from fiction that one of the rarest but most romantic situations was for the husband to provide a separate house, separate that is from both their parents, for husband and wife to live in.[21] In the early part of book two, the author's husband, Kaneie, begins construction of a splendid residence. When he talks about showing it to her, the author, in spite of her better judgment, begins to hope that he intends it as a house for them both to dwell in (cf. p. 175).

Besides providing some assistance with maintenance of the wife's housing, the husband also seems to have been expected to provide material assistance for religious observances in the way of offerings and rewards for officiating monks. Undoubtedly, however, the husband's major contribution to the marriage in a practical sense was overseeing the careers of the children, by arranging good marriages or posts as ladies-in-waiting at court for the daughters and seeking political advancement for the sons.

The most important contribution of women to the marriage was the bearing and raising of the children. The next most important contribution was the production of clothes for the husband. In several places the *Kagerō Diary* notes orders for clothing. Participating in government required elaborate costumes. From the detailed descriptions of costume in virtually all the literary works of the age, we know how important clothes were to the people of that society. Moreover, bolts of cloth themselves were a form of currency, and garments were one of the most common forms of reward or payment. The reader will note in the diary numerous occasions where garments are bestowed on people for services.

21. Examples of this from fiction of the period include Genji's establishment of the young Murasaki in the Nijō residence in *The Tale of Genji*, and the hero in *Ochikubō monogatari* providing a mansion for the Cinderella-like heroine.

It was possible for aristocratic women to work outside the home by serving at court either by holding official positions such as that of *naishi no kami*, principal handmaid, or by being employed privately as members of the entourages of empresses and imperial consorts. This latter was the case of writers like Murasaki Shikibu, Izumi Shikibu, and Sei Shōnagon. Such private ladies-in-waiting served as companions by creating amusements and making an impression on others through the writing of poetry and by participation in concerts. It was out of this kind of salon society that *The Tale of Genji* was born. There was a considerable amount of prestige attached to serving at court. Of the famous women writers of this period, only the author of the *Kagerō Diary* did not serve at court. Thus, her voice is the only one we have for the secluded married woman.

Michitsuna's Mother did share one characteristic with the other women writers of the period, and that was class background. She, like all the others, came from the provincial governor's class. This was the middle echelon of the aristocracy. Serving as a provincial governor offered many opportunities for material enrichment since the provinces were where wealth was actually produced, but since it meant living for periods of time away from the capital, the center of the universe, it carried a social taint. The daughters of provincial governors, however, were in a good place strategically to marry up the social ladder. The marriage of Michitsuna's Mother may be interpreted as a "marriage up."

The Personal Is Political, Heian-Period Style

Undoubtedly, the aspect of political life that impacted women's lives the most directly was marriage politics. During the tenth and eleventh centuries, the Fujiwara clan in particular was able to exercise hegemonic control over the imperial family, and hence the nation, by marrying their daughters into the imperial line and assuring that all emperors and potential emperors had Fujiwara mothers. As mentioned above in the section on familial relations, children were generally raised within the mother's family. One exception to this was the emperor's family. The emperor's offspring were raised within the palace. However, the emperor's children were always born in the house of their mothers (birth was considered a pollution because of its connection with blood and therefore was prohibited from taking place in the palace), and the closest relatives would always be the mother's relatives. Since the custom was frequently to have an emperor ascend the throne as a child or adolescent, the regent would usually be the emperor's maternal grandfather. Thus it was not only through grosser forms of power that Fujiwara clan chieftains controlled the imperial office, it was also through the family bonds of grandfather and grandson. Accordingly the Fujiwara leaders found dependence and weakness on the part of emperors useful. The Reizei emperor, who reigned briefly from 967–69, was actually mentally deranged. Within the interpretative framework of the time, he was considered to be suffering from "spirit possession." Even though he ascended the throne as an adult, there was need for a regent. This set a precedent for the future, and *Ōkagami* notes cannily, "It is precisely because of Emperor Reizei that the Fujiwara lords still flourish."[22]

Since marriage into the imperial line was the basis of Fujiwara power, it was important for this clan to have a good supply of daughters. This is why the author of the *Kagerō Diary* hints at the beginning of book three that she laments having only one son (cf. p. 285). More children would have been best, but if she had to have only one child, she would have been better off with a daughter. Mother of an empress was a prestigious position. Of course, without sons to assure the continuity of the Fujiwara lineage, the clan was in difficulty too. Thus, both sons and daughters were important for the game of marriage politics.

Women were important to marriage politics as prospective consorts and bearers of the next generation of players. Nonetheless, this kind of importance is different from actually holding office or making decisions about such things as promotions and allocations of estates, the "real" expressions of power. In fact, the question of how much women knew about or participated from behind the scenes in the realpolitik of the era is an intriguing one. Sometimes it seems they could play a direct role. *Ōkagami* records that the appointment of Michinaga to minister of the right, the appointment that paved the way for his total domination of court life for the next two decades, was finally secured by the tearful entreaties of his sister Senshi, the emperor's mother. It is described thus:

> After an interval long enough to excite painful misgivings, she [Senshi] opened the door and came out, wearing a triumphant smile on her flushed, tear-stained face. "At last! The decree has been issued!" she told him.[23]

This passage gives a vivid sense of Senshi's participation in political affairs.

Nonetheless, what is also abundantly clear from the literary works of the period is that the dominant literary discourse, created largely in the hands of women, had little place for the discussion of the overtly political. There seems to have been a code of etiquette that required women to censor themselves about political observation.

22. Helen McCullough, *Ōkagami*, 138.
23. Ibid., 199.

The most interesting case with respect to the *Kagerō Diary* is the account in the text of the most shocking political event of the era, the arrest and exile of Minamoto Takaakira,[24] known to posterity as the Anna Era Incident, because it happened in 969, the second year of the Anna era. A little background to the affair is in order.

In 969, Minamoto Takaakira was the minister of the left, nominally the most important position within the Heian government. As his Minamoto surname indicates, he was of imperial lineage, being the son of Emperor Daigo (885–930). The Minamoto surname was given to imperial offspring who lacked sufficient backing to be placed in the line of succession. Nonetheless, his imperial lineage gave him preferment in office, and thus he had come to occupy this powerful office. He had also married a Fujiwara woman, San no Kami, third daughter of Morosuke, father to Kaneie, the *Kagerō Diary* author's husband. Thus, San no Kami was a sister to Kaneie, albeit by a different mother. This should have assured him friendly relations with the main branch of the Fujiwara clan, but the room for ascendancy by forming alliances with the imperial family was just too narrow to avoid ferocious competition even among those closely related.

The occasion for the breakdown was Takaakira's marriage of his daughter to Prince Tamehira, fourth and favorite son of Emperor Murakami. Everyone expected Tamehira to be named the next crown prince after the present crown prince had ascended the throne. Takaakira's marrying his daughter to Tamehira brought him into direct competition with the main Fujiwara family, whose goal was always to have the reigning emperor's principal consort be a Fujiwara woman. When Emperor Murakami died in 967, his second son succeeded to the throne as Emperor Reizei, but a year later, Tamehira was passed over for designation as crown prince in favor of the fifth son, who was a mere child of nine years old. As *Eiga monogatari* puts it succinctly, Tamehira "lost the throne when he married Takaakira's daughter."[25] *Ōkagami* gives a more explicit analysis:

> Power would have shifted to Takaakira's family if Prince Tamehira had become Emperor, and the Genji [that is, the Minamoto] would have been the ones to prosper, so the Prince's resourceful uncles [Tamehira's mother, Anshi, was a full sister to Kaneie and his brothers] solved the problem by making his younger brother the heir apparent, even though it was contrary to the natural order of things.[26]

24. Seidensticker in *The Gossamer Years* and McCullough and McCullough in *A Tale of Flowering Fortunes* give the reading of Takaaki for this name. I follow *Zenshū* with this reading of Takaakira (*Zenshū*, 108).
25. McCullough and McCullough, *A Tale of Flowering Fortunes*, 99.
26. Helen McCullough, *Ōkagami*, 129–30.

The chagrin of Takaakira about this was apparent to all. As a way to put his political ambitions completely out of the way, charges that he was plotting to overthrow the current emperor were leveled against him, and he was exiled to Kyushu as provisional governor-general of Daizaifu.[27] To see one of their own in such a high position be brought so low shocked all members of the aristocracy.

As mentioned above, this is the only political event to find its way into the *Kagerō Diary*. What is interesting, however, is that the author's sympathies are entirely with Takaakira and particularly his wife. She writes of her sorrow over the news of the event and composes a long poem of condolence for Takaakira's wife (cf. pp. 179–83), who, it will be remembered, is a half sister to her husband. Nowhere in her relation of the events concerning Takaakira's fall does she indicate even obliquely that she is aware her husband is one of the chief engineers of the conspiracy that brought Takaakira down. Either she is totally ignorant of her husband's role or it cannot be mentioned.

Most interesting of all, she feels she must defend recording the incident at all. This is one place where she acknowledges that she has a conscious idea about what is appropriate for including in the diary. She writes:

> In a diary only for things related to me personally, this is perhaps something that shouldn't have been included; however, since the deep feelings of sadness about it were my own and not anyone else's, I recorded it. (cf. p. 173)

There are many things to tease out from this short passage. One is that the author is clearly operating from the assumption that her writing and perhaps by extension all women's writing should be restricted to personal life. The only excuse for mentioning the Takaakira affair is that it made her personally sad. It might be tempting to read into this that she is actually inhibited by an unwritten code of censorship that prevents her from mentioning her husband's role in the affair or expressing any chagrin over it. One might point to the fact that the narration of the Takaakira incident is placed in book two, which is where her own relations with her husband begin to go seriously awry, and perhaps she is identifying with those her husband has harmed because she is already feeling alienated from him. However, I think that would be a forced reading. In the immediate context of book two, right after bringing up the Takaakira incident, she records a poetry exchange with her husband that expresses intimacy. Moreover, there is no place in the diary where she displays any interest at all in her husband's

27. McCullough and McCullough, *A Tale of Flowering Fortunes*, 100.

official career except to lament that his rise in status actually strains the relationship because it makes it harder for him to find time to visit. In fact, the only time she is happy about an appointment of his is when he is unhappy about it. In book one, her husband, much to his distaste, is given a post in the Ministry of War, the least prestigious of the Heian government ministries, and so he stops going to work. This means he has a lot more time to spend with her, which makes her happy.

Clearly, so far as her persona in the diary is concerned, she is totally uninterested in the public career of her husband except in how it affects his availability to her. Moreover, in places she actually seems to have an inaccurate perception of what is going on. In book three for example, after the death of her husband's elder brother, Koremasa,[28] she interprets the situation as fortunate for her husband (cf. p. 319) when in actual fact, her husband's second oldest brother, Kanemichi, who assumes great power at this point, is dedicated to destroying her husband's career. This mistaken perception on her part seems to be proof that indeed she was ignorant as well as uninterested in her husband's political affairs.

Yet, how is it possible that she could ignore something so vital to the advancement of her own father and son? It is clear their careers depended exclusively on the career of her husband. There is even a place where she hints at her own knowledge of that. In book three, she ends a passage of lament over her husband's recent promotion by saying of her son that "although he cannot say anything, he seems secretly very pleased." Is her lack of interest in her husband's political affairs in the end a literary pose? Since the literary discourse she was helping to shape was derived essentially from lyric poetry and had at its core the subtle expression of feeling limited to love and sorrow, calculation about what such and such a political promotion might mean to her own family members did not have a place in it. That said, as she constructed and was being constructed by that discourse, it also became her reality. Perhaps she could not care about his political career because it did not fit into the discourse with which she was constructing her life. In this sense, a literary pose ceases to be a trivial thing.

Women's "Education"

There was no formal education for women in the Heian period, but reading between the lines of the fictional and autobiographical writings of the era, it is clear how rigorous women's informal education was. The training

28. Again, there seems to be some disagreement over the correct reading for this name. Seidensticker in *The Gossamer Years* and McCullough and McCullough in *A Tale of Flowering Fortunes* give Koretada as the reading; I follow *Zenshū* by giving Koremasa (*Zenshū*, 90).

was exclusively in the arts with poetry, calligraphy, and music as a foundation. For example, one Fujiwara patriarch's advice to his daughter was:

> First you must study penmanship [calligraphy]. Next you must learn to play the seven-string zither better than anyone else. And also you must memorize all the poems in the twenty books of the Kokin Shu.[29]

Poetry and calligraphy went together because one of the primary methods for learning both of them was copying the poems of the canon in the hands of acknowledged master calligraphers. In *The Tale of Genji* for example, one of the things that Genji takes great pains to assemble as part of his daughter's trousseau is a library of copybooks for calligraphy. "Having made the acquaintance of the more notable calligraphers, he commissioned from each a book or scroll for his daughter's library, into which only the works of the eminent and accomplished were to be admitted."[30] In this way, a woman's own hand in calligraphy developed as her understanding of the best poems of the past deepened. Since brush calligraphy was the basis for painting in the era, nearly all Heian aristocrats became accomplished artists as well. We might note the frequent reference in the *Kagerō Diary* to the author painting and the mention in the poem collection of her father bringing back paintings of Michinoku (cf. p. 387).

Of the three principle arts, music is the least mentioned in the *Kagerō Diary*, but it is there. There is the touching communication between the author and her aunt after the year's period of mourning for the author's mother is over and she finds herself playing the koto again (cf. pp. 121–23):

> So the commemoration ceremony was complete, as usual I had nothing in particular to do. Without really intending to play, as I was dusting my koto, my fingers strayed to play a few notes and it struck me that indeed the period of mourning was over. Sadly, it had passed so quickly, as I was brooding on this, from my aunt came:

ima ha tote	Now it is over,
hiki idzuru koto no	yet when I hear these notes
ne wo kikeba	plucked from the koto,
uchi kaheshitemo	they run me back to the past
naho zo kanashiki	and I am even sadder.

> At this, even though it was nothing very special, thinking about it, my tears overflowed:

29. Ivan Morris, *The World of the Shining Prince: Court Life in Ancient Japan* (Harmondsworth, England: Penguin Books, 1979), 221.
30. Seidensticker, *The Tale of Genji*, 520.

naki hito ha	The day and month that
otodzure mo sede	I cut the strings of my koto,
koto no wo wo	since the one who had gone
tachishi tsuki hi zo	could no longer hear me play,
kaheri ki ni keri	that day has come round again.

Letters and Literature

It will be noted that the exchange above between two women in the same household takes place in writing. It was not uncommon even for people in the same dwelling to exchange letters with one another. This points out the special significance of correspondence in this society. For women in particular, it was the most important means of communication with the world because they were the stationary ones while the men visited here and there. The *Kagerō Diary* can be viewed in part as a record of the author's correspondence with the world and more specifically her husband. The Japanese scholar, Sumiko Shinozuka, has been researching parallels between the development of epistolary novels in eighteenth-century England and women's writing in Heian Japan. She writes:

> In fact, truly speaking, not only the *Kagerō Diary* but the other women's diaries that followed as well can be considered a kind of long letter to one or several persons with whom the author was familiar. For instance, the *Kagerō Diary* can be assumed to be written as a letter to the author's adopted daughter.
> . . .
> It was the *Kagerō Diary* that started this tradition in Japanese women's diaries of writing a text as though it were a kind of letter. Thus, the author of the *Kagerō Diary* could develop a way to describe her thoughts and feelings in her own natural Japanese, just like Richardson did in English.[31]

The critical role that letters played in women's lives and the literature they developed may have contributed to the identification between women and the hiragana script used to transcribe vernacular Japanese.

Hiragana Script: The "Woman's Hand"

The freedom for women to correspond was made possible by the evolution of a script for writing the vernacular Japanese language. This script

31. Sumiko Shinozuka, "Women, Letters, and Literature," unpublished address at the Institute of Early Women's Writing, University of Alberta, September 1993. See also her "Shokan to bungaku: "Richaadoson no shokantai shōsetsu to kagerō nikki o chūshin ni," in *Kyōritsu: Kokusai bunka* 1.1 (March 1991): 135–45; and "Kagerō nikki to afura bein no shokantai shōsetsu," in Ikeda Tsuyako, ed., *Ōchō nikki no shinkenkyū* (Tokyo: Kasamashoin, 1995), 379–401.

was hiragana, and the date of its gaining full currency in the world at large is around 905, the date of the first imperially commissioned and quickly canonized anthology of poetry, the *Kokinshū*. Prior to this time, the only literacy possible was in the Chinese language.[32] There are instances of women composing poems in Chinese in the earlier period.[33] Moreover, there is the famous account in the *Murasaki Shikibu Diary* (ca. 1010) of the author listening to her brother's lessons in Chinese and picking them up so much faster than her brother that her father was moved to say he wished she had been born a boy.[34] While that passage indicates that some Heian women still did acquire knowledge of Chinese, it was not considered useful knowledge for a woman, and women were not encouraged to pursue it. It was the evolution of the hiragana script that gave women the freedom to write the language they spoke. We know that women were quick to take advantage of it because the script came to be known as *onnade*, "woman's hand." Moreover, a mere three decades after the script had evolved, the writing of the native language in hiragana had come to be associated with women so thoroughly that Ki no Tsurayuki, the principle compiler and author of the Japanese preface to *Kokinshū*, felt compelled to take the persona of a woman in order to write a diary in the native language.[35]

However, writing in *onnade* or "woman's hand" was never the exclusive preserve of women. In fact, the most famous examples of that kind of calligraphy that have been preserved are all in men's hands. Moreover, it seems that men did write a great number of literary texts in hiragana in the early part of the tenth century. Even the example given above of Ki no Tsurayuki writing in a woman's persona because he was writing in hiragana/*onnade* is also an indication of men doing substantial writing in that script.

The "Old Tales": Early Monogatari *Literature*

One area where it is assumed that men were the leaders in developing a native prose style was in *monogatari* or tale literature. There is a consensus that men wrote all the early romance literature, that is, prior to the

32. There was a rather cumbersome system of transcription for Japanese known as *manyōgana* developed in the eighth century, and while it played a critical role in making it possible to record some early Japanese texts, it was so difficult and complex that it did not become a generally practiced writing system. Writing in Chinese was the standard mode of writing.
33. For example, see the poem by Princess Uchiko (807–47) in Donald Keene, *Anthology of Japanese Literature, from the Earliest Era to the Mid-Nineteenth Century* (New York: Grove, 1955), 164.
34. Bowring, *Murasaki Shikibu, Her Diary*, 139.
35. The "Tosa Diary" in Miner, *Japanese Poetic Diaries*.

eleventh century, but that the primary readers of the tale literature were women. An important piece of evidence indicating that the reading of romance literature was considered a preoccupation of women is from the eleventh-century *Tale of Genji*, the greatest tale of them all. In the novel, the hero Genji comes upon his foster daughter reading tales and chides her about her enthusiasm for such a trivial diversion. However, he admits to reading tales himself from time to time and then launches into the famous "apology for fiction" that places tale literature on a par with history. He says:

> I have been rude and unfair to your romances, haven't I. They have set down and preserved happenings from the age of the gods to our own. The Chronicles of Japan and the rest are a mere fragment of the whole truth. It is your romances that fill in the details.[36]

It is clear that by the time of *The Tale of Genji*, tale literature had been considered an amusement for women for a long time. *The Tale of Genji* author was a woman, but when the author of the *Kagerō Diary* talks about the odds and ends of the old tales that are just so much fantasy, it is assumed that the old tales she read would have been written by men. It is a curious situation in world literary history. We have the production of literature for women by men, and the question arises why would men devote so much energy to producing diversions for women? Akiyama Ken, in response to this question, said that the literature was likely produced by slightly lower class serving men in aristocratic households as part of their duties.[37] This might help explain why so much of the early tale literature was anonymous.

We are hampered in our knowledge of what kinds of tales the author of the *Kagerō Diary* was referring to by the fact that so few of the early tales have survived. Two extant tales that certainly predate the *Kagerō Diary* are *The Tales of Ise* [38] and *The Tale of the Bamboo Cutter*.[39] *The Tales of Ise* is actually a poem tale, that is, a collection of anecdotes that provide contexts for poems. *The Tale of the Bamboo Cutter* is a fantasy telling the story of a magical child who actually turns out to be a creature of the moon. Another extant tale that is thought to have existed at least in some

36. Seidensticker, *The Tale of Genji*, 437.
37. From a conversation with Akiyama Ken after his guest lecture at Tokyo Women's University in June 1994.
38. Helen Craig McCullough, trans., *The Tales of Ise: Lyrical Episodes from Tenth-Century Japan* (Stanford: Stanford University Press, 1968).
39. Donald Keene, trans., "The Tale of the Bamboo Cutter," in Thomas J. Rimer, ed., *Modern Japanese Fiction and Its Traditions* (Princeton: Princeton University Press, 1978).

version before the time of the *Kagerō Diary* is *The Tale of Lady Ochikubō*.[40] *Ochikubō monogatari* contains no supernatural elements. It is the classic Cinderella story of a beautiful and good girl whose mother's death has left her at the mercy of her stepmother and ugly, selfish stepsisters. A handsome aristocrat finds out about her, courts her, and eventually marries her; they live happily ever after while her husband invents ingenious ways to wreak vengeance on her step-family. When the author of the *Kagerō Diary* talks about the tales being "so much fantasy," literally *soragoto*, "empty talk," we have no way of knowing for certain which kind of fantasy she is referring to, the supernatural fantasy of something like *The Tale of the Bamboo Cutter*, or the idealized romance of the *Ochikubō monogatari*, but it seems likely that she had works like the *Ochikubō monogatari* in mind. At any rate, it can be asserted that another aspect of women's education was also in the prose literature of the tales, which was for the most part a literature of heroines that gave young women dreams of becoming heroines in their own domestic tales.

Religion

The religion of the Heian period was a syncretic mix of Buddhism and Shintoism, as is borne out in how religion appears in the *Kagerō Diary*. When the author of the *Kagerō Diary* articulates religious thoughts, they are usually of a Buddhist nature, the most common one being the awareness of the fragility of human existence. Take for example this poem that was written when she heard that the brother of the monk who had officiated at her mother's funeral had passed away suddenly (cf. p. 119):

omohiki ya	Who would have guessed,
kumo no mori wo	that he would leave behind
uchisutete	the forest of clouds
sora no keburi ni	and rise up with the smoke
tatamu mono to ha	disappearing into the sky.

Ceremonies held in conjunction with deaths in the family were Buddhist, since in Japan Buddhism had a virtual monopoly on the management of death through ritual. However, a lot of the religious activities the author participates in are Shinto. Her offering of poems at Shinto shrines and watching processions to the Kamo Shrine are all examples of Shinto activities. In fact, all the festivals mentioned in the diary are Shinto festivals.

The aspect of religion most foreign to modern Western readers is the elaborate system of taboos that evolved from what may be called the

40. Wilfred Whitehouse and Eizo Yanagisawa, trans., *The Tale of Lady Ochikubō* (Tokyo: Hokuseidō Press, 1965).

"science" of the time, Chinese yin-yang cosmology, as it was grafted onto a native body of beliefs regarding supernatural forces. Chinese cosmology was based on the movements of heavenly bodies and the movements of forces that could loosely be called gods. The astrological calendar determined which days were lucky and which unlucky. The movements of the forces in accordance with the calendar determined which directions were safe or dangerous. Perhaps the best way to convey the spirit of these taboos is to refer to the vestiges of them that remain in present-day Japanese society. For example, a *butsumetsu* day, the most inauspicious of the six designations for days, occurs four to five times a month in the Chinese calendar. Even in contemporary Japan, people customarily avoid that day for holding celebrations, as evidenced by the fact that wedding halls will give discounts to anyone willing to hold a wedding on a *butsumetsu* day. In the Heian period, not only was belief in this system very strong, but the elaboration of the system, particularly within aristocratic society, meant that many aspects of aristocrats' lives—when they could go places, in which directions they could move—were all impacted by this system. It became a calendar for one's life. Moreover, in the general absence of "public" holidays, the periods of ritual seclusion required within the system may have functioned as periods of rest for aristocrats. Someone of the status of Michinaga, for example, spent an average of seventy days a year in ritual seclusion.[41]

Not all taboos originated with the yin-yang cosmology; some came out of Buddhism and Shinto. For instance, Buddhism required a period of abstinence and seclusion before participating in certain rites. Shinto beliefs required abstinence and seclusion as ways of overcoming ritual defilement. In Shinto any contact with blood, sickness, or death incurs defilement. Hence menstruation required seclusion. The *Kagerō Diary* author's son must refrain from participation in a Shinto festival because he becomes defiled by accidentally seeing a dead dog (cf. p. 343).

Underlying all these various taboos was the belief that breaking the rules would result in misfortune. Yet a certain amount of negotiation with the rules was possible. If one visited a sick person, for example, one could avoid defilement by remaining standing at the threshold to the room. Likewise, if the rules demanded ritual seclusion and yet it seemed absolutely necessary to go out, as long as one stayed in one's carriage, seclusion had technically not been broken. Moreover, the system could sometimes serve as an excuse to avoid doing something one did not want to

41. Francine Hérail, *La cour du Japon à l'époque de Heian* (Paris: Hachette Livre, 1995), 226. Hérail provides a good general description of the yin-yang cosmology system in Heian Japan. McCullough and McCullough give a summary of the practice of ritual seclusion in a supplementary note to *A Tale of Flowering Fortunes*, 784–85.

do. For example, later on in the *Kagerō Diary*, when relations between the author and her husband have become strained, it is curious how often her direction is forbidden to him. The author remarks herself that it seems to be only her direction that is forbidden (cf. p. 269). The very complexity of the system lent itself to this kind of use. The yin-yang calendar and various other taboos affected the ebb and flow of one's daily activities but remained an exterior aspect of religion.

The religious activity to which the author of the *Kagerō Diary* devotes the most attention and seriousness of purpose is pilgrimages, and she divides her efforts almost equally between Shinto and Buddhist sites. The rite of purification she goes to perform at Karasaki on Lake Biwa is a Shinto ritual. Her pilgrimages to Shinto sacred sites include the visits to the Kamo and Fushimi Inari shrines. Her pilgrimages to Buddhist sites are to Hase Temple and Ishiyama Temple. However, the reader will find it hard to distinguish her Shinto pilgrimages from her Buddhist ones, since the purpose of both kinds of pilgrimage seems to be the same—to pray for the fulfillment of a fervent desire. Moreover, that desire is invariably for some benefit in this life.

Sometimes the impetus for going on a pilgrimage seems to be something as lighthearted as sightseeing. In one place, the author is persuaded by her attendants, who say, "Let's go on a pilgrimage and view the maple leaves at the same time" (cf. p. 317). However, other times she seems driven to make a pilgrimage out of a sense of desperation. Her pilgrimage to Ishiyama Temple is such a case. As she describes it, she runs out of the house at dawn on foot (cf. p. 207). For someone unaccustomed to walking, the journey to Ishiyama on foot would be an act of self-abnegation. It appears that all her other pilgrimages were by ox carriage, the normal mode of transport for aristocrats in the capital area.

Undoubtedly, the most profound encounter with religion on the part of the *Kagerō Diary* author is her consideration of becoming a nun, which occurs in the latter part of book two (cf. pp. 233–53). The author goes on retreat to a Buddhist temple in a confused and tortured state of mind, and the thought of becoming a nun seems to offer the possibility of release. The occasions for and the meaning of becoming a nun in Heian Japan ought to be put in context here.

Buddhism had orders for both monks and nuns. Sometimes superfluous male offspring of aristocratic families were made monks as a way of providing them a sinecure, but that was seldom the reason a woman became a nun. Many aristocrats, both male and female, often took the tonsure in old age as a way of signaling withdrawal from activity in this world and entering preparation for the next. It was a form of "retirement," if you will, when no other formal kind of retirement was possible. Furthermore, as a response to misfortune in one's life, such as the death of a loved one or a serious illness, taking the tonsure was regarded as a sad but understandable act. However, when a young man or woman without some tragedy as a catalyst but rather of their own volition became a monk or nun, it seems to have been upsetting to others. For example, in book one of the diary, Michitsuna's Mother mentions the sudden taking of the tonsure by a cousin of her husband, Fujiwara Sukemasa, who, as she says, "without warning, abandoned his mother and wife and stole away to Mt. Hiei" (cf. p. 145). People found this "shocking and sad."[42] One gets the sense that such an act struck others as a mark of mental unbalance. In the *Kagerō Diary* author's case, when she goes on her retreat, not only is she too young for people to accept her becoming a nun as a form of retirement, but since the future of her son had not yet been settled, it would have appeared to be an antisocial act, virtually an abandonment of her duties. Moreover, it is possible that people would have inferred that her real motive for taking the tonsure was to embarrass and humiliate her husband rather than genuine religious commitment. Her husband's strong objection to her going on retreat seems to indicate he interpreted her actions in that light. In any case, the decision to take the tonsure except in certain conventional circumstances was fraught with social consequences. For Michitsuna's Mother, becoming a nun balanced on the edge between being a release and an act of resistance.

THE AUTHOR AND THE PEOPLE AROUND HER

We know exactly whose daughter, whose wife, and whose mother the author of the *Kagerō Diary* was, but we do not know her personal name. She has come down to posterity as Michitsuna's Mother. One reason why we do not know her personal name is that the personal names of women were not generally noted in genealogies. The only women whose personal names were recorded were the consorts, mothers, and grandmothers of emperors. However, there is another reason why women's names were lost, and that is because there was, and still is to a certain extent in Japan, a reserve with respect to the use of personal names. Men's personal names were for their public record, but those names, so far as we can tell from literature, were not used in daily life. A person was almost always referred to by his or her title or role. Not once in the *Kagerō Diary*, for example, does the author refer to her husband or son by their personal

42. One of Kaneie's younger brothers by a different mother, Takamitsu, also took the tonsure suddenly in 961. The disturbance this caused his family is recorded in the *Tōnomine shōshō monogatari* (Lynne Miyake, "*Tōnomine shōshō monogatari*: A Translation and Critical Study," Ph.D. dissertation, University of California at Berkeley, 1985).

names. She refers to her son as "the young one" until by an act of resistance he expresses his independence from her, and then she calls him by his official title (cf. p. 237), for to be an adult male in Heian aristocratic society was always to have a title of some kind. Thus, men's names were preserved in public records and women's names were for the most part lost because they did not have a public role.

It is not known exactly when Michitsuna's Mother was born. From a reference to a prediction about her own death that the author makes in the latter part of the diary, scholars surmise that she may have been thirty-seven years old that year because, by the Chinese astrological calendar, the thirty-third and thirty-seventh years of a woman's life were considered to be particularly dangerous. Calculating back from that year as her thirty-seventh, she would have been born about 936.[43] This would have made her between eighteen and nineteen at the time of her marriage, which also fits, so this view has become the accepted one.

Parents and Siblings

Her father was Fujiwara Tomoyasu. The Fujiwara clan dominated politics for most of the Heian period, but it was a huge family and Tomoyasu belonged to one of its less important branches. Since Tomoyasu's father had an undistinguished career and had taken posts as provincial governor, the family had descended to provincial governor class, from which it was virtually impossible to rise again to the higher ranks of the aristocracy.

Who the author's mother was is uncertain. Conjecture can only be made about the mother's identity from the author's relationship to her two brothers. The author is known to have had one older brother, Masayoshi (other possible reading, Masatō), and one younger brother, Nagayoshi (or Nagatō). These two sons of Tomoyasu had different mothers. Apparently Masayoshi's mother was Tonomonokami Harumichi's daughter and Nagayoshi's mother was Minamoto Mitomeru's daughter. However, there is no conclusive evidence as to which brother shared the same mother with her. In the *Kagerō Diary* itself, the author only makes reference to "my brother" without further specifics. However, given that the brother she exchanges poems with at the end of the mourning period for her mother in 964 must have been Masayoshi (because Nagayoshi would have been too young), the *Zenshū* commentators opt for the theory that she shared the same mother with Masayoshi.[44] Whoever the mother may have been, most of what is known about her is found in the diary itself. She hovers in the background of the first book as a steadying influence. She is referred to

43. Oka Kazuo, *Michitsuna bo*, rev. ed. (Tokyo: Yūseidō, 1970 [1986 reprint]), 12.
44. *Zenshū*, 85–86.

literally in the diary as "the old fashioned person." The depth of the author's relationship with her mother can be gauged by the author's extreme reaction to her mother's death and the frequency with which she recalls her mother in later years.

If it is accepted that Masayoshi was the brother that shared the same mother with the author, then it would follow that all the references to a brother in the diary would be to him. Masayoshi is reported to have served as governor of Bizen and Iga provinces. He married a woman who was likely an elder sister of Sei Shōnagon, author of *The Pillow Book*.[45] The author's relations with Nagayoshi as a sibling with a different mother would have been more distant. However, Nagayoshi had a distinguished reputation as a poet, and it is conjectured that the brother and sister might have had some literary connection with one another. The most definite piece of evidence for that kind of contact is the record of the presence of both Nagayoshi and Michitsuna at a poetry contest sponsored by Retired Emperor Kazan in 986. Michitsuna presented one of his mother's poems as an entry in the contest.[46] Granted, this hardly qualifies as evidence of a close relationship; nonetheless, the feeling that a brother and sister who were both skilled poets must have had some interaction persists, and it has been suggested that it was Nagayoshi who compiled the anthology of the author's poetry that is appended to all extant manuscripts of the diary.[47]

There were sisters in the family as well. In the first part of the diary, the author mentions a sister living in the same household who is visited by a husband, and it is assumed this is an elder sister (cf. p. 71). Other documents record that Fujiwara Tamemasa married a daughter of Tomoyasu, and so commentators assume his wife was that elder sister.[48] This sister leaves the household to live in a dwelling apparently provided by her husband and then follows that husband to a post in the provinces. Mention of Tamemasa and a daughter of Tamemasa (presumably the author's niece) comes up in the poetry collection at the end of the diary, which would indicate that the author maintained a close connection with her elder sister and Tamemasa through the years. The relationship through marriage with Tamemasa also links the author distantly with Murasaki Shikibu. Since the daughter of Tamemasa's younger brother was the mother of Murasaki Shikibu, the author would have been a great aunt (in-law) of Murasaki Shikibu. It is unlikely that there was any personal contact between these two authors, but this family connection may have been a route by which a manuscript of the *Kagerō Diary* could have come into

45. Ibid.
46. Ibid., 86.
47. Ibid., 87.
48. Ibid.

the hands of Murasaki Shikibu. Later in the diary, the author mentions another sister who is living with her. This is the sister we see with her at the beginning of book two jesting about starting off the New Year auspiciously (cf. p. 169). This sister also has a gentleman caller, and she stays with the author for part of her retreat to a temple in the middle part of the diary. It is assumed this was a younger sister. Finally, much later in the diary, the author sends a congratulatory poem to her father upon the birth of another daughter. This is many years after the death of the author's mother. It seems her father took a very young wife because the author herself is about thirty-six when this new younger sister is born. As a sister from a different mother, the relationship would not have been close in the first place, and the great difference in age would also have precluded much contact between the two. Nonetheless, it is curious that this sister was likely the mother of Sugawara Takasue's daughter, the author of the *Sarashina Diary*.[49] Through family ties of one kind or another, the *Kagerō Diary* author is a senior relative to three of the most important women authors in the Heian period.

Husband

So far as the diary is concerned, the most critical relationship in the author's life was with her husband. Her husband was Fujiwara Kaneie (929–90), the third son of Fujiwara Morosuke (908–60). Kaneie and the author shared the same great-great-grandfather in the Fujiwara lineage, but her husband's family was at that time the ascendant northern branch of the Fujiwara clan, which monopolized all the high offices at court. From the point of view of the author's father, this proposal must have seemed like a tantalizing prospect. He could no longer aspire to high office himself, but if his daughter were to marry one of the future leaders of the clan, the offspring of that union would have access to high positions.[50] If they were girls they might become imperial consorts, and if they were boys, they might even rise to minister of the left or right, regent, or chancellor. However, Kaneie was the third son, so in order to assume leadership of the Fujiwara clan, he would have to outlast his elder brothers. In 954 when he made the proposal, he was twenty-six and still only captain of the Right Guards, not an extremely distinguished position. Nonetheless, he had potential and influence. It is certainly more than coincidence that the author's father receives his first lucrative post as a provincial governor within the first year of the marriage.

49. Ibid., 89.
50. Ibid.

When Kaneie married the author, he already had one wife, Tokihime, whose name we know because her daughters eventually bore emperors. At the time of Kaneie's proposal to the author, he only had one son with Tokihime. Tokihime came from the same provincial governor's class as the author so they were roughly equal in rank to begin with. Tokihime went on, however, to bear Kaneie three sons and two daughters, thus becoming indisputably his principal wife. Kaneie went on to collect and discard more wives. In the course of the diary, only a year after his marriage to the author, he takes up with a woman known as the Machi Alley woman. Then, in 970 he begins an affair with one of his late uncle's handmaidens, Ōmi. We learn later in the diary that he had also had an affair during the years in between with the daughter of a former high official, Minamoto Kanetada. It is the child of this union that the author eventually adopts when the girl is already twelve or thirteen years old. From historical records, we know that he continued to marry and have affairs right up until his death. He may be regarded as following in his father's footsteps in this respect since his father, Morosuke, had nineteen children by several different wives.

Kaneie did live up to his political potential assuming both the posts of regent and chancellor toward the end of his life. However, that was some time after relations between him and the author had ended. Moreover, the fruits of Kaneie's political success were mainly enjoyed by his three sons by Tokihime. In fact, his third son, Michinaga, became the greatest Fujiwara hegemon of them all.

Of course, we only get to see Kaneie through the author's eyes in the diary. At one point in the early period of their marriage, he responds to a long poem from his wife with one of his own (cf. pp. 95–99). It is the most sustained statement from him in the work. He was an able poet and certainly a lot of the author's attraction for him must have been her skill at poetry. He also appears as something of a wit. His reaction to the author's expression of chagrin is often to try and cajole her out of her temper with jokes. Failing that he ignores her moods apparently in the hopes they will go away. Either way he had difficulty just listening to her. Nonetheless, he seems to have been deeply attached to Michitsuna's Mother. Since she had neither the wealth, social standing, nor significant number of children that would have made it a difficult relationship to sever, it can only have been a profound affection that kept him in the marriage for sixteen years.

Other Wives and Affairs Noted in the Diary

Of her husband's other wives, Tokihime is the only one with whom the author herself had any continuous relationship. When the author first records sending a poem to Tokihime commiserating over the infidelity of their mutual husband, she prefaces it with the remark that she had already exchanged correspondence with the woman before. It appears that the author was always the one to initiate the communication. Tokihime's responses seem very guarded. After all, from Tokihime's position, the author must have been seen as a great threat. The two women were evenly matched in social status, and we know from contemporary records that the author had a reputation for being both a great beauty and a skilled poet. Tokihime likely regarded the author as the bane of her existence. This finds overt expression in the poetry exchange between the two women at the Kamo Festival after some ten years of the author's marriage, where in a witty way, Tokihime accuses the author of cruelty (cf. p. 129). In the end, however, Tokihime's fertile womb won the competition between the two wives. With five children, her position became unassailable.

Of the other wives, little else is known about them beyond what the diary tells us. The Machi Alley woman, who gets her name from her place of residence, is reported to have been the unrecognized daughter of an unrecognized son of a prince. This constituted two strikes of "illegitimacy" against her, yet she was descended from royalty and still apparently possessed a residence of her own, even if not in the fashionable part of town. Why this woman, who suffers in the end such an unfortunate fate, should occasion such a consuming hatred in the author, when other affairs bothered her so much less, is an interesting question. Two factors are the author's immaturity and the timing of the affair; it came to light immediately following the birth of the author's child, when she was no doubt in an emotionally vulnerable state. Shinozuka has suggested that the author's intense hatred of the Machi Alley woman was a case of "transference" of the anger she could not express against her husband.[51] Of course, the "reason" for her emotion is ultimately unknowable.

However, the contrast in her response to her husband's affair with Minamoto Kanetada's daughter is intriguing. That affair would have occurred only about four years after the affair with the Machi Alley woman, but from the way the author recalls it, it seems as though the liaison did not upset her at all. It could have been that since the woman was older, the author did not consider her a threat right from the beginning. Whatever the circumstances, and while her passionate jealousy against the Machi Alley woman creates an unforgettable impression, the difference in her reaction to the two women suggests that it would be one-sided to see the author only as a hysterically jealous woman.

51. Shinozuka, *Kagerō nikki no kokoro to hyōgen*, 69.

Minamoto Kanetada's daughter is an example of an unmarried aristocratic Heian woman. There were apparently quite a large number of women in court society who were unable to marry.[52] Since women were expected to stay within the parent's home, there was no overwhelming economic need to marry. To remain single was sometimes preferable to marrying below one's social status. This may have been the case with Kanetada's daughter. She was of high birth but her family's fortunes were declining. After her father died, she lost her protection and became vulnerable to seduction by someone like Kaneie.

The last liaison of Kaneie to make its way into the diary was his marriage to the woman known as Ōmi, after her father, Fujiwara Kuniaki, who was provincial governor of Ōmi. She was of the same general social position as Michitsuna's Mother. However, she had been put into service as a personal attendant to Kaneie's uncle, Saneyori, when Saneyori was seventy years old. As Shinozuka notes, "She may perhaps be regarded as a sacrifice to the old man's lust."[53] Kaneie began his affair with her after Saneyori's death, and a couple of years later she bore him a daughter. That daughter Suishi eventually became principal handmaid for the crown prince and shared his bed. *Eiga monogatari* records that "Thanks to this daughter, the Lady of the Wing Chamber [Ōmi] who had had something of a reputation for loose behavior, had now become a personage of importance. It only went to show, people said, what a child could do for one."[54] *Eiga monogatari* goes on to talk about the career of Ōmi's second daughter, who was not by Kaneie, but by his son, Michitaka. One wonders if this was *Eiga monogatari*'s subtle way of saying that Ōmi's reputation for loose behavior was not unwarranted.

Children

As mentioned before, the author had only one son, Michitsuna. There are only fleeting episodes about him as a child in the diary, undoubtedly because his actual rearing would have been the responsibility of his nurse. There is the time when, at about the age of eleven, he gets caught in the middle of a quarrel between his parents (cf. p. 153). There is also the time when he frees his hunting hawks, to show his determination to become a monk if his mother is to become a nun (cf. p. 205). A mere two years later he is identifying more with his father than his mother (cf. p. 235). Then

52. Fukuto Sanae, *Heian chō no haha to ko: kizoku to shomin no kazoku seikatsushi* (Tokyo: Chūō Kōronsha, 1991), 37.
53. Shinozuka Sumiko, "Kagerō nikki nōto: atana no nai tegami," *Keisei* 73 (December 1989): 47.
54. McCullough and McCullough, *A Tale of Flowering Fortunes*, 136–37.

there are his love affairs, which occupy a large portion of the last part of the diary. Michitsuna may not have had as illustrious a career as his half-brothers by Tokihime, but it was not inconsiderable. He never had to serve as a provincial governor, and his highest post, that of major counsellor, was a respected position.

The daughter the author adopts in book three remains a shadowy figure. She was an unrecognized daughter of Kaneie by Minamoto Kanetada's daughter. As Kaneie is reported to have told the author, "A girl was born at that place I used to visit. She says it is mine. It may well be," indicating some uncertainty on his part about the girl's parentage (cf. pp. 287–91). She only comes into the diary on the day of her arrival at the author's house, where she meets her whole new family, including the father she has never seen. One wonders what the girl of twelve must have felt in such a strange situation. Afterward we see her in the diary only as a passive recipient of instruction in poetry and calligraphy, and as a source of worry for the author when one of Kaneie's younger brothers comes courting for the daughter's hand too soon. The author in the end tells us very little about her relationship with the girl, but some commentators have suggested that the author's reason for writing the diary at all was for the benefit of this adopted daughter.[55] After a promising beginning, Kaneie does not in the end take the same interest in this daughter as he does in his daughters by Tokihime or even the daughter by Ōmi. It is conjectured that this daughter ended up serving at court as a lady-in-waiting to Kaneie's second daughter, Senshi, when she became empress.[56]

Friends

Other people of importance in the author's circle were female friends. Although she does not name most of them, there is quite a number. She goes on several excursions and pilgrimages with unnamed female friends. When she secludes herself during her retreat, she is visited by a woman who comes to scold her and ends up in tears with her. She carries on a correspondence with many friends. Her long poem for the wife of Minamoto Takaakira and subsequent correspondence with her is some of the most touching writing in the work. However, it is her friendship with Kaneie's sister, Tōshi, or Lady Jōganden as she is referred to most often in the diary, that is one of the highlights in her life. She first has the occasion to get to know Tōshi when they are temporarily sharing one of Kaneie's houses (cf. p. 147). Friendship with Tōshi was as close as the author ever got to the glamour of the court. Tōshi had been married to an imperial

55. Kakimoto Tsutomu, *Kagerō nikki zenchūshaku* (Tokyo: Kadokawa Shoten, 1966), 19.
56. *Zenshū*, 92.

prince who died young. Then she was involved in an affair with the emperor Murakami. Emperor Murakami's principal consort was Tōshi's and Kaneie's elder sister, Anshi. Tōshi was in the habit of visiting her elder sister at court, and it was during one of those visits that the emperor became enamored of her. Anshi turned a blind eye to a couple of meetings but then asserted her authority and ended the affair. *Eiga monogatari*, from which the above account is paraphrased, says in summation, "Tōshi was sweet and fashionable—and probably something of a flirt, for otherwise such a thing would have been unlikely to happen."[57] When Anshi died, however, Emperor Murakami quickly summoned Tōshi to his side. They did not have long together, because a mere three years later, Murakami died. It is shortly after Murakami's death that Tōshi comes to share the same house with the author. They form a friendship that lasts throughout the period recorded by the diary.

Public Reputation of Michitsuna's Mother

We will conclude this section with a few remarks about the author's public reputation. Given that she was a woman at home without a public persona as such, she is mentioned surprisingly often in the historical record. In the *Sonpi bunmyaku*, she is noted as one of the most famous "beauties of the era."[58] Moreover, her skill as a poet and authorship of the *Kagerō Diary* are noted in *Ōkagami*. The entry is ostensibly about Michitsuna but ends up talking more about his mother:

> His mother, an accomplished poet, set down an account of the things that happened while Kaneie was visiting her, together with some poems from the same period. She named the work *Gossamer Journal* [*Kagerō Diary*], and allowed it to be made public.[59]

This nearly contemporary account gives us some idea of her reputation as a poet and also indicates that the diary was in circulation soon after its composition. A piece of internal evidence in the diary regarding the recognition of the author as a poet is the invitation to compose poems for the congratulatory screen for the fiftieth birthday of her husband's uncle, Moromasa (cf. pp. 187–89). Since Moromasa was a powerful politician, only first rank poets would have been asked to contribute poems for the final selection. Furthermore, the poetry collection at the end of the volume contains a number of poems submitted for poetry contests, again evidence

57. McCullough and McCullough, A *Tale of Flowering Fortunes*, 81.
58. Oka, *Michitsuna bo*, 12.
59. Helen McCullough, *Ōkagami*, 166.

of her activity as a professional poet. Finally, a number of her poems were included in imperial poetry anthologies for the next two hundred years.[60] The epitome of her recognition as a poet came with the inclusion of one of her poems (cf. p. 71) in the *Hyakunin isshu*, "One Hundred Poets, One Poem Each," compiled in the early thirteenth century by the great arbiter of poetic taste, Fujiwara Teika.[61] The next section will look in more detail at the artistry of both her poetry and prose.

THE ARTISTRY OF THE TEXT

It was the sheer beauty of the text that first inspired me to translate the *Kagerō Diary*. That beauty is hard to convey in English translation not only because the language of this poetry is linguistically so different from English, but also because the whole background of the literary tradition that gives the language full meaning is missing for English readers. This section will attempt to convey the literary background and some of the specificity of the language of the text.

Balance between Poetry and Prose in the Text

In the previous section, a passage from the historical document *Ōkagami* was cited as evidence of the author's reputation as a poet among her contemporaries. I would like to revisit that citation with a more literal translation:

> As for his mother, *since she was extremely skillful as a poet*, she brought together and wrote down the poems and the events of the period when his lordship [Kaneie] was visiting her, calling it the *Kagerō Diary* and letting it be spread about in the world.[62]

This indicates that so far as her contemporaries were concerned, there was something akin to a causal relationship between her being a poet and composing this work. It was not only that being a poet meant being skillful at writing; it may also have meant that one of her intentions was to create a poetry anthology. Poetry was the dominant literary form of the

60. For a good summary in English of the recognition of Michitsuna's Mother as a *waka* poet through the inclusion of her poems in public and private anthologies, poetry contests, and so on, see Edith Sarra, *Fictions of Femininity: Literary Inventions of Gender in Japanese Court Women's Memoirs* (Stanford: Stanford University Press, 1996).

61. Ariyoshi Tamotsu, *Hyakunin isshū zenyaku-chū* (Tokyo: Kōdansha, 1983), and Joshua Mostow, *Pictures of the Heart: The One Hundred Poets, One Poem Each Collection, Its Commentaries and Pictures* (Honolulu: University of Hawaii Press, 1996).

62. Tachibana Kenji, *Ōkagami/Ryōjin hishō*, in *Nihon koten bungaku zenshū* 20 (Tokyo: Shōgakkan, 1974), 259–60.

period and there was hardly any writing in Japanese that did not contain poetry. There was a range of texts that varied with respect to the degree of importance poetry had in them. These texts varied from, for example, *The Tales of Ise*,[63] where the poetry is primary and the prose essentially provides context for the poetry, to *The Tale of the Bamboo Cutter*,[64] where the storytelling of the prose is paramount and the poetry secondary. If a scale were drawn with the above two texts as the opposite poles, the *Kagerō Diary* would sit right in the middle. Particularly in the first part of the work, it is more like *The Tales of Ise*, where the main role of the prose is to provide context for the poetry. However, even by the latter part of book one, particularly in the author's description of her pilgrimage to Hase, the prose of the text comes into its own.

The Poetry and Its Literary Context

As mentioned above, Michitsuna's Mother was recognized as a skilled poet. To be skillful at poetry in this age meant to channel one's inspiration through the conduit of the poetic tradition already established by the *Kokinshū* poetry anthology. *Kokinshū* was completed around A.D. 905. It was the first anthology of Japanese poetry to be sponsored by the emperor, signaling the recognition of Japanese poetry as a serious enterprise (previously, imperially sponsored anthologies had been limited to poetry in Chinese), and it was the first major text of the literary tradition to be written in the phonetic script, hiragana. The Japanese preface (it had a Chinese preface as well, to confer the necessary air of seriousness) broke ground as the first attempt to write discursively in the native language. This preface made a declaration about the essential nature of Japanese poetry that was to determine the course of that poetic tradition for the next six hundred years:

> Japanese poetry, with the human heart for a seed, grows into the countless leaves of words. Since for people in the world, there is such a lushness of things, in response to seeing things, hearing things, we are moved to express what we feel in our hearts. Hearing the warbler in the blossoms or the voice of frogs living in water, what living thing is not moved to song [poetry]. It is poetry that without using force moves heaven and earth, causes tender feelings in invisible spirits and demons, softens the relations between men and women, and consoles the fierce hearts of warriors.[65]

63. Helen McCullough, *Tales of Ise*.
64. Donald Keene, "The Tale of the Bamboo Cutter."
65. Okumura Tsuneya, *Kokin waka shū* (Tokyo: Shinchōsha, 1978), 11.

Thus, the preface's author, Ki no Tsurayuki, stakes out the territory for Japanese poetry squarely in the domain of the expression of feeling. The characteristics of the poems compiled in *Kokinshū* define the conventions of Japanese poetry from that point forward. What are those conventions?

First, the preferred form for Japanese poetry becomes the thirty-one syllable *tanka*, or "short poem," another name for which is simply *waka*, "Japanese poem."[66] The thirty-one syllables are divided into five units called *ku* in the scheme of 5/7/5/7/7, the numbers standing for the number of syllables. *Ku* does not mean "line" exactly, although in the format the poems will be presented here, each *ku* will be the equivalent of a line. In Japanese manuscripts of the period, *waka* are usually written in one or two lines, and there has been much debate in recent years as to whether the rendering of *waka* into five lines in English is a distortion.[67] However, even if, orthographically in Japanese, *waka* are written in one or two lines, whenever *waka* are recited aloud, the *ku* breaks are registered distinctly in the rhythm. I would suggest that one of the ways one can give a sense of those rhythm breaks in English translation is with line breaks, so the translations presented in this volume will follow what has become conventional practice in English to render *waka* in five lines.

There is a perhaps a link between the choice of a brief form for the standard form of poetry, and the focus of poetry upon lyric expression. It is characteristic of feelings that they do not persist. They shift and change. To capture feeling is to create a lyric moment. Long poems must include something other than expression of feeling; the most common move is to narrative, but the *waka* being a short form could concentrate on the lyric moment. Actually Ishikawa Takuboku, a poet of this form in the twentieth century, said it eloquently:

> People say the tanka form is inconvenient because it's so short. I think its shortness is precisely what makes it convenient. . . . We are constantly being subjected to so many sensations, coming from both inside and outside ourselves, that we forget them soon after they occur, or even if we remember them for a little while, we end up by never once in our whole lifetimes ever expressing them because there is not enough content to sustain

66. *Tanka* means literally "short poem" and *waka* means "Japanese poem." Although they refer to the same form of poetry, the usage is a little different. *Waka* is used more often in the context of classical poetry up to nineteenth century, while *tanka* is generally used in the context of modern Japanese poetry since the *tanka* form is still being written by some modern poets.

67. The translator Hiroaki Sato is the most vigorous exponent of *waka* as a "single line" poem. For a summary of his views on this issue, see the introduction to his translation of *String of Beads: Complete Poems of Princess Shikishi* (Honolulu: University of Hawaii Press, 1993), 30.

> the thought. . . . Although a sensation may last only a second, it is a second that will never return again. I refuse to let such moments slip by.[68]

The choice of a brief form for the norm in poetry had other ramifications for the role of poetry in social interaction. A short form lends itself to being included in letters and facilitates impromptu composition. In conjunction with having fixed and easily understood conventions, the brevity of *waka* helped keep poetry within everyone's reach. It may not be easy to write a superb *waka*, but it is not difficult to write one that merely follows the conventions and fits the form of thirty-one syllables.

Kokinshū also determined that the main topics for Japanese poetry would be nature and love. Of the twenty books of *Kokinshū*, six are devoted exclusively to poems of the four seasons (thus subjects from nature) and five to love. Moreover, the topics of the other books, such as grief, parting, and travel, overlap with nature and/or love. As the reader will note in the *Kagerō Diary*, the language of poems of friendship is often indistinguishable from that of love poems. Although it was possible to write a love poem without natural imagery, in actual practice, they were often intertwined. Thus, nature and love constitute the essential domain of Japanese poetry.

The predilection for expressing feeling through conventional imagery of the four seasons had an important effect. It linked interior emotion to the exterior world. For example, if one wanted to write a poem to express a feeling and it was the fifth month, there was a set of natural imagery to choose from, already determined by tradition: irises, *unohana* (a kind of shrub with white blossoms), the cuckoo, summer rains. It was poetically unthinkable to use a natural image from a season other than the season one was in, even in a metaphorical way, although some natural imagery, particularly that of the sea, was not linked to any particular season and was therefore potentially available for any poem. Conventional and limiting as such a poetic practice may seem, it meant that when you wanted to express a feeling inside, you first looked outside (mentally or actually) for what flora or fauna of the season could project that feeling. An example of this in the diary is when Michitsuna's Mother and Kaneie have become physically intimate again after an estrangement. The narrative prose of the section sets the scene thus: "While still lying down [an oblique reference to their having made love], and gazing at the flowers in rank, multicolored profusion, we said the following" (cf. pp. 83–85). From

68. As cited in Donald Keene, *Dawn to the West: Japanese Literature of the Modern Era* (New York: Holt, Rinehart, and Winston, 1984), 43–44.

the scene before them, they both choose images of flowers, dew, and autumn for a poetic exchange in which they express complex emotions of erotic closeness and lingering resentment. In this case, they literally look outside to find natural images that can mirror their feelings. This practice, although guided by convention, actually grounds a poem in the here and now of the moment of composition, collapsing the line between interior and exterior worlds.

The *Kokinshū* not only established the topics that would remain the domain of Japanese *waka* poetry but it also to a great extent fixed the vocabulary to be used in poetry.[69] It has already been noted in the historical introduction how a Fujiwara patriarch enjoined his daughter to learn all of the poems of the *Kokinshū* by heart.[70] This was how the word trove and "rules" were learned. The rules were not abstracted from the poems but rather embodied in them. Thus, the *Kokinshū* was like a code book for Heian aristocrats. Given this, it will be no surprise to the reader that poetic allusion during the Heian period was most often to the poems of the *Kokinshū*, and in this respect the poems of Michitsuna's Mother are no exception.[71]

With the *Kokinshū* and the poetry it shaped for the next thousand years, we have a lyric poetry dedicated to the expression of personal emotion that is confined within very narrow conventions, thus assuring a communal unity to expression. The *waka* form embodies a code of communication that paradoxically expresses the individual person while at the same time affirming a communal mind. Michitsuna's Mother did not resist her poetic tradition. The artistry of her poetry is the artistry of her poetic tradition. Using examples from the *Kagerō Diary*, some of the technical aspects of the Heian poetic tradition will now be explicated. This section will also give the reader some insight into the problems and process of translation with regard to poetry in the text.

69. Successive imperially sponsored anthologies of poetry did add somewhat to the range of topics and approved vocabulary. The *Gosenshū*, which was completed around 958 and was therefore the only other imperial anthology to be known by the *Kagerō Diary* author, was noted for its use of use of vocabulary outside of that of the *Kokinshū*. However, the *Gosenshū* always suffered from unfavorable comparison with the *Kokinshū* and never exerted the same degree of influence. Donald Keene, *Seeds in the Heart: Japanese Literature from Earliest Times to the late Sixteenth Century* (New York: Henry Holt, 1993), 280–81.
70. Morris, *The World of the Shining Prince*, 221.
71. Michitsuna's Mother does allude to poems of her contemporaries upon occasion. The next most frequently cited and alluded to poetry collection in the *Kagerō Diary* is the *Kokin rokujō*, "Ancient and Modern Poems in Six Notebooks," an "unofficial" anthology that was not produced under official sponsorship but seemed to evolve as a reference handbook among poets of the Heian period.

Kakekotoba: *Pivot Word/Pun*

One of the most salient techniques of Heian poetry is the use of a type of pun called *kakekotoba*, "pivot word," because it pivots between two meanings. The English word "pun" seems inadequate to describe the complex phenomenon of *kakekotoba*, but I will use it because it is convenient and short. A rough approximation of how the technique of *kakekotoba* might work in English would be this:

He *leaves*
        fall yellow on the path
she *dies*
        the color of sorrow
into her *morning* gown.

Words with the same sound but different meanings are placed so that their doubled meaning can function as a juncture between two syntactic structures. In fact, Edwin Cranston, in his recently published anthology of *waka* poetry, has used the translation "juncture" for *kakekotoba*.[72] Here is an example of *kakekotoba* usage from the *Kagerō Diary*. The following poem was addressed to Tokihime, the first wife of the *Kagerō Diary* author's husband. The year before, Kaneie had taken up with a woman known in the diary as the Machi Alley woman. Michitsuna's Mother sent this poem to Tokihime to commiserate with her about Kaneie's absence from both their beds (cf. p. 75):

soko ni sahe	Even from your pond's depths,
karu to ifu naru	they say it has been reaped,
makomo gusa	the wild rice,
ikanaru sawa ni	in what marsh now does it put
ne wo todamuramu	down its roots and stay to sleep?

There are three *kakekotoba* in this poem. *Soko* in the first line means both "your place" and "bottom," as of pond. *Karu* means, "to be separated from" and "to reap," while *ne* means "root" and "sleep." The poem was written in the fifth month, which was when the stalks of *makomo*, a kind of wild rice, were harvested for making mats and pillows. The wild rice provides the unifying imagery for the poem with pond/marsh, reap, and roots. That the wild rice stalks were associated with the manufacture of bedding is also particularly appropriate. There is irony in the pun on "reap" and "to be separated from," since the Machi Alley woman's "harvest" is their loss. There even seems to be something a little naughty about the

72. Edwin A. Cranston, trans., *A Waka Anthology: Volume One: The Gem-Glistening Cup* (Stanford: Stanford University Press, 1993), xxiv.

pun available in "root" and "sleep." The imagery and puns together make this a rich and complex communication.

In the English translation, the puns have become metaphors, so it takes an effort of imagination to realize that in the original *soko ni sahe* conveys "simultaneously," "even at your place" and "even at the bottom [of the pond]." The same is true for the other two *kakekotoba*; it is like hearing two tracks of separate yet linked meaning. The density of meaning and imagery it makes possible is astonishing. Only rarely is it possible to create an analogous effect in English. However, I note the puns that occur in the poems so that the reader can be aware of their presence.

Makura Kotoba: *Pillow Words*

Perhaps one of the hardest techniques of Heian poetic diction for a Western audience to appreciate is the *makura kotoba* or "pillow word." It is often explained as analogous to the "fixed epithet" which occurs in Greek epic poetry, but the pillow word is more complex in its operation. The most intriguing thing about pillow words is that they are not definite in meaning. This is because the pillow words often come from ancient poetry and their etymological origins are obscure. Take the phrase, *sasagani no*, "of the *sasagani*," which is a pillow word for spider. *Sasagani* is a name for spider which perhaps started from a metaphor, since the *gani* part of *sasagani* may have come from *kani*, the word for crab. More important than the precise meaning of the term, however, is the incantatory ring it brings to the poem; it has the feeling of antiquity about it and signals that spider imagery is coming. Many pillow words are place names. Take for example this poem, composed by one of Kaneie's attendants for Michitsuna's Mother's serving ladies as part of the New Year's celebrations (cf. p. 277):

shimotsuke ya	Shimotsuke, hey!
woke no futara wo	This lid of a tub, we see
adjikinaku	unfortunately
kage mo uakabanu	is a mirror whereon
kagami to zo miru	your reflections do not float.

He is asking for the ladies to let themselves be seen. What does "Shimotsuke, hey!" have to do with the poem? Shimotsuke is a place-name in the area of Japan known today as Nikkō. There are two other places in the same district with the names Ooke and Futara. Ooke is homophonous for *oke*, "tub," and Futara with *futara*, "lid," so Shimotsuke became a pillow word for tubs and lids. It is not linear thinking that gives rise to pillow words but free association and usage in ancient poetry. For the most part, the pillow words have not been rendered in the present translation because they present even more difficulty than the pivot words, but again I have pointed them out in the notes to at least remind the reader that the translations are not transparent.

Engo: *Verbal Association*

Engo, literally "connected language," or as Earl Miner has translated it, "verbal association,"[73] represents another way that an associative mode of thinking became codified into a poetic technique. It is the constructing of a poem or part of a poem[74] around a cluster of words connected to a central image or motif. For example, in the poem above that has wild rice as a core image, "pond," "reap," and "root" are all *engo*-associated with wild rice. These three words are all simultaneously used as *kakekotoba*, which indicates how interwoven all the poetic techniques described here can be in usage. One of the places in the diary where the use of *engo* is conspicuous because it extends over six poems, is the poetic exchange between Kaneie and Prince Noriakira in book one (cf. pp. 101–3). The prince initiates the exchange with a poem in which the pun available on *tsuka*, "spool," in the word *tsukasa*, "court office," launches a play on textile-related vocabulary: "spool," "thread," "cut/break ties," "wind," "spin," *natsuhiki* (a special kind of summer-spun thread for linen), skeins, and so on. As in this example, *engo* often creates a sense of unity within a poem and between poems. The diary includes two long poems, *chōka*, one by Michitsuna's Mother (cf. pp. 89–93) and one by Kaneie (cf. pp. 95–97). In these long poems, the reader will notice that extended runs of associated vocabulary provide continuity in an otherwise meandering form. I have not noted the presence of *engo* specifically in the commentary to the translation largely because of the difficulty of separating it out from the use of puns, but wherever there is mention of associative language, the reader may assume that *engo* is at play.

Conclusion to the Waka *Section*

Waka poems are short but dense, not with meaning so much as with resonance; they constantly call up a shared and minutely appreciated poetic tradition. They play with language as though the words were threads in a borderless tapestry, and since the poems live in exchange, each poem

73. Earl Miner, Hiroko Odagiri, and Robert E. Morrell, *The Princeton Companion to Classical Japanese Literature* (Princeton: Princeton University Press, 1985), 273.

74. This discussion is limited to poetry, but *engo* can also be used in prose, particularly in later Japanese literature.

is always an invitation for a reciprocal creation. Michitsuna's Mother was not an original poet in her tradition; (it must be remembered that it was a tradition where originality was not the object of the game), yet she was adept at speaking her own meaning through the forms of the tradition. When we look at her prose, however, it is her originality that demands attention.

Characteristics of Michitsuna's Mother's Prose Style

It is important to stress how new Japanese prose was in Michitsuna's Mother's age. It was mentioned before that the preface of the *Kokinshū* was the first attempt to write discursively in the Japanese language. Prior to that, and for the most part, even after that, all expository writing was done in Chinese. Then in 935, the author of the *Kokinshū* preface, Ki no Tsurayuki, wrote an account in Japanese of a trip from Shikoku back to the capital, the *Tosa nikki* or *Tosa Diary*.[75] As mentioned at the beginning of the introduction, he used a woman's persona to write the diary, so much had writing of the vernacular language in phonetic script come to be associated with women. There were also the *monogatari* or "tales," presumably written by men for a largely female readership. At any rate, given that the *Kagerō Diary* was composed around 970, the Japanese prose tradition was only about sixty-five years old. Poetry was older because it had been written down in the eighth century and preserved since then as an oral tradition as well.

In that sense, the *Kokinshū* was the culmination of an already lengthy tradition. Prose, on the other hand, was very new and was appropriated by women who, being at the margins, had the freedom of irrelevance. It is hard to see this "irrelevance" now since for the last two hundred and fifty years the prose works of the Heian women writers have been declared masterpieces and the works that defined the age. Akiyama Ken has put this in perspective when he said that although the Heian period is now known as the age of *monogatari*, people of the Heian period would have been very surprised to hear it. To them the tales and prose works in general were just the diversions of women.[76] Perhaps it was both the newness and marginality of the prose medium that allowed it to be so malleable in the hands of Michitsuna's Mother.

Not all facets of interest in Michitsuna's Mother's prose are original with her; some are aspects of classical Japanese in general. In the next

75. The "Tosa Diary" in Miner, *Japanese Poetic Diaries*.
76. Akiyama, *Ōchō joryū bungaku no sekai*, 209.

section, I will first deal with general features of classical Japanese prose and then delineate Michitsuna's Mother's original contribution to the medium.

Avoidance of Pronouns

One feature of classical Japanese prose that causes headaches for modern readers and translators is the avoidance of pronouns and the general dropping of subjects. About ninety percent of the time that the reader sees an "I" in this translation of the *Kagerō Diary*, it was not there in the original. While a pronoun for "I," *ware*, did exist in classical Japanese, its actual usage was severely limited. On the other hand, gender-specific third-person pronouns did not even exist in classical Japanese. There was the word, *kare*, which in the modern language is used as the equivalent of "he," but in the Heian period, it meant only "that person"; in other words, it was the same as "*ano hito*." The unisex *hito* or "person" is used more frequently than *kare*, but neither of them are used often. Thus, in the numerous instances in the diary where the translation says of the author's husband that "he appeared," in the original it is simply *mietari*, "appeared." The reader is simply to understand "who" appeared, yet, paradoxically, the absence of explicit reference to her husband either with a pronoun or by use of his name seems to reaffirm his omnipresence in her consciousness.[77] However, as one might surmise, this very elliptical way of referring to subjects of actions can result in a troublesome ambiguity. The ellipsis of subject is general to classical Japanese, but at least in Heian fiction, the reader is aided in understanding who did or said what to whom by the fact that the narrating voice assumes a position within the social hierarchy and accordingly uses honorific forms of address and verb endings. For example, in *The Tale of Genji*, when Genji does something, the action verb is always given an honorific ending, so it is clear that he is the subject. Since the narrating voice in the *Kagerō Diary* is essentially the author talking to herself, there is no use of honorifics except in the quoted speech of others. This sometimes makes it difficult to know who the subject of a verb is. For example, in book three of the diary, in the section where Michitsuna's Mother unites her newly adopted daughter with the daughter's actual father, the author's husband, Kaneie, there is a line translated in the present work as, "*I couldn't help crying*, bringing my sleeve to my eyes many times. *He said*, 'Well, I never . . .'" (cf. p. 295), but in the original there is no subject specified for "couldn't help crying" or for "said," and

77. For a more detailed treatment of this issue, see Sonja Arntzen, "Translating Difference: a New Translation for the Kagerō Diary," *Japan Foundation Newsletter* (December 1993).

while the context makes it clear that the speaker of "Well, I never . . ." is Kaneie, commentators are divided down the middle as to whether the crying should be attributed to Michitsuna's Mother or Kaneie. Ultimately there is no way to know for sure. I have opted to follow the interpretation of the *Zenshū* commentators, because in places where expert opinion has been divided, unless I felt strongly otherwise, my practice has been to follow the *Zenshū* interpretation.

A similar problem comes up with the ungendered *hito* or "person." In book two, for example, when the author has retreated to a temple in Narutaki and Kaneie sends a member of his household office to scold the author into returning (cf. p. 241), there is no way to know whether that person was male or female, which is important in English where one must use either "he" or "she." My practice has been to make these ambiguous cases female because face-to-face conversations between men and women in this age were severely restricted.

There are other times when the author could be saying either "I" or "we." These are usually places where she describes a situation which involves her attendants. In an incident in book one, where she receives an order for sewing from Kaneie and in the end refuses to do it, the present translation says, ". . . and so it was decided; we sent the bundles back and as we suspected . . ." (cf. p. 81). This passage could just as easily be translated as "I sent the bundles back and as I suspected . . . ," but from the context of the passage, since the attendants have been included in the decision-making, it seemed reasonable to make the action collective.

Over and above the difficulties occasioned by such ambiguities as described above, the ellipsis of the first-person subject makes a difference to the construction of "self" in the diary. The fact that the "I" is understood in classical Japanese is not the same as having the "I" explicitly and constantly stated. I would suggest that the necessity of having a definite subject for every grammatically correct utterance in English is part and parcel of Western culture's traditional belief in a unitary self and separate others acting independently in a world of objects. Perhaps there is more to the writing of the first person subject with a capital "I" in English than typological convention. Is it not consistent with a dominating first-person subject viewpoint in the language and a conception that all persons are metaphysically as well as grammatically separate and distinct from one another? In classical Japanese and particularly in the *Kagerō Diary*, the general absence of a first-person pronoun creates a much more diffuse sense of self. It is a self with soft edges that bleeds into the quotations of the voices of others and the citation of others' letters. And yet, even without the constant reiteration of "I," it is a text of such intense first-person subjectivity.[78] This seems impossible to duplicate in English. I considered using small case "i" for awhile following the practice of some contemporary poetry and experimental fiction, but it seemed that such a strategy might end up drawing even more attention to the "I" than simply complying with convention. Instead I have opted to convey the sense of a diffuse self by keeping the interrupting voices of others intact in the text rather than resorting to paraphrase even where it would help smooth out a passage. In line with the same intention, I have also kept distinct through the use of italics the disrupting voice of the author's own consciousness, that is, her citation of bits of her own speech that she observes in her mind.

Tenseless Narrative

Another general feature of classical Japanese prose is what Richard Okada has referred to as "tenseless narrative":

> . . . the tenseless narrative does not mean "present-tense" narrative. The narrating easily refers to prior moments, but they are always anchored to the spatiotemporal coordinates of the particular moment in question. What happened once has relevance not as an always already reified, abstractable past point in linear time, but as the narrating moment continually represents it in a deictically determinate now.[79]

None of the suffixes from classical Japanese that are usually translated into English as past tenses, such as *nu*, *tsu*, and *tari*, are actually fixed past tenses. They all overlap with affirmation. Only the suffix *ki* is close to being a past tense, since it is used to denote actions in the past that one knows from direct personal experience. Given a grammatical description like this, one might assume that it would be the preferred ending in a text like the *Kagerō Diary*, which is the record of personal experience. Surprisingly, it hardly appears at all. Aside from the suffixes mentioned above, the most common perfective suffix is *keri*, a suffix that is used most often for narrated information that the speaker has learned

78. I am indebted to Lynn Miyake's "If 'I' were 'She' and 'She' were 'I': The Narration of the Kagerō Nikki," a conference paper at the 1993 Combined Western and Southwestern Conferences of the Association for Asian Studies, for insight into how pronoun reference creates such an intense first-person perspective. See also Watanabe Minoru's "Style and Point of View in the Kagerō Nikki," translated by Richard Bowring, *Journal of Japanese Studies* 10:2 (1984): 365–84, and the original article, "Tōjishateki hyōgen—Kagerō nikki," in *Heian bunshōshi* (Tokyo: Tokyo Daigaku Shuppankai, 1981), 90–112.

79. H. Richard Okada, *Figures of Resistance: Language, Poetry, and Narrating in the Tale of Genji and Other Mid-Heian Texts* (Durham: Duke Unversity Press, 1991), 179.

by hearsay. It is the use of this ending that gives the feeling of a tale to the *Kagerō Diary*. Another use of the *keri* suffix is for the narration of information about which the speaker experiences some sense of discovery or realization in the process of the narration. That is why *keri* is a common verb ending in the poetry of the period. Richard Okada quotes two Japanese grammarians who have attempted to explain the curious operation of *keri* by describing it in terms of bringing "the past into the present moment," or by saying that "when *keri* is used, the past is conceived of in some manner as existing at the present moment."[80] The editors of the Iwanami dictionary of classical Japanese, grappling with the same problem in description, have generalized the problem in these terms:

> There is a big difference in the way modern Europeans and ancient Japanese people conceived of time. Europeans think of time as having an objective existence and linear continuity, and they see it as something that can be divided up, so they have as a foundation the distinctions between past, present, and future. However, for the ancient Japanese, time was not an objective linear continuity. Rather, in an extremely subjective way, the future was the speaker's vague supposition or conjecture and the past was the presence of the speaker's memory or the evocation of the speaker's memory.[81]

It is an intriguing notion to narrate the past in such a way that it is recreated in the present. Just as with the construction of the self, tense in classical Japanese narrative is not connected to a world of hard and fast definitions. There is a shifting and conflation of tense just as there was a conflation of the self and other voices.

A typical passage in the *Kagerō Diary* may begin with a reference to a season or a date that will place the context of the narration in the past. The passage will then often move to a "present tense" mode of narration. Actually, since the sentences are typically long and flowing, tense is suspended for the space of the sentence and the sentence is only given a tense marking at the end which will often be one of the three perfective tenses mentioned above, or *keri*, which as described above defies summation as simply a perfective ending.

The reading experience created by this is one of an unfolding into a "present" of events one knows are in the past.[82] There are other passages where it seems that the narration of the past is more firmly in the past but

80. Ibid., 38.
81. Ono Susumu et al, *Iwanami kogo jiten* (Iwanami Press, 1974), 1439–40.
82. This description of the reading experience is, of course, based on my own experience. The reading experience of Heian readers is unknowable.

never so firmly as the equivalent in English. This is why the translation displays a much freer mixing of past and present tenses than is normally considered proper in English. By this means, I have hoped to convey what I perceive as a shifting temporal flow in the original.

Original Aspects of the Kagerō Diary Prose Style

Up to this point, I have been talking of those features of the *Kagerō Diary* prose style that it shares with classical Japanese in general. However, there are some fascinating ways in which the *Kagerō Diary* prose style is original. One is its long, undulating sentences. The sentences follow the flow of the author's mind creating something analogous to a "stream of consciousness" effect. Let us look at the following example from book two taken from the section where the author has just arrived at the temple that is the site of her retreat (cf. p. 233):

> The mountain path was not anything particular to speak about—*ah—I can only think of the times in the past when just the two of us traveled this road together; there was that time when I was ill, we were here around three or four days; yes, it was around this time of the year; he didn't even go to serve at court, together we were hidden from the world*; thinking about this and other things, I go along the long path, tears pouring down. I am accompanied by only three attendants.
>
> I get down first at the monastery's living quarters; when I look around, I see some peonies surrounded by a brushwood fence among some other luxuriantly growing plants whose name I know not; they are in such a pitiful state, their petals all fallen and scattered; the old poem, "flowers have only one season," comes to mind and repeating it to myself, I become very sad.

This passage has only three sentences, two long ones and one short one as a sort of segue. The paragraphing in the translation is in accordance with the *Zenshū* text, but there would have been no paragraph separations in the original text. If we focus on the two long sentences, we see that the first one follows the pattern of association in memory. Riding on the path to the temple reminds her of the times when she had traveled on the same path with her husband, which in turn reminds her in detail of the sweet intimacy of the time they spent together there. She virtually relives the past in the form of an inner monologue, but it occasions tears because the past stands in stark contrast to the present where not only is she by herself but she has run away to perhaps cut off relations with her husband forever by becoming a nun. Note that the author does not spell out the causal relationship between the content of her inner monologue and her tears, but rather appears simply to give us her thoughts and emotional responses as they occur. The short sentence where she remarks about the smallness of her escort, signals the return of her attention from past reminiscence to the present moment and the wretchedness of her situation.

In the second long sentence, the author surveys the scene before her, and focuses on the bedraggled peonies which become a mirror for herself. Her sense of being a flower past its prime is crystallized in her remembering a fragment of poem no. 1016 from the *Kokinshū*:

> In the autumn fields
> blooming so vigorously,
> the Maiden Flowers,
> such a struggle to be seen,
> flowers too have only one season.

The sentence moves from establishing the context of place to an image to a fragment of poetry to an expression of feeling, thereby creating the illusion of capturing thoughts and sensation as they occur. This kind of sinuous sentence, propelled by mental association in a dance with memory, is characteristic of Michitsuna's Mother's prose style and makes it very different not only from Ki no Tsurayuki's style in the *Tosa Diary*, the only immediate antecedent for diary writing in Japanese, but also from prose style in the early *monogatari*.

The last sentence in the above example can also be used to illustrate another original characteristic of the *Kagerō Diary* prose style. This is the blurring of the distinction between poetry and prose. How does the author do this? She has the prose carry as much imagistic and subjective emotional content as poetry normally does. In the sentence about the peonies above, the juxtaposition of a natural image with a feeling is common to the operation of many *waka*. Furthermore, the embedding of a poetic fragment in the sentence moves the prose even closer to poetry. Readers of the later *Tale of Genji* will not be surprised at the blurring of boundaries between poetry and prose, for it is also a hallmark of the *Genji* author's prose, but it originates with the *Kagerō Diary*.

A final characteristic of the *Kagerō Diary* prose style that arrests the reader's attention as distinctive is something that I designate as a "cinematic" style of description. One visual image succeeding another creates a montage effect. Take for example, this passage from a description of her approach to a pilgrimage site (cf. pp. 157–59):

> We left from there, and as we go along, even though the path is nothing to speak of, it still gives one the feeling of being deep in the mountains and the sound of the water is very affect-

> ing. Those famed cedars are living, even now piercing the sky, all kinds of colors of tree leaves can be seen. From among many stones, the water gurgles forth. Seeing this scene struck by the light of the setting sun, tears pour forth endlessly. The path to here had not been so especially charming. There were as yet no red autumn leaves; the flowers were all gone; one could only see withered pampas grass. Yet, here, the feeling is special, when I look out, rolling up the outer blind, pushing aside the inner blind, the color of this well-worn robe is quite different. When I pull the train of lavender gauze around me, the ties cross over my lap, how well their color complements the burnt umber of this robe, how enchanting I find it all. The beggars with their pots and bowls set on the ground before them, how sad they seem. Feeling so close to the poor and lowly, entering the temple precincts is less uplifting than I expected.

The description above is visually rich and enlivened by the narrator's shifting gaze. Imagine the above scene rendered in film. A carriage moves along a path in a forest close to a stream. A tilt shot follows cedars up to the sky, then a cut is made to a pan sweeping the foliage. A cut is made to a close-up of the stream; the sound track magnifies the water gurgling. The camera cuts to a close-up of a woman's face weeping in the slanting rays of the sun behind the blinds of the carriage, then cuts to silvery pampas grass and back to a view from the inside of the carriage of hands rolling up and pushing aside blinds. The woman's hands bring lavender ties around and crisscross them over her lap; the shot is from the woman's point of view, and the camera dwells on the colored pattern of lavender over burnt umber, then cuts to crouched figures of beggars in the indigo twilight staring up at us because we, the viewers, see them through her eyes. The point is that her prose could be translated easily into film, because even though this was millennium before the invention of film, the structure of her prose description creates an analogous effect.

Translation's Tightrope

This preceding section has attempted to give some impression of the linguistic specificity of the original text. The reader will have noticed that while the translation has taken shape by trying to render the style of the original, it remains profoundly different. There is no such thing as a transparent translation. In preparing a translation that one hopes a large audience will read, one walks a tightrope between allowing one's reading of the original to shape the translation so radically that the style may appear alien and difficult, or making the translation conform so closely to stylistic norms of contemporary English that all difference is effaced. One negotiates this tightrope perpetually and there will likely be many readers from whose viewpoint this translation will appear to have fallen off the rope in one direction or the other. Hopefully there will be other readers for whom the translation strikes the right balance. Balanced in the wind of change, I relinquish the struggle for the time being and offer the reader one of many possible versions of the *Kagerō Diary*.

The Kagerō Diary

Book One

Summary

Book one covers fourteen years in the author's married life, from the year 954 to the year 968. The author, Michitsuna's Mother, is a woman of the middle-ranking aristocracy. She is about nineteen when the proposal for marriage comes from Fujiwara Kaneie, one of her kinsmen from a distant and more powerful branch of the family. It is assumed the author began writing the diary around 971, many years after the events recorded in book one. The first indication that the diary was actually begun later is in the introductory paragraph, where she states that the events of years past are vague in her memory.

She starts the diary in the third person, giving it the feel of a fictional piece of writing. However, within one long sentence she moves to declare her purpose to write a sort of antiromance, the record of a real person's life, her own. The reader will see her struggle through book one as she alternately recaptures the moments in her marriage that accorded with the romantic ideal and laments the points at which the relationship fell short.

Running through the narration is her record of correspondence and the exchange of poetry that was an integral part of communication in the period. In fact, in many respects, book one is more like an anthology of poetry than a diary, at least in conventional Western terms. Her style of narration is elliptical and fragmentary. She is not interested in filling out the picture so that we get a clear sense of who all the actors are and what the chronology is. Her focus is rather on heightened moments of sensibility, which usually involve the composition of poetry.

there is one – She begins speaking of herself in the third person, which gives the beginning of her diary the feel of a *monogatari*, "tale."

old tales – Romantic tales perhaps like the *Tale of Lady Ochikubō,* a Cinderella story where a mistreated stepdaughter is rescued from her cruel situation by a handsome, high-ranking man.

places where I have just left it at that are indeed many – This phrase is vague in the original and has been subject to many varied interpretations ranging from "There are many things I have written that were best left unwritten" to "There are many descriptions where I've thought this will do." I have left it vague. A possible interpretation of "at that" is "as vague and fragmented as my memory."

"a tall tree among oak trees" – Conventional metaphorical expression for the position of captain of the Right Guards, which her husband-to-be, Kaneie, is known to have held at that time. From this, we also know the year is 954. He is twenty-six; she is about nineteen.

An ordinary person would have sent – Given that women (other than those serving at court) were hidden away behind ranks of relatives and servants and layers of walls and curtains (even their layers and layers of clothing seem emblematic of the barriers to intimacy), a Heian man wishing to initiate a relationship could either approach the woman through her male protectors, fathers, and brothers, as Kaneie does in this case, or try to reach her secretly through her personal female attendants and set up direct correspondence. Michitsuna's Mother, it seems, would have preferred the latter, which would have accorded more with the progress of a love affair in a romance.

my father – She uses an indirect expression, "the one who is recognized as my parent." She does this with all terms of family relation, but they are rendered more directly in this translation. Her father is of the Fujiwara clan too, a distant cousin to Kaneie. Her father's branch of the family had been relegated to the sidelines of the political world.

such a letter – A letter of proposal. An alternate interpretation of this passage is that she is surprised to see such bad handwriting because she had heard he had a fine hand, but then the mention of paper does not quite fit. It seems more likely that she is disappointed by the casualness in choice of paper and hand, that it does not seem like a serious letter of proposal. Again her expectations in this regard would have been shaped by romantic tales.

cuckoo bird – From this we know that the season of their first correspondence is early summer.

Thus the time has passed and there is one in the world who has lived such a vain existence, catching on to neither this nor that. As for her appearance, she can hardly be compared to others, and her intelligence—to say she has some is as good as saying she has none at all—so it is only natural that she has come to such a useless state she thinks again and again; it is just that in the course of living, lying down, getting up, dawn to dusk, when she looks at the odds and ends of the old tales—of which there are so many, they are just so much fantasy—that she thinks perhaps if she were to make a record of a life like her own, being really nobody, it might actually be novel, and could even serve to answer, should anyone ask, what is it like, the life of a woman married to a highly placed man, yet the events of the months and years gone by are vague; places where I have just left it at that are indeed many.

Well then, for this ultimately disappointing affair, there was, of course, the exchange of love letters; from about the time that he became "a tall tree among oak trees," it seems that he made his intentions known. An ordinary person would have sent a discreet letter using a serving maid or someone like that as a go-between to make his feelings known, but this man goes right to my father, half-joking, half-serious, hinting at the idea, and even though I told my father that it did not suit me at all, just as if he did not know, one day he sends a retainer riding on a horse to pound on our gate. Who was bringing whose messages, we had not a hint, so there is a big commotion, we were quite perplexed, and accepting the message brings on another commotion. When I look at it, the paper and so on are not what you would expect in such a letter; I had heard from of old that in such a case the hand would be perfect, but the writing in this is so bad that I feel it couldn't be that sort of letter; it is so very strange. The words were:

oto ni nomi	Only to listen
kikeba kanashi na	to your sound alone is sad,
hototogisu	cuckoo bird,
koto katarahamu to	would that I could speak with you,
omofu kokoro ari	this is what my heart longs for.

my old mother – She says "person of the older generation," but "mother" is the generally agreed upon interpretation.

I have someone write – Revealing her own hand would be the first step to intimacy, so, adopting a posture of resistance, she delays his seeing her handwriting. Since it is not written in her own hand, he will even be uncertain as to whether it is her composition or not. Of course, the posture of resistance is conventionally required.

flutter a voice – Pun on two meanings of the same word *furu*, one meaning "to brandish, wave in front of one," and the other, "to be shaky, have a quavering sound."

soundless waterfall – There is an actual waterfall of this name in the Ohara district of Kyoto.

tracks . . . letters in the sand – This poem puns on the word *fumi*, which means both "footsteps, tracks of animals or birds" and "writing" in the sense of "letters, books, and writing in general." It is a pun that occurs often in Heian poetry. There is also a pun here on *naki*, "not there," which is embedded in the word *nagi-sa*, "shore." Orthographically, *naki* and *nagi* were not distinguished in the Heian period.

wave – Metaphor for someone interfering with their correspondence, perhaps another suitor, which derives from the well-known and often quoted *Kokinshū* poem, no. 1093:

  if ever I should
change my mind and banish you
  from my heart then would
great ocean waves rise and cross
Suenomatsu Mountain

(Laurel Rasplica Rodd, *Kokinshū: A Collection of Poems Ancient and Modern* [Princeton: Princeton University Press, 1984], 372)

It is impossible that the waves could rise and cross the mountain, so the *Kokinshū* poem is like the pledge, "my heart will never change toward you." Here the allusion implies that her heart may no longer be true. The majority of allusions throughout this text are to the *Kokinshū*, the first anthology of Japanese poetry compiled by imperial command. It was completed in 905, and by the time of this diary had become the model text for the composition of Japanese verse, which is why it is alluded to so often. The poem numbers given make it possible to find the poem in any edition of the *Kokinshū*, whether in Japanese or English translation. As above, I will generally use L. R. Rodd's translations, but where the translations are not noted as Rodd's, they are my own.

serious response – The word "serious," *mame*, means "with serious intent." In other words, this is a correspondence leading to marriage.

and that was all. When we all discuss it, "How about it? Does it require a reply?" my old mother says, "It does." So feeling obliged, I have someone write:

katarahamu	Toward this village
hito naki sato ni	where there's no one to speak with,
hototogisu	cuckoo bird,
kahi nakarubeki	do not flutter a voice that
kowe na furushi so	will be quite to no avail.

With that as a beginning, there were missives one after another, but as I did not reply, there came this:

obotsukana	So faint, I strain
oto naki taki noto	to hear this soundless waterfall,
midzu nareya	you are its water,
yuku he mo shiranu	though I know not where it goes,
se wo zo tadzunuru	yet I seek the ford to meet.

When I send back, "I will answer soon," he sends this so quickly that I wonder if he was in his right mind:

hito shirezu	No one can know
ima ya ima ya to	maybe now? maybe now?
matsu hodo ni	the longer I wait
kaheri konu koso	without hearing back from you
wabishikarikere	the more wretched I become.

When this arrived, my mother said, "How awful, hadn't you better be a bit more mature about this and send him a reply." So, I had a suitable person write a suitable reply. Even with that, he was genuinely happy and corresponded abundantly.

Another time, this was attached to a letter:

hama chidori	Of the shore plovers,
ato mo nagisa ni	no tracks, at sea's edge I see
fumi minu ha	no letters in the sand,
ware wo kosu nami	is it that a strong wave has
uchiyaketsuramu	washed over me and struck them out?

That time too, using a person who could write a properly serious response, I deceived him. There was another letter. "While I am glad to have your seemingly serious response, if this time again there is nothing from you yourself, how painful it will be," and so on. Written in the margin of this grave epistle:

idzuretomo	No matter whose hand,
wakanu kokoro ha	your unknowable heart must

no cries of deer . . . – Allusion to *Kokinshū* no. 214:

here in this mountain
village autumn brings special
misery all through
the night the sound of the
belling deer awakens me (Rodd, *Kokinshū*, 109)

eyelids meet not and see . . . – Pun on *ahanu me,* "not meeting eyes," in other words, eyes that do not join lids in sleep, and *me* in the sense of "occasion," "the occasion of not meeting."

to which I reply – This is the first time she has replied directly, presumably in her own hand.

Takasago – Place-name that is a pillow word (fixed associated word) for deer.

Meeting Slope – Border point between Kyoto and the Lake Biwa region. The name Meeting Slope makes it a popular pillow word for meeting.

Nakoso – Place-name that conveniently means "come not this way."

what kind of morning – With this indirect phrase she indicates that this is the morning after they have first slept together. It is the content of his poem that answers her rhetorical question. He is no longer pleading for admittance to her presence; now he is smitten and cannot wait to see her again.

Waiting the while . . . – Contains puns: *yufugure-kure,* "evening"/"rafts," *nagare-nakare*, "flow"/ "cry," *obowi,* "Ōi (river name)"/"many."

sohetaredo	be present therein,
kotabi ha saki ni	but this time for the first time,
minu hito nogari	I wish for the unseen one.

Even though he said this, I continued to deceive him as before. With our corresponding in this serious fashion, the days and the months passed.

Autumn has arrived. In another letter he writes, "How painful it is to me that you seem to regard me with such prudence; I have borne it till now, but how can we go on like this?"

shika no ne mo	Though I am living
kikoenu sato ni	where I hear no cries of deer
sumi nagara	to waken me,
ayashiku ahanu	strangely, my eyelids meet not
me wo miru kana	and see only our not meeting.

to which I reply:

takasago no	Even from those living
onohe watari ni	on the top of Takasago,
sumafu tomo	famed for deer,
shika samenu beki	I have never heard
me to ha kikanu wo	such complaints of wakefulness.

"How truly strange it is."
After awhile, again from him:

afusaka no	How is it that this
seki ya nani nari	Meeting Slope's barrier
chikakeredo	seems so very close,
koe wabinureba	yet as I struggle to cross,
nagekite zo furu	I just spend my days in sorrow?

In return:

koewaburu	I would have you know,
afusaka yori mo	more difficult than Meeting Slope
oto ni kiku	where you struggle so
nakoso wo kataki	is the barrier I have heard of,
seki to shiranamu	Nakoso, "Come not this way."

and so on, these serious missives went back and forth until—what kind of morning was it?

yufugure no	Waiting the while
nagarekuru ma wo	till evening flows in
matsu hodo ni	flowing tears enough
namida ohowi no	to fill the Ōi River
kaha to koso nare	where the logs flow down.

Brooding on many . . . – Her poem echoes the puns of his poem. The posture of resistance has yielded to one of uncertainty and reflection.

third morning – From this we know that the marriage has formally begun. As is the normal custom of the time, it will be a visiting marriage; she will not expect him to move in with her nor will she expect to move to his residence (see introduction, pp. 9–11).

he visits me there – That he seeks her out to visit even when she is away from home is indicative of the strength of his affection.

pink – This is the *nadeshiko*, "wild pink," a type of carnation associated with autumn. Characters used to write the name phonetically also mean the "caressed child," so the flower name also puns for "beloved girl" and the like.

as much as two nights in a row – That she finds it remarkable that he stays away for two nights in a row indicates indirectly the height of his ardor during this early period of marriage.

My reply:

omofu koto	Brooding on many things,
ohowi kaha no	dusk falls on Ōi River
yufugure wa	where the logs flow,
kokoro ni mo arazu	without being aware of it
nakare koso sure	my tears flow and fall.

Then again, on about the third morning:

shinonome ni	White light before dawn
okikeru sora ha	rising in the sky . . . we parted,
omohoede	not understanding,
ayashiku tsuyu to	strangely, I felt as if I died
kiekaheritsuru	fading with the morning dew.

My reply:

sadame naku	With no permanence,
kiekaheritsuru	fading with the morning dew,
tsuyu yori mo	then what about me
soradanome suru	left to rely in vain
ware wa nani nari	on such a fleeting thing?

Things went on like this, then for one reason or another, as it comes about that I should be away from home for a while, he visits me there, and the next morning comes this note, "I had thought to spend a leisurely day with you there, but as it was not convenient. . . . What is this all about anyhow? To me, sometimes it seems as though you are hiding yourself away in the mountains." In reply, I send just this:

omohoenu	Not thought of,
kaki ho ni oreba	the hedge where this pink blooms
nadeshiko no	and broken cannot bear
hana ni zo tsuyu wa	the dew that stays not,
tamarazarikeru	tears fall endlessly.

With such exchanges going on, the ninth month arrived.

Toward the end of the month, I did not see him for as much as two nights in a row—my response when he sent only a letter:

kihekaeri	The dew that faded
tsuyu mo mada hinu	away is still here on
sode no uhe ni	these sleeves that dry not,
kesa ha shigururu	again this morning—the sky
sora mo warinashi	too cannot help drizzling.

before I could complete a reply – In passages like these, one can see her quietly exulting in the power of her person and poetry to move him. In response to her poem, he not only reciprocates with a poem of his own but also rushes to her side.

oak forest – It is to be remembered that the euphemistic title for his office at this time is "a tall tree among oak trees."

he cheated me by showing up himself – It is clear that she regards herself as being shortchanged when he does not reply with a poem. Shinozuka Sumiko, whose interpretations I have found most illuminating, has singled this passage out for attention: "not only Kaneie but almost anyone would assume that showing up in person to meet her directly would be a much more profound expression of love than taking part in an exchange of poetry. However, it seems Michitsuna's Mother felt a little differently. . . . I would conjecture that for Michitsuna's Mother, the domain of communication between hearts that could be reached through the exchange of poetry was more important than anything" (Shinozuka Sumiko, "Kagerō nikki no shudai o megutte," in *Joryū nikki bungaku kōza*, vol. 2 [Tokyo: Benseisha, 1990], 102–3).

period of abstinence – The activities of Heian aristocrats were directed by a complicated calendar based on the principles of Chinese yin-yang cosmology. This calendar, which plotted the moves of unseen forces, could determine which directions it was safe to move in, whether you should stay away from your residence for a specified period of time, whether you should stay secluded at home, and so on. Regular periods of abstinence were part of the calendar. During these periods, one abstained from contact with others, sexual activity, and certain foods. Being in violation of Shinto taboos, such as coming into contact with death or blood, could also require a period of abstinence. Underlying the whole system was the belief that staying in harmony with these prohibitions would assure health and good fortune and, conversely, breaking them would invite disaster (see introduction, pp. 22–24).

I turn my sleeves inside out – A folk belief held that sleeping with one's sleeves turned inside out would cause either one's lover to appear in one's own dream or oneself to appear in one's lover's dream.

rather trite – This is one of the places where she seems to be assessing something in the past from the vantage point of her present moment of writing. Looking back she seems to feel that this poem did not do justice to her emotions.

fire of loving – This phrase comes from the pun on *hi*, "fire," that is embedded in the word *omohi*, "love, longing." Some commentators speculate that it was her use of this conventional trope in this poem that occasions the above evaluation of the poem as trite (Uemura Etsuko, *Kagerō nikki kaishaku taisei,* vol. 1 [Tokyo: Meiji Shoin, 1983–95], 111–12). However, most tropes in this age were conventional, and she uses the same trope in other poems without seeming to be bothered by its well-worn quality.

my father, was to leave for Michinoku Province – This marks the point when her father embarks on the career path of provincial governor, a position that was lucrative but socially inferior. It is most likely that this first post was obtained through the influence of his new son-in-law, Kaneie. Characteristically, Michitsuna's Mother is not interested in recording here what this move may have meant in terms of status or economic rewards, but rather the poignancy of parting from her father.

Immediately, this reply came back:

omohiyaru	As the love longing
kokoro no sora ni	of my heart became
narinureba	one with the sky,
kesa ha shiguru to	no wonder this morning you
miyuru naruramu	looked and saw it drizzle.

And before I could complete a reply, he arrived himself.

Then another occasion, after some time had passed and I was not seeing him as often as before, on a day when the rain was falling, there was a message, "I'll come in the evening," and I sent back:

kashihagi no	Beneath the guardian
mori no shitakusa	oak forest, the grass
kure goto ni	at every dusk
naho tanome to ya	hears "keep trusting me" and
moru wo miru miru	sees the rain dripping through the leaves.

For a reply, he cheated me by showing up himself.

And thus, the tenth month arrived. It was a period of abstinence for me; continually fretting at our forced separation, he wrote:

nagekitsutsu	Lamenting, I turn my sleeves
kahesu koromo no	inside out to dream of you
tsuyu keki ni	but they are damp with dew,
itodo sora sahe	and why must the sky
shigure sohuramu	add to this an endless drizzle?

In reply, though it was rather trite:

omohiaraba	Were the fire of loving
hinamashi mono wo	thought there, sleeves would dry,
ikade kaha	how is it then,
kahesu koromo no	these turned out sleeves,
tare mo nururamu	whether yours or mine, are wet?

With things going on in this way, there came a time when the person I relied on most, my father, was to leave for Michinoku Province.

The season, late autumn, is such a sad time itself, and I still can not say that I am really used to seeing my husband; every time I see him now, I just burst into tears, and feel so sad and uneasy, there is nothing to

the one who is to go – Her father.

Sue pines – Reference again to *Kokinshū* no. 1093 (cf. p. 58), where the lover pledges that his love could never change or else waves could rise and sweep over "Sue pines" mountain. *Suwe* also means "end," and Kaneie cleverly embeds the *suwe* of *suwe no matsu* into *yukusuwe*, "the end of the road ahead," the word borrowed from the father's poem.

Yokawa – One of the three centers of the Tendai Buddhist monastery on Mt. Hiei in northeast Kyoto. It is recorded that on the fifth day of the twelfth month in this year, Kaneie's father attended a series of lectures on the *Lotus Sutra* at Mt. Hiei, and Kaneie may well have accompanied him (*Zenshū*, 134).

which I can compare it. My husband expresses sympathy for me and although he keeps saying he will never forget me, as I wonder if his heart will really be true to his words, I only feel even more sad and anxious.

Now the day has come for them all to leave; the one who is to go cannot restrain his tears, and I, the one who is to stay, am sadder than I can say. "We are way behind schedule"—even though urged thus by his attendants, he cannot leave, rolling up a letter and pushing it into an inkstone box beside him, once again breaking into tears that sprinkled down, he left the room. For awhile, I have not the heart to look at what he has left. Having watched until he went out of sight, pulling myself together, I approach, and when I look at what sort of thing was there, this poem is what I see:

kimi wo nomi	Only on you
tanomu tabi naru	I rely at this time, setting out;
kokoro ni ha	in my heart,
yukusuwe tohoku	thoughts of the long road ahead—
omohoyuru kana	may your life with her be as long.

Thinking that he intended to have this seen by my husband, I feel so sad, and place it back just as he had left it; not long after that, my husband comes to visit. As I am lost in my own thoughts and do not meet him with my eyes, he consoles me by saying, "Come now, this is a perfectly ordinary occurrence in the world. Your persistence in going on like this must mean you do not trust me." Noticing the letter in the inkstone box, "Ah, how touching," he says, and sends off after my father this:

ware wo nomi	Since you say you
tanomu to iheba	rely only on me, at the end
yuku suwe no	of the road ahead,
matsu no chigiri mo	Sue pines will betoken our vows;
kite koso ha mime	return and see us unchanged.

In this way, the days passed. Imagining my father traveling under strange skies brought sadness, and my husband's heart did not appear to be something I could rely on that much.

The twelfth month came. From him, who had gone up to Yokawa on some business, there was this, "I am snowed in. I miss you very much." I sent back with the messenger:

kohoruramu	Frozen, is it?
yokawa no midzu ni	Yokawa River—the snow that falls
furu yuki mo	there will not melt,
waga goto kiete	how unlike my thoughts of love
mono ha omowaji	in which I melt away.

gave birth to a child – The phrase in the original is the vague *monoshitsu*, "[I] did something," but from the context we know this is the birth of her first and only child, Michitsuna.

letter's tracks – The familiar pun on *fumi*, "letter, writing" and "footsteps, tracks."

three nights in a row – In the circumstances, this could easily mean he has consummated a marriage with this other woman.

Machi Alley – A small street that ran north and south between Muromachi Street and Nishi no Tōin Street. Some commentators identify it as present-day Shinmachi Street.

As we exchanged such words, the year, fleetingly and without purpose, came to an end.

Around the time of the new year, when I had not seen him for two or three days, I was to be away for awhile, so I left this with the instructions, "Should that person come, give him this":

shirareneba	My feelings of sadness
mi wo uguhisu no	unknown, like the warbler trilling forth
furi idetsutsu	with all its might,
nakite koso yuke	I have gone forth crying
no nimo yama nimo	to the fields, to the mountains.

His reply:

uguhisu no	The warbler seems
adani yukamu	capriciously to have gone forth
yamabe nimo	into the hills,
nakukowe kikaba	if I but hear its crying voice,
tadzune bakari zo	I shall seek it no matter how far.

As we carried on saying such things, something that had never been before came to be; I passed a miserable spring and summer, and then, around the end of the eighth month, somehow gave birth to a child. His care for me at that time was most tender.

Then, around the ninth month, just when he had left one day, for no particular reason, I opened a box that happened to be there and saw a letter obviously intended for another woman. Greatly astonished and thinking I would at least let him know that I had seen it, I write on the letter:

utagahashi	How suspicious,
hoka ni wataseru	I see this letter's tracks lead
fumi mireba	to another's door,
koko ya todaeni	As for here, am I to think
naramu to suramu	your visits will be no more?

As I worried, things went much as I feared, and around the end of the tenth month, there comes a time when I do not see him for three nights in a row. With an air of unconcern, he excuses himself by saying, "I just wanted to test your feelings by staying away for a while."

When evening fell, he says, "There is some business at court that I can't get out of," and leaves; I do not believe him and have a man follow him who came back saying, "It seems that his Lordship went to a certain place on Machi Alley and stayed there." So that is how it was; although I was utterly miserable, I didn't know what to say; it was about two or three

so I composed – It is very unusual for her to initiate an exchange. She might write a poem in response to an inquiry in prose from him, but this is one of the few places where she initiates the communication.

Sorrow, sorrowing . . . – This is one of her most famous poems. It has been included in several poetry anthologies, most notably in *Hyakunin isshu* (One Hundred Poets, One Poem Each), the poetry anthology that became the basis for the poem card game that has to a certain extent kept the court poetry tradition alive for a large audience up until this day. For a recent translation of *Hyakunin isshu* that gives detailed information about the text's tradition of interpretation, see Mostow, *Pictures of the Heart*.

In the Japanese poetic tradition, there are hundreds of poems expressing a woman's chagrin and sorrow at waiting alone through the night in vain for her lover to come, but this is perhaps the only poem by a woman who intentionally barred access to the lover. The last line of this poem has a staccato quality to it, almost as though the words overcome great reticence.

It is interesting that the headnotes to this poem in several anthologies and historical accounts make no mention that Kaneie had just taken up with another woman and change the context by saying Michitsuna's Mother's poem was a response to the chagrin of her husband when she took her time opening the door (Helen McCullough, *Ōkagami*, 167). This gives the poem a more conventional context, since it was almost unthinkable that a wife would bar the door to her husband.

to be so late to open – Kaneie picks up the verb *akuru*, "to dawn," literally, "to open into day," from Michitsuna's Mother's poem and puns on "to open a door." His poem along with his note seems to indicate that he is confident she would have opened the door to him if he had only stayed long enough.

Third Day Festival – The third day of the third month was the *momo no sekku*, "Peach Festival," a celebration originally imported from China. It was customary to decorate the house with peach blossoms and drink wine in which peach blossom petals had been steeped. This festival is still observed in modern Japan, where it has been designated the Doll Festival and honors girls through the display of dolls that evoke Heian court culture.

My sister's husband – This is an interpretation based on the vague phrase in the original, *ima hito kata*, "that other person." From the context, it is assumed that she is speaking of the husband of an elder or younger sister about whom we have very little information outside of what is provided in the diary. There is a record of Fujiwara Tamemasa marrying a daughter of Tomoyasu, Michitsuna's Mother's father, and from that piece of information, it is conjectured that the author is referring here to Tamemasa.

the wine drunk – The word *sugi*, "passed," can also be taken as a pun for *suki*, "drink wine."

days afterward, just before dawn, that there was a knocking on my gate. Thinking that it must be him, I felt wretched, and as I did not have the gate opened, he went off to that other place. The next morning, I felt I couldn't just leave things as they were, so I composed:

nagekitsutsu	Sorrow, sorrowing
hitori nuru yo no	when one sleeps alone the time
akuru ma ha	until night opens
ika ni hisashiki	into day, how long it is
mono to ka ha shiru	perhaps you now know it too.

I wrote this with more than usual care and sent it attached to a faded chrysanthemum. His response, "I was going to wait until dawn to see what would happen, but just then a messenger from the court came and called me away. It was just as you say":

geni ya geni	Truly, truly so,
fuyu no yo naranu	even though the fine wood gate is
maki no to mo	not a winter's night,
osoku akuru ha	to be so late to open,
wabishikarikeri	how miserable it is.

Well, it got very strange; he carried on quite openly as though there was nothing amiss when one might have expected him to try and hide the affair a little and make excuses about having to work at court and such. He became more and more inconsiderate; there was no end to it.

The year changed over and the third month arrived. We had the whole place decorated with peach blossoms for the Third Day Festival; I wait; he does not come. My sister's husband, who has hardly wanted to leave her side, did not come either. Then early on the morning of the fourth, both men arrived together. Our attendants, who had been living in a state of expectation since the night before, thinking there should be more blossoms, went out to gather them here and there. From within the house, watching them break off branches with such determination, I couldn't quite enter into the spirit of it all, and so I scribbled:

matsu hodo no	While we waited,
kinofu sugi ni shi	that day passed, the wine drunk,
hana no e ha	the flower branches
kefu oru koto zo	that you break and bring in
kahi nakarikeru	today will have no effect.

Having written it, I thought to myself, *Why not leave well enough alone, it*

"once in three thousand years"– A legendary peach tree in China was said to bring forth fruit only once in three thousand years. Kaneie turns this into a metaphor for the eternal quality of his love.

[ ] – These square brackets note a place where the manuscript is damaged and a piece of text is missing.

I seemed to feel strange – *Zenshū* notes that this locution "seemed to" indicates a sense of distance between her feelings at the moment of writing and the feelings at the time of events: "She probably wrote it that way because in the midst of her recollection, she felt that her feelings at that time were so miserable she can hardly identify with them as her own" (*Zenshū*, 139).

trees of sorrow–The word for sorrow, *nageki*, can also be interpreted as *nage ki*, "abandoned trees."

part and wither– Pun on *karuru*, "separate" and "wither."

would be disagreeable to have it seen, but he noticed my attempt to hide it and snatched it away, making this reply:

michitose wo	I should be seen as
mitsubeki mi ni ha	the "once in three thousand years" peach,
toshi goto ni	I would have you know
suku ni mo aranu	that mine is not a flower to
hana to shirasemu	be steeped in new wine each year.

My sister's husband, hearing this, responded with:

hana ni yori	Fearing that
suku tefu koto no	yesterday it would seem
yuyushiki ni	we had come only
yoso nagara nite	to get drunk on the flowers,
kurashite shi nari	we stayed elsewhere on purpose.

Nonetheless, now he was visiting the Machi Alley in a totally open manner. [ ] . . . him at least; I seemed to feel strange and to brood on regrets. Although I was caught in this inexpressible misery, what was I to do?

I have been watching the comings and goings of my sister's husband; now he is moving her to a more settled place. I who am to be left behind feel all the more the loss. Realizing that it will be difficult to see her at all, I am truly sad, and when the carriage comes to fetch her, I send this out:

nado kakaru	Why must it be thus,
nageki ha shigesa	while the trees of sorrow
masaritsutsu	grow more and more lush,
hito nomi karuru	this has become a house where
yado to naruramu	people just part and wither away.

The response was made by her husband:

omofu tefu	We care about you
waga koto no ha wo	we say, do not grieve placing
ada hito no	our leaves of words
shigeki nageki ni	in your lush tree of sorrow
sohete uramuna	for the fickle-hearted lover.

Leaving these words behind, they departed together.

Just as I thought would happen, I have ended up going to bed and waking up alone. So far as the world at large is concerned, there is nothing unsuitable about us as a couple; it's just that his heart is not as I would

the place that he has been familiar with for years – A reference to Tokihime, Kaneie's first wife, who had already borne him a son before he entered into the relationship with Michitsuna's Mother. She went on to bear him four more children through the years.

Tokihime and Michitsuna's Mother were social equals, coming from the same middle-ranking aristocratic class of provincial governors. It is clear from how Michitsuna's Mother writes about Tokihime that much as she seems to have wanted Kaneie to herself, she did not expect that his relationship with Tokihime would end. In fact, as is the case here, she seems to feel some sympathy with Tokihime when she knows that they are both being neglected. Judging from Tokihime's responses, however, the feeling of sympathy was not mutual. After all, Michitsuna's Mother was a distinct threat to the continuity of her marriage much as the Machi Alley woman was a threat to Michitsuna's Mother. Since they are from the same social class, she replies politely to inquiries from Michitsuna's Mother, but one can sense a guarded quality to her responses.

Even from your pond's depths . . . – There are three puns in this poem: *soko*, meaning both "your" and "bottom of pond," *karu*, "to reap" and "to be separated," and finally, *ne*, "root" and "to sleep."

Yodo marsh – Yodo is a place-name in *Kokinshū* associated with *makomo*, "wild rice." *Yodono* can also mean "night-time dwelling." Tokihime here demonstrates her poetic erudition and indirectly makes the point, "This is his real home."

color deeply fades – Reference again to the notion that the dew and frost of autumn bring out a deeper color in leaves before they wither and die. It looks like a paradox in English because the verb *utsurofu* means "to change color," either to a deeper or lighter shade, whereas "fade" means "to change to a lighter color." Nonetheless, the change betokens imminent demise, and in that sense, the English "fade" is a better translation. In the sixth month, which is still the season of summer rains, it is usually the fading of flowers that is invoked in poetry. For her to speak of the lower leaves changing to a deeper color is to speak ahead of season. But then, the changing/fading of her husband's love is also "ahead of season."

these gazing eyes, I grow old – Pun on *nagame furu ma ni,* "while the long rains fall" / "while I grow old gazing."

splendid will their color be – He turns her out of season motif into a positive statement to the effect, "your beauty/our love will only grow deeper as time passes."

Meeting fall—from favor – Pun on *aki*, "autumn" and "to grow tired of."

have it; it is not only me who is being neglected, I hear he has stopped visiting the place that he has been familiar with for years. As I have exchanged correspondence with that lady before, I send this to her on the third or fourth day of the fifth month:

soko ni sahe	Even from your pond's depths,
karu to ifu naru	they say it has been reaped,
makomo gusa	the wild rice,
ikanaru sawa ni	in what marsh now does it put
ne wo todamuramu	down its roots and stay to sleep?

Her reply:

makomo gusa	The wild rice,
karu to ha yodo no	whence it is reaped, is of course,
sawa nare ya	this Yodo marsh, its home,
ne wo todomu tefu	but I thought the marsh where it
sawa ha soko to ka	took root and slept was your place.

The sixth month arrived. From the first part of the month, long rains poured down. Looking out at the garden, something I wrote for myself:

waga yado no	Around my house,
nageki no shitaba	trees sorrow, their lower leaves'
iro fukaku	color deeply fades,
utsurohi ni keri	while the long rains pour into
nagame furu ma ni	these gazing eyes, I grow old.

As I pondered these things, the seventh month came.

Around the time when I was thinking to myself, *if the marriage is over and done, perhaps that would be better than just having him come infrequently*, there was a day when he visited. As I said nothing, there was an uncomfortable feeling in the room; in the course of making conversation, one of my attendants happened to mention the "lower leaves" poem that I had written the other day. Upon hearing it, he said this:

ori narade	Even out of season
irodzuki ni keru	these maple leaves have taken
momidjiba ha	a scarlet color,
toki ni ahite zo	meeting the time, how much more
iro masari keru	splendid will their color be.

At which, I drew the inkstone to me and wrote this:

aki ni afu	Meeting fall—from favor
iro koso mashite	their color is even more

he would be floored, then get up and leave – This colloquial translation attempts to capture what *Zenshū* describes as "seemingly a proverbial expression of the time." It involves a play on the meaning of *tafururu*, "to fall down" and also "to be silenced" (*Zenshū*, 141).

Smoke from salt fires . . . – Salt fires are the fires used to boil the vats of brine to make salt. This poem pivots on several puns, *fusube*, "to smolder/to be jealous," *kuyuru*, "to smoke/to suffer," and the embedded pun *hi*, "fire," within *omohi*, "thoughts."

small arrow – Miniature arrows were often attached to the pillars of the sleeping place as talismans to ward off evil.

Although I thought . . . – The subject and object for *omohi idzuru*, "to think of," are not specified, and commentators vary in their opinions as to whether she is saying "I thought you no longer thought of me" or "I thought I no longer thought of you." *Zenshū* commentators, whose interpretations I am in general following, have opted for the latter, but I have decided to render both possibilities in the translation. The poem also contains a pun on the word *ya*, "arrow/hey!" The use of such a colloquial expression as "hey" is unusual in court poetry. *Zenshū* notes that this poem was included in a later poetry anthology under the "humorous poems" category (*Zenshū*, 142). Perhaps this use of colloquialism was the reason for such a categorization. It is also interesting that she should use such playful language in an apparently serious poem.

my house was on his way – As we learn later in the diary, the author's residence was "at the edge of the training ground for the horses of the Left Imperial Guard," which would have put it on the eastern edge of the imperial palace compound at approximately present-day Ichijō Avenue and Nishi no Tōin Street. Kaneie's residence at this time is unknown.

"In the long nights of autumn, when there is no sleep" – Most commentators agree that this line is a quote from the "White-haired woman of Shang-yang" by the famous T'ang poet, Po Chü-i. The poem is about the woman of Shang-yang who came to the palace of the T'ang emperor, Hsuan-tsang, at the age of sixteen, but because of the popularity of his favorite consort, Yang Kuei-fei, never had a chance to meet her lord and died at the age of sixty without ever seeing him. A couplet from this poem is included in the popular *Wakan rōeishū* (An Anthology of Japanese and Chinese Verse for Recitation) (Kawaguchi Hisao, ed. *Wakan rōeishū. Ryōjin hishō*, vol. 73 of *Nihon koten bungaku taikei* [Tokyo: Iwanami Shoten, 1967], 106). Although this anthology was compiled after the writing of this diary, since it was an anthology of the best-known couplets of Chinese poetry, the poem's inclusion there attests to its wide currency.

wabishikere	tired and worn,
shitaba wo dani mo	the lower leaves can only
nageki shimono wo	grieve in a forgotten forest.

Thus his behavior continued; not breaking off relations entirely, he visited from time to time, but our hearts did not melt toward one another and so we drew farther apart. If he came and I was in a bad temper, he would be floored, then get up and leave abruptly. On one occasion, someone living nearby who understood the situation said this upon his leaving:

moshiho yaku	Smoke from salt fires
keburi no sora ni	going up into the sky,
tachinuru ha	is not his going
fusube ya shitsuru	up in smoke due to the fires
kuyuru omohi ni	of jealous thoughts causing pain?

And so on, our exchange of resentments had got to the point that the neighbors were even meddling; these days I have not seen him for a particularly long while.

In ordinary times, I was not like this, but when my heart was thus distracted, I had a tendency not to notice the objects around me. I thought to myself, *Will it be thus, our relations will end without there being a single keepsake for me to remember the affair by?* About ten days after this, a letter from him arrived; among other things, he said, "Send back the small arrow attached to one of the pillars of the bed chamber." *So there was a keepsake,* I thought as I untied and took down the arrow. I sent it back with this:

omohi idzuru	Although I thought
toki mo araji to	you no longer thought of me
omohedomo	nor I of you?
ya to ifu ni koso	"Hey, return the arrow,"
odorokarenure	you said and I was startled.

Thus, he as good as stopped coming at all, but as my house was on his way to and from court, at dusk and at dawn, try as I might not to listen, I could not help hearing him clear his throat as he passed by and I would be unable to melt away into sleep. "In the long nights of autumn, when there is no sleep"—yes, it is just like that; seeing, hearing, feeling these things defies description. And just when I was wishing that somehow I would not have to be subjected to such sights and sounds, I hear my attendants in low whispers saying things like, "The one who used to

the place . . . that has a lot of children – Once more a reference to Tokihime, Kaneie's first wife. This manner of referring to her is particularly interesting because at this time in the diary Tokihime did not yet have a lot of children. She had only the one son, Michitaka. This is a place where it is clear Michitsuna's Mother is writing a long time after these events with a consciousness of what eventually happened.

"How shall I do it? There is something I would ask . . ." – A quotation from a poem that was anthologized in *Yamato monogatari*, section 89. The full poem is:

> How shall I do it?
> There is something I would ask
> trout in the fish weirs,
> where is he caught, the one who
> does not ask after me?

(Katagiri Yoichi ed., *Taketori monogatari. Ise monogatari. Yamato monogatari. Heichū monogatari,* vol. 8 of *Nihon koten bungaku zenshū* [Tokyo: Shōgakkan, 1972], 327)

By quoting the first half of the poem, the author intends us to understand her real meaning, which is the second half of the poem. For another translation, see Mildred M. Tahara, *Tales of Yamato: A Tenth Century Poem Tale* (Honolulu: University of Hawaii Press, 1980), 50.

another year – The first year of the Tentoku era, that is, 957.

traces and books – The now familiar pun on *fumi*, "traces, footsteps/writing, letters, books."

only in your bay – The reader may wonder why Kaneie persists in protestations of steadfast love when his actions contradict it. When I asked this question of Akiyama Ken, he replied, "Within the conventions of *waka* poetry, the only mode of expression available to him is the avowal of devoted love."

be so fond of her never seems to come now." Hearing such whispered gossip, I feel so unhappy; the fall of every evening is just wretched.

I understand that his visits to the place that one hears has a lot of children have definitely stopped as well. How sad, thinking her pain must be even worse than mine, I send her a letter of consolation. It was around the time of the ninth month, I wrote profusely and included this:

fuku kaze ni	To the blowing wind,
tsukete mo tohamu	I attach these words of concern,
sasagani no	though the path of the
kayohishi michi ha	visiting spider has vanished
sora ni tayu to mo	completely into the sky.

Her reply, written with great care:

iro kaharu	When one sees that it
kokoro to mireba	can change the color of leaves
tsukete tofu	and hearts, this wind,
kaze yuyushiku mo	even bearing tidings of
omohoyuru kana	concern, is somehow terrible.

Yet, seemingly unable to break off relations with me entirely, he visited from time to time and winter came. Going to bed, rising, I had only my little one for a companion; without meaning to, I would find myself reciting the old poem, "How shall I do it? There is something I would ask trout in the fish weirs . . ."

We crossed into another year and spring came. Around this time, he forgot to take a book he had been reading and had me send it to him. On the wrapping paper, I wrote:

fumi okishi	This beach, this heart where
ura mo kokoro mo	you left your traces and books
aretareba	so wild a shore it is,
ato wo todomenu	the plover's tracks wash away
chidori narikeri	as soon as they are made.

His reply sent back as a sort of excuse:

kokoro aru to	"Your heart has strayed,"
fumi kahesu to mo	so you say returning my book,
hama chidori	but as for the tracks
ura ni nomi koso	of this shore plover, they are
ato ha todomeme	left behind only in your bay.

As his messenger was there, I sent back:

place that was in such ascendancy – The Machi Alley woman's place.

choosing an auspicious direction – That is, choosing a direction in accordance with the astrological calendar.

he rode out in a single carriage with her – For him to ride in a single carriage with her is to make a public display of his intimacy with her.

ritual pollution – Due to the connection of childbirth with blood, birth was considered polluting.

bizarre – She seems to regard it as bizarre that he would communicate with her so casually about the matter.

sumo tournament – The sport of Sumo wrestling had been part of the court's annual celebratory activities at least from the eighth century. The tournament was held in the seventh month, which was closer to the present calendar's August.

two bundles of cloth – One of a wife's chief contributions to the marriage relationship was the production of clothing for the husband and his household. For someone of Kaneie's rank, participation in court ceremonies and festivities required a large quantity of fashionable and beautiful clothing. Later, in book three, we will see her describing with nostalgia some of the garments that she had made for her husband. Her skill as a designer and seamstress may have been one of the qualities that attracted Kaneie to the author in the first place.

Cloth was very valuable and therefore recycled, which is why he sends both old and new cloth. The production of the clothing was a joint activity for the women in the household, as we can see from their participation in the discussion and eventual decision about the request. The obvious chagrin of Michitsuna's Mother and her women attendants could be because some of the requested garments might be women's clothing intended for the Machi Alley woman, or simply because the request comes at a time of estrangement.

Some of the more outspoken attendants – The phrase in the original here is *namagokoro aru hito*, "persons with a raw heart," the basic meaning of *nama* being "uncooked." Accordingly *nama* can be extended to mean "immature," "inexperienced." I have further extended this to "outspoken." Furthermore, I differ from the *Zenshū* commentators here in interpreting this remark about the attendants as part of the narrative prose in this section as opposed to part of quoted speech.

hama chidori
ato no tomari wo
tadzune tote
yukue mo shiranu
urami o yasemu

"Look where the plover
left its tracks on the shore,"
you say, but, gazing out
over the bay, I can only resent
not knowing where it went.

and, exchanging such words as these, we came into summer.

At the place that was in such ascendancy these days, it became time for the birth of a child, and choosing an auspicious direction in which to remove her for the lying in, he rode out in a single carriage with her, raising a continuous din that could be heard over the entire capital. It was such a racket, so painful to my ears, and did he really have to pass right by my gate? I scarcely felt like myself at all, unable to say anything, and hearing noisy complaints from the lowliest servants to my closest attendants, who were saying things like, "Such a thing, it tears one apart. And there are so many other streets he could have taken," I thought that all I wanted to do was die, yet things do not go as we want. From now on, I thought wretchedly, if the best is not to be, then it would be better to break off relations entirely so that I wouldn't have to see him. About three or four days after this, there is a letter from him. Thinking over and over to myself as I read it how awfully cold it was, I noticed this, "Someone has not been feeling well here, so I have not been able to come and visit. However, just yesterday, a safe delivery was accomplished. I haven't wanted to trouble you with the ritual pollution." This surpassed all for being bizarre. I merely sent back, "Message received." When I heard that in response to my servant's inquiries, the messenger had responded, "The household was blessed with a boy," I felt as though my chest were blocked. About three or four days later, he showed up himself as though nothing were the matter. With a look on my face of *what are you doing here,* I did not welcome him in, and finding things very uncomfortable, he left. This happened often.

The seventh month arrived and around the time of the annual sumo tournament, two bundles of cloth, one of used and one of new cloth, are delivered. "Please, sew these," is the message. I am appalled, what on earth does he mean by this. Just looking at them, I feel my eyes darken with anger. My mother says, "How regrettable. There must be no one over there who can do these." Some of the more outspoken attendants gathered around and said, "This is really the limit. Suppose we don't do it and just see what sort of bad things they'll say about us." And so it was decided; we sent the bundles back and as we suspected, we heard he had to divide them up here and there to get them done. He must have

plumes of words – Plumes of the pampas grass were conventionally likened to putting things forth clearly; therefore the phrase "put forth plumes" could also mean "to express one's meaning clearly."

east wind – The word for east wind, *kochi*, also means "here" and can be used to express "come here."

a good exchange – It is interesting to note that the author's sense of what constitutes a "good exchange" is not necessarily related to the content of the verses. There is no need to overtly express conciliation in the poems; it is the engagement in the poetry exchange that is the most important.

While still lying down – There is very little of the explicitly erotic in the diary. However, the inclusion of this phrase about lying down implies that they are still lying in bed after making love, and it charges the next section and particularly the poems exchanged with a muted erotic quality.

wild-looking hue – In the classical lexicon the word *iro*, "color," is full of connotations ranging from the "world of the senses" and "the beauty of a woman" to "sensual love." Its meaning in this poem is nonspecific, partaking of all those connotations.

white dew – Again this is a reference to the notion that it is the dew of autumn that brings out the most brilliant color in the flowers and leaves. With the images of the pampas grass a few poems before, it is clear that the setting of the diary has shifted to autumn. As with "color" above, the meaning of dew here is indeterminate but points to a constellation of connotations, which here include the season of autumn, tears, sorrow, and a hint of eroticism introduced with the notion of wetness.

found it very cruel, for more than twenty days, there were no inquiries from him.

Then, on what occasion I can't quite recall, there was a letter from him. It said, "I would very much like to come and see you, but it seems you are feeling very cold toward me. Certainly, if you were to say 'Come,' in fear and trembling, I would be at your door." I thought not to send a response to this, but as on all sides there were cries of "That would be too cruel of you. It would really be too much," I sent back:

ho ni idete	Not putting forth plumes
ihaji ya sara ni	of words, rather will I charge
ohoyoso no	the pampas grass to
nabiku wobana ni	sway whither it will,
makasete mo mimu	in general, I will watch.

He sent back:

ho ni ideba	When the plume comes forth
madzu nabiki namu	whither first will it sway,
hana susuki	flowering pampas grass?
kochi tefu kaze no	With the east wind, which says
fukamu mani mani	"come hither," and so it does.

As there was a messenger to take back a response, I wrote:

arashi nomi	At a house that is
fukumeru yado ni	only buffeted by storms,
hana susuki	flowering pampas grass,
ho ni idetari to	even if it puts forth plumes
kahi ya nakaramu	of words, what good does it do?

and so on, we had a good exchange and he came to visit again.

While still lying down and gazing at the flowers of the front garden blooming in rank, multicolored profusion, we said the following. It seems we both had feelings of resentment toward each other. When he breaks the silence with this:

momo kusa ni	The wild-looking hue
midarete miyuru	of these myriad flowers,
hana no iro ha	is it due only
tada shiratsuyu no	to the white dew fallen there,
oku ni ya aruramu	or have their hearts turned cold?

I reply:

late rising moon – In the lunar calendar, the dates of the month correlated with the phases of the moon, so we can infer that this exchange was taking place after the twentieth of the month.

desperate – This word is an interpretation. The original has only *sa*, "like that." The implication appears to be that she does not feel so desperate for him to stay that she would stoop to pleading. It is remarkable how well the author conveys the meaning of what was not said in this conversation.

so he stayed – With these words, she signals her victory in this dance of emotion, poetry, and will.

leaves of words – Pun on *koto no ha*, "words," which includes the word *ha*, "leaves."

the tree trunk itself – Pun on *mikara,* "myself," which includes the word *kara,* "tree trunk."

mi no aki wo	Thinking of autumn,
omohi midaruru	these rank-growing wild flowers,
hana no uhe no	were they to speak,
tsuyu no kokoro ha	of the heart of the dew
iheba sara nari	upon them, it would be thus.

Saying such things, it was painful between us as always.

As the late rising moon was just about to emerge from behind the mountain ridge, he makes as though to depart. Then, perhaps seeing the expression on my face as I think *surely, tonight at least he doesn't have to go*, he says, "Well, if you really think I ought to stay . . . ?" But I didn't feel that desperate, so I say:

ikaga semu	What is there to do?
yama no ha ni dani	Since your heart is like the moon
todomarade	that does not linger
kokoro mo sora ni	at the edge of the mountain
idemu tsuki woba	but would emerge into the sky.

He replies:

hisakata no	You say this heart-moon
sora ni kokoro no	emerges into the o'er-spread sky,
idzu to iheba	yet will it leave
kage ha soko ni mo	its reflection
tomarubeki kana	behind in this pond.

and so he stayed.

On another occasion, there was something like a typhoon and he came calling about two days later. "With a wind like the other day, no matter what, an ordinary person would have inquired after our well-being," I say, and he seemed to think there was some truth to this, yet with nonchalance he replies:

koto no ha ha	With leaves of words
chiri mo ya suru to	all scattered and pinned to
tome okite	the ground—today
kefu ha mi kara mo	has not the tree trunk itself
tofu ni ya ha aranu	come to inquire after you?

I reply thus:

chirikitemo	Even scattered,
tohi zo shite mashi	could they not have come this way
koto to ha wo	those leaves of words,

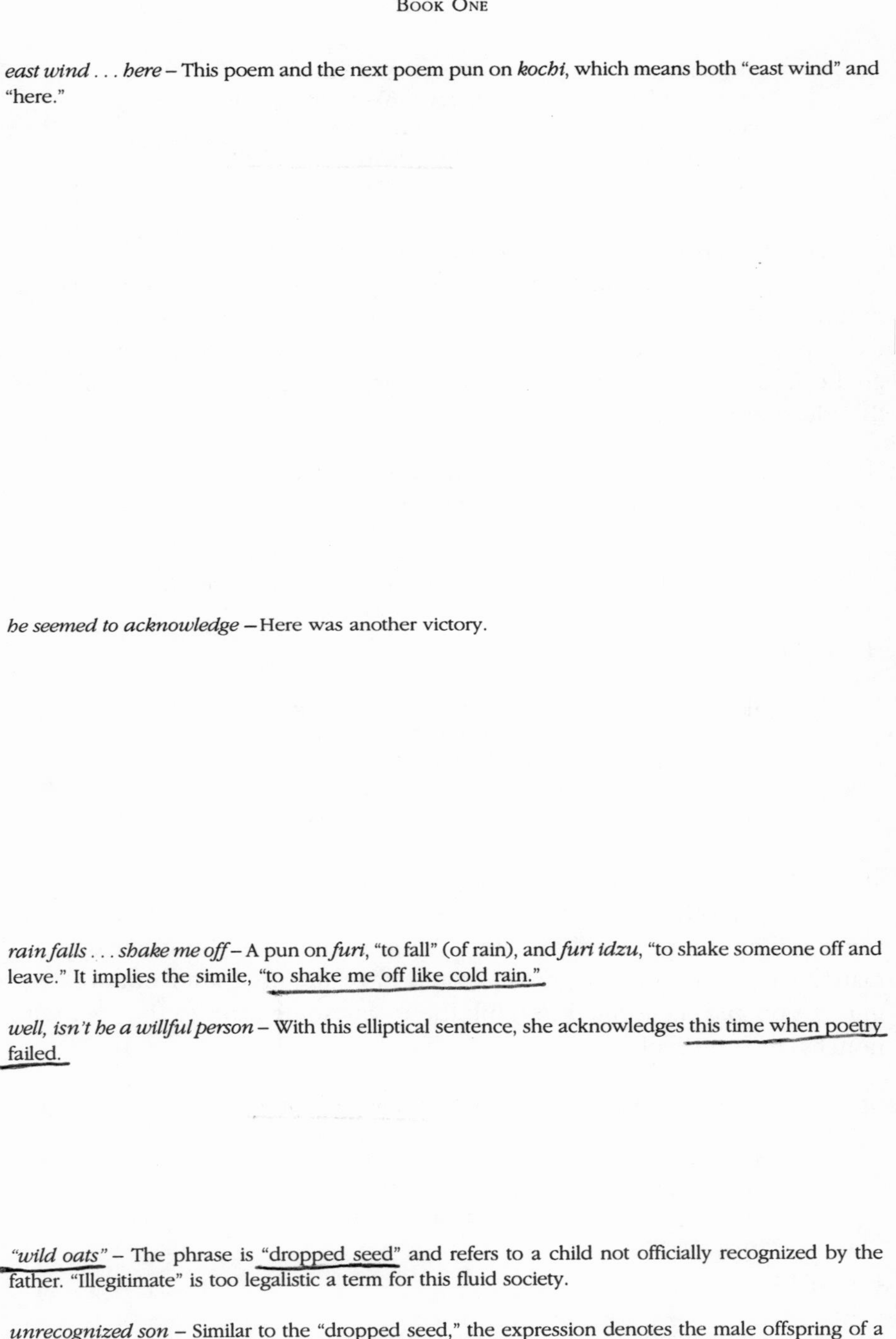

east wind . . . here – This poem and the next poem pun on *kochi*, which means both "east wind" and "here."

he seemed to acknowledge – Here was another victory.

rain falls . . . shake me off – A pun on *furi*, "to fall" (of rain), and *furi idzu*, "to shake someone off and leave." It implies the simile, "to shake me off like cold rain."

well, isn't he a willful person – With this elliptical sentence, she acknowledges this time when poetry failed.

"wild oats" – The phrase is "dropped seed" and refers to a child not officially recognized by the father. "Illegitimate" is too legalistic a term for this fluid society.

unrecognized son – Similar to the "dropped seed," the expression denotes the male offspring of a prince from a union with a low-ranking attendant.

kochi ha sabakari	the east wind surely blew that hard
fukishi tayori ni	to bring their inquiries here.

He rejoins with:

kochi to iheba	That east wind blows so
ohozo unarishi	wildly, how could one ever
kaze ni ikaga	trust it to inquire
tsukete tohamu	after the right person,
atara na date ni	it might end up somewhere else.

Being in no mind to be beaten on this one, I say further:

chirasaji to	Those leaves of words
oshimi okikeru	that you say you are loath
koto no ha wo	to scatter elsewhere,
kinagara dani zo	then, at least, this morning could
kesa ha tohamashi	you not have said something first?

At this, he seemed to acknowledge that what I said was reasonable.

At another time, around the tenth month, he says, "There is some business I simply must attend to" and makes as though to leave. While it is not quite raining hard enough to be called "winter downpour," it is quite miserable and still he intends to go out. In some astonishment at this, I can't help saying:

kotowari no	Though I see this is
wori to ha miredo	a time you have reason to go,
sa yo fukete	yet, the night deepens
kakuya shigure no	and the cold rain falls thus
furi ha idzubeki	must you shake me off and go?

but even at this—well, isn't he a willful person?

Things going along in this fashion, it seems that after the birth of her child, that "splendid" personage of Machi Alley lost favor; in the midst of my feelings of hatred, I had wished to see her live long enough to suffer just as I had; now not only had that come to pass, but to top it all off, was not the child that had been the occasion of all that annoying clatter dead? The lady was the "wild oats" of an unrecognized son of a prince. Needless to say, she was extremely base. Just for a time, she had been able to cause a stir among unknowing people; now suddenly it had come to this—how must she be feeling? When I thought she must be even a little more miserable than I had been, at that moment, I felt as though I

I felt as though I could breathe again – Literally the expression is "my chest clears." This passage is one that has occasioned a lot of comment. It shocks because it bares thoughts that we as human beings may have but tend not to make public. For that reason, the passage is often singled out as an example of her honesty. For instance, Murai Jun has said, "Here the hatred of the author for the Machi Alley woman is nakedly expressed. Due to this, there are some readers who criticize the author, but as for me, I am inclined to feel respect for this author who has written down her true feelings to this degree with no prevarication as the truth of her heart" (Murai Jun, *Kagerō nikki zenhyōkai* [Tokyo: Yūseidō, 1978], 81).

"swept the pillow" for him at his former place – This means he is again being welcomed to Tokihime's place. Pillows were usually made of wood so they were swept clean of dust after not being used for a while.

"It is because you are so young" – In this elliptical citation of criticism from an acquaintance may be seen the implied norm of forbearance to which she was expected to conform. Her refusal to conform is attributed to her immaturity.

just write it all down – This introduces her long poem. Since the production of long poems was very rare at this time, it is an unorthodox form of expression for her to choose. The question arises of why she would choose poetry over prose in this situation. Shinozuka Sumiko suggests that "it can be said particularly of book one that there is a gap between Michitsuna's Mother as a composer of poetry, whether *waka* or long poems, and Michitsuna's Mother as a writer of prose, almost as though she were a different person. She chose the long poem form precisely because she had that much to say. There is no doubt she would not have been able write it in the form of a prose letter. . . . We can also see here the strength of Michitsuna's Mother's ability to write poetry" (Shinozuka, *Kagerō nikki no kokoro to hyōgen*, 80).

color of your leaves of words – Pun on *koto no ha*, "leaves" and "words."

left beneath a neglected tree sorrowing – Pun on *nageki/nagekareki*, "tossed out, neglected tree" and "to sorrow, lament."

Winter . . . regrets for him – Reference to her father's departure for the north country in late autumn of the year before last and the grief she felt that first winter that he was gone.

he had left words – Reference to her father and his parting poem for Kaneie.

quick as frost falls and melts – This simile is implied in the original with an image that is embedded in the associative vocabulary of *shimo*, "frost," and *okitsu*, "fell" (as of frost), as well as "left" (with respect to his words), and *hodo mo naku*, "quickly."

could breathe again. Now, I hear they have "swept the pillow" for him at his former place. However, as for here, since he visits as irregularly as before, there are times when I think there is no affection left between us. My little one here has just begun to say a few words. Whenever his father takes leave of us, he always says, "See you soon," and the little one hearing this goes around imitating him.

Thus again, it is still not a world in which I can feel at ease even though meddlesome people say things like, "It is because you are so young"—I just find it too cruel of him when he says things like "Have I done anything wrong?" with such an air of innocence and unconcern that I don't know what to do. There are just these millions of thoughts milling around in my mind; when I get so riled up that I want to tell him every bit of what is on my mind, I am so upset that I just can't say anything at all.

I think to myself, *what if I just write it all down and show it to him:*

omohe tada	Just think on this,
mukashi mo ima mo	in times past and now too,
waga kokoro	my heart knows no peace,
nodokekarade ya	will it be thus forever?
hatenubeki	That autumn when first
misomeshi aki ha	we met, was not the color
koto no ha no	of your leaves of words
usuki iro ni ya	so pale even then that when
utsurofu to	they faded, I was left
nageki no shita ni	beneath a neglected tree
nagekareki	sorrowing only.
fuyu ha kumowi ni	Winter—in the midst of
wakare yuku	regrets for him who
hito o oshimu to	left for a place far beyond
hatsu shigure	the clouds from which fell
kumori mo ahezu	the first cold drizzle drenching me,
furi sohochi	so forlorn I felt,
kokoro bosoku ha	yet, as I heard he had left
arishikado	words for you, those words,
kimi ni ha shimo no	"Do not forget her," thus would
wasuru na to	it be so, I thought.
ihiokitsu to ka	Yet, quick as frost falls and melts,
kikishikaba	so suddenly there
sari to mo to omofu	was distance between us;
hodo mo naku	my father far away,
tomi ni harukeki	me adrift, knowing nothing,
watari nite	one with the white clouds,
shiragumo bakari	as my heart took to empty skies,
arishikaba	time passed, heavy mist
kokoro sora nite	stretched between us and severed
heshi hodo ni	our relations—

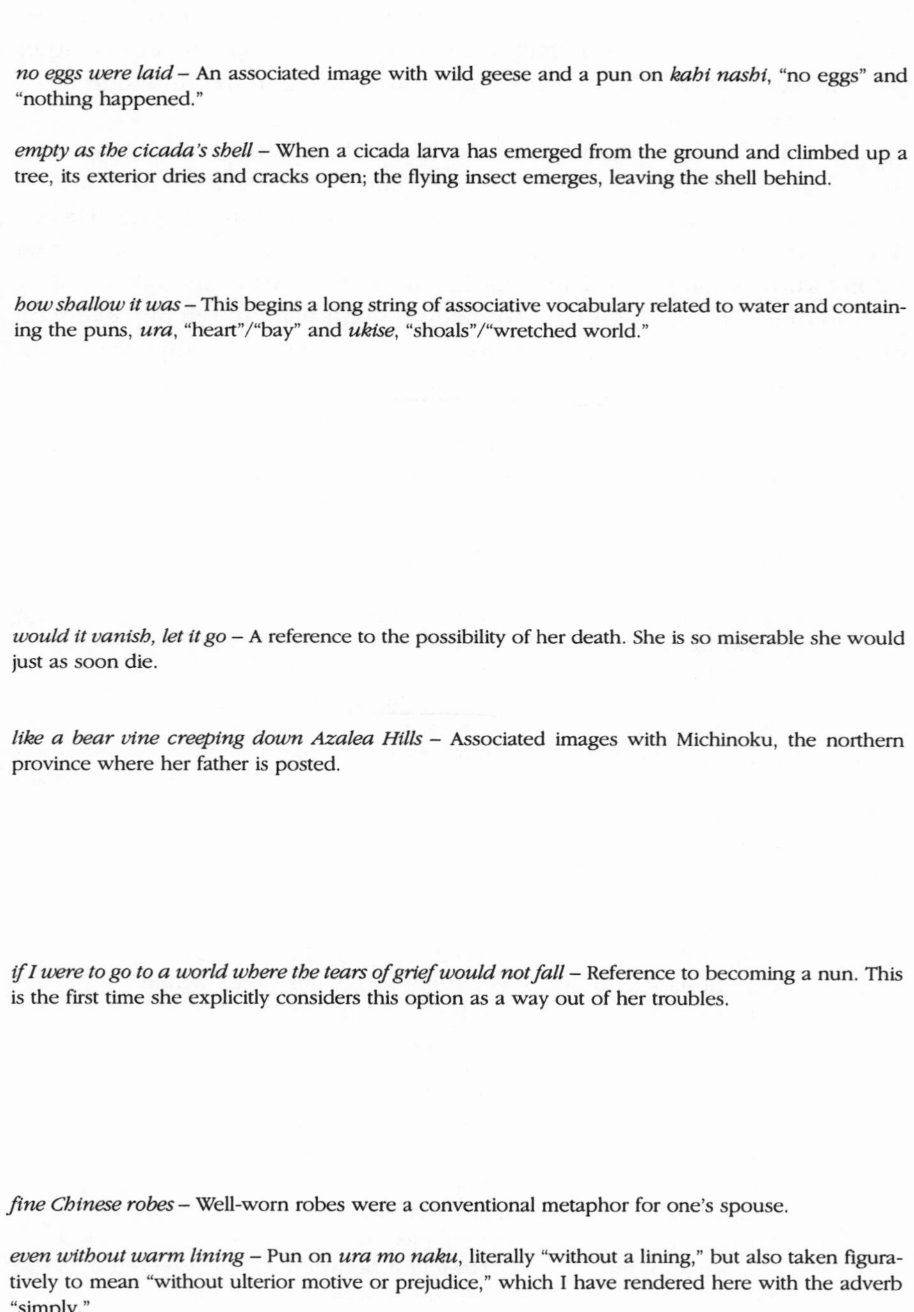

no eggs were laid – An associated image with wild geese and a pun on *kahi nashi*, "no eggs" and "nothing happened."

empty as the cicada's shell – When a cicada larva has emerged from the ground and climbed up a tree, its exterior dries and cracks open; the flying insect emerges, leaving the shell behind.

how shallow it was – This begins a long string of associative vocabulary related to water and containing the puns, *ura*, "heart"/"bay" and *ukise*, "shoals"/"wretched world."

would it vanish, let it go – A reference to the possibility of her death. She is so miserable she would just as soon die.

like a bear vine creeping down Azalea Hills – Associated images with Michinoku, the northern province where her father is posted.

if I were to go to a world where the tears of grief would not fall – Reference to becoming a nun. This is the first time she explicitly considers this option as a way out of her troubles.

fine Chinese robes – Well-worn robes were a conventional metaphor for one's spouse.

even without warm lining – Pun on *ura mo naku*, literally "without a lining," but also taken figuratively to mean "without ulterior motive or prejudice," which I have rendered here with the adverb "simply."

kasumi mo tanabiki
taenikeri
mata furusato ni
karigane no
kaheru tsura ni ya to
omohitsutsu
furedo kahi nashi
kakushitsutsu
waga mi munashiki
semi no ha no
ima shimo hito no
usukarazu
namida no kaha no
hayaku yori
kaku asamashiki
ura yuwe ni
nagaruru koto mo
taenedomo
ikanaru tsumi ka
omokaramu
yuki mo hanarezu
kakute nomi
hito no ukise ni
tadayohite
tsuraki kokoro ha
midzu no awa no
kieba kienamu to
omohedomo
kanashiki koto ha
michinoku no
tsutsuji no oka no
kuma tsudzura
kuru hodo wo dani
matade ya ha
sukuse tayubeki
abukuma no
ahimite dani to
omohitsutsu
nageku namida no
koromo de ni
kakaranu yo ni mo
fubeki mi wo
nazo ya to omohedo
afu hakari
kake hanarete ha
shika suga ni
kohishikarubeki
karagoromo
uchikite hito no

yet, I lived in hope
that in spring with the line of
returning geese, you too
would return to your old home.
Time passed and no
eggs were laid, nothing happened,
going on like this
my life became as empty
as the cicada's shell,
as thin as its wings, your love,
nor is it only
just now that it has become so.
From the first time
how shallow it was, that is why
my heart flows in a river
of tears, the bay never fills.
What heavy load of
sins from former lives binds me
to you? I would leave
but I cannot get away,
thus I float and drag
upon the shoals of this wretched life,
this suffering heart,
a bit of foam upon water,
although I think
would it vanish, let it go,
the only sad thing is
not to wait until my father
from that far northland
like a bear vine creeping down
Azalea Hills returns.
Tell me how could I not wait
and cut off the ties
of former lives between parent
and child? Over and
over, I think to myself
I must see him once more.
What if I were to go to a world
where the tears of grief
would not fall onto my sleeves?
But if I place on
the scales spending my life without
meeting you, I know
in a moment, I would be
wanting you again.
When I think of how I am simply used
to you as someone
gets used to fine Chinese robes
even without warm lining,

leave this world – Reference again to becoming a nun.

with heaven's drifting clouds – Allusion to *Kokinshū* no. 784:

as distant as those
drifting clouds in the heavens
has my love become
and yet each day I see him
here before my searching eyes (Rodd, *Kokinshū,* 274)

This poem is a particularly appropriate allusion here because it was composed by the family of a woman to criticize her wayward husband, who had ceased visiting in the evening.

our young pine – Her infant son, Michitsuna.

seaweed you don't see me – There is a pun here on *miru,* a type of seaweed, and *miru,* "to see."

shells of meeting – The word for shell, *kahi,* is homophonous with meeting. The two halves of a bivalve shell meeting is also an image in the background of the pun.

If the white waves roll up – Metaphor for his visiting her.

ura mo naku
nareshi kokoro
omohite ha
ukiyo wo sareru
kahi mo naku
omohi ide naki
ware ya semu
to omohi kaku omohi
omofu ma ni
yama to tsumoreru
shikitahe no
makura no chiri mo
hitori ne no
kazu ni shitoraba
tsukinubeshi
nanika taenuru
tabi naru to
omofu mono kara
kaze fukite
hitohi mo mieshi
amagumo ha
kaherishi toki no
nagusame ni
ima komu to ihishi
koto no ha wo
sa mo ya to matsu no
midori go no
taezu manebu mo
kiku goto ni
hito waroge naru
namida nomi
waga mi wo umi to
tatahedomo
miru me mo yosenu
mitsu no ura ha
kahi mo araji to
shirinagara
inochi araba to
tanomekoshi
koto bakari koso
shiranami no
tachi mo yorikoba
tohamahoshikere

then if I think to leave this world,
this vulgar world behind,
it would be no use, memories
would pursue me and
bring tears, such would it be.
Thinking this way,
thinking that way, always thinking,
while I brood thus,
if I consider the dust piled up
on mountains of our
bedclothes, it cannot even match
the number of nights
that I have slept alone.
Something is severed,
I feel as though you have gone
on a trip far away.
Even on that day after
the typhoon blew
when I finally
saw you again, you swept
away with heaven's drifting clouds.
In consolation,
parting you said, "See you soon."
Thinking these words
must be true, our young pine
waits endlessly
mimicking your voice,
each time I hear it,
I think ill of you, tears just fall.
If I compare myself
to a sea filled to the brim,
there is no seaweed
you don't see me
nor on Mitsu Bay
are there shells of meeting.
No good it does to cry,
even knowing this to be so,
"while there is life, rely on me,"
you said, I remember it well.
If the white waves roll up
on my shore, this is what
I long to ask them about.

This I wrote and placed on the two-tiered shelf for him to find.

In a few days, he visited as usual, since I did not go out from my inner chamber to meet him, it was painful for him to stay, so he went

I received this from him! – Her surprise at receiving a long poem back from him is registered with an exclamatory particle here. This was quite an effort on his part, and he does express his feelings openly, which is perhaps why although his poem is critical of her and offers nothing in the way of apology, it still serves as a basis for reconciliation.

fades with each meeting, not so . . . – With a pun on *aki*, "autumn" and "to grow tired of," and a play on the range of meaning that *tsune* can have, from "usual" to "always," Kaneie can say simultaneously, "Love is usually thought to wane with each meeting" and "Meeting each autumn [the anniversary of our marriage], my love is always true."

"protect this child" – Reference to her father's parting poem.

tree of sorrow – Perennial pun on *nageki*, "neglected tree"/"sorrow."

green pine who pines – He picks up her reference to their son as a young pine and then makes the conventional pun on *matsu*, "pine"/"to wait." Pines by association call up Tago Bay in the Suruga district, which in turn evokes the famous view of Mt. Fuji from Tago Bay.

around Mt. Fuji – Mt. Fuji was an active volcano in this era, hence its use as a metaphor for hidden passions and jealousy.

cut the tie – This begins a string of associative language related to thread, including the pun *mahikuru*, "to wind on a spool" and "come."

confused and lost . . . falcon – An extended pun elaborates the sense of this passage. *Hashitaka no suzu* means "falcon's bells"; *hashitaka no suzuro nite* means "having nothing to hang on to, unsettled."

flew to ask after you – Contains pun on *tobikuru*, "to fly and come" and "ask and come," which makes a bridge between the falcon image and his relation of a particular visit.

but you lay down alone – Reference to the night she barred the door to him.

the wakeful moon shone with every drop of its light on your fine wooden door – A metaphor for himself pounding on her door.

away taking only the letter. Then, I received this from him!

orisomeshi
toki no momidji no
sadamenaku
utsurofu iro ha
sanomi koso
afu aki goto ni
tsune narame
nageki no shita no
kono ha ni ha
itodo ihioku
hatsu shimo ni
fukaki iro ni ya
nari ni kemu
omofu omohi no
tae mo sezu
itsu shika matsu no
midorigo wo
yukite ha mimu to
suruga naru
tago no uranami
tachi yoredo
fuji no yamabe no
keburi ni ha
fusuburu koto no
tae mo sezu
amagumo to nomi
tanabikeba
taenu waga mi ha
shiraito no
mahikuru hodo wo
omohaji to
amata no hito no
we ni sureba
mi ha hashitaka no
suzuro nite
natsu kuru yado no
nakereba zo
furu su ni kaheru
mani mani ha
tohikuru koto no
arishikaba
hitori fusuma no
toko ni shite
nezame no tsuki no
maki no to ni
hikari nokosazu
morite kuru

The maple leaves when
first we met, colored with the season
were inconstant and
faded, just so it is thought
love usually
fades with each meeting, not so
is this love of mine.
Since those words, "protect this child,"
beneath the tree of
sorrow were spoken, even
when frost first fell,
did not the color of these
leaves turn deeper still?
I long, I burn, a fire
that never ends.
I want to go and see
our little green pine
who pines for me, yet although
as often as the
waves of Tago Bay pound in
on Suruga shore
have I come, around Mt. Fuji
the smoke smolders
from a fire of jealousy
that never ends,
and while it becomes drifting clouds
that trail between us,
I am not one to cut the
tie that binds me as
fast as thread is wound to a spool.
"He does not love her
enough to come," so many
say bitterly,
confused and lost, I am a falcon,
bells on its feet, who,
finding no welcoming perch,
returns to his old nest.
As things went along, there was
that time when I flew
to ask after you, but you
lay down alone, and
although the wakeful moon
shone with every
drop of its light on your
fine wooden door,
not even your shadow
deigned to peep through.

Who then would see dawn with the woman of one night? – Reference to a casual liaison. He frames this as a rhetorical question implying the answer, "Surely not I."

become bound to someone unbound – Another possible interpretation for *kakaranu*, which I have translated as "unbound," is "someone who would not occasion your complaining." Either way he is going so far as to suggest that she consider taking a different husband.

Chinese robes – Once again he takes up a phrase from her poem and alters its context.

just lay them over the bamboo frame – It was the custom of the times to scent robes by laying them on bamboo frames over censers of incense.

kindled by our memories passing through the censer's lattice eyes – The embedded pun of *hi*, "fire," in *omohishi ide*, "recall," brings the notions of heat and memories together. The openings in the censer and the bamboo frame are called *me*, "eyes," and Kaneie uses it as a pun for his own eyes.

in the vale of Hemi in the country of Kai – An area in present-day Yamanashi Prefecture famous at that time for the production of fine horses for the court, and thus preparing the introduction of the string of images and vocabulary associated with horses.

the colt – Their son, Michitsuna.

kage dani miezu	Since that occasion, it is true
arishi yori	my heart did begin
utomu kokoro zo	to have cold feelings toward you.
tsuki someshi	Who then would see dawn
tare ka yodzuma to	with the woman of one night?
akashikemu	What heavy load of
ikanaru tsumi no	sin brings you to this pass, you ask?
omoki zo to	I say, none other
ifu ha kore koso	than this complaining is your sin.
tsumi narashi	Do not wait to see
ima ha abukuma no	your father, right now, become bound
ahi mo mide	to someone unbound.
kakaranu hito ni	Yet, I am not like a tree
kakarekashi	or rock, my feelings
nani no ihaki no	for you, I cannot suppress.
mi naraneba	Layer on layer
omofu kokoro mo	cotton grasses grow by the shore
isamenu ni	betokening how we
ura no hamayufu	ended up distant from each other.
ikukasane	Even if these layers
hedate hatetsuru	of Chinese robes are drenched
kara goromo	in a river of tears,
namida no kaha ni	just lay them over the bamboo frame,
sohotsu to mo	then the fragrant heat
omohishi ideba	kindled by our memories
takimono no	passing through the censer's
kono me bakari wa	lattice eyes would dry at least
kawakinamu	these eyes of mine.
kahi naki koto ha	It is to no avail—
kahi no kuni	in the vale of Hemi
hemi no mimaki ni	in the country of Kai,
aruru uma wo	there is a mare
ikadeka hito ha	grown so wild to her groom
kaketomemu to	one wonders
omofu mono kara	how could she ever be caught?
tarachine no	Then, what about the colt
oya to shiruramu	who will know only his dam,
katakahi no	growing up one-sided,
koma ya kohitsutsu	yet, longing for his sire
inaka semu to	will he not cry?
omofu bakari zo	To the very degree I think on this,
ahare narubeki	I grow desolately sad.

and so on.

As the messenger was still there, I send this:

natsuku beki	Let loose by the groom
hito mo hanateba	who should care for her, the mare

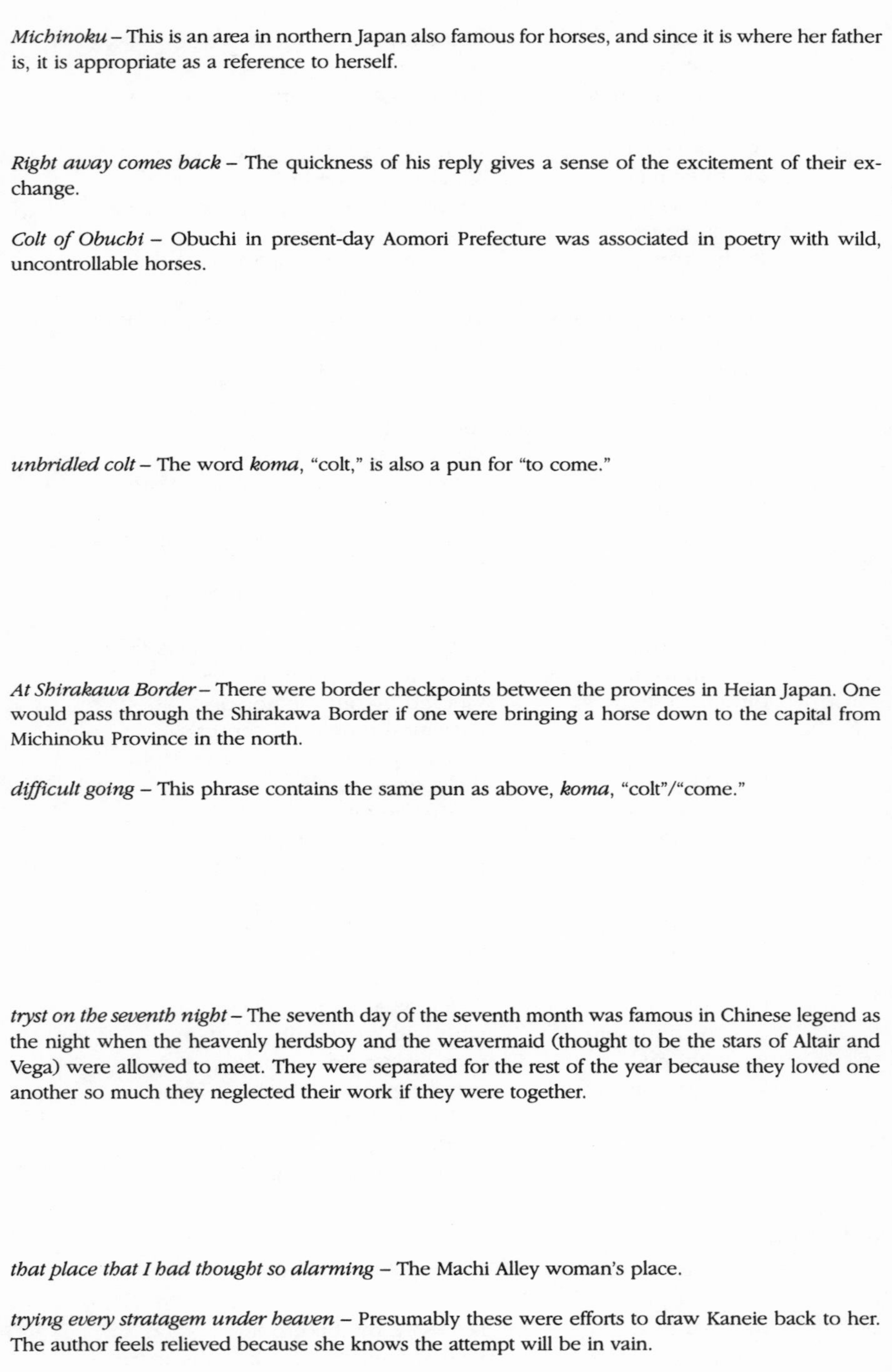

Michinoku – This is an area in northern Japan also famous for horses, and since it is where her father is, it is appropriate as a reference to herself.

Right away comes back – The quickness of his reply gives a sense of the excitement of their exchange.

Colt of Obuchi – Obuchi in present-day Aomori Prefecture was associated in poetry with wild, uncontrollable horses.

unbridled colt – The word *koma*, "colt," is also a pun for "to come."

At Shirakawa Border – There were border checkpoints between the provinces in Heian Japan. One would pass through the Shirakawa Border if one were bringing a horse down to the capital from Michinoku Province in the north.

difficult going – This phrase contains the same pun as above, *koma*, "colt"/"come."

tryst on the seventh night – The seventh day of the seventh month was famous in Chinese legend as the night when the heavenly herdsboy and the weavermaid (thought to be the stars of Altair and Vega) were allowed to meet. They were separated for the rest of the year because they loved one another so much they neglected their work if they were together.

that place that I had thought so alarming – The Machi Alley woman's place.

trying every stratagem under heaven – Presumably these were efforts to draw Kaneie back to her. The author feels relieved because she knows the attempt will be in vain.

michinoku no	of Michinoku
muma ya kagiri ni	runs to the horizon's limit,
naramu to suramu	this must be the end, she thinks.

What must he have thought of it? Right away comes back:

ware ga na wo	Just because my name
wobuchi no koma no	is the Colt of Obuchi
areba koso	when I behave wildly,
natsuku ni tsukanu	did you think if you went to
mi to mo shirareme	tame me, I could not be caught?

And I reply:

koma uge ni	To the unbridled colt
nari masari tsutsu	less and less inclined
natsukenu wo	to come this way,
ko naha taezu zo	is attached this little rope,
tanomi ki ni keru	unbreakable it entreats you.

He replies:

Shirakaha no	At Shirakawa
seki no sekeba ya	Border, I've been stopped it seems,
koma ukute	difficult going,
amata no hi wo ba	for many days I have been
hiki wataritsuru	leading this north country colt.

There is a note with it, "I'll cross the border day after tomorrow." It was the fifth day of the seventh month. And as it was around the time of a long abstinence for him, I send back a reply like this:

ama no gaha	If you have a mind
nanuka wo chigiru	to tryst on the seventh night,
kokoro araba	am I to think that
hoshi ahi bakari no	from now on we shall only meet
kage wo miyo to ya	like the stars of heaven's river?

He seemed to think there was some justice in what I said and began to treat me with a bit more consideration, and the months go by.

As for that place that I had thought so alarming, I was relieved to hear that she was now frantically trying every stratagem under heaven. While I was spending the time worrying myself to pieces, thinking, *I have never known what to do about this relationship right from the start, as he was promoted to the fourth rank* – This was a significant promotion for Kaneie, who was thirty-four years old at the time. When she married him, he was fifth rank and captain of the Right Guards. In 956, he was promoted to the post of lesser counselor, still within the fifth rank. The position of lesser counselor was not one with great responsibilities but as part of the government office directly serving the emperor, it did allow access to the inner court and an opportunity to be in the presence of the emperor. With his promotion to the fourth rank, he was obliged to retire from his post as counselor. The promotion to the fourth rank was of major importance in the court hierarchy because it involved a significant increase in entitlements of income-producing land, servants, cloth, and other goods. It was a feature of the Heian court system that remuneration was based primarily on rank rather than office (McCullough and McCullough, *A Tale of Flowering Fortunes*, 802, 829). Yet service in office was important for placing oneself in a position to be promoted in rank.

assistant to some stuffy sort of ministry – This is the War Ministry. The low esteem in which this ministry was held in the Heian period can be seen in the author's dismissive tone here and by Kaneie's own lack of interest in the post. Moreover, as his assigned post of assistant could be done by someone in the fifth rank, it is no wonder he found it distasteful. Thus, although the promotion in rank was welcome, his actual posting condemned him for the time being to political obscurity. Ironically, this low point in her husband's political career is actually one of the happiest periods in the marriage from her perspective.

the prince, who was in charge of the ministry – This is Prince Noriakira, who would have been about thirty-nine at the time. He was noted as a man of elegant tastes, being skilled in the composition of Chinese poetry and the playing of the koto. He was not, however, in the first circles of power as is indicated by his posting in the unpopular War Ministry. McCullough notes that the ministry "had little to do aside from choosing and rehearsing contestants for the Court's archery matches" (McCullough and McCullough, *A Tale of Flowering Fortunes*, 810). Nonetheless, Noriakira had the aura of royal prestige about him, which can be felt in the respectful tone the author reserves for him in the diary. This was one of the high points in the author's married life, when she is able to participate in her husband's playful and courtly correspondence with royalty.

Probably one of the reasons Kaneie wanted to have Michitsuna's Mother for a wife was her skill at poetry composition. He may actually have expected her not only to help him with the composition of poems for occasions like this interaction with the prince, but also to be the collector for his poems, creating just such a record as the following.

Like scattered threads – With this image, the prince introduces the textile motif that they spin out with elaborate wordplays on vocabulary associated with cloth, spinning, and weaving through the series of six poems. The following translations of the poems are quite free in an attempt to convey the playfulness in the exchange. The puns in this and the following poem are *tsukasa*, "office," containing *tsuka*, "spool," and *kuru*, "to come"/"wind on a spool."

summer-spun thread –Natsuhiki, "summer spun," is a pillow word for thread. This poem is founded on an allusion to a verse of a popular song, which puns on *me*, the word for wife and a weight measure for cloth: "Of white summer-spun thread, I have seven measures, let me weave them into robes and wear them as wives." The other pun in the verse is on *furu*, "to pass" (of time)/"to string the warp threads on a loom." I left this pun out of the translation.

As numerous as seven – Kaneie takes up the allusion to the popular song introduced in the previous poem by bringing in the number seven. He doesn't mean literally that he has seven wives.

unbearable as it is, it must be the result of my own deplorable sins in a previous existence, and such, it so happened that having served as a lesser counselor for some years, he was promoted to the fourth rank and accordingly retired from his present position at court. In the next round of promotions, since he was given a position he did not particularly like as assistant to some stuffy sort of ministry, the world of affairs came to seem distasteful to him, and as there was nothing else for him to do but to visit here and there, he would come to stay leisurely for two or three days at a time with me.

One day, there comes this missive from His Highness, the prince, who was in charge of the ministry toward which my husband did not feel attracted:

midare i no	Like scattered threads
tsukasa hitotsu ni	wound onto a single spool,
narite shimo	we ended up in the
kuru koto no nado	same office, yet it seems that
tae ni taruramu	you would like to break those ties.

His respectful reply:

tayu to ieba	When you say "break ties,"
ito zo kanashiki	How sad it makes me feel!
kimi ni yori	There is nothing to do
onaji tsukasa ni	but be wound together on
kuru kahi mo naku	the same spool of office.

A response comes back right away:

natsuhiki no	Traveling around
ito kotowari ya	to gather summer-spun thread
futa me mi me	for two skeins, three skeins,
yori ariku ma ni	I understand perfectly
hodo no furu ka mo	how the time passes away.

His respectful reply:

nana bakari	As numerous as
ari mo koso sure	seven are the skeins I have
natsu hiki no	of summer-spun thread.
itoma ya ha naki	How could I say I had no
hito me futa me ni	time were there only one or two?

Again, from the prince:

With time's passage . . . – The textile motif in this poem is maintained with a pun on *i*, "thread," embedded in *itodo*, "how could," and a pun on *futomo,* a form of the verb *furu*, "to pass," and "to string on the loom," but in this case they are there to keep the associative language play going rather than to strongly convey metaphorical meaning. I have suggested the presence of the textile motif with the word "unravel," which is not explicitly in the poem.

in avoidance of a forty-five day period of abstinence – If the movements of unseen powers determined that one would have to remain secluded in one's own residence, one could avoid it by moving somewhere else temporarily. Her father is presumably away attending to his duties as provincial governor.

Extending into the sixth month – The fifth month was the season for the monsoon rains. This year the rains seem to have continued longer than usual.

this message that was quite mad – Presumably she considers it mad because it makes fun of their very real and practical problems.

one stares out at the long rain – This sense is actually conveyed in the pun on *nagame*, "to stare, gaze out" and "long rain."

kimi to ware	With so many threads
naho shira ito no	entangling you, as for you and me,
ika ni shite	in the end, perhaps we
uki fushi nakute	had best cut our ties while we
taemu to zo omofu	still can with no hard feelings.

"Two or three women would really be too few but as I have probably already overstepped the bounds of propriety, I shall stop here."

His respectful reply:

yo wo futomo	With time's passage,
chigiri okiteshi	vows between men and women
naka yori ha	may unravel,
itodo yuyushiki	but could we ever see such
koto mo miyuramu	an awful thing between us?

Around that time, somewhat after the twentieth of the fifth month, in avoidance of a forty-five day period of abstinence, I moved into my absent father's residence, which was only separated by a hedge from the residence of the prince. Extending into the sixth month, the rain poured down ferociously and we were all cooped up on account of it. Since the house is quite run down, we had a big commotion dealing with rain leaking in. Noticing this, the prince deigned to send over this message that was quite mad:

tsuredzure no	With nothing to do,
nagame no uchi ni	one stares out at the long rain,
soso kuramu	yet over at your place,
koto no sudji koso	there seems to be such a flurry
okashikarikere	of activity, how very charming.

His respectful reply:

idzuko ni mo	Since everywhere
nagame no sosoku	a flurry of activity pours on
koro nareba	us with the long rains,
yo ni furu hito ha	there must be no one in the world
nodokekaraji wo	who can take it easy.

Again, he deigned to correspond, "So you can't take it easy?"

ame no shita	An unsettled time indeed,
sawagu koro shimo	for all under these rainy skies,
ohomidzu ni	in the midst of this flood,

muddy path of love – pun on *kohidji*, "muddy" and "path of love."

You who with the night . . . – This translation follows the interpretation of Murai Jun in taking the *yo* in the first line as "night" rather than "world" (Murai, *Kagerō nikki zenhyōkai*, vol. 1, 102). However, I do not agree with Murai in assuming that the reply poems throughout this section are actually by Michitsuna's Mother spoken in her own voice. From that perspective, in this poem, Michitsuna's Mother would be empathizing with the prince's lovers on the basis of her own experience. While this is an interesting interpretation, it seems to me that this exchange is still ostensibly between Kaneie and the prince.

As we looked at this together – There are only a few places in the diary where she notes explicitly that they did something together. They mark places of exceptional intimacy and harmony (see Shinozuka, *Kagerō nikki no kokoro to hyōgen*, 94).

he said something like, "How outrageous of him" – It is difficult to know what Kaneie means by this remark. Perhaps he is remarking on the crazy turn the poetic exchange has taken. Having started with joking about the problems with a leaky roof, the prince's bantering has lead to an exchange where male and female speaking positions have become blurred. The prince's last poem is particularly ambiguous. It may be taken as a reproach of Kaneie for not visiting, which would mean that the prince is assuming a feminine persona. Yet, the first line speaks of Kaneie as the one "damp with tears," which in association with the previous poem would put Kaneie in the feminine position of waiting for the prince.

his usual place – Presumably his first wife, Tokihime's place.

pinks – The author spoke of herself as a pink in an earlier poem (cf. p. 63). Here a different name, *tokonatsu*, which can also mean "eternal," is used for the same flower. However, given that it is the same flower with the meaning of "maiden," the reference still has connotations of woman. A pun on *woru*, "to pick, break off" and "be in a place," along with the *tokonatsu* pun makes it possible to derive two paraphrases of the poem's meaning: "Do you not know that the pinks soothe thoughts of love and that I have picked them from your hedge," and "Do you not know how being at your hedge soothes my thoughts of eternal love." This poem could easily be interpreted as being flirtatious.

I show this to him – Since the prince's poem and note could easily be interpreted as an amorous advance, it is interesting that she does not hide it from her husband. Moreover, although the correspondence that follows is characterized by ambiguity and indirection, it is nonetheless evident that the prince is not upset to think that Kaneie might have seen the poem, nor is Kaneie disturbed to have seen it. In a conversation about this passage, Akiyama Ken remarked that Kaneie was likely flattered to have the prince show an interest in his wife. Her stock goes up, as it were, since she is desired by a member of the royal family. Of course, this good humor might have evaporated had the flirtation exceeded the realm of play.

The water is high . . . – There are two puns in this poem: the first one is *ura mo nagisa*, "the bay too, the beach," and the embedded *ura mo naki*, usually meaning "no ulterior motive" and here interpreted by the *Zenshū* commentators to mean "nothing between the hearts" (*Zenshū*, 160). The second one is the frequently occurring pun on *fumi*, "footprints"/"letters." Variations on these same puns recur in the following poems.

tare mo kohidji ni	who has not been drenched
nurezarame ya ha	on the muddy path of love.

His respectful reply:

yo to tomo ni	You who with the night
katsu miru hito no	visit one after another
kohidji wo mo	on love's muddy path,
hosu yo araji to	I imagine there is never
omohi koso are	a time when your lovers' tears dry.

And again from the prince:

shikamo winu	It is not like that,
kimi zo nururamu	you are the one damp with tears,
tsune ni sumu	for me who lives in
tokoro ni ha mada	the same place, always,
kohidji dani nashi	there are no muddy paths of love.

As we looked at this together, he said something like, "How outrageous of him."

On a day when my husband had taken advantage of a break in the rain to visit his usual place, there comes a missive from the prince. My attendant said, "Although I sent word, 'The master is away,' the messenger said, 'Deliver it anyway.'" When I looked at what had been brought:

tokonatsu ni	Picked from your hedge, these
kohishiki koto ya	pinks, tokens of eternal love
nagusamu to	soothe my love's longing,
kimi ga kaki ho ni	do you not know how happy
woru to shirazu ya	I am simply to be near you?

"However, since this can come to nothing, I must bid you farewell."

A couple of days later when my husband appears, I show this to him, telling him, "This is what happened," and so on, he says, "With this much time passed, it is not suitable to send a reply poem," so we just send a note, "Recently, we have not had the honor of your communication." The prince deigned to send this in response:

mizu masari	The water is high,
ura mo nagisa no	no beach welcomes the plover's tracks,
koro nareba	your felicity leaves
chidori no ato wo	no room for my approach, I
fumi ha madofu ka	wonder, did my letter go astray?

in "man's hand" – This is one of the most difficult passages to decipher in the diary. The three participants are playing a cat-and-mouse game with each other. The fact that Kaneie and the author ignore the prince's poem about the pinks has puzzled him. He is trying to find out whether Kaneie saw the poem or not. When he says, "Is it true I shall hear from you yourself?" in the context of the communication between the two men alone, he may mean that he expects a personal visit from Kaneie. In the context of the communication involving the three of them, he may be looking for a direct response from the author. After all, his sending the poem about the pinks may simply have been to acquire a poem of hers in her own hand just for the fun of it.

This brings us to the matter of "hands," which further complicates this passage. Why does the author specifically mention that the prince wrote in "woman's hand" and their response was in "man's hand"? "Woman's hand" was the name for the cursive style of writing Japanese that was preferred by women (see the introduction, pp. 19–20). It was not written exclusively by women, however, since it was a mark of courtliness for a man to be able to write it fluently. "Man's hand" refers to a stiffer writing style in which the graphs are closer to the square forms of Chinese characters (see illustrations on pp. 108–9).

The prince's choice to write in woman's hand could be construed as a display of his elegance, or as an indication that his correspondence is meant for the author as well as Kaneie. Or, if his previous letter had been written in woman's hand, he may be simply being consistent so as not to arouse suspicion. Whatever the prince's motives in the choice of hands, Kaneie's response in man's hand has the effect of bringing the communication solidly back into the "man's world" again.

purification ceremonies – She refers to the Shinto purification ceremonies, which were normally performed at the edge of a river or a lake in the sixth month. She will describe in detail one of these purification ceremonies in book two.

Tanabata Festival – The festival celebrating the legend of the herdsboy and weavermaid stars on the seventh day of the seventh month.

departed spirit's bad influence – In this period, disease was thought to be primarily caused by the malign influence of spirits of the dead. Therefore Buddhist rites to pacify those spirits were the usual prescription.

mountain temple I have visited before – From later evidence in the diary, it is assumed she is speaking of Hannya Temple at Narutaki, located in the northwestern hills of Kyoto.

Obon Ceremony – The festival to celebrate the souls of departed ancestors who it was thought returned from the world of the dead at this time of the year. One therefore had the opportunity to fete them with offerings of food and other gifts before sending them back.

watching this together – From this phrase alone we know that Kaneie came to visit her at the temple. Again a feeling of warmth and intimacy suffuses the scene. She makes nostalgic reference to this occasion again in book two when in very different circumstances she returns to this temple (p. 233).

The year changed over – It is 963. She has been married for nine years.

admitted to serve in the inner chambers – Although his actual post does not seem to have changed at this time, Kaneie was once more granted the privilege of access to the inner chambers of the imperial court.

Kamo Purification Rites – These were Shinto rites of purification performed on the bank of the Kamo River in the fourth month by the high priestess of the Kamo Shrine. It entailed a grand procession that people liked to watch as a parade.

his villa next door – From this remark, it seems that the author is once again staying at her father's residence.

"This is what I have been thinking. Your complaint of no news is misplaced. Is it true that I shall hear from you yourself?" This was written in "woman's hand." Though it seemed graceless to reply in "man's hand":

ura gakure	If hidden on the
miru koto kataki	beach, those tracks are hard to see,
ato naraba	it seems we must wait
shihohi wo matamu	until the tide dries even though
karaki waza kana	a bitter thing it will be.

Again from the prince:

ura mo naku	In those tracks there was
fumi yaru ato wo	nothing to keep us apart,
watatsuumi no	on the open sea,
shiho no hiru ma mo	what need is there to wait for
nani ni ka ha semu	the tide to dry to see the shore.

"Or so I think; I hope there has been no misunderstanding."

Things going on in this way, the time for the purification ceremonies passed and the next day was the day of the Tanabata Festival. It was the fortieth day of a forty-five day period of abstinence for me. These days, I have not been feeling well and have been troubled by a cough; wondering if it might be the result of some departed spirit's bad influence, I think to try a Buddhist rite, and as my place is so cramped and the weather so awfully hot, I go up to a mountain temple I have visited before. Since it is the fifteenth or sixteenth of the seventh month, it is time to celebrate the Obon Ceremony. Looking out I see a procession of servants hurrying to bring offerings, carrying them in the oddest of ways, some on their shoulders, some balanced on their heads, watching this together, we find it so engaging and laugh. Then since I was feeling quite back to normal and the abstinence period had past, I went back to the capital. Autumn and winter sped by with my barely noticing them.

The year changed over, there was nothing particularly different. The times when his heart was unusually affectionate were times when all seemed peaceful. From the first of this month, he was once again admitted to serve in the inner chambers of the court.

It was the day of the Kamo Purification Rites in the fourth month, when the prince from before graces us with this letter, "If you are going to view the event, I would like to ride in your carriage." In the margin, he had also written a little poem that began "This year for me . . . [missing text]." The prince had not lately been at his villa next door. We thought he

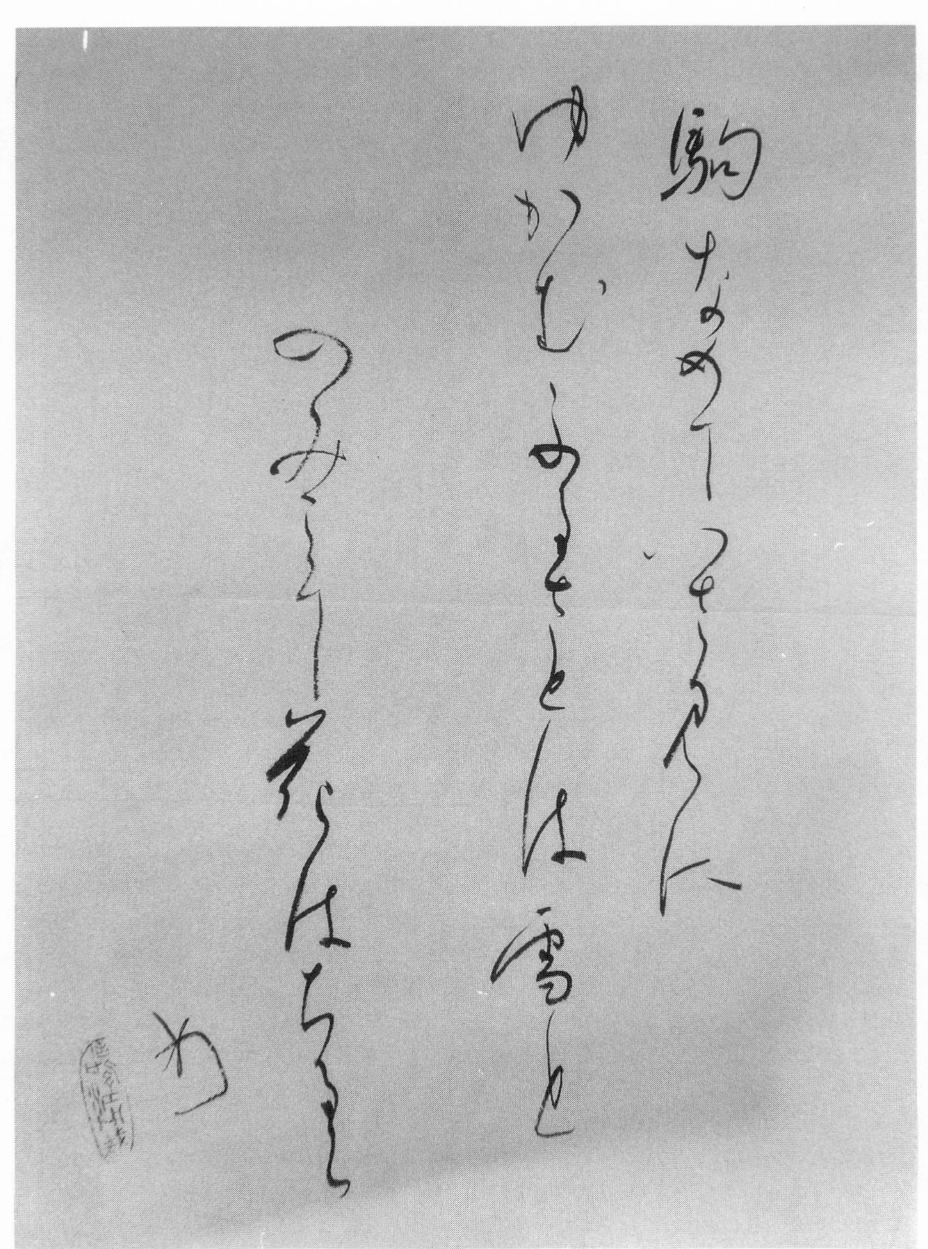

Example of calligraphy in "woman's hand" by the contemporary Japanese calligrapher Shiko Kataoka (see pp. 106–7).

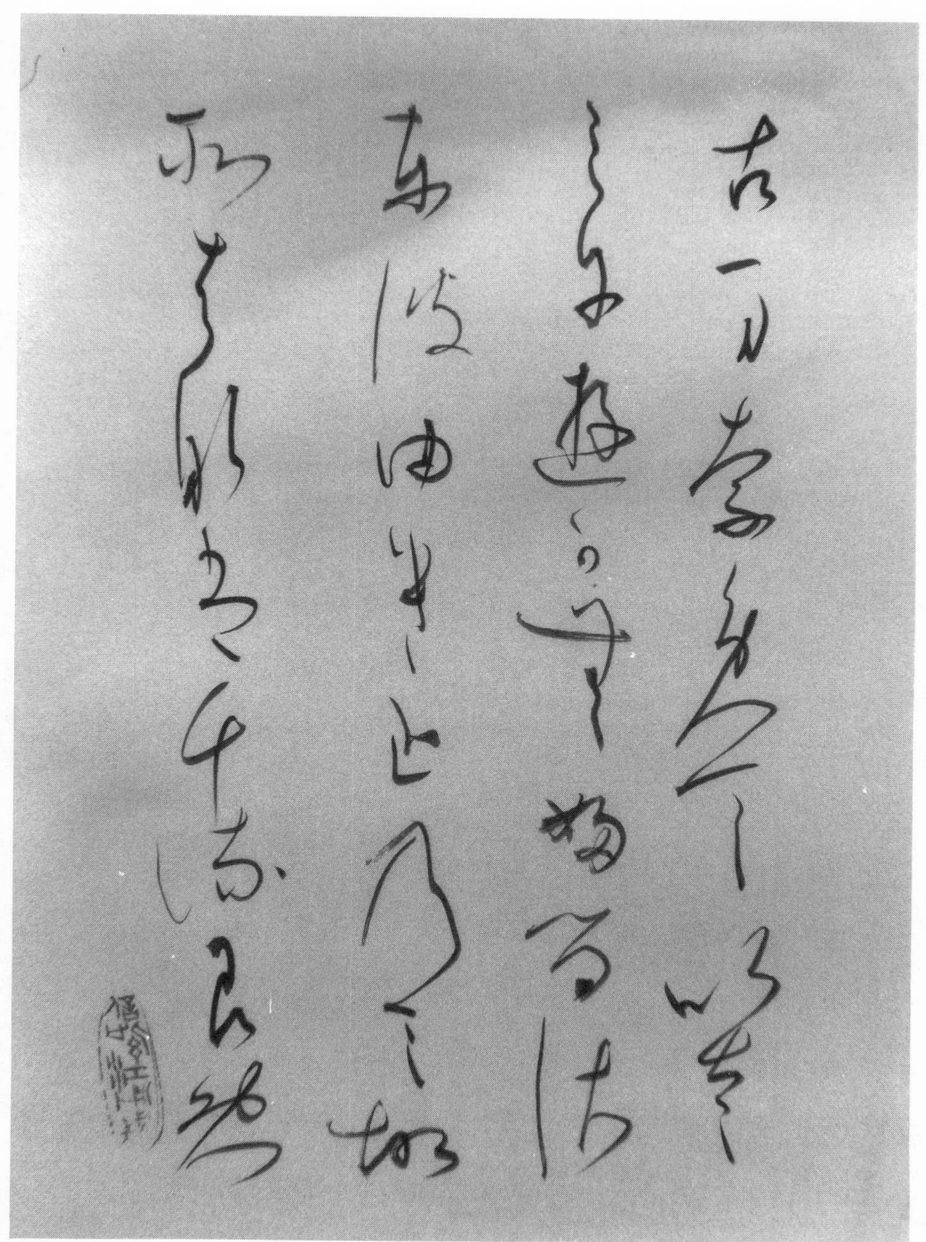

Example of calligraphy in "man's hand" by the contemporary Japanese calligrapher Shiko Kataoka (see pp. 106–7).

We thought he was off visiting a place near Machi no Koji, and inquiring about this – The details are not given for their movements, but *Zenshū* commentators assume that Kaneie and Michitsuna's Mother go off in a carriage together to pick up the prince (*Zenshū,* 162–63). There seems to be some uncertainty about his location, but they appear to have guessed right that he is visiting someone (presumably a wife or lover) in the Machi no Koji area.

Requesting an inkstone – Kaneie requests an inkstone from the Machi no Koji house in order to send in a note. This detail informs us that Kaneie and the author are in a carriage and not back at her house when this note is written. The author's presence is assumed because she would not report on this if she had not seen it. It is most likely that she also helps with the composition of the poem.

Thus, it came about that we went out together – The original contains the phrase *morotomo ni,* "together," which the author uses very sparingly to indicate times when she felt a particular sense of intimacy with Kaneie. In this case, she is not only together with Kaneie but also with the prince. This experience would have been a very unusual one for her.

the bank of the Kamo River – It seems that both her father's residence and the prince's fronted the Kamo River.

brief purification rite – Pouring water from the river over one's hands while praying to have one's sins and defilements washed away was a purification rite. It might have been a customary thing to do when one walked by the river.

wish for it . . . digging efforts – Pun on *horu,* "to wish, desire"/"dig."

However, when I think of what I have written up to this point, I really wonder how it is – This is a difficult passage. For a history of commentators views on it, see Uemura, *Taisei*, vol. 2, 93–94. The original is very elliptical: *saredo, sakizaki mo ikaga to obohetaru kashi* could be rendered literally as, "However, the preceding, how [is it]? I am wondering." The question is, to what does "the preceding" refer: her account of the immediately preceding poem, or is it everything she has written up to that point? I prefer the latter. I also think that the author is actually pausing here to ponder how her diary will appear to her readers.

Spring passed by – This is a new year, 964.

"cries at sunset" – Pun on the name of the type of cicada, *higurashi*, and "sunset."

was off visiting a place near Machi no Koji, and inquiring about this we were told, "Yes, he is here." Requesting an inkstone, he wrote this:

kimi ga kono machi no minami ni tomi ni osoki haru ni ha ima zo tadzune mawireru	Just as a late spring quickly visits you in the south of this city, I have come as fast as I could to attend you and here I am.

Thus, it came about that we went out together.

That season passed. At another time, when the prince was in residence next door, we passed by his garden. Last year we had noticed some luxuriantly growing pampas grass that had lovely flowers and looked very graceful. My husband had requested, "If you are going to divide the roots sometime, please be so kind as to give me a little." Now, time had passed and we were with a companion going along the bank of the Kamo River; we just pointed out to our guest, "That is the prince's place," and my husband sent a servant in to pay his respects. He told him, "Just give this message to his servants, 'I should like to visit but now is not such a good time as I have someone with me. I thought I might inquire about the pampas grass that I spoke of some time ago.'" We went on our way. Since we just performed a brief purification rite, we were back before long. One of the servants called out, "Pampas from the prince," and there it was, carefully dug up and placed in a long box with a slip of green paper attached to it. When we looked at it, this was what was written:

ho ni ideba michi yuku hito mo maneku beki yado no susuki wo horu ga wari nasa	When it flowers, it beckons people off the road, my garden's pampas grass, thus your special wish for it, and my special digging efforts.

It was so charming but since I have forgotten what sort of poem we sent back, I will have to leave it at this. However, when I think of what I have written up to this point, I really wonder how it is.

Spring passed by, and around summer, I felt that he was getting a lot of night duty. He would come early in the morning and stay the day but it seemed strange to me that he should always leave at night; just as I was thinking this, I heard for the first time that year the voice of the *higurashi*, "cries at sunset," cicada. It startled and moved me so:

ayashiku mo yoru no yuku he wo	How strange it is where does it go at night

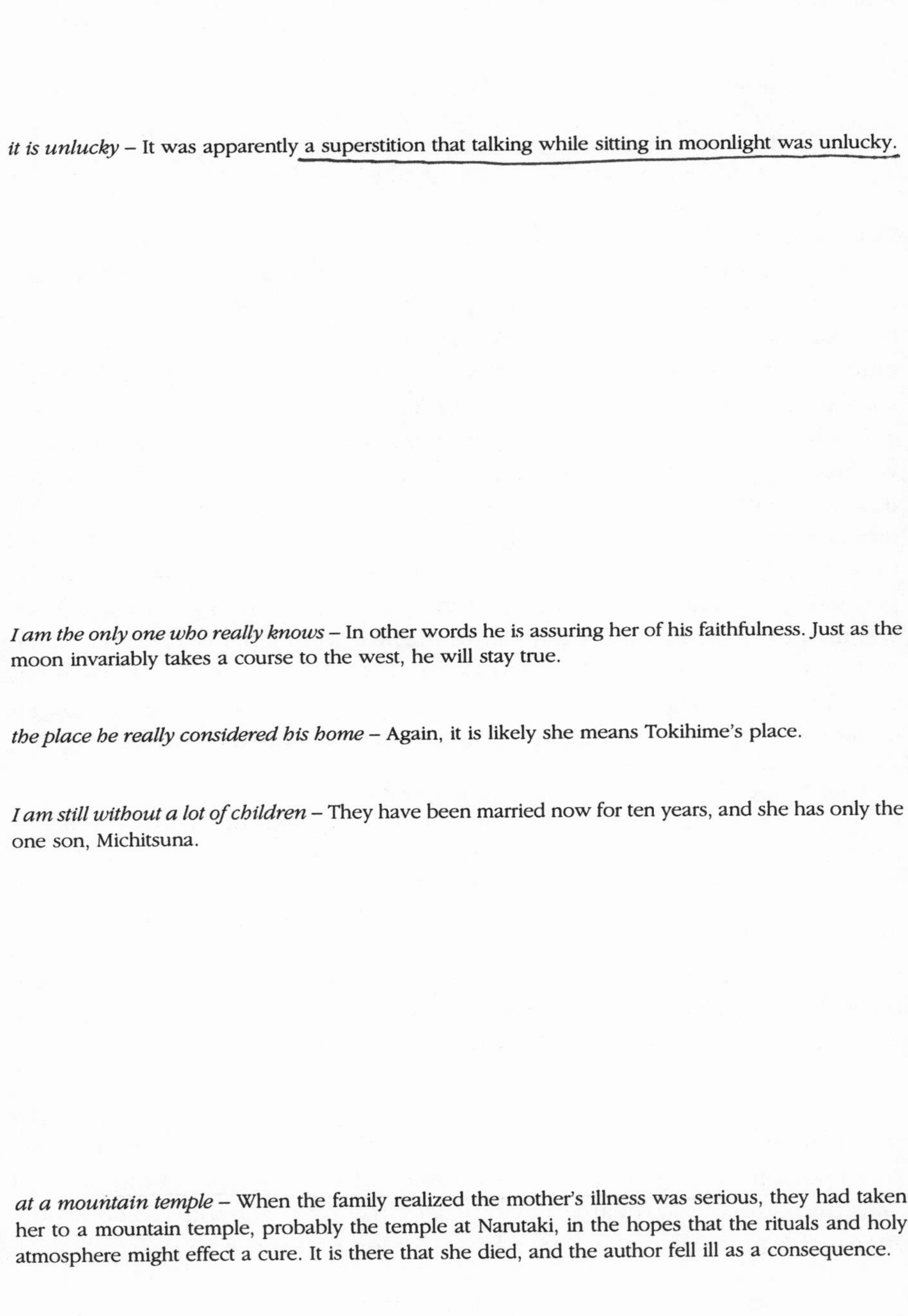

it is unlucky – It was apparently a superstition that talking while sitting in moonlight was unlucky.

I am the only one who really knows – In other words he is assuring her of his faithfulness. Just as the moon invariably takes a course to the west, he will stay true.

the place he really considered his home – Again, it is likely she means Tokihime's place.

I am still without a lot of children – They have been married now for ten years, and she has only the one son, Michitsuna.

at a mountain temple – When the family realized the mother's illness was serious, they had taken her to a mountain temple, probably the temple at Narutaki, in the hopes that the rituals and holy atmosphere might effect a cure. It is there that she died, and the author fell ill as a consequence.

shiranu kana	this I cannot know,
kefu higurashi no	yet I heard the voice of
kowe ha kikedomo	"cries at sunset" here today.

When I said this, he seemed to find it difficult to leave. Thus, uneventful days passed and his heart seemed not to flag in faithfulness.

One full moon night, even though it is unlucky, we talked to each other lying in the moonlight, as I spoke of all the things that had made me sad over the years, it brought back memories of the past, thus sunk in my thoughts, I could not help saying:

kumori yo no	Where the moon goes
tsuki to waga mi no	on a cloudy night or where
yuku suwe no	this self of mine
obotsukanasa ha	will end up, which I wonder
idzure masareri	is the most uncertain?

He replied in a playful manner:

oshihakaru	As for the moon,
tsuki ha nishi he zo	we can presume it goes west,
yuku saki ha	where will things end up?
ware nomi koso ha	Surely I am the only
shirubekarikere	one who really knows.

Thus, although he seemed to be someone I could depend on, as the place he really considered his home was different from mine, it is just not a world I would have wished for. Despite my having consorted with this most fortunate man for months and years, I am still without a lot of children, and thus, my position is uncertain and these worries are the only things of which I have a surplus.

Things being as they were, nonetheless, while at least I had my mother, it was one thing—but then, she succumbed to a lengthy illness, and finally around the beginning of autumn, passed away. My feelings of utter helplessness and loss were much greater than usual for people at such a time. Of all the family members, I was the one who lost myself in thoughts of, *I don't want to stay behind, let me die now too,* such that—what a thing it was—my arms and legs became stiff and unmovable and it seemed as though I couldn't breathe. Things being as they were, having met with this fate at a mountain temple, since the person to whom I had so many things to say was down in the city, I called our young one to my side and with difficulty managed to say, "I will likely die here. What I would like you to convey to your father is this, 'As for myself, do not go to any trouble when I die, but for my deceased mother, over and beyond

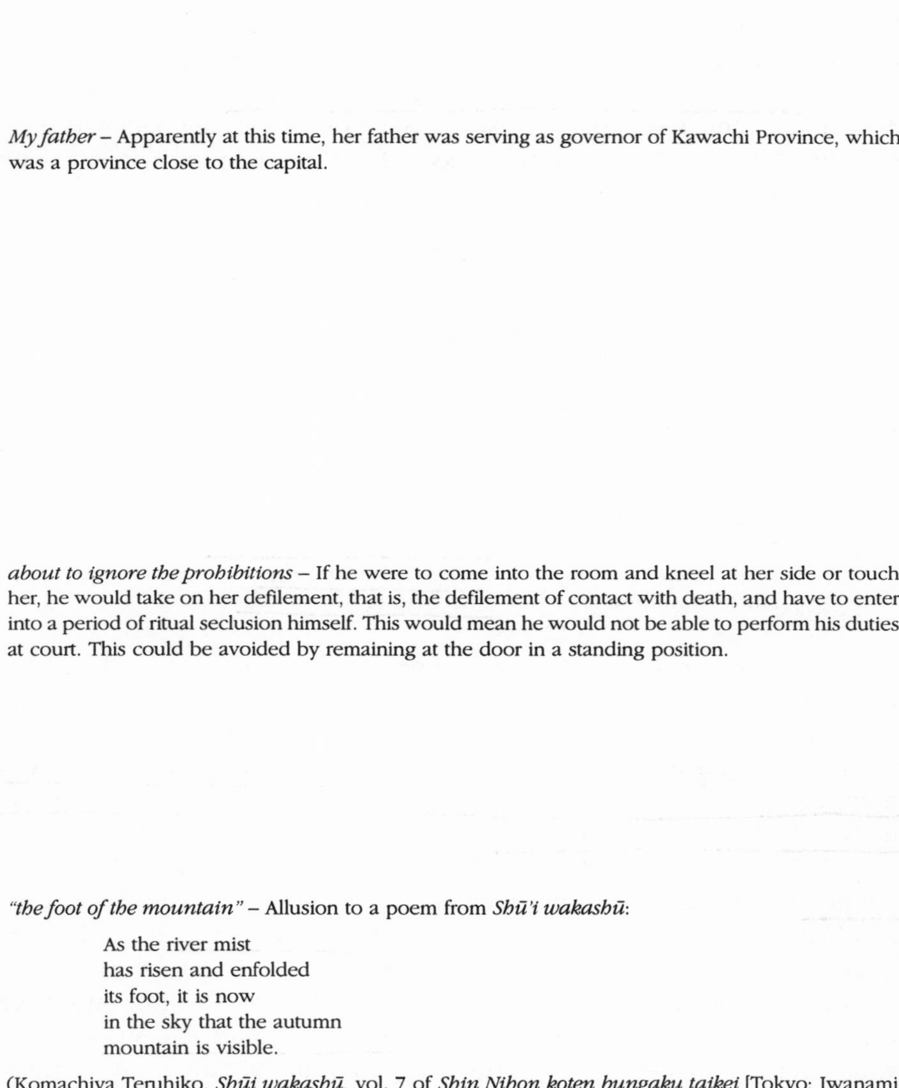

My father – Apparently at this time, her father was serving as governor of Kawachi Province, which was a province close to the capital.

about to ignore the prohibitions – If he were to come into the room and kneel at her side or touch her, he would take on her defilement, that is, the defilement of contact with death, and have to enter into a period of ritual seclusion himself. This would mean he would not be able to perform his duties at court. This could be avoided by remaining at the door in a standing position.

"the foot of the mountain" – Allusion to a poem from *Shū'i wakashū*:

As the river mist
has risen and enfolded
its foot, it is now
in the sky that the autumn
mountain is visible.

(Komachiya Teruhiko, *Shūi wakashū,* vol. 7 of *Shin Nihon koten bungaku taikei* [Tokyo: Iwanami Shoten, 1990], 58.)

intoning the Buddha's name – This refers to the chanting of the name of Amida Buddha, who is thought to dwell in the Western Paradise.

what others do for her, please hold special services.'" Then, just saying, "What is to be done?" I could no longer speak. After the long days and months of my mother's suffering, people of the household had somehow accepted that it was over and nothing further could be done; now with this illness of mine, everyone was caught up again in worry; there were so many people bewildered saying, "What are we to do?" "How has it come to this?" and having already cried would begin to cry again. Even though I was unable to speak, I was still conscious and could see. My father, the person most concerned about my welfare, came, and said, "You still have one parent. How could you have come to this?" He urged me to swallow some broth, and drinking things such as this, my body began to mend. However, still brooding on things, I felt as though I was not really alive. I remembered how on some of those days when my mother was suffering so and was unable to talk, the only thing she would say, thinking about the uncertainty of my life, which I lamented night and day, was "Alas, what is to become of you?" This she would say often under her breath; remembering this brought me to a state of barely feeling alive.

He heard about my mother's death and came to visit. I was hardly conscious, aware and not aware of things around me. He was met by one of my serving maids, and when she told him of my condition, "She really is in such a bad way," he burst into tears and seemed about to ignore the prohibitions concerning defilement to come to my side, but was dissuaded. "Really, your lordship, you must not," so he stayed standing. His whole bearing and attitude were such that it seemed he really cared deeply for me.

Thus, all the various tasks connected with the funeral service were attended to; many people took great pains and so it was accomplished. Presently, we were together at this melancholy mountain temple with nothing in particular to do. At night, I would lie awake, grieving until dawn; when I looked at the mountain's countenance, I saw that just as in the old poem, "the foot of the mountain" was truly enfolded in mist. I thought, *In the capital, who do I really have to go home to? No, better just stay here and die*, yet even thinking this, I was pained for my little one who would have me live.

In this way, the tenth of the month passed. I listened to the monks telling stories when they took a rest from intoning the Buddha's name. They said, "There is a place where you can actually see a person who has passed away. It seems that the form of the person disappears when you get close. But from a distance you can see it." "Where is this country?" I asked. "It is called 'Comfort to the Ears Island.'" Hearing them speak about it one after another, how much I wanted to know where it was. Feeling sad, I could not help saying:

my elder brother – This is the first mention of her elder brother, Masayoshi, who shares the same mother with the author and is therefore on close terms with her throughout her life (cf. p. 26). From periodic references throughout the rest of the diary, it appears he was often living at the same residence as the author.

The closest members of the family, particularly the children by the same mother, would have been all in seclusion together at the mountain temple for the week following the mother's death.

"where insects pipe lonely calls" – Allusion to poem number 853 from the "Poems of Grief" section of *Kokinshū*:

that single clump of
waving plume grass planted by
my lord long ago
is now an overgrown field
where insects pipe lonely calls (Rodd, *Kokinshū,* 294)

high enough office to serve in the inner court – None of her male or female relatives serve at court, so no special provisions need to be made for their accommodation during the ritual confinement.

ari to dani	If only she exists,
yoso nite mo mimu	even from afar, I would see her,
na ni shi ohaba	tell me more about
ware ni kikaseyo	this place, "Comfort to my Ears,"
mimiraku no shima	if true to its name it be.

And as I spoke, my elder brother hearing this broke into tears, saying:

idzu koto ka	Where is it? Just hearing
oto ni nomi	the sound of "Comfort to my Ears
kiku mimiraku no	Island," I would seek
shimagakure ni shi	to find the one who has
hito wo tadzunemu	hidden herself away there.

With things going along like this, although each day he came to ask after me, paying his respects while standing, just at that time, I had no heart for anything, and it was also irritating that he could not stay on account of defilement. I was in a dazed condition; we did carry on a correspondence that was somehow difficult, but I guess because I was not in a state of mind to remember things, I have forgotten all that we said.

I was in no hurry to go home but it was not something to leave up to one's feelings. This day when we are all to leave has come. When we were coming here, my mother lay across my lap, and worrying only about how to make her more comfortable, I was bathed in sweat, yet, even so, there was hope in my heart and I still felt there was something I could do. This time, no matter how comfortable I was and able to ride with such an awful lot of space in the carriage, the trip home was miserably sad. Even getting home, getting down from the carriage and looking around, without being fully aware of it, I was all the more sad. Here where we used to come out on the veranda and sit together were the plants we had cared for; from the time when she became ill, they had just been abandoned, yet here they were growing in a great tangle blooming profusely. Performing a Buddhist rite in mother's memory, everyone was lost in their own thoughts. I alone remained just gazing at the scene around me in a vacant way, and intoned the old poem, "plume grass . . . where insects pipe lonely calls," and feeling like this:

te furenedo	Even with no care,
hana ha sakari ni	the flowers are blooming in
nari ni keri	splendid profusion,
todome okikeru	it must be thanks to the dew
tsuyu ni kakarite	left behind to nourish them.

Since no one in the family was of high enough office to serve in the inner court, we could pass our period of ritual confinement in the

The ceremony for the forty-ninth day – In Buddhist belief it is thought that the soul of a dead person remains for forty-nine days after death. At the end of forty-nine days, the soul is then reborn according to its accumulated karma. Services were held every seven days after death, but the service on the forty-ninth day was the largest and in a sense the funeral proper.

my husband took care . . . – It appears that Kaneie takes care of the arrangements for the funeral, and, as we learn later in the diary, he continues to take responsibility for the mother's memorial services for many years. This was one of the ways he supported her economically.

intentions for the ceremony – People would commission works of Buddhist art as an expression of their prayers for the future of the deceased. The intention is to have the departed person be reborn as a Buddha.

nominal ordination – When an illness appeared grave, it was common to administer a nominal ordination in the hopes that it might save the person's life.

"Cloud Forest" hermitage – Unrin'in, a temple of the Tendai school of Buddhism located in the Murasakino district of northern Kyoto.

same place, each making a chamber for themselves with curtains. In the midst of all this, I alone could not get my mind onto other things; at night, from the time when I heard them start to invoke the Buddha's name, I would just cry continuously until dawn. The ceremony for the forty-ninth day was held with everyone present at the house. Since my husband took care of most of the arrangements, a lot of people attended. As an expression of my own intentions for the ceremony, I had an image of the Buddha painted. After that day was over, everyone went their separate ways. I was left feeling even more bereft; there was no help for it, but he, having some compassion for my helplessness, visited much more often than before.

Then, when in an absentminded sort of way, I set about putting in order the things that had been scattered about when we left for the temple, just looking at the things that she had used everyday from dawn to dusk, or the letters that she had written, nearly stopped my heart. At the time when she was weakening, on the day when she received the Buddhist precepts for nominal ordination, she had died just like that with the reverend priest's stole laid over her. Now I found that stole among the other things. Thinking that I should really return it, I got up very early in the morning to write a note. The moment I set down on the paper, "This, your venerable stole," my eyes clouded over with tears; I carried on, "Thanks to this":

hachisuba no	Wrapped with this she
tama to naruramu	became a jewel on the lotus leaf,
musubu ni mo	this morning, wrapping it
sode nuru masaru	tears dampened my sleeves once more,
kesa no tsuyu kana	dew on this holy vestment.

and with this poem I sent it back.

A little later, I heard that the elder brother of the owner of the stole, who was also a monk and whom we had had offer prayers and services, suddenly died. What must the brother be feeling? I felt very sorry for him, and at the same time it seemed that all the people I depended on were disappearing. Thinking thoughts like that I felt quite disturbed, and often made inquiries after the younger monk and sent offerings. Due to certain circumstances, he was serving at the "Cloud Forest" hermitage. When the Forty-Ninth Day Ceremony for his brother was complete, I wrote this:

omohiki ya	Who would have guessed,
kumo no mori wo	that he would leave behind
uchisutete	the forest of clouds
sora no keburi ni	and rise up with the smoke
tatamu mono to ha	disappearing into the sky.

"whether in the mountains or in the fields" – Allusion to poem number 947 from the "Miscellaneous" section of *Kokinshū*:

where shall I go to
renounce this sorrowful world
whether in the mountains
or in the fields my heart surely
will be distracted and stray (Rodd, *Kokinshū*, 321)

one brother and an aunt – Her brother, Masayoshi. The aunt is unidentifiable, but she is most likely one of her mother's sisters.

The year changed – It is 965.

removing our mourning clothes – It is now the end of their official year of mourning. They remove the clothes and purify them by immersing them in the river.

dusting my koto – The koto is a horizontal zither. She would have been prohibited from playing it during the year of mourning.

from my aunt came – The original is just *anata yori*, "from over there," but it is assumed to be the author's aunt. The aunt would have been staying in a separate room and would have sent this in writing.

and sent it along; mind you, my own feelings of misery and loss were like those in the old poem, "whether in the mountains or in the fields."

Feeling empty and alone, I passed through autumn and winter. In the same place are living with me one brother and an aunt. Although I think of my aunt as a parent, still there are times when I weep until dawn longing for the past. The year changed, spring and summer passed by, and soon it was time to commemorate the first anniversary of mother's death; for this time only we held the service at the same mountain temple as before. Remembering so many things from the year before deepened the sadness I was already feeling. From the moment the monk leading the service began to speak, "Clearly, it is not that you have come here seeking the autumn mountain scenery; you are here to have made clear to you the heart of the scriptures to which your eyes have been closed. . . ." Hearing just that much, I became unaware of everything around me and I barely noticed all the things that came afterward. Once everything that should have been done was done, we returned. Quickly removing our mourning clothes, we performed a purification ceremony with our grey clothes and even our fans. As we were doing that, this poem came to me:

fudji goromo	Setting my mourning weeds
nagasu namida no	out in the flow of
kaha midzu ha	the river, my tears flow
kishi ni mo masaru	even more than when I wore them,
mono ni zo arikeru	the water overflows the bank.

I cried wretchedly, but just left it at that without saying anything to anyone.

So the commemoration ceremony was complete, and as usual I had nothing in particular to do. Without really intending to play, as I was dusting my koto, my fingers strayed to play a few notes and it struck me that indeed the period of mourning was over. Sadly, it had passed so quickly. As I was brooding on this, from my aunt came:

ima ha tote	Now it is over,
hiki idzuru koto no	yet when I hear these notes
ne wo kikeba	plucked from the koto,
uchi kaheshitemo	they run me back to the past
naho zo kanashiki	and I am even sadder.

At this, even though it was nothing very special, thinking about it, my tears overflowed:

naki hito ha	The day and month that
otodzure mo sede	I cut the strings of my koto

my sister – This would appear to be the same older sister that moved out with her husband, Tamemasa.

move far away – She is likely accompanying Tamemasa on a tour of duty in the provinces.

inauspicious behavior – To cry too much at parting was thought to bring on misfortune.

mountain barrier – She is thinking of the Ōsaka Barrier, the border checkpoint between the capital and Ōtsu.

a new year arrived – The year 966.

koto no wo wo	since the one who had gone
tachishi tsuki hi zo	could no longer hear me play,
kaheri ki ni keri	that day has come round again.

Meanwhile, among all my family, my sister was one on whom I particularly relied, but this summer, it had come about that she would have to move far away. Now that the official period of mourning was complete, she is getting ready to leave. Thinking about this I feel so bereft, I am quite dazed. Now, finally, it is the day of departure and I go to see her. I take as parting gifts just one outfit of clothes and some trifles placed in a lidded box. Her household is in a terrible commotion with all the fuss. Both she who is going and I are unable to look one another in the eye; we just stand in front of each other unable to stop our tears. Everyone says things like, "What are you crying for?" "Get a grip on yourselves." "How very inauspicious behavior for a departure." Then just as I was thinking how terrible it would be to see her get in the carriage to leave, someone came from my own household to relay a message from him. "Hurry back. I have just got here," and the carriage was brought up for me. My sister, who was wearing a double, dyed overrobe, and I, who was only wearing a thin overrobe of red ochre, parted by taking off and exchanging these robes. It was just past the tenth day of the ninth month. When I came back to my house, I cried wretchedly until he said, "Why on earth do you behave so? You'll bring bad luck."

Then, at night, I was thinking to myself, *They must have got as far as the mountain barrier either yesterday or today.* The moon was so affecting, I was gazing at it, and my aunt was still awake playing the koto. She said this:

hiki tomuru	The gates creak open
mono to ha nashi ni	at Ōsaka Barrier,
afusaka no	no one stops them nor
seki no kuchi me no	will my playing draw them back,
ne ni zo sohotsuru	in these sounds, I am drenched.

She was indeed one who felt the same as I. I answered:

omohiyaru	Imagining I hear
afusaka yama no	the sound of the creaking gate
seki no ne ha	at Mount Ōsaka,
kiku ni mo sode zo	just hearing that, my sleeves begin
kuchi me tsukinuru	to molder with the dampness.

While I spent my time imagining their journey, a new year arrived.

it is not convenient – He does not seem to regard her place as appropriate for holding the various rituals for his cure. Or, he may not want to cause her the inconvenience. One can understand that he would like to be back in his own residence where he can be attended by those servants who have looked after him since he was a child.

not likely you will remain single – It is difficult to know what is in the background of this remark. Does he mean, "With your beauty and talents, another man will surely marry you," or "You will not be able to survive without the support of another man"? It could be a bit of both.

how on earth could you ever come to me – This remark indicates how unusual it was for a woman to visit the residence of a man. There seems to have been a feeling of impropriety about it.

elder brother – Again we assume she is referring to Masayoshi.

someone who took that amiss – Most likely Tokihime.

Around the third month, one day when he had just come here, he took ill, and I was bewildered by this suffering, about which it seemed nothing could be done; it seemed very serious. He said, "Much as I would like to stay here, as it is not convenient for the various things to be done, I had better go back to my own residence. Please do not take offense at this. This comes so suddenly, I feel as though I may not have long to live; it can't be helped. Ah, if I die, how very sad it is that I have done nothing that would have you remember me." Seeing him cry, I lose control and begin to cry miserably too, at which he says, "Don't cry. It makes me suffer more. The worst thing about all this is to have to part from you in such an unexpected way. What will you do? It is not likely you will remain single. Yet, if it comes to that, don't marry again until the period of mourning for me is over. Even if I don't die, this may be the end of us. Even if I manage to stay alive, I will likely not be strong enough to visit you and even were there a time when I might be stronger, how on earth could you ever come to me . . . oh, if I die thus, this will be the last time we see each other," and so on, lying there, he speaks so miserably and weeps. Calling together the various attendants, he says to them, "You can see how fond I am of her. To think that if I die this way, I will never see her again makes me feel wretched." When he said this, everyone broke into tears. As for myself, I was even more overwhelmed, unable to say anything, I just wept and wept. At that moment, he began to feel worse; his carriage was brought up for him to depart, he was raised up and brought toward it leaning on others. He looked directly at me, and kept looking fixedly; how miserable he appeared. And as for me who was to stay behind, there were no words to express it. My elder brother said, "Why are you inviting bad luck in this way. Surely, it is not as you think. Quickly let us be on our way, your lordship," and they drove off, my brother holding him in his arms. I cannot begin to say all that I thought and felt. I sent letters two and more times a day. There might have been someone who took that amiss, but it couldn't be helped. As for a reply, he had one of the older female attendants from over there write for him, "'It is unbearable not to be able to respond to you myself,' was all his lordship was able to say." I heard that his condition was even worse than before and I could see no way of going to see him myself as he had suggested, so as I fretted and wondered what on earth I could do; ten or more days passed.

Then, with all the performing of special services, it seems that he has become a little better and begins as might be expected to respond himself. "How strange it all has been, I lay ill for so many days with no improvement, never having experienced such distress before, it was a great anxiety," and so on, taking advantage of when no one was looking, he wrote at length, "I am quite conscious now and while I know there is

I feared what people might think – People might think that she was lowering herself to be summoned like a servant woman or that she was using the pretext of his illness to try to usurp Tokihime's place. Nonetheless, despite her concerns, her visit to his place is clearly one of the most romantic episodes in her marriage.

broken my fast – During an illness, one refrained from eating meat or fish of any kind.

dawn is breaking – She wants to leave in the dark. This description ironically parallels a secret visit by a male lover. The male lover usually leaves before dawn.

no way you could come openly to me in the day, come at night; so many days have passed since we have been able to meet." I feared what people might think and felt very uneasy. He replied immediately to my objections by simply repeating the same thing. Thinking there was nothing but to do it, no sooner had I said, "Send for a carriage," then we were drawing up to a side wing some distance from the main part of his residence, where a room had been very nicely prepared, and by the edge of the veranda, he was waiting lying down. As the lights are extinguished just when I step down from the carriage, it is very dark and I don't know the way in, "How silly, I'm right here," he says, taking me by the hand and leading me in. "What took you so long?" So saying he begins to relate in bits and pieces what had happened in the last few days, and after a little while, he says, "Bring a light; it's so dark," and to me, "There is really nothing for you to be anxious about, you know," and so a faint light was placed behind a screen. "I have not yet broken my fast and eaten fish, but tonight, once you got here, I thought we would eat some together. Bring in the meal," he ordered and trays were brought in. Once we had eaten a little, monks arrived. The night was getting late and monks were preparing to chant a service for his health; however, when he said, "Please be excused now. Today, I have been feeling a bit better," a reverend monk responded with, "I see it is as your lordship says," and withdrew.

Then, just as dawn is breaking, I say, "Please, call the servants to prepare my departure," but he responds, "What, it's still so dark, wait a little yet." And so we remain until it is quite light. Then he calls his men servants to raise the wooden shutters and we gaze out at the garden. "See, how do you like the way the flowers and shrubs are planted?" He draws me out to look. "Look at what time it has gotten to be, how embarrassing," I say urging him to let me depart. "What, you can't leave now, some rice gruel is just on its way." And thus, with one thing and another, broad daylight arrived. Finally, he said, "Well now, shall I accompany you back home? I doubt you will ever venture such a thing again?" to which I responded, "Even just for my coming here, what are people going to think? If it were thought that I had come to drag you off back with me, how awful it would be." "If that is the case, there is nothing else to do. I shall have my men draw up a carriage." When the carriage was drawn up, with faltering steps, he walked right up to where I was to get in; I gazed at him, moved by the sight, and just as I said, "When might my lord be up and around," tears welled forth. "Since it is so distressing to be apart, I would hope to be able to visit as soon as tomorrow or the day after." What a wrenching scene it was. When the carriage was drawn a little way off to where the oxen were hitched up, I kept looking at him. I saw that he had returned to the place where we had been together and was looking in this

strange indeed – A pun on *ura*, "shore"/"heart" brings the sea imagery into this poem. The imagery evokes her rolling ride in the carriage back home as well as providing the hyperbole of "drenched in sea waves" to express her grief at parting.

Kamo Festival – A festival of the fourth month that involved a grand procession from the Lower Kamo Shrine to the Upper Kamo Shrine. People watched lined up in carriages on either side of the route. This festival is still held every April in Kyoto (see illustrations on pp. 366-69).

the one from that place – Tokihime.

heartvine – The heartvine or hollyhock plant is the symbol of the Kamo Festival, and its leaves and flowers are used to decorate the shrine buildings and the costumes of the people in the procession. The name of the heartvine in Japanese, *aoi*, or in the old spelling, *afuhi*, is a pun meaning also "meeting day" and was often used in poems composed around this festival (see illustration, p. 131).

Though I heard . . . – This is the first half of a thirty-one syllable *waka*. By sending her half a poem, the author is challenging Tokihime to complete it. It is a very clever opening. With two puns, one on *afuhi*, "heartvine"/"meeting day" and the other on *tachibana*, a type of orange, with *tachi*, "to stay," embedded in it, it yields two simultaneously perceived meanings: "Though I hear this is a heartvine, there is this orange from somewhere else" and "Though I heard this is a day for meeting, you stay over there." Moreover, it is terribly fitting that she present the poem with gifts of the flowers and fruit that provide the wordplays for the poem.

After quite some time – This phrase hints of derision. With impromptu poetry, the mark of skill is to be quick in responding. That it takes Tokihime (with likely the help of her serving women as well) a long time to reply is an indication of some trouble on their part to frame an appropriate ending to the poem. Judging from the absence of any of Tokihime's poems in later poetry anthologies, it seems likely that poetry was not one of Tokihime's strong points.

yellow flesh's sharp tartness – Tokihime does, however, come up with an appropriate response. Her capping lines hinge on a pun on *kimi*, "yellow flesh"/"you." On one level, her lines may mean, "Today, I see the tartness of the citron's yellow flesh" or on another, "Today, I see your cruelty." There is a biting quality to her capping lines. Uemura Etsuko, editor of the *Taisei* compendium, speculates that this battle of poetry from carriages watching the Kamo Festival might have given Murasaki Shikibu the idea for the famous fight of the carriages scene in the Aoi chapter of *The Tale of Genji* (Uemura, *Taisei,* vol. 2, 306).

he said – The speaker of this utterance is not identified explicitly. There has been debate among commentators as to whether it is Kaneie or some member of her household who makes this remark (Uemura, *Taisei,* vol. 2, 303). I follow *Zenshū* and Uemura Etsuko in assuming that it is Kaneie. It is the wit of the remark that seems to have Kaneie's stamp on it.

direction watching despondently as the carriage was drawn away. I too couldn't help looking back until I couldn't see him any more.

Then, while it was still daylight, a letter arrived from him. He wrote many things and this:

kagiri ka to	Even more than when
omohitsutsu koshi	I came away from you thinking
hodo yori mo	this may be the end,
nakanaka naru ha	to part with so many things
wabishi karikere	unfinished was wretched.

My reply, "Having seen that you were still far from well, now I am still distracted and anxious. 'So many things unfinished,' truly, it is so . . ."

ware mo sa zo	For me too, no peace
nodokeki toko no	or ease in our berth of one
ura narade	night's short passage
kaheru namidji ha	drenched by waves, the sea road
ayashikarikere	homeward was strange indeed.

Then, even though he still seemed to be somewhat ill, with an effort of will, he came to visit after only two or three days. But gradually as he returned to his former state of health, he also resumed his former pattern of visiting.

Around this time, the fourth month, I was going to watch the Kamo Festival and the one from that place was going out to see it too. Seeing that such was the case, I parked my carriage across from hers. Since there was not much to do while waiting, I draped some heartvine over a branch of tachibana oranges and sent this over to her:

afuhi to ka	Though I heard we would
kikedomo yoso ni	be bound together with heartvine,
tachibana no	over there you stay, this citron's . . .

After quite some time, this arrived:

kimi ga tsurasa wo	yellow flesh's sharp tartness
kefu koso ha mire	today truly I see in you.

One of my company remarked, "You are someone she must have hated for years, why does she only say 'today'?" Returning home, when I told him about what happened, he said, "Well, at least, she didn't say:

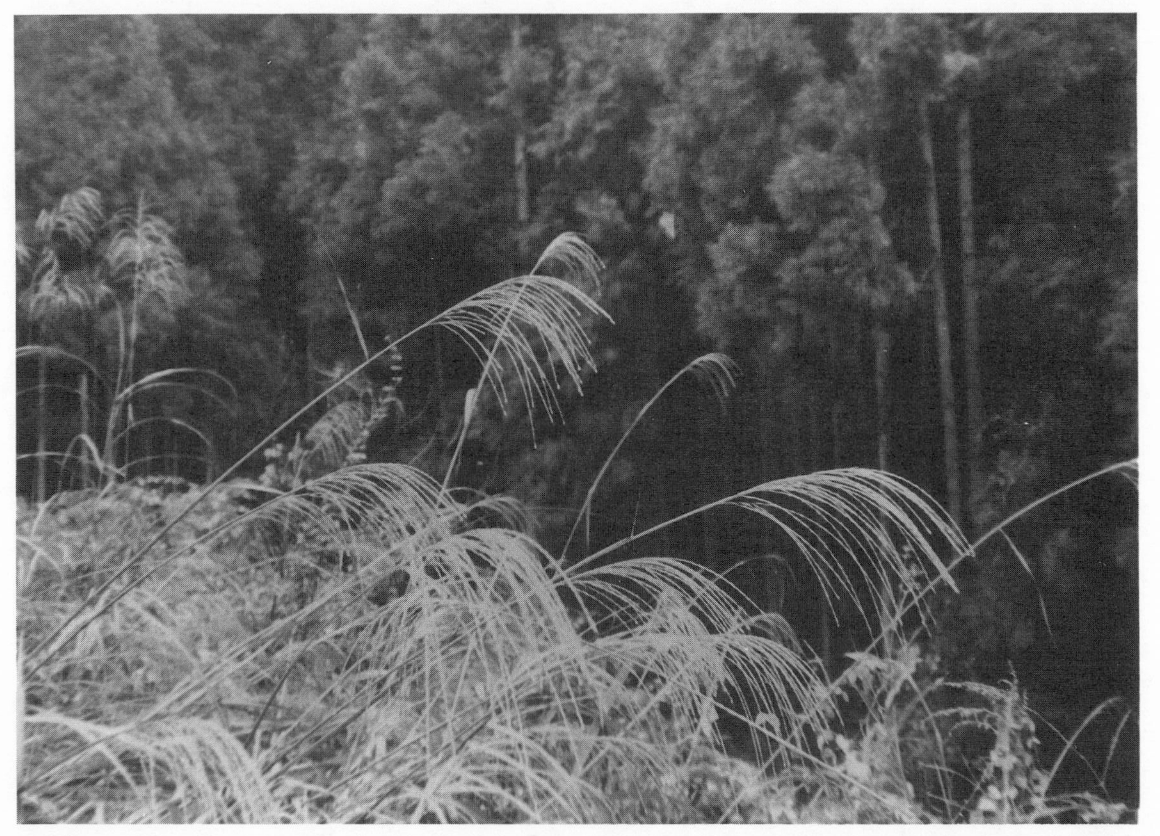

Pampas grass, *susuki*. "When the plume comes forth/ whither first will it sway,/ flowering pampas grass?" (p. 83). See also pp. 82, 111, and elsewhere.

Heartvine, *afuhi/aoi,* often rendered in English as "hollyhock," the plant decoration for the Kamo Festival. *Afuhi* is a homophone for "meeting day." "Though I heard we would/ be bound together with heartvine . . ." (p. 129). See also pp. 128, 304–5, 386–87.

Gosechi Festival – This festival was part of the fifth day of the fifth month celebrations at court. It usually involved the emperor sponsoring a horse race and an archery from horseback contest. Due to bereavements in the royal family, there had not been a Gosechi Festival for two years; that is why the author specifically mentions that one was to be held "this year" and why it was so special.

. . . roots, for the Fifth Month Festival – It was the custom for the Fifth Month Festival to pick iris roots and festoon one's house with them as a charm for warding off disease. The longer the roots the better, and contests were held to compare length of roots.

prince's boxes – Their friend from before, Prince Noriakira.

between Fourth and Fifth Avenues – This is the first time she gives us the location of her father's residence. From the previous mention when she moved there temporarily to avoid a period of abstinence, we know that it was also close to the Kamo River. By oxcart, it would have been more than an hour's distance from the author's residence.

my house – Presumably the author's house, located outside the eastern edge of the palace compound, is one she inherited from her mother. It is clear in the following passage that she expects her husband to contribute to the upkeep of the house. This seems to have been one of the normal expectations of a husband, at least judging from evidence in *The Tale of Genji*. One of the indications of Genji taking on responsibility for a woman is his sending parties of workmen to do repairs on her house.

kuhi tsubushi tsubeki	yellow flesh that I would like
kokochi koso sure	to tear to pieces and eat up . . .

did she?" and so we thought it was most amusing.

This year, a Gosechi Festival was going to be held and everyone was all excited. I wanted to see it in the worst way but there were no places left. Having heard him chance to say, "Well, if you really want to see it . . .," when he said, "Let's play a game of backgammon?" I said, "Right! Let's play for seats at the Gosechi Festival," and the dice fell in my favor. I was so happy and set about making arrangements for attending the festival. Later that night, when things were quiet, I drew an inkstone to me and as though I was practicing calligraphy, I wrote:

ayame gusa	Having counted the
ohi ni shi kazu wo	good throws of the dice, now counting
kazohetsutsu	the iris in the pond,
hiku ya satsuki no	plucking their roots, for the Fifth
sechi ni mataruru	Month Festival, I wait.

showing it to him, he broke out laughing, and said:

kakure nu ni	Who knows how many
ofuru kazu wo ba	irises may be growing in
tare ka shiru	the hidden marsh,
ayame shirazu mo	yet, not even knowing that,
mataru naru kana	you wait counting on going.

Yet, as he had meant all along to have me see the festival, he had arranged for me to share two bays of special box seats adjoining the prince's boxes, so I was able to see the festival in splendid style.

In this way, our marriage had continued for ten plus one or two more years, looking like a match others would not find disagreeable. Yet, actually I had spent all this time, dawn until dusk, ceaselessly lamenting that it was not a marriage like others. This is understandable for someone in a position like mine—on the nights when he neglects to visit, I feel forlorn about having so few people in the household. And these days, as for the only man I can really rely on, my father, he has just been marching around the provinces for the last ten years and more. Even on the rare occasions when he is in the capital, since he lives between Fourth and Fifth Avenues and I live alongside the stables for the Guardsmen of the Left, we are so far apart. Thus, my house, with no one to take it in hand, falls into a worse and worse state of disrepair. And that my husband can

called our young one to him – Michitsuna is twelve years old at this time. This scene where an estranged husband takes his rage out on his wife by causing pain to the child of the union needs little cultural translation.

pilgrimage – This is the first pilgrimage she describes in the diary. As the passage indicates, the first impulse to go on a pilgrimage might come from a desire to enjoy seasonal scenery. The ninth month is closer to October in the modern calendar, and October is still a preferred month for sightseeing in the Kyoto area. Nonetheless, as well as the potential pleasure in the trip, the desire for receiving assistance from higher powers was an important motive. Here, with the choice of a Shinto shrine, she is putting her hopes in the native gods.

to a certain place – From her reference to Inari Mountain in the second of the three poems, we know this is the Fushimi-Inari Shrine to the south of Kyoto. The fact that there is a lower, middle, and upper shrine also helps identify the site. This shrine complex is still a thriving religious center (see illustrations on pp. 138–39).

made an offering of them – Presenting poems for offerings to the Shinto gods was an ancient custom based on a reverence for the magical power of words in general and more particularly poetry. She does not present poems when she goes on pilgrimages to Buddhist temples. These poems do not convey the specific content of her distress or wishes, but it is likely she is going to pray for happiness in her marriage, a good future for her son, and the birth of more children (Uemura, *Taisei,* vol. 2, 365–66).

If this be the entrance . . . – This playful poem turns on the pivot word, ***kami no keshiki***, which means both the face of the god and the scenery of the upper shrine. In effect, the author is saying, "If the gods here have miraculous powers, then show me the upper shrine without my having to walk all the way there." Today the walk from the lower to the upper shrine is about an hour, and presuming that the positioning of the shrines was approximately the same in the Heian period, that would have been quite a walk for a woman not used to exercise.

come and go from this house without noticing a thing makes me feel especially forlorn; when I think that it must indicate a lack of deep regard for me, a thousand weeds of worry grow rank in my mind. He says he is overrun with busy affairs, well, he must be more overrun than my run-down house is overrun with mugwort. With my brooding on such things as these, the eighth month arrived.

One day when we were passing a quiet time together, we began to argue over a trifle and ended up, both he and I, saying nasty things to one another; he had a fit of anger and left. He walked out onto the veranda and called our young one to him, and among other things said, "I will no longer be coming here." As soon as he had left, my son came into the room convulsed with sobbing. "Now, now, what's the matter?" I said, but he didn't answer. Of course, I could imagine how it was for him, but as it seemed foolish to have everybody else hear about it, I stopped questioning him and did what I could to calm him down. Thus, as many as five or six days passed without a word from him. He had never done anything like this before, it seemed crazy, and here I was thinking that it was a kind of joke, but as our relationship was such a fragile thing, it could actually end just like this, I thought. Brooding despondently, I happened to notice the basin of water he had used for dressing his hair the day he had left; there it was, just as it had been. There was dust on it. Has it come to this? Startled I wrote:

taenuru ka	Is this the end?
kage dani araba	I would ask your reflection
tofu beki wo	if it were there, but
katami no midzu ha	on the water left behind as a
mikusawi ni keri	memento, a film has formed.

On the very day I was brooding on such things as these, he appeared. It was difficult between us as usual. At times like this, I felt just as though my chest was being crushed, my heart could not feel at ease, I was wretched.

The ninth month arrived; the world seemed beautiful; I thought to myself, *how about going on a pilgrimage, and telling the gods all the worries of this useless, insubstantial self.* So making up my mind, I went very inconspicuously to a certain place. I wrote the following poems and, tying them into a bunch, made an offering of them. First, I went to the lower shrine:

ichishiruki	If this be the entrance
yamaguchi naraba	to the mountain miraculous,
koko nagara	while I rest here

trusting the cedars – It was a custom to take home branches or seedlings of the cedars at this shrine. If the branches stayed green a long time or the seedlings grew, it was considered a good omen for one's prayers.

Upward and upward . . . – There are two puns in the poem: *kamigami*, "upward"/"the gods," and *saka*, "slope"/"flourishing fortune."

another shrine – Again, a reference in the poems and the mention of the lower and upper shrines indicate the identity of the shrine. This time she went to the Kamo Shrine in the northern part of Kyoto. This would have been relatively close to her house. The upper and lower Kamo Shrines are separated by about three kilometers. Both are located on the Kamo River.

The upper reaches dammed? . . . – The Kamo Shrines, upper and lower, are located respectively on the upper and lower reaches of the river, hence her reference to the river. The Cleansing Stream, *mitarashi*, is the name of a small tributary of the Kamo River that ran through the shrine complex and was a place for doing ablutions before going to worship.

On sakaki leaves – The *sakaki* is a broad-leaved evergreen regarded as sacred to the Shinto gods. Its branches are used in various rituals. There are always one or two *sakaki* trees within a shrine complex, and it seems it was the custom then as now to tie pieces of paper with one's prayers to the branch of the *sakaki* tree (see illustration on p. 140).

Kamo Shrine – The name of the shrine is not as explicit in the original as it is here in the translation. It is embedded into the phrase *itsu shikamo*, "I wonder when."

kami no keshiki wo
mise yo to zo omofu

I would have you show me your face,
the aspect of the upper reaches.

At the middle shrine:

inari yama
ohoku no toshi zo
koe ni keru
inoru shirushi no
sugi wo tanomite

Inari Mountain,
for many years have I come
climbing your slopes,
trusting the cedars to show
the sign of a prayer's worth, yet . . .

At the top:

kamigami to
nobori kudari ha
wabure domo
mada saka yukanu
kokochi koso sure

Upward and upward,
climbing, descending, for the gods,
although I am worn out,
there are still slopes I climb not
nor do my fortunes flourish.

Toward the end of the same month, I made a pilgrimage in the same manner to another shrine. I made two prayer offerings of poems. At the lower shrine, this:

kami ya seku
shimo ni ya mikudzu
tsumoruramu
omofu kokoro no
yukanu mitarashi

The upper reaches dammed?
Or at the lower reaches does
rubbish plug the flow?
The Cleansing Stream runs not
as I thought nor does my life.

Another:

sakaki ba no
toki ha kaki ha ni
yufu shide ya
katakuru shinaru
me na mise so kami

On *sakaki* leaves
ever green, ever . . . unchanging
prayer tags are bound,
at me alone, with hard eyes
do not look, oh, ye gods.

Another at the upper shrine:

itsu shikamo
itsu shikamo to zo
machi wataru
mori no koma yori
hikari mimu ma wo

When, I wonder, when,
here at the Kamo Shrine where
I go on waiting,
might I see the sacred light
shining down between the trees?

Another:

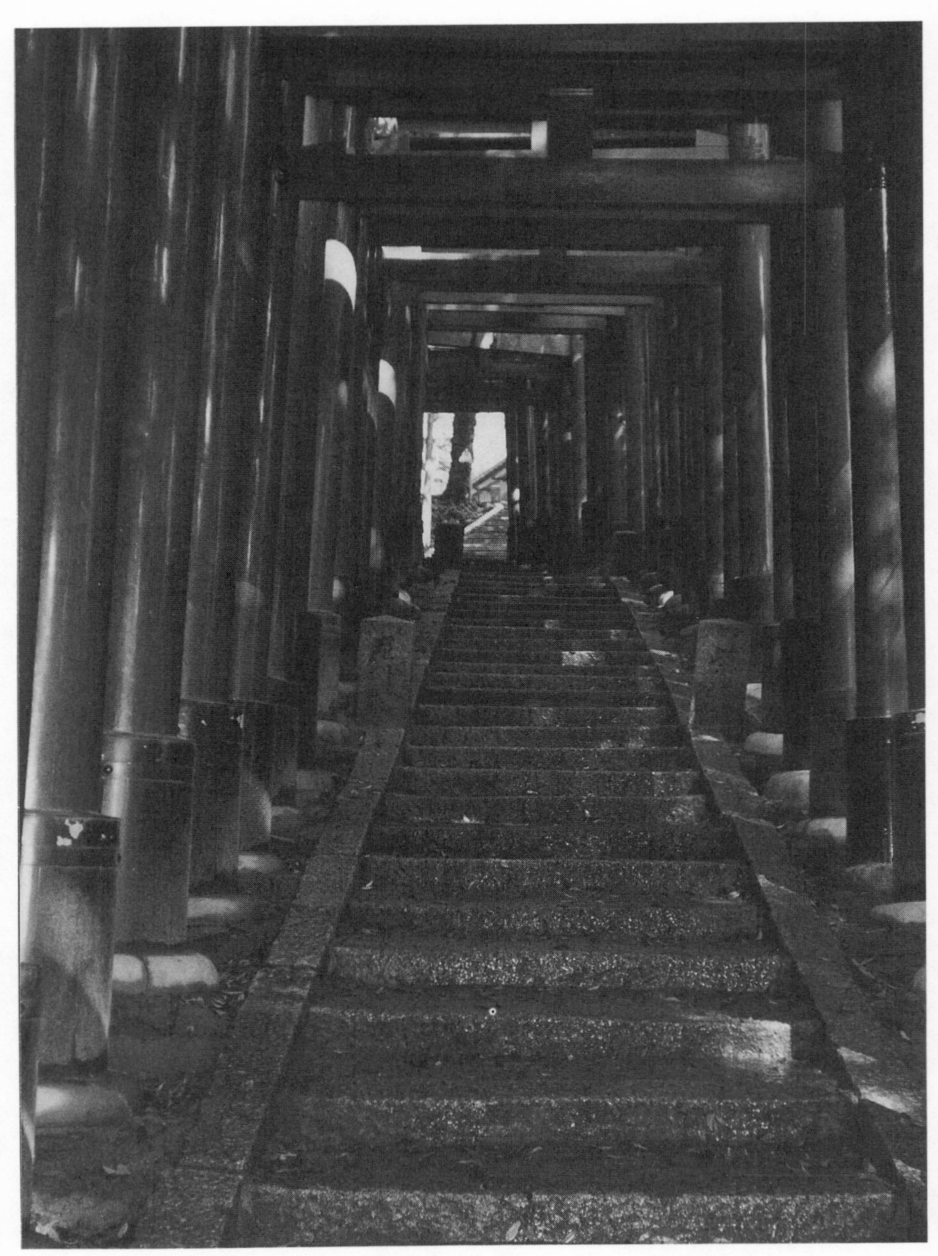

Pathway at Fushimi Inari Shrine. Michitsuna's Mother made a pilgrimage here in the autumn of 966. "If this be the entrance/ to the mountain miraculous . . ." (p. 135). See also pp. 134, 136–37.

Uppermost shrine at Fushimi Inari. "Upward and upward,/ climbing, descending, for the gods . . ." (p. 137). See also p. 136.

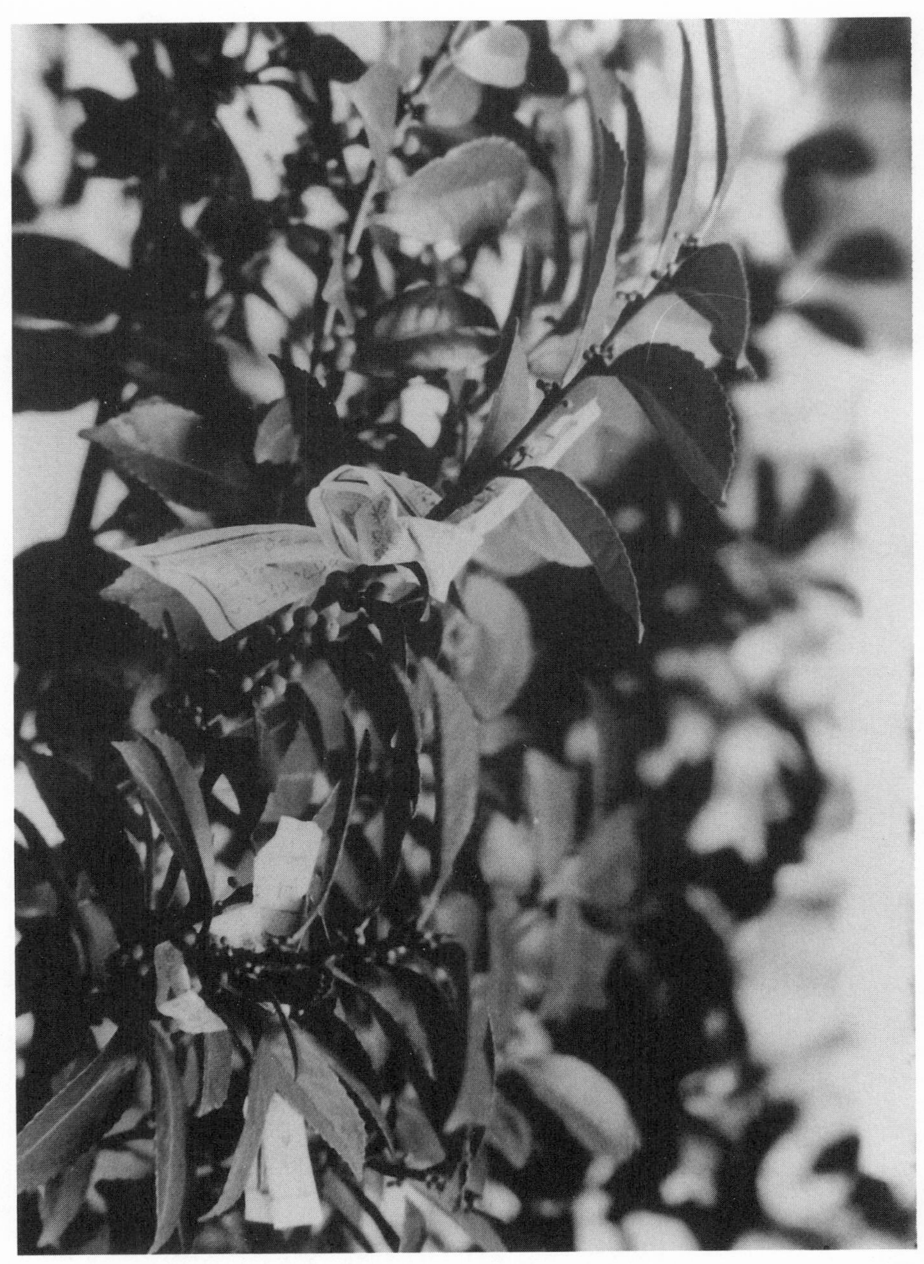

Prayer tags tied on *sakaki* leaves, a custom still observed at Shinto shrines. "On *sakaki* leaves/ ever green, ever . . . unchanging/ prayer tags are bound . . ." (p. 137). See also p. 136.

Tree in a Shinto shrine precinct. "When, I wonder when,/ . . ./ might I see the sacred light/ shining down between the trees?" (p. 137).

White hempen cords – Another decoration of Shinto shrines is white ropes.

on an occasion when the gods were not listening – This is an interesting remark that has prompted different interpretations. *Zenshū* commentators, for example, surmise that upon looking at all the poems she has composed for these pilgrimages, she realizes that they express only her frustration at not having her prayers answered and therefore are not fitting offerings for the gods (*Zenshū*, 186). It is also possible that this remark is another place where she is speaking from the perspective of hindsight. The gods could not have been listening on that occasion because her prayers were not answered.

first of the new year – The year is 967.

"pile them up in tens" – She is referring to a poem from section 50 of *Tales of Ise* that is based on the idea that piling up eggs is a nearly impossible thing to do. The poem is composed by a man who is irritated by the reproaches of a lady:

How can I love someone
Who would care nothing for me
Even were I able
To pile up hen's eggs
Ten high and ten wide.

(Helen McCullough, *Tales of Ise*, 103. See also Watanabe Minoru, *Ise monogatari* [Tokyo: Shinchōsha, 1976], 64.)

the junior consort of the Ninth Avenue Palace – Fushi, Kaneie's younger sister, likely of a different mother, who was actually made junior consort to Emperor Reizei in 968, about a year after the occasion that is recorded here. This is another indication that book one was written later than the events it describes. The Ninth Avenue Palace was the residence of Kaneie's father, Morosuke. Thus Fushi was the junior consort sponsored by the Ninth Avenue Palace.

unohana – Botanical name, *deutzia*, a dense shrub that puts forth a mass of white blossoms around the fourth month.

"that it can be done" – Based on the allusion to the *Tales of Ise* poem above, there is also the teasing message, "So I can love you even if you do not love me." This is what prompts the junior consort's protestations of love.

However countless . . . – There are two puns in this poem: *kahi*, "egg"/"effect," and *kahesu*, "to repeat"/"hatch."

the fifth prince – Emperor Murakami's fifth son, Morihira, who is a child of eight at this time. He eventually ascended the throne as Emperor Enyū (r. 969–84).

emperor – Emperor Murakami (r. 946–67). He died on the twenty-fifth of the fifth month.

east prince – The crown prince, Emperor Murakami's second son, who was eighteen years old and ascended the throne at this time as Emperor Reizei, for what turned out to be a short two-year reign from 967–69. His short reign was due to his mental instability. Nonetheless, his infirmity was actually useful to the main Fujiwara family, because even though the emperor was in his majority, there was need for a regent. This established the precedent for having a Fujiwara regent even while the reigning emperor was an adult (see introduction, p. 14). The exchange of poems above about the eggs was with the woman who became Emperor Reizei's junior consort in 968, the following year.

assistant master of the crown prince's household – Although the diary has not been recording it, Kaneie has been moving steadily upward in position since his posting with the Ministry of Military Affairs. He had just risen to the position with the crown prince's household at the beginning of the year.

yufudasuki	White hempen cords
musubo horetsutsu	bound up like me in knots,
nageku koto	if this lamenting
taenaba kami no	were to be cut off, I would
shirushi to omohamu	see it as a sign from the gods.

Saying such things, on an occasion when the gods were not listening, I muttered away.

Autumn ended, winter came, the end of the year and first of the new year kept everyone busy regardless of their station in life; I passed the time sleeping alone.

Around the end of the third month, upon seeing some goose eggs, I wondered, *Now, how one might "pile them up in tens"?* So as a pastime for my fingers, I took some long threads of raw silk yarn and knotted them, tying the eggs in one after another. When it was done and I suspended it, the eggs were so very nicely piled on top of each other. Rather than just put them away like that, I sent them to the junior consort of the Ninth Avenue Palace. I attached it to a branch of *unohana*. I didn't send any special message with it, but simply put in the margin of an ordinary letter, "These ten goose eggs piled up show that it can be done." Her reply:

kazu shirazu	When we compare
omofu kokoro ni	the countless loving thoughts
kurabureba	I have for you,
towo kasanuru mo	even a pile of ten
mono to ya ha miru	can we say it looks like much?

As to this, my reply:

omofu hodo	However countless
shirade ha kahi ya	your thoughts, they have no effect
arazaramu	unless over and
kahesu gahesu mo	over they are hatched into
kazu wo koso mime	forms whose number I can see.

After that, I heard that she sent the string of eggs to the fifth prince.

The fifth month arrived. Hardly was it bruited about that around the tenth, the emperor had begun receiving medicine, when just after the twentieth, he passed away. The east prince was to succeed him immediately. As for my husband, who had been serving as the assistant master of the crown prince's household, since it was now rumored that he would

head chamberlain – Since he had already been serving the crown prince, now that the crown prince had become emperor, it was natural that Kaneie should assume a position of responsibility within his court. There were two head chamberlains in the Imperial Secretariat, and Kaneie has become one of them. It was a powerful and influential post.

Misasagi – A hilly area in the northwestern corner of Kyoto that was preferred for imperial burials.

Lady Jōganden – Tōshi, another younger sister of Kaneie, who was originally married to Prince Shigeakira. He died in 954. Ten years later in 964, she was brought into the court of Emperor Murakami, who had just lost Anshi, an elder sister to Tōshi and younger sister to Kaneie. There had been an affair between Tōshi and Emperor Murakami some years before; thus her summons after Anshi had died seems to indicate the emperor's lingering affection for her (see introduction, pp. 32–33). They were together for only three years before his death.

This world's frailty . . . – There is a pun on the embedded *mi*, "see," in Misasagi, the mountain name.

I shan't be long . . . – In the reply poem, Lady Jōganden turns a different pun out of Misasagi. She makes the first syllable *mi* part of *ukimi*, "sorrowful self."

assistant commander of the Guards – Fujiwara Sukemasa, a cousin of Kaneie's.

no reason for suffering – Underlying this remark is the assumption that someone living a "normal" life would only choose to become a monk due to some personal tragedy.

a friend – She was the sister of Tamemasa, the husband of the author's elder sister. It is likely that they became friends through mutual connection with the elder sister.

. . . clouds had cloistered you – The word *ama*, "nun," is embedded in the compound *amagumo*, "rain and clouds."

In a hand just the same as before – The consensus of opinion regarding the meaning of this remark is that given the changes in her friend's life, particularly her transformation into a nun, the author expected to see some change in her friend's handwriting but finds it touchingly the same as before (Uemura, *Taisei*, vol. 2, 415).

become head chamberlain, in the midst of the public sadness, all that was heard over here were congratulations for the promotion. As I responded to some of the well-wishers myself, I felt somewhat like a person of importance, yet at the same time, in my heart, my personal feelings of dissatisfaction with the marriage were still the same. Nonetheless, it did seem as though things had been turned upside down and gotten quite lively around here.

When I heard that the place of burial was going to be Misasagi, I felt sad imagining how it must be for those whom he had favored. After a few days had passed, I sent a message asking after the well being of the Lady Jōganden and along with it:

yo no naka wo	This world's frailty,
hakanaki mono to	such have you seen in the scene
misasagi no	of his interment,
umoruru yama ni	by that Misasagi mountain,
nagekuramu ya zo	how you must have been lamenting.

Her reply, how sad it seemed:

okureji to	"I shan't be long, my lord"
uki misasagi ni	at heart, this sorrowful self
omohi iru	dwells on Misasagi
kokoro ha shide no	and is it not already with you
yama ni ya aruramu	on the mountain crossing to death?

At the completion of the service to mark the forty-ninth day after the emperor's passing, it was the seventh month. The assistant commander of the Guards, who had been in the service of the former emperor, without warning abandoned his mother and wife, stole away to Mt. Hiei and became a monk even though he was still young and seemed to have no reason for suffering. Just as people were making a great fuss about it, saying how shocking and sad it was, I heard that his wife too had become a nun. Since she was a friend with whom I had corresponded for some time before, I inquired after her, expressing my surprise and sadness:

okuyama no	Sorrowful was I
omohi yari dani	just imagining the deep
kanashiki ni	mountains when I heard
mata amagumo no	their clouds had cloistered you too.
kakaru nani nari	How could this have come about?

In a hand just the same as before, she replied:

yama fukaku	Although I thought to
irinishi hito mo	follow him who had entered

middle captain . . . third rank – Kaneie was promoted to middle captain in the tenth month of this same year, 967. However, he was not promoted to the third rank until the following year. Retrospectively for the author, however, it all seemed to happen very fast.

a suitable place – This marks the first time that the author has lived in a residence provided by Kaneie.

Lady Jōganden – Kaneie's sister with whom the author had exchanged the poems of consolation over Emperor Murakami's death. Having been married to a prince and a favorite of an emperor, she was someone who had lived most of her life at court. Her moving into the same residence provides the author with an opportunity to get close to someone who has been out in the world. Through the following passages, one feels the author's enormous curiosity about her housemate. Although they are living in the same house, they will not necessarily see one another often because the apartments are quite separate. The first interaction she records is typically an exchange of correspondence and gifts.

New Year's Eve – The new year is 968.

next door – Possibly she is referring to Kaneie's principal residence, which is nearby and would be busy with New Year's well-wishers given his importance at court.

"in the morning what will be awaited" – Quotation from a poem in the *Kokin rokujō* poetry anthology:

> Like a rough-hewn jewel,
> the New Year has just arrived,
> in the morning
> what will be awaited is
> the warbler's first song. (*Zenshū,* 190)

The warbler's first song stands for Kaneie's first visit.

with a wen on one leg – *Kata kobi*, "wen on one leg," also means "one-sided love."

yoke – The word for "yoke," *afuko*, can also mean "opportunity to meet."

tadzunuredo	deep into the mountain,
naho amagumo no	cloistered thus, by rain and clouds,
yoso ni koso nare	all the more am I kept apart.

How very sad it was.

In the world, such as it was, happy events one after another befell my husband; one moment he was promoted to middle captain, the next, to the third rank. He said, "Living in places apart, so many things get in the way of visiting you that it's most inconvenient; I've found a suitable place for you near here," and so he moved me to a place where he could come secretly even without a carriage; people must have thought that things were going just as I wanted them. It was around the middle of the eleventh month.

Around the end of the twelfth month, Lady Jōganden came to stay in the western apartment of this dwelling. On New Year's Eve, I thought I would try the custom of "chasing away misfortune," so while it was still light, I set my attendants to shouting and banging things, and while I was thus amused, the new day and new year dawned. Early in the day, over at my guest's apartment, as there were no gentlemen callers, it was quite quiet. It was quiet for me too, and when I listened to the commotion next door, it brought to mind the old poem, "in the morning what will be awaited," and just as I was smiling to myself about this, one of my attendants brought out something she had made to keep her fingers busy. It was a collection of New Year's treats strung together so they could be presented as a gift, and making a shoulder yoke out of wood, she had laid this on a wooden doll, which had a knot just like a wen on one leg. I draw it toward me, stick a strip of colored paper to its leg, write this, and present it to her ladyship:

kata kohi ya	Pity the poor woodsman
kurushikaruramu	with a wen on one leg as painful
yamagatsu no	as one-sided love.
afuko nashi to ha	Yet it isn't as though he hasn't
mienu mono kara	a yoke nor we time to meet.

In response, she ties up bundles of shreds of dried seaweed called sea pine and sends the doll back with these bundles attached to the ends of its yoke. Onto the skinnier leg, she had stuck a wen fashioned out of wood so now that leg was bigger than the original one. When I look closely, I see this:

yamagatsu no	Finally the time comes
afu ko machi idete	for the poor woodsman to meet

compare wens and swollen love – Even in this playful exchange, it is evident that the language of poetic discourse for expressing friendship between women is not different at all from the language for romantic love between men and women.

"anyone else but me" – Allusion to a poem from section 37 of *Tales of Ise*:

For anyone else but me,
do not loosen your undersash,
even though your love
may be like the morning-glory
that waits not for evening.

In the original context for this poem it is addressed by a man to a woman he suspects is licentious (Watanabe, *Ise monogatari*, 51).

There are a number of possible interpretations for what Kaneie means by citing a piece of this poem as a joke. He may not have been referring to the author at all but simply teasing his sister by suggesting she has a lover who would not like her to see anyone but him. He could be poking fun at the author's jealous tendencies by saying "I would like to see you but your housemate wants me to see only her." The other possibility is that he is implying that the author has a lover who would find the visits of Kaneie annoying. Though this would seem to be the most far-fetched, it appears from the author's reply poem that she takes it that way.

Pine Mountain – The author alludes to the famous poem from *Kokinshū* about the impossibility of infidelity that has already been cited twice before. The import of that poem is, "That I should be unfaithful to you is as impossible as a wave engulfing Pine Mountain."

Pine Island – Lady Jōganden deftly turns the pine motif into one not associated with infidelity and makes the meaning of the poem complimentary to both her brother and his wife.

east prince – This is the same young prince, Morihira, who had been the final recipient of "the pile of ten eggs." As the prince's foster mother, Lady Jōganden will once again be in the center of things at court. The very next year, this lad will ascend the throne as a child emperor, and Lady Jōganden's position will be of even more importance. She eventually is given the title *naishi no kami*, principal handmaid, which despite the menial sound of the English translation was actually a position of considerable power and prestige. For a description of the evolution of the Naishi no Tsukasa, "Handmaid's Office," and the principal duties of its members, see McCullough and McCullough, *A Tale of Flowering Fortunes*, 820–21.

one night, I went to her apartments – As far as we are informed by the diary, this is the first and last time the ladies meet face to face.

"You would think he could do without a nanny" – There is something charming about these two women sharing a joke that characterizes this powerful man as a small, petulant child.

kurabureba	his beloved, when we
kohi masari keru	compare wens and swollen love,
kata mo arikeri	this side is surely the largest.

As the sun rose higher, it seemed that they were partaking of their New Year's feast just as we were too, and the fifteenth of the month was celebrated in the same way as usual.

The third month arrived. A letter from my husband obviously intended for my guest, her ladyship, was mistakenly delivered to me. Looking at it, I could see he couldn't help referring to me; among other things, this was written, "I've been thinking of coming to visit you recently, however, there is someone who might take it amiss. Don't see 'anyone else but me,' as the old poem goes." Since they had been on such friendly terms over the years, I surmised this was why he could write such a letter; yet, I couldn't just leave it like this, so I added in very small handwriting:

matsu yama no	Although this is a
sashi koete shimo	world where Pine Mountain could
araji yo wo	never be engulfed,
ware ni yosohete	yet he would compare me
sawagu nami kana	to a noisy, busy wave.

and thus, telling a messenger, "Please take this to her ladyship," I returned it. When she had seen it, she immediately sent back this:

matsushima no	Since he is a wave
kaze ni shitagafu	that follows the wind of love
nami nareba	toward Pine Island,
yoru kata ni koso	even from where the letter went
tachi masari kere	his heart's pull can be seen.

Since her ladyship was to serve as foster mother to the east prince, she would soon be leaving for court. "What a shame to have to part like this," she said and often repeated an invitation to visit, "even if just for a little bit." So one night, I went to her apartments. No sooner had I got there when we heard his voice in the other wing. "Dear, dear," her ladyship said, but as I paid no attention to her urging, she followed this with, "It sounds as though it is his bedtime; no doubt he'll get cranky. Better be quick." "You would think he could do without a nanny by this time," said I, still dragging my feet, but as servants came from my quarters to hurry me along, there was no peace for us so I returned. The evening of the next day, she returned to court.

Then, in the fifth month, when her ladyship was excused from court duty on the occasion of the formal removal of mourning clothes on

cut off – The verb *tayuru* that the author used in her poem can have connotations of a life "cut short."

Seeing the other side . . . – There are two puns in this poem: ***kaha***, "other side"/"river," and ***yukanu***, "not going," extending to ***yukanu kokoro***, "a blocked heart."

the first anniversary of the former emperor's passing, there was talk that she would come and stay here as before; however, she complained, "I have been having bad dreams," so she ended up staying over there. Thereafter, as she kept having these ominous dreams, she apparently said, "If only there were some way to be delivered from this." Then one night in the seventh month, when the moon was very bright, she sent me this:

mishi yume wo	These long autumn nights
chigahe wabinuru	as I struggle to alter
aki no yo zo	the dream that I see,
negataki mono to	now, I have understood
omohi shirinuru	how hard they make it to sleep.

I replied:

samo koso ha	It is as you say,
chigafuru yume ha	to transform one's dreams is
katakarame	difficult indeed,
ahade hodo furu	as painful as I feel it
mi sahe uki kana	to live on never meeting you.

She replied immediately:

afu to mishi	In a dream, I saw you
yume ni nakanaka	half in, half out of that dream
kurasarete	I am now living
nagori kohishiku	so fond of the memory,
samenu narikeri	I waken not to consciousness.

And I to her again:

koto tayuru	This reality where
utsutsu ya nani zo	we are cut off each from each,
nakanaka ni	why must it be so?
yume ha kayohidji	The dream road of which you speak
ari to ifu mono wo	is neither here nor there.

And again from her, "What is this you say, 'cut off each from each,' how very inauspicious to speak thus":

kaha to mite	Seeing the other side,
yukanu kokoro wo	not able to cross this river
nagamureba	as I brood and feel blocked,
itodo yuyushiku	is it meet for us to speak
ihi ya ha tsubeki	thus in such an ill-omened way?

passed the whole night – They would be exchanging these poems by messenger so the process would take a considerable time. It was a way for the author to provide company at a distance for Lady Jōganden on a sleepless night.

fervent desire – Likely a reference to her desire for another child, particularly a daughter.

Hase – Hase Temple located about a three day's journey away up the Hase River valley in Nara Prefecture, a popular place of pilgrimage particularly for women in the Heian period. It is still a thriving religious center.

Purification Ceremony – Before the Enthronement Rites a lustration was performed by the new emperor on the banks of the Kamo River.

Enthronement Rites – Held in 968 for the accession of Emperor Reizei.

my daughter – Chōshi (b. 957), Kaneie's eldest daughter by Tokihime, eleven years old at the time of this event.

acting consort – The role played by the emperor's consort in the ceremony was taken by an acting consort when either the emperor was too young to have an actual consort or, as in this case, his consort was indisposed. (Reizei's consort, Kaishi, was pregnant.) Serving as acting consort implied one was next in line to become a consort.

pro forma start – Since the day she actually wanted to leave the city was inauspicious, she made a start for form's sake a day earlier, presumably a good day to begin a trip on.

Hōshō Temple – No longer extant, it was located in the southeast corner of Kyoto.

Uji – On the banks of the Uji River, where many nobles had villas.

people riding in the back – The text specifies neither number nor gender here. Some commentators suggest this refers to Michitsuna; others say it refers to lady attendants.

I see the fishing weirs – Fishing weirs were a common subject for poetry and painting, but this would have been her first opportunity to see them with her own eyes.

loaded on a boat – The carriage would have been transported by boat across the Uji River and then unloaded on the other side.

Nieno Pond – Location no longer known.

Izumi River – Old name for Ōtsu River.

Having come secretly on my own like this, connecting with everything – In this and other phases throughout her description of the Hase trip, one notices how being outside her normal environment has sharpened her perception and sparked a sense of wonder. Her description of her trip marks a turning point in her ability to write an extended prose narrative.

Hashi Temple – A temple located on the north bank of the Ōtsu River just where there was a bridge across the river.

My reply:

wataraneba	Not crossing over,
wochikata hito ni	we become persons apart
nareru mi wo	on opposite banks,
kokoro bakari ha	only in our hearts will the
fuchise ya ha waku	depths and shallows be clear.

and so we passed the whole night.

Well then, I have had a fervent desire for so many years; I decide that no matter what I must make a pilgrimage to Hase. I wanted to go in the eighth month, but as I cannot always arrange things as I would like, here it is the ninth month and I have made up my mind to go. Even though he says, "Next month is the Purification Ceremony in preparation for the Enthronement Rites and my daughter will be going out from here to serve as acting consort. How about waiting until that is over? Then we could go together," as that is not really my affair, I just decide to leave secretly. However, the day I fixed upon is inauspicious so we make a pro forma start a day earlier, staying the night around the neighborhood of Hōshō Temple. Starting from there at dawn, we arrive at Uji village around noon.

Gazing out, I see the surface of the water sparkling in between the trees and find it so moving. Since I want to attract as little attention as possible, I have left with very few attendants, and although this is probably lax of me, I cannot help thinking if it were someone other than me, what a big fuss and commotion they would be making.

The carriage is pulled around and the outer curtains drawn up; just the people riding in the back are let down. In the direction of the river, when I roll up the blind and look out, I see the fishing weirs stretched across. As I have never seen lots of boats plying to and fro like that, it is all so moving and fascinating. When I look behind, there are my servants tired from the journey, eating some rather poor-looking limes and pears with their hands; that too seems touching. After eating lunch, the carriage is loaded on a boat, and as we go along smoothly from place to place; they say "Here's Nieno Pond" and "Here, Izumi River," where there are so many birds flocking together; the scene soaks into my heart; it is moving and enchanting. Having come secretly on my own like this, connecting with everything, I feel tears welling up. We cross Izumi River too.

We stopped for the night at a place called Hashi Temple. It was evening when I got down from the carriage and rested; the first thing to come out of what must have been the temple kitchen was a dish of sliced

Uji River. Michituna's Mother stayed overnight at Uji both going and returning from her two pilgrimages to Hase Temple (see pp. 153, 159, 161, 261, and 263).

Ox-drawn carriage. In most of her pilgrimages, Michitsuna's Mother traveled in this type of conveyance (see pp. 153, 161, 197, 199, and elsewhere).

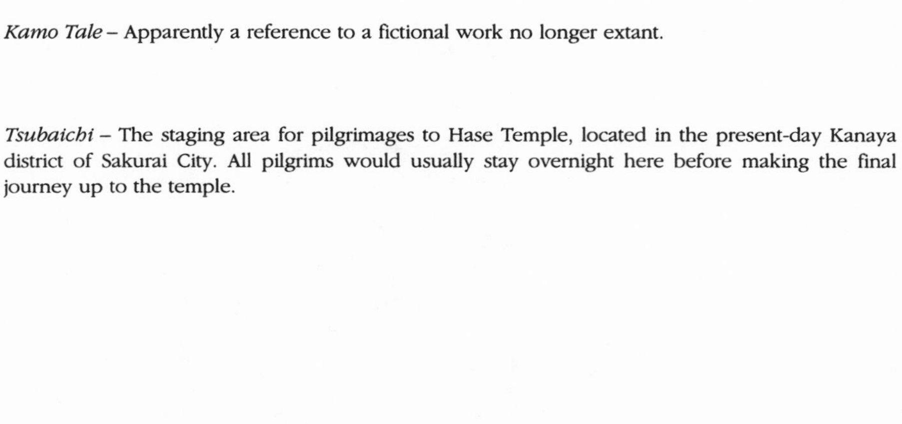

Kamo Tale – Apparently a reference to a fictional work no longer extant.

Tsubaichi – The staging area for pilgrimages to Hase Temple, located in the present-day Kanaya district of Sakurai City. All pilgrims would usually stay overnight here before making the final journey up to the temple.

Having heard all this – She has been very coy with her message, refusing to specify any date of return. However, aware that the messenger will report the disgruntlement of her attendants as well, she assumes that Kaneie will understand that she will not be away any longer than the three days as originally planned.

famed cedars – An allusion to poem number 1009 in *Kokinshū*:

> Hase River,
> by the ancient river bed,
> there are two cedar trees.
> I long to meet you again
> and be like two cedar trees.

radish with lime dressing. Traveling like that, all the things I encountered were so curious and wonderful, that I still remember them.

The next morning we cross the river and go on our way; I notice some houses surrounded by brushwood fences and think to myself, *I wonder which one might be the house mentioned in the Kamo Tale*; how moving it is.

That day too we stayed at some kind of temple, the next day at a place called Tsubaichi, a market town. The next morning, when the threads of frost are still white on the ground, there are many people both coming and going, their legs wrapped in cloth leggings, all in various states raising a lively commotion. The shutters are open at the place where we are staying and while I am waiting for wash water to be warmed, I look out and see all these people crossing paths; I think to myself that they must all have their own concerns and worries that would bring them on a pilgrimage like this.

A little while later, a fellow arrives holding a letter aloft. He stands there and says something like "A letter from his lordship." I look at it. It said:

> I've been worrying yesterday and today. Why did you run off like that? You went with so few attendants; are you all right? I seem to remember you said you would go on retreat for three days. Let me know what day you are coming back. At least I could come and meet you.

In reply, I wrote:

> It seems that we have arrived smoothly to this place, Tsubaichi. However, taking this opportunity, I am thinking of going from here even deeper into the mountains, so I cannot tell you exactly the date of our return.

Meanwhile my attendants, discussing among themselves, say such things as "Being on retreat for even three days is bad enough . . ." Having heard all this the messenger returned.

We left from there, and as we go along, even though the path is nothing to speak of, it still gives one the feeling of being deep in the mountains, and the sound of the water is very affecting. Those famed cedars are living, even now piercing the sky; all kinds of colors of tree leaves can be seen. From among many stones, the water gurgles forth. Seeing this scene struck by the light of the setting sun, tears pour forth endlessly. The path to here had not been so especially charming. There were as yet no red autumn leaves; the flowers were all gone; one could

train – The *mo*, a train attached at the back with the ties falling in front, worn on formal occasions. Her donning the train indicates that she is getting ready to enter the temple precincts.

hosted here and there – Kaneie has likely informed acquaintances along the route.

Miyake in the Kuze district of Yamashiro – Site of the imperial court rice fields, present-day Kuzegun.

Your heart only . . . – Two puns in this poem tie together the author's feelings with the image of the fish weirs at Uji. One is *kokoro u*, "heart's suffering" (*kokoro*, "heart," is embedded in the phrase *hitogokoro*, "your heart"), which pivots into *udji no ajiro*, "fish weirs of Uji." The other is *hiwo*, which is taken as both "trout" and *hi wo*, "days" (plus object marker). Though it is not translated literally here, the phrase "*tamasaka ni yoru hiwo*" can mean the "days you visit by chance."

only see withered pampas grass. Yet, here, the feeling is special, when I look out, rolling up the outer blind, pushing aside the inner blind, the color of this well-worn robe is quite different. When I pull the train of lavender gauze around me, the ties cross over my lap; how well their color complements the burnt umber of this robe, how enchanting I find it all. The beggars with their pots and bowls set on the ground before them, how sad they seem. Feeling so close to the poor and lowly, entering the temple precincts is less uplifting than I expected.

In the temple hall, unable to sleep, having nothing else to do, I listen intently to the noises outside and hear a blind person, who does not seem all that poorly off, pouring forth in a loud voice all his troubles without any thought that others might hear; moved by this, my tears just pour down.

The following day, even though I think I would like to stay a little longer, just when it gets light, I am bustled into departing. Even though I intended our return to be unobtrusive, being hosted here and there, we go along in quite a social whirl. We should have reached the capital by the third day, but as we were caught by nightfall, we stayed at a place called Miyake in the Kuze district of Yamashiro. Although it was a frightening place, since it was dark, there was no choice but to wait until dawn. When it was scarcely light and we had just set out, a black clad figure with a quiver on his back comes riding up at a gallop. At some distance, he dismounts and kneels down respectfully. I could see it was one of his guardsmen. "What is it?" they ask on all sides; whereupon he says, "Yesterday, around dusk, my lord arrived at the Uji estate, 'Go and see if they are on their way back yet,' he ordered, so here I am." Hearing this, my servants in front urge the oxen forward with cries of "Get along now."

When we get close to the Uji River, a mist drifts in and we can no longer see where we have come from; it makes one uneasy. The cart is unhitched from the oxen; with a lot of effort and activity the servants manage to get things arranged; a number of voices cry out, "Stop my lady's carriage on the bank." Beneath the mist, I can see the fish weirs as before, it is indescribably beautiful. I suppose he himself is probably on the other bank. So I write this and have it sent across:

hitogokoro	Your heart only
udji no ajiro ni	inquires of the trout happening
tamasaka ni	into Uji weirs,
yoru hiwo dani mo	my heart suffers your visits
tadzunekeru kana	to be so happenstance and rare.

When the boat came back once more to this side, it carried his answer:

Suffering in my heart . . . – Kaneie picks up the puns of the previous poem. He adds a further nuance by using the word *uchi*, "within," which can be understood three ways: with *kokoro* it means both "within my heart" and "heart's suffering," on its own it also represents the place name Uji.

his son, a captain of the Guards – This is Kaneie's son by Tokihime, Michitaka. It is curious that the author seems to recognize him by sight. In book two, when Michitaka comes to visit her at a mountain hermitage, he apologizes for not having been to see her for a long time (p. 251). Perhaps he sometimes accompanied his father to visit the author. It would have been a way that Kaneie could have encouraged a relationship between Michitaka and Michitsuna.

Azechi grand counselor – Kaneie's uncle, Fujiwara Morouji.

"Once the flower blooms . . ." – General reference to her flowering fortune due to her husband's rise in importance and perhaps the career awaiting her son.

kaheru hi wo	Suffering in my heart
kokoro no uchi ni	I have been counting the days
kazohetsutsu	till you return, like
tare ni yorite ka	counting trout, for whom else
ajiro wo mo tofu	would I ask at the Uji weirs?

While I am reading this, the carriage is loaded onto the boat and we cross in a lively tumult. Some attendants of not particularly distinguished yet quite respectable background stand mixed in with the attendants of some lord's office in between the shafts of the back of the cart. A few rays of sunlight can be seen; here and there the mist is clearing away. On the other bank, his son, a captain of the Guards, and some others are lined up looking this way. In among them, he stands dressed for travel in a hunting costume. They bring the boat in at a place where the bank is very high so there is nothing else to do but lift the cart up on their shoulders. Placing the shafts on the veranda of the villa, they bring it to rest.

Preparations have been made for the breaking of our fast, and when we sit down to eat, someone tells us that the Azechi grand counselor, who owns a villa on the other side of the river, "is in residence to view the fish weirs." We were just saying, "He has probably heard we are here and we should likely go and pay our respects," when someone comes bearing a beautiful branch of scarlet maple leaves to which are attached a pheasant and some trout. There is an invitation as well, "Having heard that you were here, I thought we might share a meal together, even though it is a day when I have nothing special to offer." His reply is, "Having just been informed of your lordship's presence, we shall hasten to attend upon you . . ." and so on; he takes off an inner robe and lays it on the messenger's shoulder for a return gift. It seems the messenger crossed back again just like that.

Then, it seems that more food, carp, and bass were brought over. The merriest of our lot gather together and, getting drunk, even say things like "What a splendid sight, the sun shining on your moon wheels." They begin to decorate the carriage by sticking branches of flowers and maple leaves into the back of the carriage; the attendants of his household say, "Once the flower blooms, soon will come the day of the fruit." The people in back exchange jests with them as they all make ready to cross to the other side. Then, saying "They are sure to give us enough to make us drunk" and choosing as attendants those who like to drink, he crosses over. My carriage is pointed in the direction of the river; resting the shafts on a stand, two boats tow it across on a barge. Well, by the time the festivities were over, everyone got thoroughly drunk and set off on the road home singing. With shouts of "Let's hitch up the oxen, come on hitch

close to the Purification Ceremony – Thus it is evident that he came to meet her at Uji even though he was still in the midst of making arrangements for the Purification Ceremony. On the one hand, it makes his gesture all the more chivalrous. On the other hand, perhaps he also wanted to assure her cooperation in the final preparation of costumes.

"do such and such" –These would be tasks undoubtedly to do with manufacture of costumes for the event.

time-consuming – Presumably for her husband.

birds singing anew – Embedded allusion to poem number 28 in *Kokinshū:*

> With the singing of
> a myriad birds in spring
> everything is
> brought to life anew except
> for me who alone grows old.

am I, is the world, here or not – In the original, the phrase is simply, *aru ka naki ka*, "exist or not exist," with no specified subject for the verb. My interpretation is that this ambiguity encourages a reading where the subject I's existence and the existence of the objective world are both brought into question. See also below for the use of this same phrase in conjunction with the term *kagerō* in poetry of the time.

mayfly or . . . – The word in the original, *kagerō,* means both "mayfly," a symbol for a fleeting, ephemeral life, and "the shimmering of heat waves," a symbol for insubstantiality. Thus as a pun it signifies indeterminacy both on the temporal plane and in the material world. The title for the diary is taken from this passage.

Two poems from anthologies contemporary to the author indicate that *kagerō* in the sense of the shimmerings of heat waves was linked with the phrase, *aru ka naki ka*, "does [it] exist or not," "is [it] here or not." The first one is from the *Kokin rokujō* and specifically connects *kagerō* with suffering in human relations:

> Relations in the world
> and all the things I have suffered about
> exist in a world
> that is here and not here
> like a *kagerō.*
>
> *yo no naka to / omohishi mono wo / kagerofu no / aru ka naki ka no /*
> *yo ni arikere*

(Kawaguchi Hisao, *Tosa nikki. Kagerofu nikki. Izumi Shikibu nikki. Sarashina nikki*, vol. 20 of *Nihon koten bungaku taikei* [Tokyo: Iwanami Shoten, 1965], 171.)

The second one is from the *Gosenshū*:

> I say neither that
> it is sad or it is miserable,
> since this is a world
> that will vanish like a *kagerō*
> one hardly knows is here or not.
>
> *ahare tomo / ushi tomo ihaji / kagerofu no / aru ka naki ka ni /*
> *kenuru yo nareba*

(Hasegawa Masaharu et al., *Tosa nikki. Kagerō nikki. Murasaki Shikibu nikki. Sarashina nikki*, vol. 24 of *Shin Nihon koten bungaku taikei* [Tokyo: Iwanami Shoten, 1989], 94. See also Katagiri Yōichi, *Gosen wakashū*, vol. 6 of *Shin Nihon koten bungaku taikei* [Tokyo: Iwanami Shoten, 1990], 358.)

them up" ringing in my ears, I came back to the capital in some discomfort, feeling poorly and dead tired.

The day after we returned was very close to the Purification Ceremony. "Now, I would like you to do such and such," came his requests. "Yes, and how should it be done?" said I, getting caught up in the bustle. The day of the event, the ceremonial carriages followed one upon another. The women and male attendants followed along too; everything was so bright and colorful, I almost felt as though I was a part of the parade myself, all so very stylish. The next month came the Enthronement Rites, and the inspection of everything to make sure it was perfect was most time-consuming. I too was busy with preparing to attend the ceremony, and then it was the end of the month, which was the end of the year, and so we all got very busy all over again.

Thus, the years and months have piled up. As I lament that this has not been the life I wanted, even voices of well-wishers mingled with the birds singing anew bring no happiness; all the more I sense how fleeting everything is; the feeling arises—am I, is the world, here or not—this could be called the diary of a mayfly or the shimmering heat on a summer's day.

Book Two

Summary

Book two covers only three years, from 969 to 971. After a rather hopeful start, the tone of the narration becomes more and more distraught as the author's dissatisfaction with her marriage increases. Kaneie takes up with another woman again, and while this is a catalyst for the author's anguish, she struggles more with her own state of mind than with him. She takes two pilgrimages that help briefly by removing her from her immediate situation, but her mind has begun to run in obsessive patterns from which there seems to be no relief. She finally withdraws to a mountain temple, against her husband's express wishes, to consider becoming a nun. During her retreat, however, through conversations and exchanging poems with people other than her husband, she achieves some distance from her situation. Even though her period of resistance ends in what might be termed a rout by her husband and son, she comes down the mountain a different person.

Most scholars of the text agree that she probably started the diary project sometime during the three years covered by book two. Many suggest 971, the year of the crisis in her marriage. The evidence for that is the degree of the narrator's closeness to the events she relates. There is not the pulling back and contemplating events from the perspective of hindsight that we see in book one. Nonetheless, a dual perspective of a different sort emerges in book two. In the midst of her experiences, the author begins to achieve some objectivity about her situation. While in the first part of book two, the author is often crying out her pain within a mental prison, by the end, she is able to step outside the bars of the cage and observe herself as she suffers. There is a higher proportion of prose than poetry in book two. Gaining mastery of prose language itself may have been a way she reestablished some sense of control over her life.

New Year's morning – This is New Year's day of the second year of Anna, which occurred in terms of the Western calendar on January 21, 969.

avoiding inauspicious speaking – The term is *kotoimi*, literally, "word taboo," and seems to refer to the custom of avoiding speaking about inauspicious subjects at the beginning of a new year.

my sister – Commentators assume this is a younger sister. The original text here has only the author's customary *harakara to oboshiki hito*, "the person thought to be a sibling."

"Sew heaven and earth into a bag . . ." – Opening of a well-known poem for invoking good luck at the beginning of the New Year. The whole poem is, "Sew heaven and earth into a bag, put good luck in and nothing more you shall want."

"Thirty days and . . ." – This can be understood as a playful alternate ending for the sister's poem.

my young one – Michitsuna, who is entering his fourteenth year.

such a figure – Around this time, Kaneie had begun to surpass his elder brother Kanemichi in terms of court rank and power.

two fifth months – The court followed a lunar calendar with twenty-eight days in each month. From time to time it was necessary to insert intercalary months in order to have the lunar year match the seasons of the solar year. In the second year of Anna, there was to be two fifth months.

I think we've really done it with this New Year's well-wishing – The general consensus among commentators about the meaning of this passage is that the author is saying that the exchange of New Year's greetings this year between her and her husband has been somehow exceptional (Uemura, *Taisei*, vol. 3, 18–19). However, her expression is ambiguous with respect to her feelings. Is she happy about the exceptional nature of it or does it seem uncomfortably excessive to her?

the servants over there – Presumably the servants of Tokihime, Kaneie's first wife chronologically and by this time a clear winner in the competition of producing children. As indicated at the end of book one, her eldest daughter, Chōshi, was already being groomed to become an imperial consort. Yet Michitsuna's Mother's pull on Kaneie was still strong enough to have him drop the affairs of his daughter and come all the way to Uji to meet the author on the way back from her pilgrimage. It is likely that the tensions of the competition between the two women were felt among the servants of the two households and could result in altercations.

living so close – As recorded in book one, two years ago, Kaneie had moved the author to a house within walking distance of his residence.

Thus while days passed empty and fleetingly, the year came to an end and New Year's morning has come. Oddly enough, for years our household has not observed the custom of avoiding inauspicious speaking at the beginning of the year, so wondering to myself if that was why things had turned out as they had, getting up and crawling out of bed, I say, "Hey, everyone, come here—for this year at least let's avoid speaking inauspiciously, and we'll see if it has any effect in the world." Hearing this, my sister, still in bed, says, "I've got something to say," and chanted the old poem, "Sew heaven and earth into a bag . . . ," and so it gets more and more amusing. "Well, as for me," I say, "Thirty days and thirty nights of every month, let him be by my side." At this, one of my attendants breaks out laughing, "Surely you'll get your wish. Why don't you write that down exactly as you just said it, and send it to his lordship." In response to this, my sister gets up and says, "What a good idea. It would bring the best luck in the world," and she laughs and laughs. So, I write it down and had my young one present it. These days, he is such a figure in the world that his house was teeming with New Year's well-wishers; apparently he was just about to leave for court when my message arrived, and although he was in a rush to get away, there was this response. I suppose he is referring to the fact that there will be two fifth months this year:

toshi goto ni	Since every year
amareba kofuru	your love overflows the bounds,
kimi ga tame	is it for your sake
urufuzuki wo ba	this year they had to put in
oku ni ya aruramu	an extra month?

Well, I think we've really done it with this New Year's well-wishing.

The next day, there occurred an incident between the servants over here and the servants over there that occasioned a lot of unpleasantness. He, for his part, rather sympathized with me. It all seemed very regretful, and I couldn't help thinking that it was due to my living so close; as I was brooding over the disagreeableness of it, he came up with a plan

now in the midst of feelings of the ephemerality of it all, I might have thought myself lucky then – This is an elliptical and difficult passage in the original. I follow *Zenshū* and Uemura (*Taisei*, vol. 3, 46) in interpreting the phrase, "in the midst of feelings of ephemerality," as an interjection expressing the feelings she has at the moment of writing. As she remembers how fortunate she actually was then, she muses that she might have and perhaps should have been more content, yet she was not.

One speaks of being "clad in brocade" . . . return to my "old village" – There are two proverbial expressions drawn from the Chinese histories that bring together "brocade" and "returning to one's old home." One is "After becoming rich and successful, not to return to your old home town is like wearing brocade at night." In other words, if one's old friends and relatives do not get to admire one's success, it is hardly worth having it at all. The other one is "to return to one's old village clad in brocade," which expresses the satisfaction of returning to one's home village as a success (Uemura, *Taisei*, vol. 3, 43–44). The author may be referring to either or both of those expressions here. However, her allusion to these expressions seems to pull in two ways. In one sense, it amplifies her feeling in retrospect that the days she is writing of here were her "brocade days." In another sense, the expressions evoke the desire she had in those days simply to "return home," which is assumed to be her mother's old residence just outside the eastern edge of the palace compound.

third day of the third month – The peach blossom festival (see book one, pp. 70–73).

the people here – Her serving women. This is the first time where contact between her serving women and his attendants has been mentioned, but it must have been something that had been occurring all along. One can imagine how much her ladies must have depended on this contact for enlivening social interaction. Here we get a glimpse of how the expectations of others also rode on the ups and downs of marital relations between Kaneie and Michitsuna's Mother.

Queen Mother of the West – In Chinese mythology, the Queen Mother of the West, possessor of the elixir of immortality, was thought to reside in the Kunlun Mountains to the far west. *Seiwau no sono* means "the Western Queen's garden," but *sono watari* can also mean "around your place," so with a pivot word, the magical garden of the west and Kaneie's residence are made equivalent, a flattering bit of wit.

open freely from young buds . . . without a care – There is a pun on *mayu mo . . . hirakuru. Mayu* means "eyebrow." Since the buds of willow leaves are long, "willow eyebrows" was a conventional metaphor for willow buds. *Mayu ga hiraku*, literally, "to open one's eyebrows," was an idiomatic expression meaning "to feel relieved, without a care."

to move me to another residence. Once I was installed in that place a little distant, since he came to visit every other day in splendid state, now in the midst of feelings of the ephemerality of it all, I might have thought myself lucky then. One speaks of being "clad in brocade"; it wasn't that, but I think I wanted to return to my "old village."

On the third day of the third month, having prepared for the festivity, it was disappointing to have no guests, so the people here wrote this message and sent it over to his attendants. In jest, it said:

momo no hana	Peach blossom steeped
sukimonodomo wo	wine we have and go to seek
seiwau ga	elegant tipplers
sono watari made	as far as the Queen Mother
tadzune ni zo yaru	of the West's garden or yours.

He came quickly with quite an entourage. The feast was put out, and drinking and carrying on, he stayed the whole day.

Around the tenth of that month, his retainers divided themselves into two teams, the "fore" and "after," to have an archery contest with the small bow. With both teams, taking turns to practice, it was very lively around here. One day when the whole of the "after" team was gathered here to practice, they begged the lady attendants to come up with a prize; they couldn't think of anything particularly appropriate right on the spot, so as a rather forced joke, this was written on a piece of blue paper attached to a willow branch:

yama kaze no	When the mountain wind
mahe yori fukeba	blows from ahead,
kono haru no	surely the threads
yanagi no ito ha	of this spring willow will wind
shiri he ni zo yoru	themselves around those coming after.

In reply, so many verses were spoken, I couldn't possibly remember them all and would have you imagine them. But one of them went like this:

kazu kazu ni	Since we draw our bows
kimi katayorite	with each of you pulling for us,
hiku nareba	just as willow threads
yanagi no mayu mo	open freely from young buds,
ima zo hirakuru	now we go forth without a care.

Just as we were deciding to hold the match at the end of the month, an incident broke out in which several people were banished for who knows what terrible crime, and the whole world was convulsed by the upset, so our plans ended up in disarray.

the minister of the left residing in the West Palace is banished – This incident is known as the Anna Disturbance (since it happened in the second year of the Anna era). The minister of left, Minamoto Takaakira, was banished on the charge that he was plotting a rebellion to place his own son-in-law, Prince Tamehira, on the throne. When Emperor Reizei ascended the throne, the designation of crown prince passed over Tamehira and went to the fifth prince, Morihira, even though he was only a child. If Prince Tamehira had eventually ascended the throne, he would have been the first emperor in a long time without a Fujiwara consort. That would have meant the possible production of heirs to the throne outside the Fujiwara maternal lineage, which ultimately could have led to an eclipse of Fujiwara power. The Fujiwara northern branch scions, Kaneie and his older brothers, had already exerted pressure to have Tamehira passed over in the succession line, but apparently they felt they could not rest as long as Tamehira still had a powerful father-in-law at court. It is assumed that despite their rivalry with each other, Kaneie and his brothers cooperated to have charges of treason trumped up against Minamoto Takaakira.

As we shall see, this incident touched Michitsuna's Mother deeply. She gives no indication that she knows or suspects that her own husband has been one of the engineers of Takaakira's downfall. Indeed, she never acknowledges that Minamoto Takaakira posed a threat to the political future of her husband and his family. She only expresses her profound sympathy for Minamoto Takaakira, his wife and children. Whether her silence on the political ramifications of this situation concerning her husband is due to ignorance or discretion remains a puzzle (cf. pp. 15–16).

Atago . . . Kiyomizu – Atago is in the western part of Kyoto; Kiyomizu is in the eastern part.

diary only for things related to me personally . . . – This is one of the rare places where the author explicitly states an authorial intention. She views the diary as properly a record only of personal things and therefore appears to have to defend this insertion of worldly and political affairs. The defense for the inclusion is that it occasioned strong emotion in her.

this year's fifth months – It will be remembered that this year had two fifth months.

period of abstinence – Since a few weeks later Kaneie embarks on a pilgrimage to Mitake, commentators speculate that this abstinence and fast may have been in preparation for that.

fall one after another – There is a pun on *fure*, "to fall" (of rain) and "to pass" (of time).

Around the twenty-fifth or twenty-sixth of the month, the minister of the left residing in the West Palace is banished. The whole capital is in an uproar; trying to see how things are, people rush to the West Palace. When the minister himself understands how serious the situation is, he does not show himself to anyone and steals away. In the uproar—some say he is in Atago, some say in Kiyomizu—he is finally found out and when he hears that he is indeed to be banished, his terrible grief is beyond expression. There is no one among those who know and are concerned with the affair, not to mention even someone like myself not connected with it at all, who does not dampen their sleeves for him. His various sons too are separated and scattered, whither they know not, to live under the sky of a strange country, some taking the tonsure, all meeting with unspeakable misery. The minister too becomes a monk, but, nevertheless, he is forced to accept the duties of a post in Kyushu and is exiled there. For that period of time, this affair was all one heard about.

In a diary only for things related to me personally, this is perhaps something that shouldn't have been included; however, since the deep feelings of sadness about it were my own and not anyone else's, I have recorded it.

In the first of this year's fifth months, a little after the twentieth, there was a period of abstinence, and my husband, who was to begin a long fast, retreated to a mountain temple. It must have been while I was brooding, lost in thought watching the rain fall heavily, that I received a letter from him in which he said something like, "This seems to be a place where I am strangely depressed," to which I replied:

toshi mo are	Such a time as this,
kaku samidare no	when the water of the fifth month
midzu masari	rains overflows and
wochikata hito no	the days you must be far away
hi wo mo koso fure	also fall one after another.

and sent it away. In response he wrote:

kiyomidzu no	If the rain keeps
mashite hodo furu	falling until pure water
mono naraba	overflows the brim,
onaji numa ni mo	better had I to come down
ori mo tachinamu	and soak in the same marsh with you.

And as we thus exchanged messages, the intercalary fifth month arrived.

Around the end of that month, I came down with some kind of illness—hard to say what it was. Although I suffered greatly with it, I

burning of poppy seeds – A Shingon ritual to burn away evil karmic influences.

new residence – There is uncertainty as to just what residence this is. Three years later Kaneie is spoken of for the first time as "the captain of the right of the Higashi Sanjō residence," so it is speculated that it is this residence that is under construction now.

standing at the entrance – It was believed that by remaining standing at the entrance of the room one did not contract the pollution of being in contact with someone who was ill.

"not regretting to die yet sad" – This is acknowledged to be an allusion to a poem by the well-known mid-Heian poet, Ki no Tsurayuki, which has two alternate endings. One version is:

> Not regretting
> to die, yet sad have
> I become,
> not knowing the way
> to turn my back on the world.

The second version ends:

> not knowing whither
> my lover's heart will go. (*Zenshū*, 208)

We cannot know which version the author had in mind, yet both fit her state of mind well here.

one stalk of lotus pod – Given that this is the end of the intercalary fifth month, approximately the first week of July, it is very early to find a lotus gone to seed, and it is likely as an unseasonable rarity that Kaneie has brought it for a gift.

"I want to show it to you soon" – With this quotation, one senses her hope that he intends to share the residence with her.

The flower blossoms . . . – From the reference to "floating leaf," we know the flower is the lotus, whose unseasonably early seed pod she has before her. There is a pun on *mi*, "fruit" and "self"/ "body."

could only think *so be it.* I just bore it, not wanting to appear as though I were clinging to life; nonetheless, the people around me could not just leave things as they were, and they performed such rituals as the burning of poppy seeds, all to no effect and so time passed. Since I was in ritual abstinence, he was not visiting as usual, but on his way back and forth from overseeing the construction of a new residence, he would stop by and standing at the entrance inquire, "How is she?" One evening when I was feeling weaker and lost in thoughts of "not regretting to die yet sad," he stopped on the way back from the usual place and sent in with a servant one stalk of lotus pod. Apparently he said something like, "Since it is getting dark, I will not come in. Please show this to her; it is from my place." In reply, I just had the servant say, "I feel more dead than alive," and lying back yielded to melancholy thoughts . . . *ah, truly, that splendid place he is building—but who knows if I will live, and as I never know what is really in his heart, even though he says, "I want to show it to you soon," things will turn out as they will*, yet, when I thought it may all come to naught, I became sad. I wrote:

hana ni saki	The flower blossoms
mi ni nari kaharu	and changes into this fruit,
yo wo sutete	casting off this world,
ukiba no tsuyu to	I shall vanish with the
ware zo kenu beshi	dew drop on a floating leaf.

My thoughts gone as far as this, the days passed with my condition the same, so I felt quite forlorn.

Suppose I don't get better was all I could think of, and while I had not a dewdrop's worth of attachment to my own life, it was just that continually thinking about what would happen to this only child left behind, I could not hold back the tears. Since my appearance must have shown how strangely different my feelings were from my usual self, he had distinguished monks come and do their best, but nothing seemed to do any good. I thought, *continuing like this, I must surely die, and if it were to come suddenly, and it would end up that I had not been able to express what was on my mind, how much I would regret it; at least while I am alive, I had better speak my thoughts just as they are*, so leaning against an armrest, this is what I wrote:

> You have always bade me live long and I have always thought to see you through to the end, but it seems that I may have reached the limit, and since I have been feeling strangely uneasy, I write this. As I have always said, I have never thought that I would be long in this world, nor have I a speck of regret for leaving it, except for our young one; for him I have concern.

Since I am one so deep in sin – From here on through the poem, she is speaking out of the general belief that people who have not attained enlightenment are somehow kept back in this world by their attachments and remain in spirit form observing the world they have left behind. Moreover it was believed that the spirits of the deceased, particularly those who have died with bitter feelings, can bring misfortune to those who have wronged them. In essence here, she is gently threatening her husband that if he neglects or mistreats her son, she will know and may punish him from beyond the grave.

Mountain paths . . . – One metaphor for dying was crossing the mountain of death.

As for your exams – There is some controversy over what the author is referring to here because the word she uses is only *tohi*, "question," but I follow the majority opinion that she means the questions of study for his upcoming exam. Michitsuna is fifteen and will therefore be preparing to write academy exams. Although in the mid-Heian period, rank and office were decided primarily by birth and family connections, the ritual taking of Chinese-style civil service exams was maintained. It is touching to hear this mother of a thousand years ago exhorting her son to study.

period of abstinence for mourning – This may mean the general forty-nine day period of mourning after a death, or the three month period of mourning specified for husbands.

governor general's wife – This is Minamoto Takaakira's wife. The post he had been forced to accept in Kyushu was honorary governor general of Daizaifu, hence the term of address here. It would be good at this point to be reminded how close the relationships were between the families struggling for power at the center. Takaakira's wife was actually a younger sister of Kaneie, albeit by a different mother. Despite the fact that they shared the same father, the fault lines of family politics placed Kaneie and his sister on opposite sides, which makes Michitsuna's Mother's sense of identification with the sister all the more remarkable.

the West Palace was burned – It is recorded the West Palace burned on the first day of the fourth month. It was most likely not an accident. Takaakira's palace was the only major aristocratic residence on the west side of the capital. Its burning hastened the decline of that quarter of the city (Hérail, *La cour du Japon a l'époque de Heian*, 98).

Even when you frown at him in jest, it seems to make him so miserable; I beg you, as long as his offense is not great, please don't show him your displeasure. Since I am one so deep in sin:

kaze dani mo	Would that the wind
omohanu kata ni	send me to the realm of no-thought,
yosezaraba	but if it does not,
kono yo no koto ha	even from the world beyond
kano yo ni mo mimu	I shall see what happens here.

Even when I am gone, if someone treats my child unkindly, I shall feel the pain of it. Over the years, I have always worried that your regard for us might end, yet seeing that your heart has not changed, I entreat you, please take good care of our son. Having always thought that eventually I would have to leave him in your charge, now that such has actually come to pass, please see him through. And might I hope too that you will not forget some of the things that we alone shared, some of the times when I was moved to say, "How lovely." Unfortunately, due to these circumstances, I have not been able to say these things to you face to face as would have been better:

tsuyu shigeki	Mountain paths are heavy
michi to ka itodo	with dew, the path up death's
shide no yama	mountain, how much more so—
katsu gatsu nururu	What shall I do with these sleeves
sode ika ni semu	already damp growing damper?

This was what I wrote and in the margin added, "After I am gone, please tell him that his mother said, 'As for your exams, study hard so you will not make the slightest mistake.'" Then sealing the letter, I wrote on top, "To be looked at after the period of abstinence for mourning." Crawling over to a Chinese box beside me, I placed the letter inside. Those looking on might have thought it a strange thing to do, but I did it because if my illness were to go on for a long time and I hadn't at least put that much down on paper, how very pained at heart I would be.

Like this, my condition was the same for a while; I did not go to any great lengths with services and purifications, just kept at it bit by bit until toward the end of the sixth month I began to feel a little better and aware of things around me. It was then that I heard that the governor general's wife had become a nun and I felt so sad for her. It seems that three days after her husband was banished, the West Palace was burned to the ground and so she had moved to a residence of her own, the Momozono villa, and there was living wretchedly, brooding on the past. Hearing about this, I grieved too, and since there seemed no way to clear my mind, I

so many as to be excessive – There is a hint of apology in this expression. She is once again going to write in the unconventional form of a long poem.

Mt. Atago – One of the places where Takaakira is rumored to have hidden, but also here a pun on *ata*, "retribution from a former life."

mountain cuckoo – In summer, the cuckoo replaces the warbler as the seasonal bird. The cuckoo is used here as a comparison to Takaakira's wife, following Takaakira's lamentations with her own.

brooding thoughts the fifth month's long rains – Pun on *nagame*, "to gaze out, brood" and "long rains."

time falls with the rain – Pun on *furu*, "to pass" (of time)/"to fall" (of rain).

one fifth month followed yet another and overlapping robes – Pun on *kasanetaritsuru*, form of *kasaneru*, "to follow one after another" and "to overlap." The image of robes sticking together and molding is associated with the rainy season when moisture permeates everything.

gathered together all the burdensome thoughts that I had lain with, so many as to be excessive, and wrote them out even though it was pitiful to see:

ahare ima ha	Ah, how sad, that now
kaku ifu kai mo	saying these things will make no
nakeredomo	difference, yet I
omoihshi koto ha	would remember how it felt
haru no suwe	at the end of spring,
hana namu chiru to	the tumult as flowers fell
sawagishi wo	for you forever,
ahare ahare to	so sad, so very sad, we said,
kikishi ma ni	upon hearing that
nishi no miyama no	deep in the western mountains,
uguhisu ha	your warbler trilled forth
kagiri no kowe wo	a final note and hid himself
furitatete	on Mt. Atago.
kimi ga mukashi no	Yet some fate from former lives
atago yama	pursued him into
sashite irinu to	the wilds, for although we heard
kikishikado	that he had hidden,
hito goto shigeku	then the clamor of rumors
arishikaba	grew rank like weeds
michi naki koto to	choking the paths he would travel.
nageki wabi	Poor man he lamented,
tani gakurenaru	and just as mountain water
yama midzu no	in deep valleys
tsuhi ni nagaru to	finally flows to the sea,
sawagu ma ni	he must go, midst
yo wo udzuki ni mo	all this tumult, the fourth month
narishikaba	came with misery.
yama hototogisu	The mountain cuckoo in place
tachikahari	of the warbler took
kimi o shinobu no	to the skies, longing for her lord,
kowe tahezu	crying without end,
idzure no sato ka	in which village then did she
nakazarishi	ever stop crying?
mashite nagame no	Still deeper into brooding thoughts
samidare ha	the fifth month's long rains
ukiyo no naka ni	plunged us all, ah, among those
furu kagiri	here in this sad world
tare ga tamoto ka	where time falls with the rain,
tada naramu	who had sleeves untouched?
taezu zo urufu	Ceaselessly drenched as one
satsuki sahe	fifth month followed yet
kasanetaritsuru	another and overlapping
koromode ha	robes stuck together
uhe shita wakazu	under- and overrobes, hard to
kutashiteki	part as they molded.

the beloved children – Takaakira's sons who have been banished as well.

one little egg – One young child was left with the mother.

what will become of it should it never hatch – Pun on *kahi*, "egg" and "result."

ninefold realm – Ninefold is an epithet for the imperial court.

nine provinces – Literally the meaning of Kyushu.

forest of lamentation – Pun on *nageki*, "abandoned tree" and "lament."

sister of the sea – Pun on *ama*, "fisher" and "nun."

the bay and your heart – Pun on *ura*, "bay" and "heart."

deep seaweed of sorrow – Pun on *nagame*, "brood sadly," and name for a type of seaweed.

migrating geese . . . just for a while – Pun on *kari*, "wild geese" and "temporary."

mashite kohidji ni
oritateru
amata no tago ha
ono ga yoyo
ika bakari ka ha
sohochikemu
yotsu ni wakaruru
mura tori no
ono ga chiridjiri
subanarete
wazuka ni tomaru
su mori ni mo
nanika ha kahi no
arubeki to
kudakete mono wo
omofuramu
iheba sara nari
kokono he no
uchi wo nomi koso
narashikeme
onaji kazu to ya
kokono kuni
shima futatsu woba
nagamuramu
katsu ha yume ka to
ihinagara
afubeki go naku
narinu to ya
kimi mo nageki wo
koritsumite
shiho yaku ama yo
narinuramu
fune wo nagashite
ika bakari
ura sabishikaru
yo no naka wo
nagamekaruramu
yuki kaheru
kari no wakare ni
araba koso
kimi ga yodoko mo
arazarame
chiri nomi oku ha
munashikute
makura no yuku he mo
shiraji kashi
ima ha namida mo
minatsuki no
ko kage ni waburu

Still sadder, the muddy paths
down which they must tread,
the beloved children each
reaping his own fate,
and how much will they be
soaked in tears,
parted in four directions
like a flock of birds
scattered each from the other
distant from the nest;
as for the one little egg
that stays in the nest,
what will become of it should
it never hatch?
To think on these things must tear
your heart to pieces,
to speak it anew makes it worse.
Accustomed as he was
only to the ninefold realm
of the inner court,
while the number is the same,
he must be brooding
over those nine provinces
and two islands,
and for you, saying to yourself,
Is this a dream?
Can it be, will I never
meet him again?
Meanwhile you log a forest
of lamentation,
becoming a sister of the sea,
boiling brine for salt,
setting your skiff adrift
how desolate
must be the bay and your heart,
in this world reaping
the deep seaweed of sorrow
plying to and fro.
If like the migrating geese,
your parting was just
for a while, your sleeping mat
would not be so hard.
The dust just piles up in vain,
your pillow afloat
on tears, whither it goes
you surely know not,
now even your tears exhausted
in this sixth month,
in tree shadows, suffering

cicada splits its shell – In the midsummer or early autumn the cicada emerges from seven years' existence as a grub in the earth and crawls to a tree branch to let its shell dry and split, from whence it emerges as a flying insect.

Under the forest of Ōaraki . . . – Allusion to a poem in *Gosenshū*, miscellaneous, book two:

I have no one
to rely on, no way to tell,
since I am just
the fruit of grass under
the forest of Ōaraki. (Katagiri, *Gosen wakashū,* 356)

Michitsuna's Mother recycles the central pun from this poem, ***kusa nomi***, "just grass," or ***kusa no mi***, "fruit"/"self of grass." The author brings this long poem to closure with a reference to her own unhappiness and insecurity, which gives her the basis for sympathizing with the governor general's wife.

Gosenshū was the next imperially sponsored poetry anthology after *Kokinshū* and was completed between 953 and 958 (Keene, *Seeds in the Heart*, 277). Thus in this case, the author is making an allusion to nearly contemporary poetry.

'that place' . . . perverse and tasteless – The author uses the phrase "that place" when thinking of the reaction from the point of view of Takaakira's wife. Combined with her fears that this action might appear "perverse and tasteless," it encourages the interpretation that the author is aware that her husband has had a part in the downfall of Takaakira, and therefore she fears that Takaakira's wife would find expressions of sympathy from someone close to Kaneie distasteful. For examples of that line of interpretation, see Uemura, *Taisei*, vol. 3, 204–5. However, *Zenshū* commentators prefer to explain her hesitation here in terms of social etiquette. They posit that it was not the custom at this time for women to exchange long poems with one another. Assuming that she had not had prior correspondence with Takaakira's wife, to begin correspondence with what amounts to an extravagant and old fashioned mode of expression would give her pause (*Zenshū,* 215).

official document paper – In other words, to make it look as though it were from a man.

Tōnomine . . . lay monk – Fujiwara Takamitsu, an older brother by the same mother whose withdrawal from the world to a hermitage on Tōnomine in 961 was rather similar to that of Kaneie's cousin, Sukemasa, which was described in book one (see p. 145). The *Tōnomine Shōshō monogatari*, "The Tale of Captain Tōnomine," presumably written by a serving woman to Takamitsu's wife, records the events of his withdrawal from society and the reactions of his friends and family. It is written mainly in an epistolary style and is thought by some to precede the *Kagerō Diary*.

pilgrimage to Mitake – Mitake is the same as Kinbusen, a mountain in Yoshino in Nara Prefecture that was a site of pilgrimage for esoteric Buddhism. Only men were allowed to make the pilgrimage there, and it required a three month period of abstinence in preparation. This may have been the pilgrimage for which Kaneie started a period of abstinence right after the Anna incident. The decision of the actual day of departure is sudden.

utsusemi mo	the cicada splits
mune sakete koso	its shell, just so your breast
nagekurame	is rent lamenting.
mashite ya aki no	Even more so when the first
kaze fukeba	winds of autumn blow,
sagami no wogi no	the rushes in the brushwood fence
naka naka ni	heedlessly
so yo to kotahemu	will whisper "it's so" in response.
origoto ni	So each time you hear
itodo me sahe ya	it, your eyes will not close,
ahazaraba	if you meet not by day,
yume ni mo kimi ga	at night in dreams neither
kimi wo mide	will you meet your lord,
nagaki yo sugara	all the long autumn night through,
naku mushi no	one with the throbbing
onaji kowe ni ya	incessant voices of the insects
taezaramu to	your melancholy thoughts,
omofu kokoro ha	so many you will feel
ohoaraki no	it can be borne no more.
mori no shita naru	Under the forest of Ōaraki,
kusa nomi mo	this fruit of grass
onajiku nuru to	is dampened in the same way—
shirurame ya tsuyu	do you know this dew at all?

Then at the end, I added:

yado mireba	Seeing your dwelling
yomogi no kado mo	with mugwort now blocking the
sashinagara	gate, so desolate,
arubeki mono to	how could anyone have dreamed
omohikemu ya zo	that it would have come to this?

Having written it, I laid it aside, and it was noticed by my attendants, "How sad and moving a thing it is. What if you were to show it to her ladyship?" Such ideas being put forth, I said, "But truly for them to know that it came from 'that place' might make them think it perverse and tasteless." So I had someone copy it out on official document paper, fold it formally, and attach it to a carved stick. If they were to ask, "Where is this from?" I instructed the messenger, "Say, 'From Tōnomine,'" which was to have him say it was from her brother by the same mother, the reverend lay monk. As soon as the household had received the letter, the messenger returned. Whatever they thought of it over there, I do not know.

Things going on in this way, I began to feel like a normal person again, then, a little after the twentieth, he suddenly decides to leave for a pilgrimage to Mitake, and as he is to take our young son along with him, we have quite a time getting everything ready for their departure. Not only that, but on the evening of that same day, I was to move back to my

back to my original residence – This is presumably the house she inherited from her mother that was on the eastern edge of the palace compound. In 966, she mentions the run-down state of that place (book one, pp. 132–33). In 967 she records the move to a place assumed to be of Kaneie's choice and proprietorship where "he could come secretly even without a carriage" (book one, p. 147). Then after the servant's altercation, she is moved to another residence not so far away, but mentions that she would like to go back to her "old village" (book two, p. 171). Perhaps her own residence had been under repair during these last two years, and now she was able to move back to it.

our son who still needs to be looked after - Michitsuna is in his fourteenth year.

governor general's wife – Takaakira's wife again.

That person – Some commentators think this may even have been Tokihime, but there is no way to know for sure.

so in the same hand – That is, having the person from before write.

sister of the sea – Referring not only to her present state as a nun but also echoing the poem the author had sent her.

original residence now that renovations were complete. Since he had left behind some of the retainers he might have been expected to take with him, I actually did move. From then on, as he had gone so far to take along our son who still needs to be looked after, I was preoccupied with thoughts of, *How are they? How is it going*? On the first of the seventh month, at dawn, my son came and announced, "Father has just now returned." As this place is quite a distance from his residence, I thought he would find it difficult to visit for a while, but then, around noon, looking very weary and travel worn, surprisingly enough, there he was.

Now, around that time, I learned from others that somehow or another, her ladyship, the governor general's wife, had discovered where the letter had come from, and she had dispatched a messenger to deliver her reply to the place where I had been living in the sixth month, but the messenger made a mistake and took it to someone else. That person had taken it in and apparently not even thinking it strange had sent a reply, but then I heard that her ladyship, upon reading the reply, knew that her letter had been delivered to the wrong place. Yet if she sent the same useless poem again, and that were to become known, what a twisted situation it would be and how she would be thought lacking in taste, so she was confused. As I listened to this with interest, I thought things couldn't be left like this, so in the same hand:

yama biko no	Although I have heard
kotahe ari to	there was a response from
kikinagara	the mountain echo,
ato naki sora wo	troubled, I have searched the
tadzune wabinuru	traceless skies to no avail.

I wrote this on pale turquoise paper, folding it as a formal letter and attaching it to a very leafy branch. However, as again the messenger just disappeared after delivering the letter, whether we had ended up in the same situation as before or she was acting out of a sense of reserve, at any rate, there was no response. This exchange had gotten quite strange, I thought. Then, after quite some time, having sought out an intermediary who could deliver it with certainty, she wrote thus:

fuku kaze ni	To the blowing wind,
tsukete mono omofu	were attached her melancholy thoughts,
ama no taku	did they not reach you,
shiho no keburi ha	smoke from the brine fires kindled
tadzune idezu ya	by the sister of the sea?

It was in a youthful hand, on light gray paper, and came attached to a branch of cypress. I respectfully replied:

a branch of pine whose needles had changed color – By this point, the reader may have begun to wonder, what is the significance of pale turquoise paper attached to a leafy branch, light gray paper coming with a sprig of cypress, nut brown paper attached to a pine? It is clearly important to the author that these details be noted, and it is likely a Heian audience would have understood the subtleties involved in these choices, but the precise nature of that aesthetic code is lost to us.

Longevity Celebration – Held when someone reached fifty years old. This celebration for the minister of the left is recorded as having been held on the twenty-first day of the seventh month. Since this section begins, "the eighth month arrived," either the author's memory is vague or the stir of preparing gifts for the occasion extended for a couple of weeks around the event.

minister of the left of the Koichijō residence – Fujiwara Moromasa, younger brother to Kaneie's father. He replaced Minamoto Takaakira as minister of the left and is generally thought to have been the mastermind behind the plot to expel Takaakira.

chief of the Left Guards – There is some controversy over who this was at the time; *Zenshū* commentators opt for the dominant opinion that it was Fujiwara Yoritada, a nephew of Moromasa, cousin to Kaneie (*Zenshū,* 217).

congratulatory screen – A customary gift on such an occasion was a free-standing screen with illustrations of beautiful and auspicious scenes to which were added poems. It was a mark of respect to be asked to contribute poems for such screens. A number of distinguished poets would be asked to present a complete set of poems for the illustrations, from which the final set would be selected.

presses me to contribute some poems – This is a place in the diary where we can gauge the level of respect her poetry commanded. These poems are also comparatively rare examples of her public, "professional" poetry.

screen with pictures – The conventional practice was for the poet to write the poems in the persona of a figure pictured in the scene (see Joshua Mostow, "Self and Landscape in Kagerō Nikki," *Review of Japanese Culture and Society* [December 1993]: 15).

a thousand birds – The word for plovers in Japanese, *chidori*, has the word *chi*, "one thousand," embedded in it. By association, this evokes the notion of long life and generations of progeny.

Awatayama – A mountainous district to the east of Kyoto.

leading the horse in – In big houses, the stables were actually part of the house.

aruru ura ni	From the rough wild shore,
shiho no keburi ha	the smoke from the brine fires
tachi keredo	rose up . . . but
konata ni kahesu	alas there was no wind
kaze zo nakarishi	to carry it hither.

I wrote this on nut brown paper and attached it to a branch of pine whose needles had changed color.

The eighth month arrived. Around that time, a great fuss is being made over the Longevity Celebration of the minister of the left of the Koichijō residence. We hear that the chief of the Left Guards is going to prepare a congratulatory screen. Using an intermediary difficult to refuse, he presses me to contribute some poems. It is to be a screen with pictures of various places painted on it. The request rather leaves me cold; I send it back many times, but, as he insists, there is no choice, so in the evenings and when gazing at the moon, I think up one or two poems.

For the illustration of a congratulatory banquet being held at someone's house:

ohozora wo	How many times have
meguru tsuki hi no	the sun and the moon made their
iku kaheri	rounds of the vast sky;
kefu yuku suwe ni	down the road, how many more
ahamu to suramu	days like today will we meet?

For a scene in which a traveler halts his horse on a beach and listens to the voices of the plovers:

hito kowe ni	In a single voice,
yagate chidori to	all of a sudden one hears
kikitsureba	a thousand birds,
yo yo wo tsukusamu	generation upon generation
kazu mo shirarezu	lives innumerable.

A scene of someone leading a colt through Awatayama, stopping at a house in the neighborhood and leading the horse in:

amata toshi	For so many years,
koyuru yamabe ni	I have lived by these mountains,
ihewi shite	crossing them time and
tsunahiku koma mo	time again, even the most
omonare ni keri	stubborn colt is used to me.

In a pond in front of someone's house, the full moon of the eighth month is reflected; as some women gaze at it, a person playing a flute passes by on the big avenue outside the garden wall:

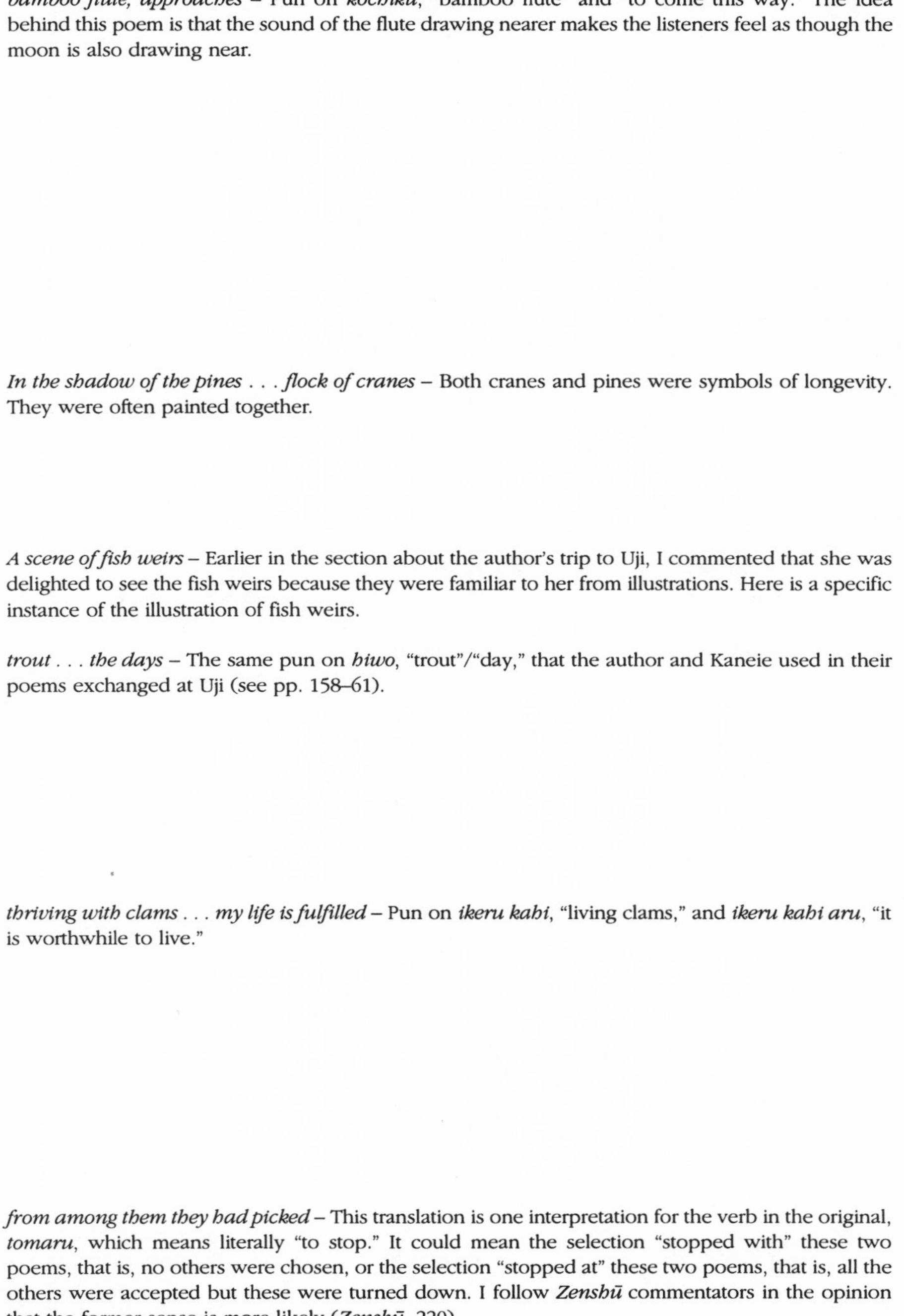

bamboo flute, approaches – Pun on *kochiku*, "bamboo flute" and "to come this way." The idea behind this poem is that the sound of the flute drawing nearer makes the listeners feel as though the moon is also drawing near.

In the shadow of the pines . . . flock of cranes – Both cranes and pines were symbols of longevity. They were often painted together.

A scene of fish weirs – Earlier in the section about the author's trip to Uji, I commented that she was delighted to see the fish weirs because they were familiar to her from illustrations. Here is a specific instance of the illustration of fish weirs.

trout . . . the days – The same pun on *hiwo*, "trout"/"day," that the author and Kaneie used in their poems exchanged at Uji (see pp. 158–61).

thriving with clams . . . my life is fulfilled – Pun on *ikeru kahi*, "living clams," and *ikeru kahi aru*, "it is worthwhile to live."

from among them they had picked – This translation is one interpretation for the verb in the original, *tomaru*, which means literally "to stop." It could mean the selection "stopped with" these two poems, that is, no others were chosen, or the selection "stopped at" these two poems, that is, all the others were accepted but these were turned down. I follow *Zenshū* commentators in the opinion that the former sense is more likely (*Zenshū*, 220).

kumowi yori	From beyond the clouds,
kochiku no kowe wo	the voice of a bamboo flute,
kiku nahe ni	approaches—listening,
sashikumu bakari	it seems the moon's reflection
miyuru tsuki kage	is right here in our cupped hands.

In a pine grove on the shore in front of a rustic house, a flock of cranes is playing. "Two poems for this one" are the instructions:

nami kake no	Standing on the sweep
miyari ni tateru	of beach where waves roll in,
ko matsu bara	the little pines grove;
kokoro wo yosuru	it would appear hearts of cranes
koto zo arurashi	are drawn to it in good will.

matsu no kage	In the shadow
masago no naka to	of the pines, on the fine white sand
tadzunuru ha	seeking something,
nani no akanu zo	but what more could anyone
tadzu no muratori	possibly want?—flock of cranes.

A scene of fish weirs:

ajirogi ni	The trout are drawn to
kokoro o yosete	the fish weirs and I am drawn
hiwo fureba	to the scene, thus
amata no yo koso	the days passed and so many nights
tabine shite kere	have I slept a traveler's sleep.

A scene of fishing boats along with fisherman's fires on the beach:

isaribi mo	The fisherman's fires
ama no kobune mo	and little fisher's boats too
nodokekare	are peaceful; I have come
ikeru kahi aru	to this beach thriving with clams
ura ni kinikeri	feeling my life is fulfilled.

A woman's carriage on the way home from viewing maple leaves comes to another house with many maple leaves:

yorodzu yo wo	Even people who live for
nobe no atari ni	a myriad generations
sumu hito ha	on this wide plain
meguru meguru ya	as the seasons go round and round,
aki wo matsuramu	they must still look forward to autumn.

Thus, I was forced to compose so many uninteresting poems; when I heard that from among them they had picked the "fisherman's fires" and "flock of cranes," I somehow felt let down.

quite harried for no particular reason – So she says, but *Zenshū* commentators point out that the latter part of this year contained a number of events with which members of her extended family were involved, including the abdication of Emperor Reizei and assumption of the throne by Emperor Enyū, promotion to the third rank for Kaneie, permission to serve in the palace granted to her son, Michitsuna, her sister-in-law Lady Jōganden's promotion to principal handmaid, and the death of Fujiwara Moromasa, for whom the congratulatory screen had been made (*Zenshū,* 220).

Placing the piled up snow . . . – While this poem is saying something as simple as, "I'm so miserable I could die," her mode of expression is unusual. The expected treatment of this image for this sentiment would be, "Just as the snow soon melts away, I too will likely melt away [die] from this misery." This poem is the inverse of that, "the snow will melt soon, but I will not." It makes the poem more cold and stark.

last day of the year – The new year is the first year of the Tenroku era, 970.

that splendid residence – The residence that has been under construction at Higashi Sanjō.

dress rehearsal – The dress rehearsal provides the author and her household with the opportunity to see the performance they will not be able to attend. For this reason, they treat it more like an actual performance than a rehearsal.

Ō no Yoshimochi – The Ō family was famous in the fields of music and dance. Yoshimochi is noted in another contemporary chronicle as particularly skillful.

take off robes for him – The custom of the time when one wanted to reward someone was to take off one of one's own garments and give it to the person. Multiple layers of clothing were the style of the period. Clothes and cloth in general were virtually a form of currency.

the "Butterfly" piece – In this piece, apparently the dancer had a headdress festooned with yellow *yamabuki* blossoms and held a branch of *yamabuki* in his right hand (Uemura, *Taisei*, vol. 3, 337).

How well this fit – The saffron-colored singlet complements the yellow flowers of the costume.

So it is held with great to do over at his residence – Again, rather than a mere rehearsal, this is a private performance for a select number of those who matter at court.

might think it strange – In his excitement, he dispenses with all formalities.

Doing such things as these, autumn ended and winter arrived. In the midst of feeling quite harried for no particular reason, there was a day in the eleventh month when the snow piled up very deeply and for whatever cause, I couldn't help feeling depressed in both body and heart, feeling sad over his coldness. Gloomily gazing out, I wrote how I felt:

furu yuki ni	Placing the piled up
tsumoru toshi wo ba	snow alongside the
yosohetsutsu	years piled up—
kiemu go mo naki	that this self has no fixed time
mi wo zo uramuru	to melt away, I grieve.

While I was thinking such thoughts as these, the last day of the year and then the middle of spring arrived. As for him, it is rumored how he is in a rush to move, tomorrow, no tonight, into that splendid residence on which he has lavished such care; as for me, just as I thought, I am to remain where I am and I suppose that's best. Such being the case, I have been consoling myself with thoughts of *you've learned from bitter experience,* and so on, when I get caught up in the preparations for the archery contest to be held around the tenth of the third month at the palace. My young one has been chosen to participate as a member of the "after" team. Since it has been declared that the winning team will present a dance, these days everything else is forgotten in the rush to attend to this. Every day, the house resounds with the sound of music for the dance practice. Going off for archery practice, he comes back with prizes won for his skill. Looking on, I feel terribly pleased.

The tenth day arrived. Today, they hold a sort of dress rehearsal here. The dance master, Ō no Yoshimochi, receives a lot of presents from the lady attendants. All the other participants to a man take off robes for him. Announcing, "His lordship is observing abstinence," nonetheless all his retainers come. In the evening, just as the rehearsal is coming to an end, Yoshimochi comes out and dances the "Butterfly" piece; afterward someone removes a saffron singlet and bestows it on him. How well this fit the occasion. Then again on the twelfth day, they say, "We have to gather the whole of the 'after' team together for dance and archery practice, but it is inconvenient to hold it here because there is no archery practice ground." So it is held with great to do over at his residence. I hear that "practically all the high-ranking courtiers are attending; it seems the dance master Yoshimochi will be buried in congratulatory robes." For my part, as I wonder and worry, *how is it going? how is it going?* the night grows late and my son returns with a great many people in train. Then, in a little bit, he himself arrives and not caring whether people might think it strange, comes right into my room, "This one danced so charmingly, it will

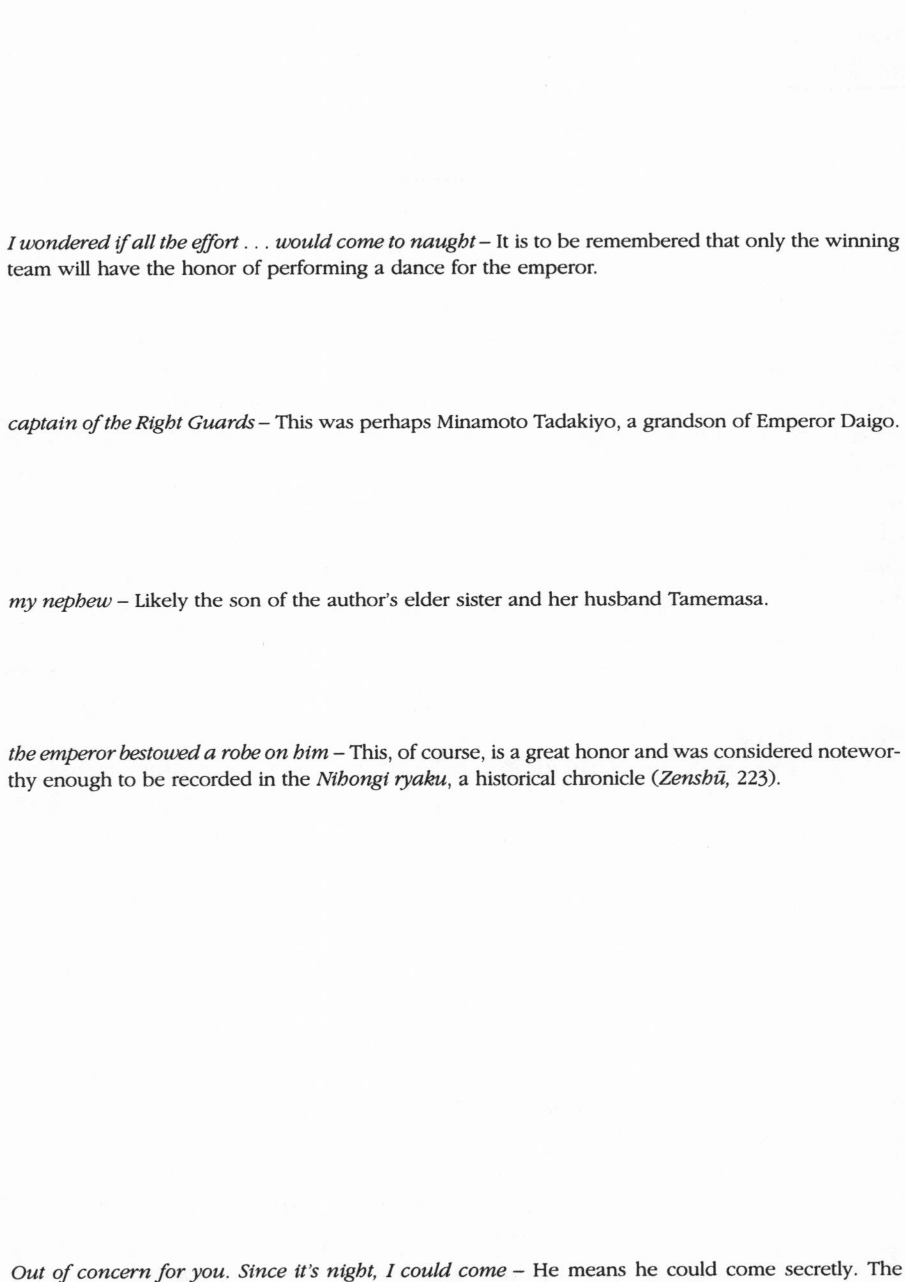

I wondered if all the effort . . . would come to naught – It is to be remembered that only the winning team will have the honor of performing a dance for the emperor.

captain of the Right Guards – This was perhaps Minamoto Tadakiyo, a grandson of Emperor Daigo.

my nephew – Likely the son of the author's elder sister and her husband Tamemasa.

the emperor bestowed a robe on him – This, of course, is a great honor and was considered noteworthy enough to be recorded in the *Nihongi ryaku*, a historical chronicle (*Zenshū,* 223).

Out of concern for you. Since it's night, I could come – He means he could come secretly. The fragmentary nature of his speech here conveys his agitation and preoccupation.

be the talk of the court. It was so touching, everyone was in tears. I'm still observing abstinence tomorrow and the next day, how very trying. But I will come while it is still early on the fifteenth and attend to all the details." Having said these things, he left, but I didn't feel my usual chagrin; I felt so happy; there was no limit to my joy.

The day arrives; he comes early; a lot of people gather to attend to the dance costumes; there is great excitement, seeing people off, praying for the success of my son's bow. Sometime before, my husband had said, "The 'after' team is bound to lose. They picked some rather odd archers." When I heard such things, I wondered if all the effort he had put into the dance would come to naught and as I worried about what was going to happen, the day turned to night. Since the moon was very bright, I did not even have the outer shutters lowered; as I fervently prayed, first one, then another attendant runs in to tell the tale of the event. "He has taken this many shots." "It seems our young lord's opponent is the captain of the Right Guards." "He shot with all his might and defeated his opponent." Moved by each report, *yes, yes, such joy and happiness, there is nothing like it.* Then another messenger comes in with the news, "While the 'after' team was expected to lose, with our young lord's arrows hitting the mark, the match ended in a tie." Since it was a tie, the 'before' team led the dancing with a piece entitled "King Ryō." The dancer was my nephew who is about the same age as my son. When they had all been learning their dances, he had come here to watch and my son had gone there, so they had both taken an interest in each other's dancing. Then, my son danced next and as a result of the general appreciation for his performance, it seems the emperor bestowed a robe on him. Directly, they returned from the palace with the young "King Ryō" also riding on behind. He proceeded to tell me what had gone on, how proud his son had made him, how all the high-ranking courtiers had been so enchanted they had cried, and so on, repeating the story over and over in tears himself as he told it. He called for the archery master and, when he came, loaded him up with all kinds of gifts. Forgetting that I had ever been sad, I experienced a happiness beyond comparison. For about two or three days afterward, friends and acquaintances, even some priests, came one after another to congratulate us on the young lord's success. Listening to their words, I felt so strangely happy.

Thus the fourth month arrived. From about the tenth of that month to the tenth of the fifth month, complaining that, "I've been feeling rather unwell," he stayed away for much longer than usual. Then about seven or eight days later, he did come, but saying, "It took all I had to come. Out of concern for you. Since it's night, I could come. I'm still far from well. I am

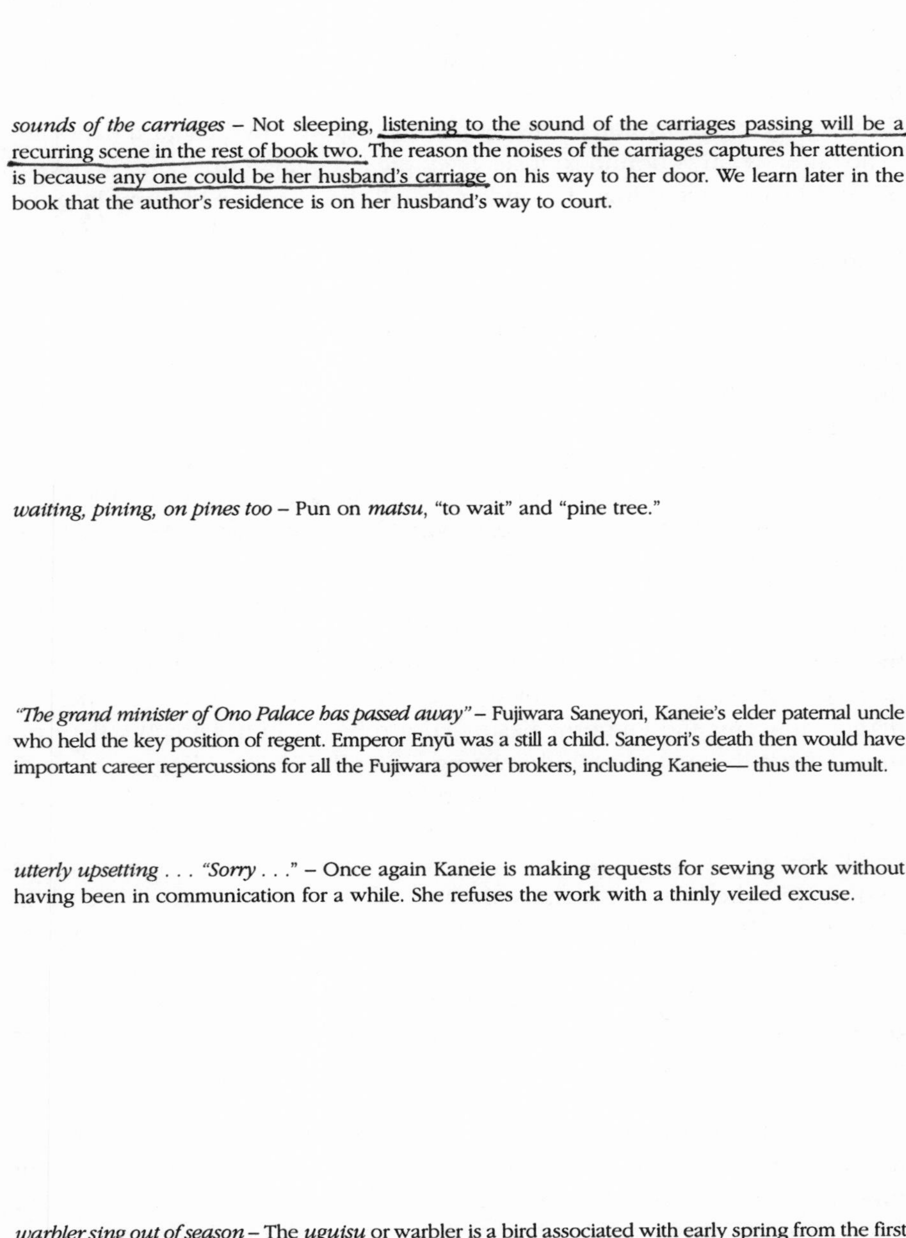

sounds of the carriages – Not sleeping, listening to the sound of the carriages passing will be a recurring scene in the rest of book two. The reason the noises of the carriages captures her attention is because any one could be her husband's carriage on his way to her door. We learn later in the book that the author's residence is on her husband's way to court.

waiting, pining, on pines too – Pun on *matsu*, "to wait" and "pine tree."

"The grand minister of Ono Palace has passed away" – Fujiwara Saneyori, Kaneie's elder paternal uncle who held the key position of regent. Emperor Enyū was a still a child. Saneyori's death then would have important career repercussions for all the Fujiwara power brokers, including Kaneie— thus the tumult.

utterly upsetting . . . "Sorry . . ." – Once again Kaneie is making requests for sewing work without having been in communication for a while. She refuses the work with a thinly veiled excuse.

warbler sing out of season – The *uguisu* or warbler is a bird associated with early spring from the first month to the third month. It would be odd to hear it sing in the middle of summer.

not even reporting for duty at court. If someone were to see me walking about like this, how embarrassing it would be," and so on, he left. Yet, after I heard that he had recovered, I felt that the time of waiting for him to visit went on too long. It felt strange, and while I spent my nights thinking to myself, *I'll just see if he comes tonight*, it ended up that a long time had passed without him sending even a note. Although I found this most unusual and unsettling, I pretended not to be concerned, yet, at night, the sounds of the carriages rumbling outside would set my heart pounding. Sometimes, I would fall asleep and wake to find I had spent another night alone and feel all the more uneasy. My young son made inquiries every time he went to visit, but there was nothing in particular to report. There was not so much as a note asking "How are you?" Rather than going on like this, I kept thinking about sending him a note asking, "What on earth is happening? Don't you find this strange?" And thus I spent my days and nights, when one day raising up the shutters and looking outside, I saw that it had been raining that night and the trees were laden with dew. Looking at this scene, this is just what I felt:

yo no uchi ha	Through the whole night,
matsu ni mo tsuyu ha	of waiting, pining, on pines too
kakarikeri	the dew has fallen, yet,
akureba kiyuru	when the sun rises, the dew vanishes
mono wo koso omohe	and one suffers all the more.

Time passed in this way, and then at the end of the month, there was a great commotion in the world over the news, "The grand minister of Ono Palace has passed away." After such a long time, I received this note from him, "As the world is in an uproar, I will be in abstinence and won't be able to attend upon you for awhile. By the way, I will be in mourning dress; have these garments prepared as quickly as possible." Finding this utterly upsetting, I responded, "Sorry, but it seems all the serving women who could do this have returned home for the moment." This seemed to offend him, for he sent not a word back. With things in this state, the sixth month arrived. When I counted back, it was more than thirty days since I had received a visit from him at night, and more than forty days since he had visited during the day. To say this strange state of affairs was sudden would be an understatement. Even though our relationship had never gone quite as I would have liked, it had never come to this kind of crisis before; even my attendants looking on thought it very strange and unprecedented. I felt barely conscious of what went on around me, lost in melancholy thoughts. Feeling very ashamed before others' eyes, one time when I was lying down trying to stifle tears, I heard a warbler sing out of season and this is what I felt:

rites of purification – The sixth month was traditionally a time for performing Shinto rites of purification, which had to be done on the bank of a river or on a beach. The object of the purification was to rid oneself of evil influences and thus bring good fortune into one's life. For the author, although she does not state it explicitly, her hopes must have been on turning her marriage around for the better.

Karasaki – On the west shore of Lake Biwa, close to present-day Ōtsu city. This was a favorite place for performing purification rites.

Another woman similar to myself – There is no way of identifying who this woman might be. It is interesting, however, that she had women friends whom she could invite along on such occasions. Later in book three we see the author accepting invitations of this kind from others. When she says "similar to myself," it is hard to know how far to extend the sense of similarity. Does she mean just the same age and place in life, or does she mean it is a woman who is also having marital difficulties?

Kamo River – The river that flows along the eastern edge of Kyoto.

just seeing this landscape, so different from the capital – The landscape of the capital was conventionally thought to be moving because it had been so enriched by descriptions in poetry and other forms of literature. The mountain paths would not have been made accessible to one's perceptions in that way.

checkpoint – There were border checkpoints between the various regions of Heian Japan. This checkpoint was at the middle point of the road between Kyoto and Ōtsu.

it is enchanting – One wonders why freight carts would be so captivating, but an answer is to be found in the fact that lumbering activities were a pictorial subject for screens. Similar to her experience of the fish weirs at Uji, her excitement at seeing them is partly the astonishment of seeing with her own eyes something she has imagined from pictures (Mostow, "Self and Landscape," 11).

useless to try and explain such feelings – Indeed it is. Her state of mind here seems very complex. The release of being out of the city, and perhaps even more being out of the circular ruminations on her marriage, bring on a flood of feeling that cannot be specified as sadness or happiness.

Ōtsu – The village on Lake Biwa.

box lunches – The custom of eating lunches in wooden boxes with divided compartments goes back to the Heian period. They do not seem to have brought the boxes with them but had them delivered. Ox carriages travel very slowly. Riders on horseback could cover the distance much faster, so presumably the box lunches would be sent out from home at a later time in the day with riders. We note a few lines below that a party is sent back with news of the progress of the expedition.

uguhisu mo	Warbler, do you too
go mo naki mono ya	suffer from sadness that
omofuramu	has no fixed term,
minatsuki hatenu	that you still cry well out
ne wo zo nakunaru	of season in the sixth month.

While things continued in this fashion, around the twenty-fourth of the month, feeling at a loss for what to do, strangely unable to settle down, I think, *there must be a cool place somewhere where I might relieve the tension of my mind and at the same time perform rites of purification at a water's edge*, and so I decide to make a pilgrimage to Karasaki. Leaving well before dawn, the moon is still very bright. Another woman similar to myself accompanies me, so together with one attendant, we are just three in the carriage, with only seven or eight men of the household riding on horses, such is our entourage. Around the area of the Kamo River, dawn breaks faintly. Past there, the road becomes a mountain path: just seeing this landscape, so different from the capital, perhaps because of my state of mind recently, I feel everything with such poignancy. Just when we reach the checkpoint and stop the carriage for a while to feed the oxen—freight carts drawn one after another bringing strange fresh wood down come forth from the dim light of the forest—what shall I say, I feel as though my state of mind has been turned around, it is enchanting. Going along thus on the mountain road, I feel touched again and again. When I strain to see and scan the boundless lake ahead, I notice what I take to be two or three birds; then on second thought I realize they must be fishing boats. At this, I was simply unable to stop the tears from pouring down. I think it is useless to try and explain such feelings, and it seemed all the more so for my companion who was also moved to tears. Feeling quite embarrassed, we were unable to look one another in the eye.

Our destination still a long way off, we are driven by some very miserable looking houses in the village of Ōtsu. That too gives me a very odd feeling, and when we pass through there, we come out onto the wide sweep of the beach. Looking back the way we had come, the view of the houses gathered along the lake shore with all their boats lined up on the beach in front is very beautiful. There are also boats rowing to and fro. Going along bit by bit, it finally ends up being noon. "Let's give the horses a rest for a while," someone says, and so at a place called Shimizu, under the shade of a single tall sandalwood tree that we had seen from far off, the carriage was unhitched and the horses led to the shore to cool off in the water. Someone says, "Let's wait until the box lunches are brought here. It seems Karasaki is still a long way." My young one has a very tired-looking face, so bringing out the provisions bag, I give him something to

although I felt something was missing – This passage has required emendation by editors to make sense. Commentaries vary in their emendations, but this translation again follows the *Zenshū* edition.

the net for the ceremony – The precise nature and procedure of the purification ritual is no longer known, but poems related to the ceremony mention the throwing out of a net, and illustrations of Karasaki on screens also show the casting of a net. Judging from this passage, some kind of augury is made on the contents of the net.

shells that one could say "shell" bode well – This is an attempt to catch some of the playful, punning quality of her remarks, which in the original are a puzzling mix of puns and allusion.

The people in the back – When the author started out, she mentions only one attendant in the back, but now there seem to be more, or perhaps it is people riding on the outside of the carriage. At any rate, it makes a funny scene.

letting ourselves be seen – In Heian etiquette, a high-ranked lady never let herself be seen, but the special ritual nature of the occasion seems to bring a relaxing of the rules.

"Oh little waves of Karasaki in Shiga" – Song of Shinto worship.

"cries at sunset" cicada – The same cicada that she writes a poem about in book one (p. 111).

Running Well – Hashirii, just on the Lake Biwa side of the checkpoint, was famous for having a fresh, cool spring where travelers slaked their thirst.

made half a poem – As a game, the companion makes up half the poem for the author to supply the last two lines.

Running Well . . . – The interest in this joint poem lies in a thicket of puns. In the companion's first three lines, the place name Hashirii, or Running Well, is punned upon. Then the author's capping lines contain two puns, one, *kage*, "reflection," which can also mean "fawn-colored horse," and *yodomu*, "rest," which can also mean "hesitate" or, of horses, "go slowly." It becomes a joking rebuke, "Why be envious, do you really expect the horses to go slow?" and it also weaves in an image of the fresh, flowing water.

eat. Just at that point, the box lunches arrive and are distributed to everybody. A party is also dispatched to let them know at home, "We have arrived at Shimizu."

Well, then the carriage was hitched up; we set out again and reached Karasaki. There, the carriage is turned around, and as we head out toward the purification site, we see that the wind is rising and waves are getting high. The boats going to and fro are putting up their sails. There are some men gathered on the shore, our retainers say to them, "Sing us a song," and so they go along singing in voices it would be difficult to describe. The time came to perform the purification rites, and although I felt something was missing, we arrived at the site. The carriage was set right beside the water's edge on a very narrow spit of land at the lower end of the purification site. The net for the ceremony was dropped, the waves came in one after another, and when they hauled the net in, some shells that one could say "shell" bode well were caught in it. The people in the back strain forward so much to see that they nearly fall into the water, and letting ourselves be seen, we are offered the sight of strange and rare things from the shore; it is a merry bustle of activity. Some young men line up off to the side at a little distance, and sing the famous sacred song that begins, "Oh little waves of Karasaki in Shiga." How lovely it sounded. Even though the wind is blowing strongly, as there is no tree shade, it is very hot. I start to think it would be good to return to Shimizu without delay. Around midafternoon, when we had completed our rites, we start back.

Such an experience does not fade quickly, and I was deeply moved gazing at the passing scenery as we went along. When we reached the entrance to the mountains, it was almost evening; the "cries at sunset" cicada were in splendid full song. Listening to them, this is what I felt:

naki kaheru	Crying at the return,
koe zo kihohite	these voices sound as though they strive
kikoyu naru	one against the other . . .
machi ya shitsuramu	have you been waiting for me,
seki no higurashi	sundown cicada at the border?

This I said to myself without telling others.

We had sent a few riders to speed ahead to a place called Running Well. When we reached there, the ones who had gone ahead looked so rested, cool, and cheerful as they came up to help unhitch the carriage that my friend made half a poem:

urayamashi	How enviable,
koma no ashi toku	the quick legs of the ponies
hashiri wi no	Running Well,

having curtains drawn around us – So that they would not be seen.

preparing the watery rice with one's own hands – This was apparently dried cooked rice that was mixed with water for traveler's fare. The novelty of preparing food with her own hands brings a pleasure akin to the experience of camping out.

Awatayama – A mountainous area on the road to Ōtsu. The place-name has already come up in the descriptions of the screen illustrations (pp. 186–87).

Of this painful world . . . – This poem puns on the word, *mitsu*, which means "I have seen" as well as being the name for the beach area of Ōtsu on Lake Biwa, and hence another way of referring to Karasaki. The word *namida*, "tears," also has the word *nami*, "waves," embedded in it, and *nagori* can mean "remains" or "water left behind by waves or the tide."

to which I added:

shimidzu ni kage ha yodomu mono kaha	can reflections rest on flowing water, or horses check their pace?

The carriage was brought close to the flowing water, and having curtains drawn around us in the back, we all got down. Soaking hands and feet in the cool water, I feel as though all my troubled thoughts cleared away. We sit on rocks, trays being laid on top of the water conduit. We eat; the joy of preparing the watery rice with one's own hands made the thought of leaving painful, but voices urge, "The sun has already set." I think, *no one could possibly be sad in a place like this,* but as the sun had set, we had to leave.

When we had gone along for a bit, at a place called Awatayama, there were people from the capital waiting for us with torches. I hear, "Earlier today, his lordship paid us a visit." How very strange, I felt that he had actually waited for a time when he knew I would be out. "And after that?" everyone wanted to know more. As for me, I arrived home just feeling upset. Getting out of the carriage, I felt unbearably miserable when the people who had stayed behind came up saying, "He paid us a visit. When he asked after you, we told him the situation and so on. 'Well, I wonder what she had on her mind. I seem to have come at a bad time.' That's what he said." Listening to this, I feel as though I am in a bad dream.

The next day, I was very tired. The day after that, my young one was leaving to visit his father's residence. I wondered if I should just come out and ask him about his strange behavior, but felt too depressed for that, yet, when I remembered my feelings at that beach, I was unable to keep it to myself:

ukiyo wo ba kabakari mitsu no hamabe ni te namida ni nagori ariya to zo mishi	Of this painful world, I have seen this much at Mitsu Beach, remains of waves, I wondered of tears, could there be any more left to shed?

Having written this, I told my son, "Just deliver this, and before he has a chance to see it, return home." He came back shortly saying, "I did as you asked." I wondered how he would react when he saw it, and secretly I guess I hoped for some kind of response. However, he revealed nothing, and so the month came to a close.

A little while ago when I had a lot of time on my hands and was having the garden attended to, I had the gardeners gather together a few

your spouse, the lightning – The word for lightning in Japanese is *inadzuma*, "rice plant spouse." This name seems to come from the folk belief that the ears of rice swell due to the influence of the lightning from the summer storms that accompany their ripening.

Lady Jōganden – Kaneie's younger sister Tōshi, who has already appeared several times in the diary. She shared the same house with the author for a short time in book one. The fifth prince that she became guardian to at the end of book one has now ascended the throne as Emperor Enyū. Lady Jōganden became principal handmaid in the fall of the previous year.

the year before last – Lady Jōganden actually became principal handmaid just the previous year. This discrepancy may be due either to fuzzy memory on the author's part, or it may be a clue as to when she actually started to write the diary. Many commentators suggest 971 as the year she began to write. If the author were speaking in terms of the time of actual writing, then it would be "the year before last" from that perspective.

her relations with her brother were contrary – Although the last time Lady Jōganden was mentioned in the diary, she was on good terms with Kaneie, it seems that relations between them had become strained. It is speculated that the source of the estrangement was the fierce competition between Kaneie and his older brother, Kanemichi. Kaneie had begun to outstrip his elder brother in rank from about the year before, which must have chagrined Kanemichi. Kanemichi's son Akimitsu was married to Lady Jōganden's daughter, which would likely cause her to favor Kanemichi.

end of her web's thread – Referring to the possible end of her marriage to Kaneie.

but you are not a spider . . . – The sense seems to be, "If you were a spider, one could understand that threads break, but surely your marriage has come through many years on something more substantial than that, so how can it be that it is broken?" There is a pun on the word *i*, "thread," embedded in *ika*, "how."

I have sent letters but you have not responded – Shinozuka speculates that the reason she may not have recorded his sending these letters and has not responded to them is because he never sent an answering poem to her "Mitsu Beach" poem. It was a poetic response to that she was waiting for, and therefore the other inquiries did not count (Shinozuka, *Kagerō nikki no kokoro to hyōgen*, 272).

the sort of thing it appeared to be – She uses the verb form *arumeri* here. The *meri* ending indicates supposition based on sight. It seems slightly odd here that she should speak in terms of supposition about something she quotes, but it subtly indicates her sense of estrangement from his communication.

period of mourning – The period of mourning for his uncle, Saneyori. It is also revealed shortly in the diary that Kaneie makes use of the period of mourning to start an affair with one of his uncle's mistresses.

of the numerous rice sprouts and plant them under the eaves outside my room. Charmingly their ears had begun to swell, but even though I was careful to have them well supplied with water, the leaves began to change color and droop, seeing this I felt very sad:

inadzuma no	In the roof's shadow
hikari dani konu	where even the light of
yagakure ha	your spouse, the lightning
nokiba no nae mo	does not come, you too seem to languish
mono omofu rashi	rice sprouts under the eaves.

That was how it appeared to me.

Lady Jōganden had become principal handmaid the year before last. Strangely, she had not inquired how things were going over here, but that might have been due to the fact that her relations with her brother were contrary to what one might expect, and so she might have come to feel distant from me, too. Thinking she might not know how things had gone awry here, as part of a letter to her, I sent this:

sasagani no	The spider has reached
ima ha to kagiru	the end of her web's thread
sudji nite mo	yet throwing these lines
kakute ha shibashi	to you, for awhile at least,
taeji no zo omofu	she would like to keep in touch.

Her reply to me was full of tender feeling:

taeki to mo	It has been broken—
kiku zo kanashiki	just to hear that makes me sad;
toshi tsuki wo	through years and months
ika ni kakikoshi	how was your web spun, but you
kumo naranaku ni	are not a spider, how can this be?

When I saw this, realizing that she must already have heard some gossip, I felt even worse, and while I was passing my days in brooding, a letter arrived from him. "I have sent letters but you have not responded; since you have seemed out of sorts, it seemed best to stay away. However, I am thinking of coming today" was the sort of thing it appeared to be. As this and that attendant urged me to respond, I did, and evening fell by the time I had written it. Before one would have thought my answer could have reached him, he appeared. Since my attendants said such things as, "He may have had his reasons for staying away. Please look as though you're not upset." I did my best to change my feelings. "It's because I've been in a period of mourning that I have been absent; I have no intention

As there are some things I simply must attend to . . . – He leaves the sentence unfinished, but it is his excuse for not coming that day.

it is natural for me to hope he might have a change of heart – There are two different lines of interpretation for this statement. One line (notably Uemura and *Zenshū* commentators) takes the subject of the hoping or expectation here as Kaneie, thus giving "It is likely he expected me to have a change of heart." The other line of interpretation (notably Kakimoto and Shinozuka) makes the author the subject. I am specifically following Shinozuka here with this translation (Shinozuka, *Kagerō nikki no kokoro to hyōgen*, 274).

If only he would grow up – Michitsuna is about fifteen years old at the time.

if you became a monk, how could you possibly manage without your hawks – As a monk, he would not be able to indulge in lifetaking activities like hunting with hawks.

untied them all, and let them go – This act either expresses Michitsuna's complete devotion to his mother at this point, or it expresses the pain he feels at this suggestion by injuring himself to show her how such an idea distresses him. Either way, this scene shows the strong emotional bond between this mother and her only son.

Obon – A Buddhist observance of the seventh month. At this time, it was believed that the spirits of the deceased came back to their former homes, and it was required to make offerings and hold special services to assure their peace of mind for another year.

my husband's household office – To provide the offerings and arrange for services for her deceased mother was one of her husband's material contributions to their marriage.

Maigre Feast – Vegetarian feast prepared for the monks performing services.

of ceasing my visits entirely. Really, I find your sulking strange." Since he said these things so blithely and unfeelingly, I felt repulsed.

The next morning, he says, "As there are things I simply must attend to . . . ; I'll come soon either tomorrow or the day after." I do not think it is really true, yet it is natural for me to hope he might have a change of heart—the thought occurs to me—*what if this were to be the last time I would ever see him*—then, little by little, the number of days he does not come increases. So it is coming to pass as I thought; I become even sadder than ever.

I continued to sink deeper into a depression; all I could think about was if only I could die as my heart desired, but when I think about my only child, I get very sad. If only he would grow up and I could leave him in the care of some dependable wife, then I could die in peace, but failing that, how bereft he would be; thinking about that, it seems very difficult to die. When I said to him one day, "How would it be, if I were to take the tonsure and try separating myself from the suffering of this world," even though he is still not capable of deeply understanding things, he began to sob piteously. "If you were to do that, I would surely become a monk myself. How could I involve myself in the affairs of the world after that?" And as he broke out sobbing again, I too could no longer hold back my tears, but in the midst of our misery, I tried to make a joke out of it. "Well then, if you became a monk, how could you possibly manage without your hawks," at which he got up quietly, ran to his tethered hawks, untied them all, and let them go. Even the attendants looking on couldn't help crying, and I was sad the whole day long. This is just how I felt:

arasoheba	Quarrel between us
omohi ni waburu	miserable, I would become
ama gumo ni	a nun, yet how sad,
madzu soru taka no	first to see his hawks soaring
kanashikarikeru	to the sky, he to shave his head.

At the end of the day, a letter appeared from my husband. As I thought that it was full of nothing but boldfaced lies, I sent back, "I'm not feeling very well at the moment."

As it is a day or two after the tenth of the seventh month, everyone is busy with preparations for the celebration of Obon. Up until now, the offerings for my mother's spirit have been done at my husband's household office; since we had grown apart, I wondered if he might not do it this year—ah—it would be something that would sadden my mother's spirit as well. I waited awhile to see what would happen, thinking to myself, I may have to arrange for the Maigre Feast myself. I spent my days

'Not regretting to die but sad. . . .' – An allusion to Tsurayuki's poem with the two alternate endings that was on her mind when she was ill at the beginning of book two (pp. 174–75). *Zenshū* commentators suggest the ending she intended to have remembered here was, "not knowing whither my lover's heart will go" (*Zenshū*, 236).

Ōmi – This woman is assumed to be the daughter of Fujiwara Kuniaki, at one time in his career governor of Ōmi, hence her name. She is then yet another member of the provincial governor's class, like Michitsuna's Mother and Kaneie's other wife, Tokihime. She was put into service with Kaneie's uncle, Saneyori, when Saneyori was seventy. After Saneyori died, it seems Kaneie did begin an affair with her. A couple of years later she bore Kaneie a daughter, Suishi, who eventually was made consort to Emperor Sanjō. From humble beginnings then, Ōmi was able through this liaison with Kaneie to rise to a high position as mother of an emperor's consort.

one of the late emperor's daughters – Some sixteen years later, historical chronicles record a brief marriage between Kaneie and Emperor Murakami's third daughter, Princess Hōshi. She was then at the advanced age of thirty-nine. It is conceivable casual relations between them might have begun at this time, but it remains uncertain.

Ishiyama Temple – On the shore of Lake Biwa in the opposite direction from Karasaki. This temple too was a popular site of pilgrimage for women in the Heian period.

my own sister – Presumably the same sister who was with her at the beginning of book two.

I run out of the house – Something of her distress can be read in the verb, "run out." This also would seem to indicate that she left for this pilgrimage on foot. Going on foot was considered more meritorious for a pilgrimage. Furthermore, she seems to decide on the spur of the moment, and arranging for a carriage would take time and could not be done secretly as is her wish. Her mention several times later on of her physical discomfort also seems to indicate she was on foot.

catch up with me – There is no word for "me" or "us" in the original text. In this period, women of her status were hardly ever alone completely, so it is hard to imagine her without a companion. It seems likely she slipped out with only her closest female attendants, and then a number of the other household servants, probably male, were dispatched to catch up with her once she was missed.

I am not even afraid – This is an indication of the degree of her agitation.

Awatayama – The road is the same one she took to Karasaki at least as far as Lake Biwa, so the same place-names appear.

Yamashina – Another place along the road to Ōtsu.

with tears trickling down, but as usual, he took care of the provisions and sent them along with a letter. I wrote this and sent it back with the messenger. "You have not forgotten the person who passed away . . . 'Not regretting to die but sad. . . .'"

The more I think about this situation the stranger it seems. I have not heard that he has shifted his affections to a new woman, but suddenly just as I was thinking about this, I hear from someone who knows of my affairs, "There are the serving ladies of his late uncle, the minister of the Ono Palace; he has likely become infatuated with one of them. There is one woman, Ōmi, who has apparently been acting strangely, and it seems she is a rather licentious woman. He wouldn't want her to know that he visits here, so he has probably cut off relations here in preparation for winning her." Another person listening to this, says, "For heaven's sake, he didn't have to do that. If she is really as easy a woman as one hears, why should he have to go to all the trouble of scheming like that?" So went the conversation. Someone else suggested "If it is not Ōmi, then it is one of the late emperor's daughters." And so on, it might be this one, it might be that one; it is just so very strange. I am urged by my attendants, "It is as though all you can do is stare helplessly at the setting sun. Why not go off on a pilgrimage somewhere?" It's true, these days, I can think of nothing else: in the morning, I talk about it; at night, I grieve about it. Yes, if that is the way it is, even though this is the season of terrible heat, isn't it true, I can't just stay as I am; I make up my mind to go to Ishiyama Temple around the tenth of the month.

As I intend to go secretly, I don't even let my own sister know, and, gathering my courage, I run out of the house just at the time I thought it might be growing light. But around the area of the Kamo River—how they found out about it, I don't know—some people from the household catch up with me. Even though it is quite bright by the light of the remaining moon at dawn, we meet not another soul. On the riverbank, I am told and can see that there are corpses lying around, but I am not even afraid. When we have gone as far as Awatayama, I am in such discomfort, we stop to rest for a bit. I don't understand what is happening to me; tears just pour down. When I think someone might be coming, I compose my tearful face as though nothing has happened, and we just keep going at a run.

At Yamashina, it becomes completely light; I feel very exposed and hardly know myself. Since my attendants, having placed themselves ahead and behind, are walking along with a hangdog air, the people we meet coming toward us or walking alongside us think us suspicious and noisily whisper to one another; how wretched it makes me feel.

Finally, we get as far as Running Well, where it is suggested we have our box lunches. They set up a curtain; we have just started eating,

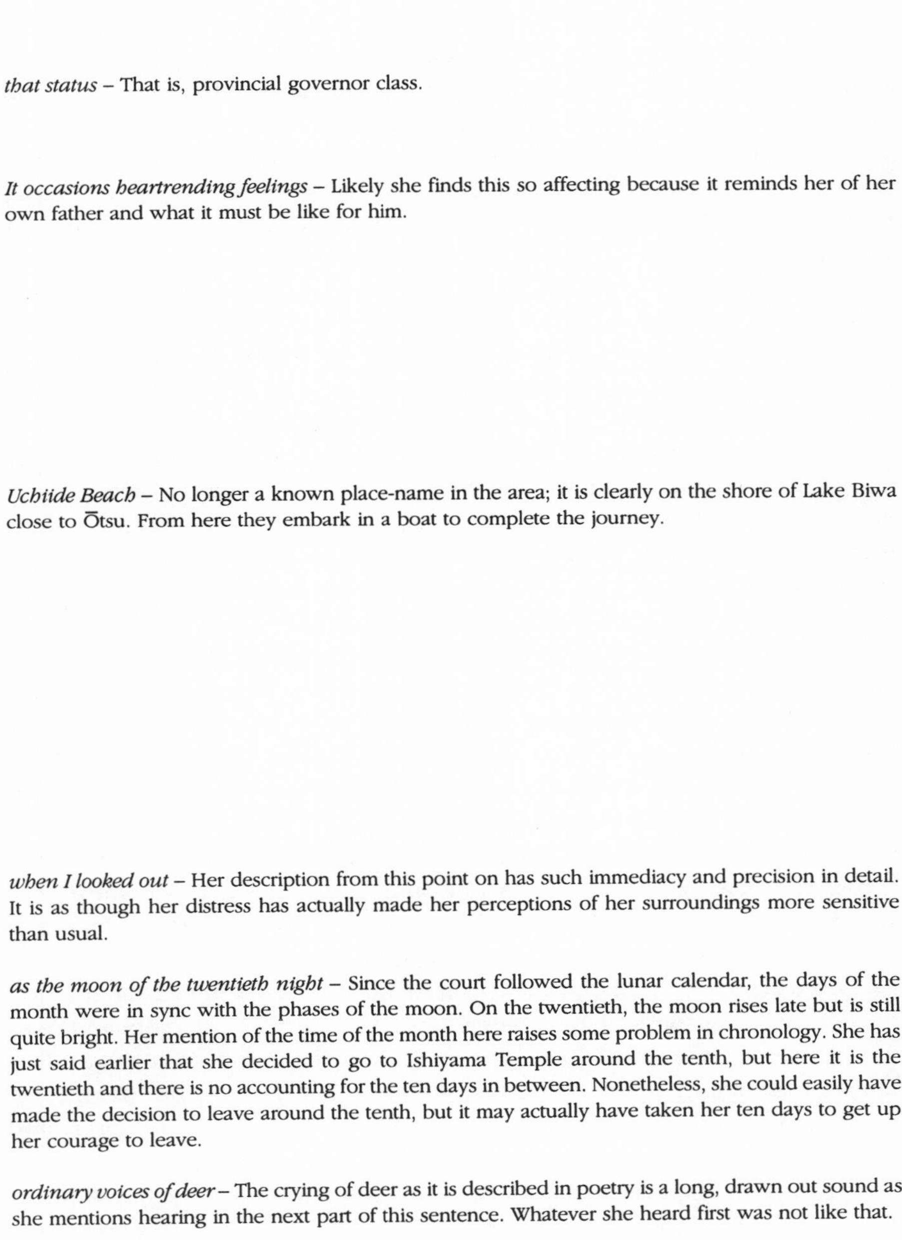

that status – That is, provincial governor class.

It occasions heartrending feelings – Likely she finds this so affecting because it reminds her of her own father and what it must be like for him.

Uchiide Beach – No longer a known place-name in the area; it is clearly on the shore of Lake Biwa close to Ōtsu. From here they embark in a boat to complete the journey.

when I looked out – Her description from this point on has such immediacy and precision in detail. It is as though her distress has actually made her perceptions of her surroundings more sensitive than usual.

as the moon of the twentieth night – Since the court followed the lunar calendar, the days of the month were in sync with the phases of the moon. On the twentieth, the moon rises late but is still quite bright. Her mention of the time of the month here raises some problem in chronology. She has just said earlier that she decided to go to Ishiyama Temple around the tenth, but here it is the twentieth and there is no accounting for the ten days in between. Nonetheless, she could easily have made the decision to leave around the tenth, but it may actually have taken her ten days to get up her courage to leave.

ordinary voices of deer – The crying of deer as it is described in poetry is a long, drawn out sound as she mentions hearing in the next part of this sentence. Whatever she heard first was not like that.

when some outriders come up making an alarming amount of noise. *What are we to do? Who might this be? If any of their attendants were to recognize any of my attendants, how awful it would be.* Just as I was thinking that, a large number of mounted guardsmen with a caravan of two or three carriages came up, making a big commotion. Someone says, "It's the carriage of the governor of Wakasa." They pass by without stopping and I feel relieved. *How poignant,* I think to myself, *just like someone of that status to drive along with great pride and abandon, while, back in the capital, morning to dusk, he has been bowing and scraping. Just so, he would drive along with a great commotion the moment he is out of the city limits.* It occasions heartrending feelings. Some straggling lower-ranking servants from that procession, such as those assigned to leading the oxen and some others, come close to my curtain and begin to noisily wash themselves. I find their behavior so rude, it is outrageous. Finally, when one of my attendants says, "Hey, stand back from there," the servants respond with, "Don't you know, everybody coming and going stops here. Who are you to scold us?" Watching this exchange, how could I ever describe my feelings.

After that procession had passed by, we set off ourselves and passed the checkpoint. I arrived at Uchiide Beach in a half-dead state. The people who had gone on ahead had fashioned out of some reeds a kind of roof for a boat. Barely conscious, I crawled into the boat, and now we set out rowing to cover a vast distance. As for my state of mind, I felt so awfully sad, so anguished, so wretched, it was unmatched by anything I had ever experienced before.

Around early evening, we arrived at the temple. As a bed had been prepared in our lodgings, I went to lie down. Not knowing what to do, feeling such anguish, I cry as I lay there tossing and turning. Night fell; I washed with some warm water and went up to the temple hall. Even though I try to speak of my condition to the Buddha, I am so choked with tears that I cannot get the words out. Night deepened further; when I looked out from the hall, I could see that the hall was up high and there was a ravine below. There were trees growing thickly on one side of the ravine; it was very dark with trees but as the moon of the twentieth night grew bright with the deepening of the night, here and there, where the moonlight filtered between the trees, I could see the path by which I had come all the way. When I looked down, at the bottom of the ravine, I could see a pond shining like a mirror. When I leaned against the balustrade and looked very closely, on one of the slopes in the grass, there were some dimly white creatures rustling about making strange cries. "What is that?" I asked and was told, "That is the deer talking." Just when I was wondering why their crying did not seem like the ordinary voices of deer,

my innards – In the original, it is literally that she feels her liver is being crushed.

looked just like a picture – Again a reference to the kinds of scenes depicted on screens.

to spare him from the eyes of others, I had left behind the one for whom I care more than any other – She thinks of Michitsuna. Perhaps there are mares and foals in the scene before her, and that is why she thinks of her son. Or the horses may recall for her the colt imagery that she and her husband used to speak of Michitsuna in their exchange of long poems so many years ago, when Michitsuna was a small child. Since she had left in such a distraught state and without many attendants, it would have been embarrassing for Michitsuna to have been dragged along.

that bond – The original word, *hodashi*, meant a hobble for a horse, which fits with the imagery of horses, but the word came to mean more generally the bonds that keep us in this world.

Sukuna Valley – The lower reaches of the Seta River, which is not far from Ishiyama Temple. The legend of the valley swallowing up people does not seem to have been recorded elsewhere.

shibuki – Obviously some kind of edible green, but it is not known to what vegetable it corresponds today.

yuzu – A small sour orange with very little juice but a divine aroma. It is still a distinctive feature of cooking in the Kyoto area.

spoke all there was to say – It seems necessary to verbalize one's troubles to the Buddha before one can expect help.

chōshi – A long-handled metal ladle used for pouring sake in a ceremonial way.

big court slipper – Ceremonial shoes that had turned up toes (see illustration on p. 213).

A monk who lighted the votive lights for me – This monk was probably assigned to assist the devotions of the pilgrim. It seems that in the process he has become good friends with her attendants.

from a ravine a little distance away came the sound of very young voices crying faintly in a drawn out sort of way. Were I to describe my feeling listening to them, to say I was spellbound goes too far. I was absorbed in the service, yet still in a kind of daze, when, from the other side of the hill across from this building, my ears were struck by the indescribably cruel voices of farmers chasing some beasts out of the fields. All these impressions coming together, I felt often as though my innards were being crushed; in the end, I was left feeling blank. The evening service over, I went back down. As I was feeling very weak, I remained in my room.

When I looked out at it becoming dawn, there was a lovely gentle breeze from the east; with the mist rising, the other side of the river looked just like a picture. I could see far away on the other river bank some pastured horses foraging for food. It was so very moving. Since, in order to spare him from the eyes of others, I had left behind the one for whom I care more than any other, I thought, *now having gotten away from it all, I would like to devise a way to die here*, but then the first thing that came to mind was that bond and feeling the love; I was sad. I cried every tear there was to cry. One of the men among my attendants says, "It is quite close to here. Let's go have a look at Sukuna Valley." Someone else says, "They say the entrance to that valley draws you in and you never get out. It's a dangerous place." Hearing things like this, I thought, *without even intending it, if only I could be drawn in and swallowed up*.

As one thing after another had exhausted me, I had not been able to eat anything. Someone said, "You know there is some *shibuki* growing in the pond out back." "Collect some and bring it in," I said, and so it was brought. It was arranged in a dish with slices of *yuzu* for garnish; I found it delightful.

Then evening fell. In the great hall, I spoke all there was to say; my tears cleared away. Just as the dawn is about to break, I doze off and see the head monk of this temple put water in a *chōshi* and bring it to pour on my right knee. That is what I saw. I woke up with a start, *this must have been something the Buddha has shown me*, so I think, and all the more I feel awed and sad.

When someone said, "It is dawn," I came quickly down from the hall. Though it was still very dark, the surface of the lake spread out whitely—*yes, yes*, I say to myself, *we have to go*. When I looked down I saw that the boat our party of about twenty people was going to board appeared about the size of a big court slipper; somehow, there was a strange poignancy to it. A monk who lighted the votive lights for me was standing on the bank to see us off; with each dip of the oars bearing us away, he looked more forlorn. He seemed to have thought it sad to stay behind at this place where he had gotten to know us, at least that is how

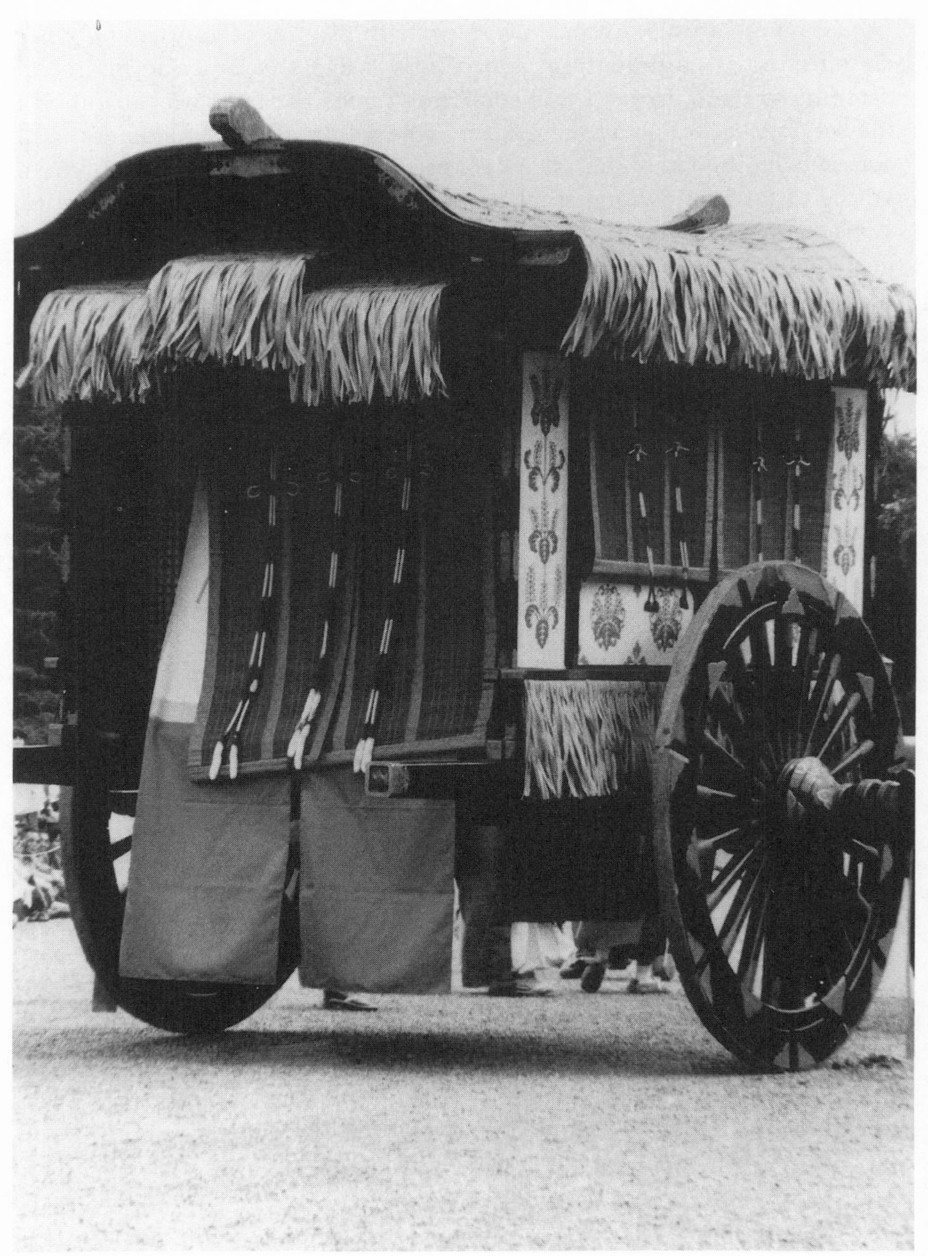

Ox-drawn carriage (close up). Note the bamboo blinds that allowed riders in the carriage to see out but not be seen. See pp. 215 and 371, where the author describes seeing her husband, Kaneie, in a carriage with another woman.

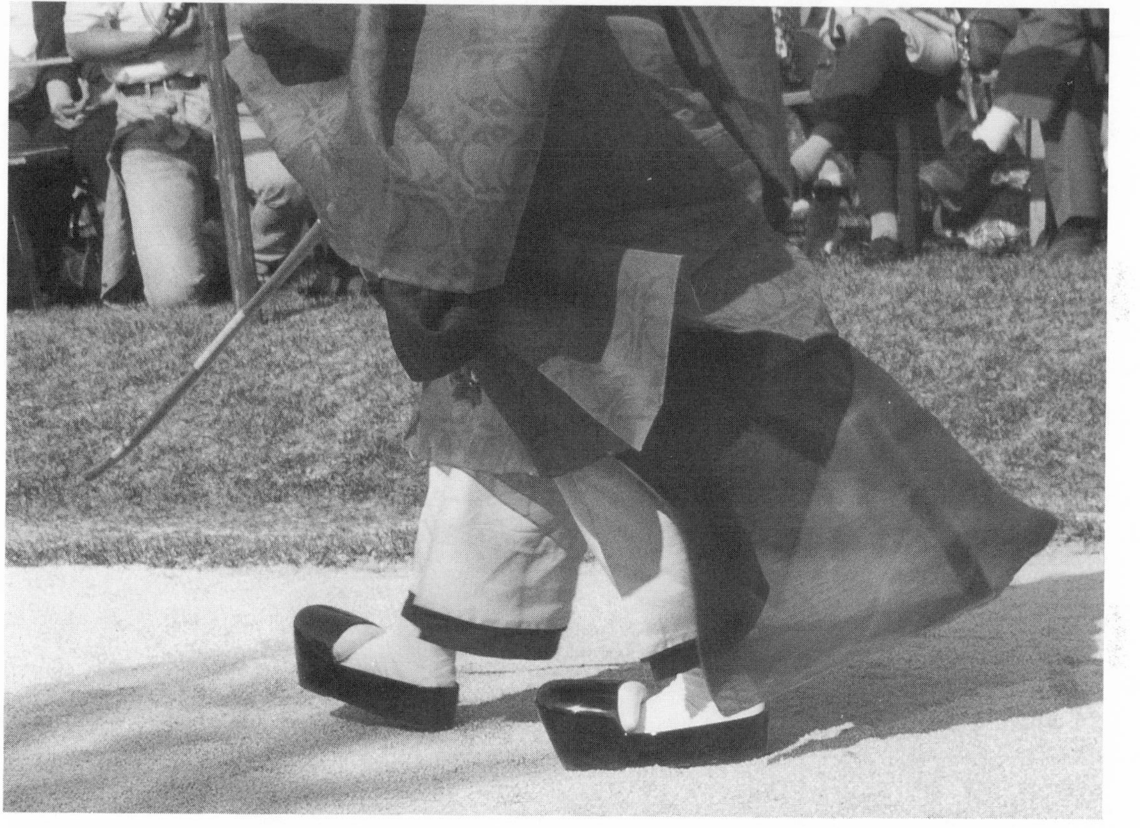

Court slippers. Michitsuna's Mother describes the boat they took from Ishiyama Temple as looking like a "big court slipper" (p. 211). See also p. 210.

Ikaga Point . . . Yamabuki Point – Place-names famous in poetry but now of uncertain location.

The voice sounded so poignant to me – It is touching because the people have come to meet them.

carriage that had come to meet us – For the return, it appears that arrangements have been made for an ox carriage (see illustration on p. 212).

Grand Sumo Tournament – The tradition of holding sumo wrestling matches at court was already a long one. The most important tournament of the year was usually held toward the end of the seventh month.

he looked to me. One of my men called out, "We'll come for sure next year in the seventh month." "Let it be so," he replied; as we drew farther away, he became like a shadow; that too was sad.

Looking up at the sky, the moon was very slender and its reflection was mirrored on the surface of the lake. A breeze sprang up and busied the surface of the lake; with a whispering sound the ripples stirred. Hearing one of my young men sing out the song with the line, "Your voice is weak, and your face so pale," the tears fell drop by drop. Gazing out over Ikaga Point and then Yamabuki Point, we rowed in among the reeds. Around the time when things still weren't clearly visible, in the distance there was the sound of oars of a boat coming this way with people singing in a rather forlorn way. Since the boat was going in the opposite direction we ask, "Where are you going?" and they reply, "To Ishiyama, to meet your party." The voice sounded so poignant to me. As it turned out they had been told to come and meet us, but due to their leaving late, we had already left and thus it seemed we were crossing paths. So, we stop and some of our party transfer to their boat, and all go along singing as they like. Just as we approach Seta Bridge, it grows vaguely light. Plovers are soaring high in the sky, crossing paths in their flight. Sights that moved me in a melancholy way like this were without number. At last, we reached the shore, and the carriage that had come to meet us was there. We arrived back in the capital around midmorning. My attendants gathered around. "We thought you had gone to the ends of the earth. What a stir and commotion it has been!" When they said such things, I replied, "Really! You can talk all you want but do you really think I am in a position to actually do something like that?"

The time for the Grand Sumo Tournament at court arrived. As my young one wanted to attend, I had a costume made for him and sent him along. He was to go first to his father's and then ride with him in his carriage; at nightfall, I expected him to come back here with the boy, so when I was informed that he had gone elsewhere, I was more taken aback than ever. The next day, just as the day before, the lad went to court again. My husband paid no attention to him, and at nightfall he left early saying, "I have this and that to attend to at the office, someone see the lad home," and so our son came home alone again. How must he feel? If things were normal between us, the boy and he would return here together; in his young heart, the boy must brood about this. When I see him enter the house looking so crestfallen, I feel awful not being able to do anything about it, but what will have any effect? I feel as though I am being torn to pieces.

In this manner, the eighth month arrived. On the evening of the second, he suddenly appeared. I find this strange. "Tomorrow is a day of

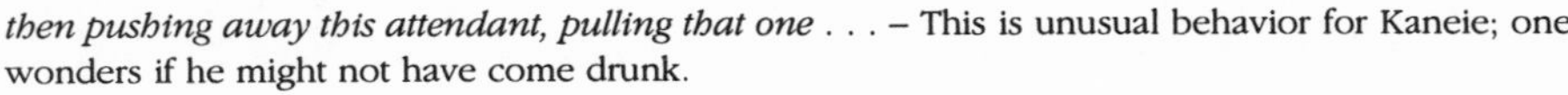

then pushing away this attendant, pulling that one . . . – This is unusual behavior for Kaneie; one wonders if he might not have come drunk.

major captain – More precisely, he has been appointed major captain of the Right Palace Guards.

retired emperor – Emperor Reizei, who just abdicated last year.

Enthronement Rites – The Great Harvest Festival that was celebrated the autumn after a new emperor has been designated. It constituted the official enthronement.

official ceremony of manhood – This was the recognition of the attainment of adulthood and involved the bestowing of the tall black hat worn at court.

Minamoto grand counselor – It is assumed this was Minamoto Kaneakira, elder brother to Takaakira.

forbidden direction – Apparently the author's house was in a forbidden direction for Kaneie that day, but since it is already late, he risked staying put.

Great Purification Ceremony – A preparatory ceremony for the Enthronement Rites. This ceremony was apparently held on the twenty-sixth day of the tenth month.

and some of my household – Likely her sister and a suitable number of attendants.

so close to the Phoenix Carriage – The carriage of the emperor. As a major captain of the Inner Palace Guards, Kaneie is entitled to attend the emperor's carriage closely.

it is quite unsettling – Perhaps it is unsettling because she must worry about whether her son is meeting his father's expectations or not.

change our lad's clothes – Michitsuna has been awarded court rank, the lower fifth rank, which is starting at the low end of the highest echelon. He is now entitled to wear the fifth rank color, which is vermillion.

ritual seclusion, lock the doors tight!" he shouts all over the house. I am startled and feel anger boil up, then pushing away this attendant, pulling that one toward him, whispering in their ears, "We just have to put up with her, don't we," then imitating me in a simpering way, he upsets my attendants. I was quite struck dumb, and, sitting across from him, I must have ended up looking drained and completely beaten. The next day, all day long, he just keeps repeating, "It's not that my heart has changed; it is you who keep seeing everything I do in a bad light." There was no use saying anything.

On the fifth of that month, on the occasion of the autumn promotions, it seems he was promoted to major captain—how lofty he was becoming, how very felicitous an event. Strangely enough, however, after his promotion we do see a little more of him. He says, "I'm thinking of requesting official court rank for our son from the retired emperor for the upcoming Enthronement Rites. We had better hold the official ceremony of manhood. I'm thinking of the nineteenth," and thus he decides. Everything was done according to custom. The Minamoto grand counselor bestowed the court headdress. When the ceremony was over, although this was a forbidden direction for him, on the excuse that it was late at night, he stayed. Nonetheless, in my heart, I couldn't help feeling that our relationship might be coming to an end.

The ninth and tenth months seem to pass in much the same way. In the world at court, there is a stir about the Great Purification Ceremony leading up to the Enthronement Rites. Myself and some of my household are provided viewing seats for the ceremony, and so we go to have a look. There he was, so close to the Phoenix Carriage; while I couldn't forget our painful relations, I feel quite dazzled by his appearance; the people around me say things like, "My . . . how superior he has become." "How splendid he is!" Hearing this, I feel more helpless than ever.

The eleventh month arrived, and although one might have expected him to be very busy with preparation for the Enthronement Rites, I had the feeling that we were seeing him a little more often. Since our son has officially become a man, he comes to train him in the manners of the court even if the boy isn't very interested yet, and when he comes to attend to this, it is quite unsettling. On the day the Enthronement Rites ended, he came quite late at night, saying, "Although I really should have stayed right to the end, as it was getting late, I made a fake excuse about having a pain in my chest and came back here. I wonder what people will say? Tomorrow, let's change our lad's clothes and he and I shall go out together." Saying such things, it felt a little like the old days between us. The next morning, he said, "It seems as though the attendants who should be accompanying me haven't all made it here. I will have to go back to my

there is a man who visits the south apartment – This is the apartment presumably of her sister.

in a place away from my bed – Her mention that she avoided her own bed is a telling detail in this description of her anguish.

residence to get everything arranged properly. Get the lad into his costume and have him come along," and so they departed. As my son went along with him so happily, I was moved with deep joy. Since then, there has been the usual excuses about abstinences.

Hearing that on the twenty-second as well my son is to attend upon his father, I think it might be an occasion for him to visit here; as I wonder, *will it be so*, the night grows painfully late. But the one I have been worrying about appears all alone; I am stunned and feel torn apart. "Father has just now returned home," he says, and as the night grows later still, I wonder, *if his feelings were as they had been in the old days, would something like this have happened*; at this thought, I am wretched. For a while after that, there is not a word from him.

The first day of the last month of the year arrived. During the day on the seventh, he peeked in. As I was embarrassed to have him see me, I pulled a curtain of state between us. Seeing that I seemed out of sorts, he said, "My, the day has grown late. Since I have a summons to be at court. . . ." and left directly. The seventeenth arrived without his having visited again.

Today, from about noon on, the rain pattered down, sadly falling on and on. So much for thoughts of, *I wonder if he'll come. . . . When I think of the old days, it must not have been love, but just his basic lustful nature that brought him to me, not letting wind or rain stop him; now when I think about it, since there was never a time when I felt really secure, my expectations have been exaggerated—ah—to think he wouldn't let wind or rain get in his way, that's no longer something I can expect,* and so I spend the day gazing out, sunk in brooding thoughts.

With the sound of the rain pattering on, it became time to light the lamps. These days, there is a man who visits the south apartment. When I hear his footsteps, I think, *so, he has come. How touching and charming of him to have come on such a night,* and right alongside that feeling comes boiling up a swirl of emotion; when I speak out, one of my attendants who has known me for years, faces me and says, "It is sad, in the old days, even rain and wind worse than this would not have kept him away." The moment she says this, I feel hot tears rolling down:

omohi seku	I stifle these thoughts
mune no homura ha	but the flames in my breast
tsurenakute	do not appear,
namida wo wakasu	they just go ahead
mono ni zarikeru	and boil up these tears.

repeating this over and over to myself, I stayed up all night in a place away from my bed.

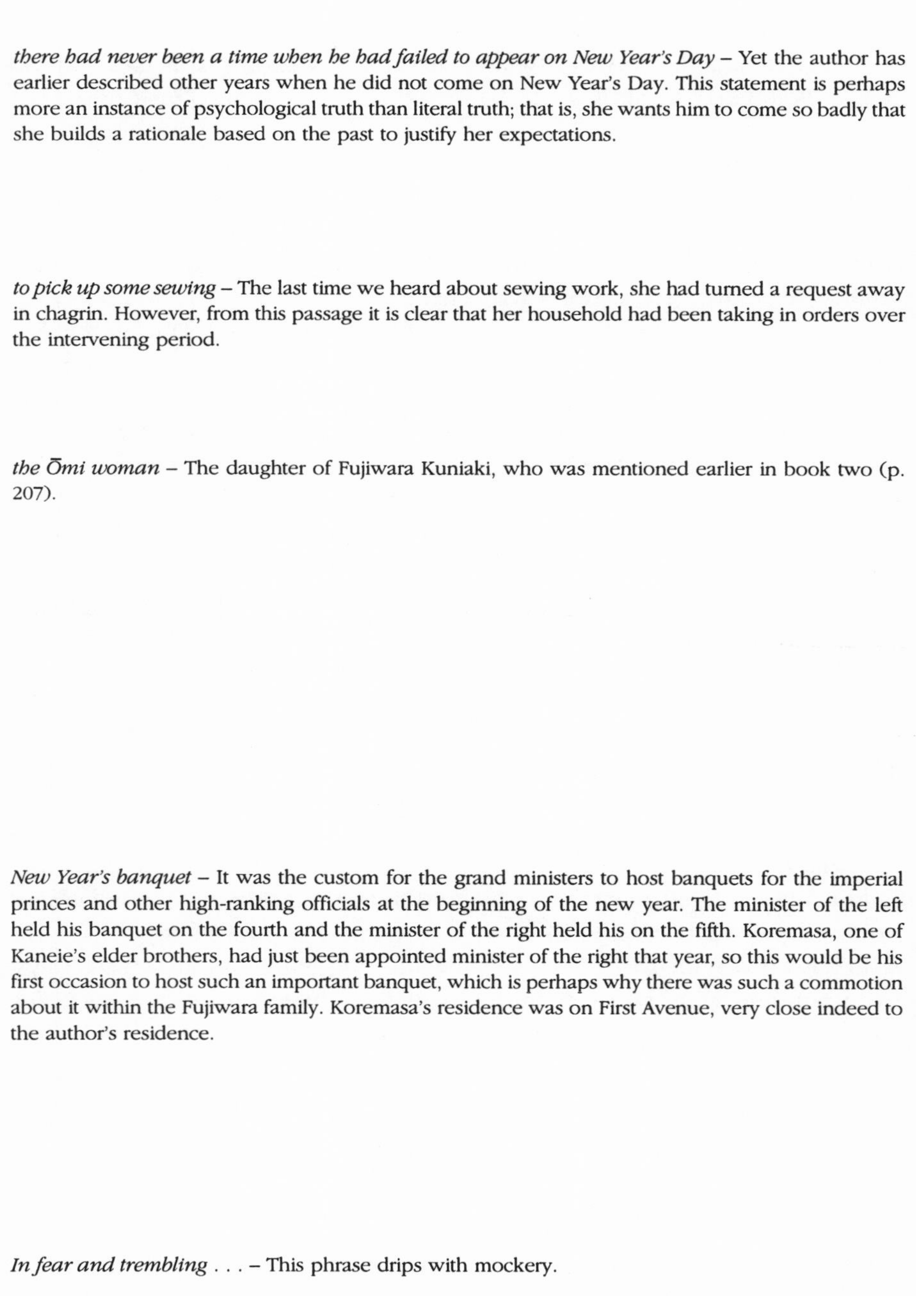

we crossed into another year – The second year of Tenroku, 971, seventeenth year of her marriage.

there had never been a time when he had failed to appear on New Year's Day – Yet the author has earlier described other years when he did not come on New Year's Day. This statement is perhaps more an instance of psychological truth than literal truth; that is, she wants him to come so badly that she builds a rationale based on the past to justify her expectations.

to pick up some sewing – The last time we heard about sewing work, she had turned a request away in chagrin. However, from this passage it is clear that her household had been taking in orders over the intervening period.

the Ōmi woman – The daughter of Fujiwara Kuniaki, who was mentioned earlier in book two (p. 207).

New Year's banquet – It was the custom for the grand ministers to host banquets for the imperial princes and other high-ranking officials at the beginning of the new year. The minister of the left held his banquet on the fourth and the minister of the right held his on the fifth. Koremasa, one of Kaneie's elder brothers, had just been appointed minister of the right that year, so this would be his first occasion to host such an important banquet, which is perhaps why there was such a commotion about it within the Fujiwara family. Koremasa's residence was on First Avenue, very close indeed to the author's residence.

In fear and trembling . . . – This phrase drips with mockery.

That month, with his only coming as many as three times, we crossed into another year. As the observances of the season were no different than usual, I do not record them.

Now thinking back over the years, no matter what was going on, there had never been a time when he had failed to appear on New Year's Day. Thinking it must happen, I prepared myself for a visit. Around midafternoon, there was the noise of his outrunners clearing the way. Just as my attendants were bustling about getting ready, unexpectedly, the procession passed us by. Making the best of it, I thought he must simply have some urgent business to attend to before coming, yet, with no sign of him, night fell. The next morning, in a letter sent with a servant dispatched to pick up some sewing, there was this, "I did pass by your house yesterday but then it grew late, so . . ." Although I hardly felt like replying to that, someone said, "It's New Year's, don't start the new year by getting angry." So I wrote only a slightly sullen reply. In the course of speaking about my uneasy feelings to my attendants, I heard that he was exchanging letters with the Ōmi woman whom we had suspected before. So that must be what was afoot, and that it was being bruited about as a rumor was a source of chagrin. The second and the third day passed. On the fourth, in the late afternoon, again there was the noise of his procession approaching, even louder than the other day. "His lordship is arriving, his lordship is arriving," the call was passed continuously around the house. I could not help thinking, *if the same thing occurs as the other day, it will be unbearable*; nevertheless, my own heart began to pound in anticipation. As he drew nearer, my servants pushed open the middle gate and stood waiting kneeling respectfully, but it was all to no avail; the procession drew by us. I would have you imagine how much worse I felt today than even the time before.

Then, on another day, there is a commotion about the New Year's banquet. As it is being held so close to here, I think to myself without anyone knowing, *even though things are the way they are, I'll just see if he shows up tonight.* The sound of every carriage rumbling by crushes my breast. At a good hour, not too late, one can hear the sound of everyone returning. So many carriages are driven directly by my gate; every time I hear a carriage pass by, my heart feels a jolt. When finally I listen to what must be the last one, I feel numb to everything. Early the next morning, since he seemed unable to let things be, a letter arrives from him. I do not reply.

Then again about two days later, this arrived from him, "I know I've been neglecting you lately, but it really has been a very busy time for me. How would it be if I were to come over tonight. In fear and trembling, I await this opportunity to attend upon you." I had word sent, "Since she

like a rock or a tree – Kaneie used this simile in the long poem he addressed to her many years ago (p. 97). She seems to use the phrase to imply that she rejected his advances.

"everything is brought to life anew except for me" – Allusion to poem 28 of *Kokinshū,* which she cites at the end of book one:

> With the singing of
> a myriad birds in spring
> everything is
> brought to life anew except
> for me who alone grows old.

he had visited for three nights in a row the place we had heard about – This refers to the lady known as Ōmi. Visits for three nights in a row constitute a marriage.

why not even let that happen – Veiled reference to becoming a nun.

sister's impending delivery – From this mention we learn that not only does the younger sister have a visiting husband, but she is about to bear a child from the union.

Kure bamboo – A kind of bamboo associated with longevity. Shinozuka reminds us that it was last spring around this time that Michitsuna was experiencing his triumphs as an archer and dancer. Being reminded of that happier time by this note from a friend must have served by contrast to make her feel even sadder (Shinozuka, *Kagerō nikki kokoro to hyōgen*, 358).

is not feeling well at the moment, she is unable to reply," and just when I had given up all hope of seeing him, he appeared looking as though nothing were wrong at all. I was quite dumbfounded; he teased me so openly, I found it most annoying. When I told him what had been on my mind for these many months, his attitude was one of "What's wrong with you?" and making no reply at all, he pretended to fall asleep. He was listening while asleep; then he feigned awakening with a start, and laughingly said, "Well, shall we go to bed early?" Even though it got to the point where he seemed to feel abashed, I spent the whole night like a rock or a tree, and early in the morning he left without saying a thing.

After that, he made an effort to act as though everything were normal, sending over work to do with a note like this, "I know you have your reasons for being out of sorts. I would like this work done in this way. . . ." I found it provoking and said so, turning the work away; thus our communication ceased all together until past the twentieth of the month. Amid the spring scenery, which inspired the old poem, "everything is brought to life anew except for me," as I listened to the voice of the warbler, there was not a time when tears did not well up. The tenth day of the second month arrived. Rumors that he had visited for three nights in a row the place we had heard about were as numerous as blades of grass. As the equinox approached, time weighed heavily on my hands. Thinking that rather than just continuing as I was, it would be better to perform a fast and go to a monastery, I started the preparations. When I had the mattress and the mats of the bed chamber cleaned and changed, seeing the dust raised in the cleaning, I thought to myself wretchedly, *I never dreamed it would come to this*:

uchiharafu	Shaking out bedding,
chiri nomi tsumoru	where the dust has just been
samushiro mo	piling up, I think
nageku kazu ni ha	even the dust motes are no more
shikaji to zo omofu	numerous than my sorrows.

The moment I made up my mind to start a fast as soon as possible and retreat to a mountain temple, the thought arises, *yes, why not even let that happen, how easy it would be for people to lose touch with me, and I could turn my back on the world, couldn't I.* But my attendants say things like, "For fasting, autumn would be so much better." Not only that but I really cannot avoid having some concern for my sister's impending delivery, so I shall wait until the next month.

Anyway, just when I had completely lost interest in everything in this world, a friend from whom in the spring of last year I had begged a clump of Kure bamboo, sent word, "I have the bamboo for you." I sent

I won't be long in this world – This could refer to either her leaving the secular world to become a nun or her wishing to die.

Saint Gyōgi – A legendary monk of the eighth century.

toward the realm of no more thoughts – Since the wind blew from the east, the bamboo stalks are leaning toward the west, which makes her think of Amida Buddha's Western Paradise, the Pure Land. Thus, while she is sad to see the bamboo blown over, she takes comfort from the direction of their falling.

"the mountains of no thoughts" – The phrase, *omohanu yama*, "mountains of no thoughts," means the same as "mountains of no suffering." It is an allusion to the following poem from the *Gosenshū*:

> There are other seasons—
> when the full bloom of the cherry
> is too painful,
> would that I could go into
> the mountains of no thoughts. (Katagiri, *Gosen wakashū*, 24)

observing a directional taboo – From time to time in the yin-yang cosmology upon which the Heian calendar was based certain directions would become forbidden and one would have to spend a period of time at another residence.

residence of my father – In book one she mentions a residence of her father in the area of Fourth Avenue, and it may be this residence.

the long fast I intended to go on – This would be in preparation for going on the retreat to a temple that she had spoken of at the beginning of the year.

"Not even seeing the moon . . . strange" – Allusion to a poem from the collection of the early Heian poet, Ono no Komachi:

> So strangely,
> my heart is difficult
> to console,
> not seeing even the moon
> over Abandoned Crone mountain. (*Zenshū*, 255)

Since the word for moon can also mean month, the allusion can be seen as a complaint about not having seen him for months.

back, "I'm sorry, but I rather think I won't be long in this world, so how could I indulge in such a frivolous activity." To which she replied, "You take too shortsighted a view of things. Did not Saint Gyōgi plant fruit trees by the side of the road for the sake of generations to come?" And she sent the bamboo all the same. Thinking, *let sympathetic people come later and say, "Ah, this is where she once lived,"* with tears pouring down, I had them planted. Two days afterward, it rained heavily, and a wind blew fiercely from the east. One or two stalks leaned over; wanting very much to right them, as I long for a break in the rain, I composed:

nabiku kana	Leaning over—
omohanu kata ni	toward the realm of no more thoughts,
kuretake no	the Kure bamboo
ukiyo no suwe ha	points to this painful world's end,
kaku koso arikere	thus it shall be for us all.

Today, the twenty-fourth, the rain pattering down gently is very moving. In the evening, there is an ever so rare letter from him. Among other things, it says, "Not feeling brave enough to face your frightening countenance, the days have passed." I leave it unanswered.

The twenty-fifth, the rain still hasn't let up; time heavy on my hands, I feel sensitive to things, as in the mood of the old poem, "the mountains of no thoughts." Thinking about these things, tears are the only thing of which there is no end:

furu ame no	Falling along with
ashi to mo otsuru	the patter of falling rain
namida kana	are these tears—
komaka ni mono wo	as they splinter finely
omohi kudakeba	these restless painful thoughts.

Now, it was the end of the third month. Time weighs heavily on my hands, and thinking to take the opportunity of observing a directional taboo to spend some time elsewhere, I move to the residence of my father, who is away on duty in the provinces. As the birth about which I was worried had taken place smoothly, I was just thinking again about the long fast I intended to go on, attending to a lot of things in preparation for it, when this arrived from him. "It may be supposed you consider my crimes even heavier than before. Nonetheless, if you could forgive me, I would like to come tonight. How about it?" My attendants seeing this letter, raised such a din, "You are just going to end up estranging him completely, and that would be a bad thing to do. At least this one time, please send a reply. You simply must do it." So I sent just this, "Not even seeing the moon . . . strange." Though I never expected it to happen, he

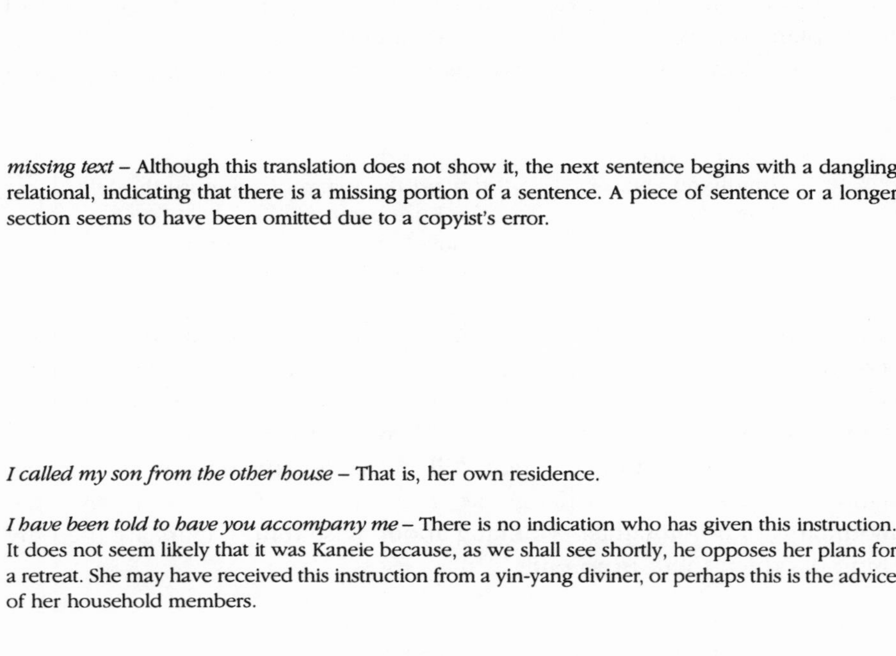

missing text – Although this translation does not show it, the next sentence begins with a dangling relational, indicating that there is a missing portion of a sentence. A piece of sentence or a longer section seems to have been omitted due to a copyist's error.

I called my son from the other house – That is, her own residence.

I have been told to have you accompany me – There is no indication who has given this instruction. It does not seem likely that it was Kaneie because, as we shall see shortly, he opposes her plans for a retreat. She may have received this instruction from a yin-yang diviner, or perhaps this is the advice of her household members.

at that time there was hardly a woman without a rosary . . . – This remark gives us a glimpse into the relationship between women and religious practice in the Heian period. One can imagine how, given the uncertainty of marriage for women, they might turn to religion for solace. In her younger days, it seems that the author had considered women's infatuation with religion itself to have been a cause of their estrangement from their husbands, but now she finds herself in the same situation.

came over promptly. With total disregard for the time of day, he showed up at my father's place when it was already late at night. There was the usual whirl of many emotions for me, but added to that, this was such a cramped place, milling with people, that I felt I could barely breathe, and pressing my hands to my chest, I stayed awake until dawn. Early in the morning, saying, "There is this and that affair, I must attend to," he rushed away. Though I knew better, I found myself wondering, *Will he come today? Will he come today?* and so the fourth month arrived without another word from him.

[A portion of the text appears to be missing here.]

This place is so close to his residence, there are even some attendants who, unable to relax, say things like, "His lordship's carriage is readied at the gate. Doesn't it look as though he's coming here?" It is most painful. More than ever before, I feel as though my heart is being torn to pieces. Even the people urging me to make replies to inquiries oppress and distress me.

On the first day of the fourth month, I called my son from the other house, "I am to start a long fast. I have been told to have you accompany me." Saying this, I began. From the first, I had not intended to have my devotions be an elaborate thing; I just burned some incense in an earthenware container, placed it on top of an armrest, and, leaning over it, intoned prayers to the Buddha. The sense of my prayers was just this: *I have become a person of no happiness. Thinking how miserable it was that over the years my heart has never known any peace and now it has come to this awful turn in our marriage, please let me quickly perfect my practice and achieve enlightenment.* Performing my devotions in this manner, the tears trickled down. Ah, I remember one time when I heard that at that time there was hardly a woman without a rosary dangling from her wrist and a sutra in her hand, I had said, "What a miserable sight they must be; that sort of woman is bound to lose her husband"; now where had it gone, that desire to criticize. From dawn to dusk, with unsettled heart, not letting up for a minute, even though I had no sense of getting anywhere, I poured myself into the practice. Ah, but the thought came again and again—*how strange I must look to people who had heard me condemn other women in the same situation, "And when she had such a fragile marriage herself, how could she say such things."* There was not a time when that thought came to mind that the tears did not well up. Before the eyes of others, I felt so ashamed to present such a miserable appearance; I passed each day from dawn till dusk constantly repressing tears.

hair cut short and parted at the forehead – That is in the style of a nun. Heian women wore their hair very long, and even when they took the tonsure, they did not normally shave their heads completely but left their hair in a short bob.

I record them here so that – It is always intriguing when the author lets us in on her reasons for recording specific events in her life. For one thing, it clearly indicates that she intended her diary to be read by others. The image of the snake inside her eating her liver is powerful, yet most readers would likely agree that we are in no better situation to judge the meaning of her dreams than she was.

put up the iris decorations – As has come up earlier in the diary, it was the custom on the Tango Festival, held on the fifth day of the fifth month, to festoon the eaves of a house with iris roots and leaves to ward off disease and misfortune in the hot summer months ahead.

I no longer distinguish things, don't know what to do with irises – Pun on *ayame*, "the pattern, principles of things" and "iris."

in between my devotions – From this we know that she has continued her religious practice back at home.

I was obstructed by what you people said – Her attendants had dissuaded her earlier that year from going on retreat at a mountain temple.

just 'slip this under the gate' – During a period of ritual seclusion, one was not supposed to have direct communication with others even by letter.

On about the twentieth day of my practice, in a dream, I see myself with my hair cut short and parted at the forehead. I know not whether it bodes well or ill. About seven or eight days later, I dream that there is a snake moving around inside me eating my liver, and to cure this I have to splash water on my face. I have no idea whether this dream too bodes well or ill, but I record them here so that people who might see how I ended up may judge whether these dreams were sent from the Buddha or not.

The fifth month arrived. From the people who had stayed behind at my residence came this, "Even though you are not here, it would seem to invite misfortune not to put up the iris decorations. How would you have us proceed." Indeed, thinking to myself, *what further misfortune is there to invite?*

yo no naka ni	Am I still someone
aru waga mi ka ha	in this world? Having reached
wabinureba	such a wretched state,
sara ni ayame mo	I no longer distinguish things,
shirarezarikeri	don't know what to do with irises.

was what I would like to send, but since there is no one who would understand, I pass the time keeping my heart to myself.

In this way, when the period of directional taboo is over, I move back to my usual residence, where time lays even heavier on my hands. As it is the rainy season, the plants grow into a tangle; in between my devotions, I have the clumps dug up and divided.

There was one day when that constantly upsetting person passed by my gate making the usual ostentatious fuss in clearing the way. I was in the midst of my devotions when my servants raised a great tumult with "His lordship arrives, his lordship arrives." Thinking to myself, *as usual, he will probably not stop*; still my heart went thump thump within my breast. When he indeed passed on by, my attendants all looked one another in the face. I myself was unable to say anything for three or four hours. One of my attendants said, "How strange. What can his lordship be thinking of?" and even broke into tears. I managed to pull myself together a little, "It is awfully humiliating, but is it not because I was obstructed by what you people said that we are still residing in this place and thus subjected to this sort of affront?" This was all I said, but words could not express the searing pain I felt in my chest.

On the first of the sixth month, a messenger delivers a letter from him, saying, "Although his lordship is observing a period of ritual seclusion, he would like to just 'slip this under the gate.'" Thinking this both strange and unexpected, when I looked, this was what it was: "Your period of

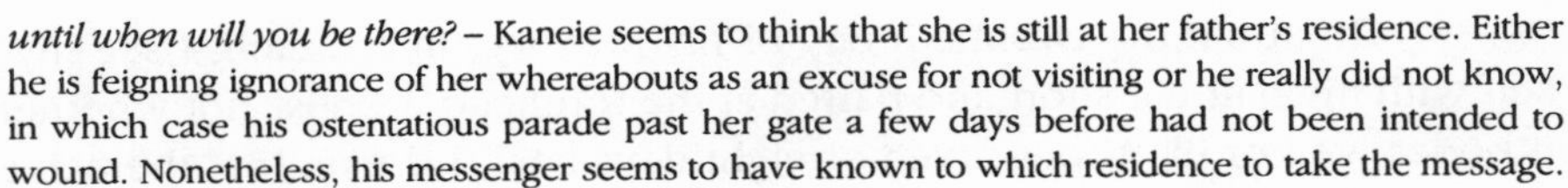

until when will you be there? – Kaneie seems to think that she is still at her father's residence. Either he is feigning ignorance of her whereabouts as an excuse for not visiting or he really did not know, in which case his ostentatious parade past her gate a few days before had not been intended to wound. Nonetheless, his messenger seems to have known to which residence to take the message.

monastery in the Western Hills – We find out later that this is Hannya Temple in the Narutaki district of northwest Kyoto.

no place for this nor haven for my heart – Pun on *okamu kata*, "place where one could put something" and "place where one could confer one's heart."

'since I am still the same me' – Line from a poem in the *Fujiwara Tadafumi Collection*. It is actually a poem sent by a woman to Fujiwara Tadafumi. The woman has gone on a retreat to Ishiyama Temple and is reproaching him for not visiting:

> Wherever I go,
> since I will be the same me,
> even if I dwell
> in mountains shrouded in clouds,
> you will never visit me.

Fujiwara Tadafumi would still have been alive at the time of these events recounted by the author. Therefore, this is another example of her alluding to contemporary poetry (Uemura, *Taisei*, vol. 5, 176–77).

This season is not really a convenient one – By the solar calendar, this is already July, the hottest time of the year.

directional taboo must be over by now; until when will you be there? That residence is a rather inconvenient place so I have not visited. As for my planned pilgrimage, I met with a defilement and canceled it." Thinking it highly unlikely that he had not heard by now that I was back here, I am more depressed than ever, but controlling myself, I write a reply, "How rare a thing to hear from you, I hardly recognized who it was from at first. We have been back here for quite some time now, but indeed, how could you have known? Anyway, there have been so many times, when in your manner of passing, one could never have guessed this was a place you used to visit. But, no doubt this is all due to my having tarried in the world till now. I shall say no more."

Then, brooding every time I recalled these things, I felt uncomfortable. Thinking it very likely that I would be subjected to the same humiliation as before, I decided that I simply must get away for awhile. There was that monastery in the Western Hills where I usually went; it is to there I would repair. Telling myself it would be best to do it before his present period of ritual confinement was over, I left on the fourth day of the sixth month.

Since this was the very day I suspected that his period of ritual confinement would be lifted, my mind was all in a flutter. Packing up things for the departure, under the quilt, they found some medicine wrapped up in folded paper that he used to take every morning; it had been here all the time we were away. Finding it the attendants cried out, "What might this be?" Taking it just as it was, I wrote in the folds of the paper:

samushiro no	Having given up
shita matsu koto mo	waiting under the quilts
taenureba	with any sense of hope,
okamu kata dani	sad now there is no place for
naki zo kanashiki	this nor haven for my heart.

Then in the accompanying letter, I said, "As it says in the poem, 'since I am still the same me,' yet thinking there must be some realm where I would not be subjected to your passing by my gate, today I seek that place. I am sure this too will strike you as a strange tale that you did not ask to hear." I sent this with my young son who was going, as he said, "to inform father that I shall be on retreat for a while." After telling him, "If he asks after me, say, 'She left immediately after writing this and I am to follow right afterward,' then come back," I had him bear the message.

Being struck by the sight of my letter, he must have felt the agitation of my heart; his reply was this, "I know you have a lot of reasons for being upset, but you might at least let me know where you are planning to go. This season is not really a convenient one for devotions; just this

How alarming . . . – This is the first time in a long time that Kaneie has answered with a poem. She has succeeded in getting his attention. He picks up the bedding image in her poem and launches into sea imagery by pivoting on the pun *toko*, "bed," which is also a place-name *toko no ura*, "Toko Bay."

One might wonder why he finds her departure for a retreat so upsetting. He has been occupied elsewhere, ignoring her and chagrined by her ill temper; why does he not just let her go and even become a nun if that's what she wants? As we shall see in the succeeding pages, he seems genuinely alarmed by her departure and actually goes to some lengths to get her back. It is hard to know whether he does this because of an abiding affection that persists despite his chagrin, or her leaving him is too great a wound to his pride and reputation. Perhaps, as so often with human beings, it is a bit of both.

the two of us traveled this road together – She and Kaneie had come to this temple in the summer of 962 (book one, p. 107).

"flowers have only one season" – From *Kokinshū* no. 1016:

In the autumn fields
blooming so vigorously,
the Maiden Flowers,
such a struggle to be seen,
flowers have only one season.

When my period arrives – Menstruation was considered a defilement, so she would not be able to stay at the temple. Having left so impetuously and seemingly distraught, she appears oddly self-possessed as she considers this note. Her servant's agitation seems to inspire calm in her.

one time, I would like you to listen to me— do not go! I will be over right away as there is something I want to discuss with you:

asamashiya	How alarming!
nodoka ni tanomu	This bed on which I relied
toko no ura wo	so serenely
ura kaheshikeru	has been overturned by waves,
nami no kokoro yo	your heart storms Connubial Bay.

Most distressing!"

When I saw this, I departed with even greater haste.

The mountain path was not anything particular to speak about—*ah—I can only think of the times in the past when just the two of us traveled this road together; there was that time when I was ill, we were here around three or four days; yes, it was around this time of the year; he didn't even go to serve at court, together we were hidden from the world*; thinking about this and other things, I go along the long path, tears pouring down. I am accompanied by only three attendants.

I get down first at the monastery's living quarters; when I look around, I see some peonies surrounded by a brushwood fence among some other luxuriantly growing plants whose name I know not; they are in such a pitiful state, their petals all fallen and scattered; the old poem, "flowers have only one season," comes to mind, and repeating it to myself, I become very sad.

Just as I was about to bathe in preparation for going up to the main hall, a messenger from home came running up all flustered. It was a letter from those who had stayed behind. It said:

> Just now someone bearing a letter from his lordship arrived. Conveying his master's words, he said, "It seems my lady is planning to leave for somewhere. As a first measure, you are to go and stop the departure. His lordship will come here shortly himself." When he had finished, we told him the situation here, "Her ladyship has already left. Her attendants are just now following after her." He said, "What can she be thinking of? His lordship seemed so worried, what am I to tell him?" As we described the situation in recent months, how you had been performing a fast and so on we broke into tears, and he said, "Anyway, the first thing I must do is inform his lordship directly." Thus, no doubt you will be hearing from his lordship. Please prepare yourself.

Seeing what was written there, I thought to myself, Oh dear, they have foolishly exaggerated everything, how annoying. When my period arrives

standing in his carriage – It turns out that he is still in ritual seclusion. As long as he stays in his carriage, he will not be breaking the ritual taboo.

a block of stone stairs – One *chō,* or about 130 meters.

they only say things that might weaken my spirit – It seems her attendants are siding with Kaneie and Michitsuna.

And I'm not coming back here again! – Michitsuna's opposition to the retreat and his sympathy with his father become clear. He has changed considerably from the year before, when he let his hawks go as a sign he would accompany his mother into monastic orders.

tomorrow or the day after, I am going to have to leave the monastery anyway; reflecting on this, I bathed quickly and went up to the hall.

Since it is hot, I push open the doors for awhile; looking out I could see that the hall stands in quite a high place. The monastery is in a kind of pocket with hills surrounding it; the thickness of the trees is fascinating, but as this is still the time of no moon, just now, it is very dark. Since the first service of the night was to begin, monks were gathering in a hurry; with the doors pushed open, I began to chant when, as in the style of mountain temples, a conch shell was blown four times to announce the hour.

From the direction of the main gate came the sound of loud voices, "His lordship arrives, his lordship arrives." Quickly letting down the blinds that had been raised, I looked out and saw between the trees the lights of two or three torches. When my young son rushed out to attend to things, he found his father standing in his carriage, "I have come to fetch your mother. As I am still in ritual seclusion due to a defilement until today, I cannot get down. A carriage will have to be brought up somewhere around here." When my son related this to me, I was shaken. I sent back to begin with, "What can you be thinking of to behave so strangely? I have only come here thinking to stay one night. For you to come here when you are still in ritual seclusion, really, there can be no reason for it. The night is growing late. Please return home quickly." But after that, many exchanges went back and forth. As my son had to climb up and down about a block of stone stairs every time, he got tired and it was very painful for him. Everyone feels sorry for him, "How sad for him" and such; they only say things that might weaken my spirit. My son tells me, "Father is very angry. He says, 'This is all your fault. You haven't said anything to her to make her change her mind.'" And then he cries tears on top of tears. Nonetheless, I ended it with, "What do you think, that I would go now?" "All right, all right, as I am still under ritual seclusion, it is not as though I can stay here. It can't be helped. Hitch up the carriage." When I heard that I felt so relieved. My son, who had been running back and forth, said, "I will see father home. I'll ride on the back of his carriage. And I'm not coming back here again!" Breaking into tears once more, he left. He being the one I counted on, I felt this was an awful thing for him to say but I said nothing, and it seemed as though everyone had departed. But then he came back, sobbing as he told me, "Although I told father I wanted to see him home, he said, 'You will come when I call you' and left." I felt how painful this was for him but tried to console him by saying such things as, "How silly. This is not something that will lead to your father abandoning you." By that time, it was about two hours past midnight. The road back to the

fewer attendants than he usually has – In his haste, he probably was not able to put together a proper guard. The streets late at night in Kyoto had their dangers, and her servants express their worry for his safety with this comment.

young lord – This is the first time the author refers to her son by his official court title. Last year, at the age of fifteen, in tandem with his "coming of age" ceremony, he had been promoted to the fifth rank, for which the general title was *taifu*. The fifth rank was a major dividing line among the Heian aristocracy. This rank brought entitlements of income-producing fields, servants, cloth, and other goods (McCullough and McCullough, *A Tale of Flowering Fortunes*, 829). All the better positions in government were open to those of the fifth rank and above. To be able to start one's career at the fifth rank, as Michitsuna does, gives him an advantage in the fierce competition for high positions at court. However, the fifth rank was not itself a office with duties; the rank simply qualified him to be chosen for a office when a suitable one became available.

From this point forward, except for one isolated instance, the author will always refer to Michitsuna by his title. This shift in naming subtly reflects her recognition of him as an adult. His resistance to her the other night and his identification with his father seem to have brought about this change in her perception.

"So strange and unexpected . . . I shall return very soon" – In contrast to her dogged resistance of the night before, this note is remarkably conciliatory. She even states an intention to return soon. It is as though she has begun to think that his coming to get her was out of affection and that perhaps there is a way for them to become close again. Yet, this reaction from him was won by her withdrawal from contact. Withholding is her only weapon in this struggle of wills. So although this note seems to indicate she is not opposed to going back home, it will be very difficult for her to actually do so.

Sitting with the blinds rolled up – It must be a strange feeling for her to be so exposed in an unfamiliar place.

"hito ku, hito ku" - Recalls a humorous poem from *Kokinshū,* no. 1011:

> I came here only
> to gaze on the plum blossoms
> but still the wood thrush
> laments hitoku hitoku
> a man has come man has come (Rodd, *Kokinshū,* 348)

Uguisu may be translated either as the bush warbler or wood thrush.

as everyone in the city was talking about how I had become a nun – The gossip of the people in the city becomes a barrier to returning home.

my aunt – Presumably this is the same aunt that shared her sorrow over the death of her mother.

fireflies seem to glow with a startling brilliance – This phrase calls up a poem anthologized in the *Kokin rokujō*:

> The night deepens,
> the love I have waited for,
> now he comes and
> is it fireflies that glow
> so much they startle us? (*Zenshū,* 266)

As Uemura remarks, if she intends to allude to this poem, it is very ironic (*Taisei*, vol. 5, 289).

capital was very long. Various people sympathized with him, "Since he left the capital in such a hurry, he had many fewer attendants than he usually has when he travels around the city." With people saying such things, it grew light.

Since there was business to be attended to in the capital, a servant was dispatched. The young lord said, "I am still worried about father's return last night. I am going to pay a call at his residence to inquire after him," and since he was going there anyway, I sent this letter with him. "So strange and unexpected was your arrival, and then noticing how late it was getting, all I could do was pray for the Buddha to see you safely home. Anyway, I hope you understand I was confused as to what you were really feeling, and I was so terribly embarrassed myself that I found it very difficult to return just at that moment," and so on, explaining in detail, and adding in the margin, "As I came up to this monastery, I thought all the way along, this was a path you had seen in the old days, too, and overwhelming feelings of nostalgia came over me; it seems I shall return very soon." This I sent attached to a branch of pine that had some moss stuck to it.

When I saw the dawn, there was something like mist or a cloud hanging over the scene; I passed the time sunk in melancholy. Around noon, the one who had gone out returned. He said, "As for your letter, father was not in so I left it with his attendants." Even had that not been the case, I thought it unlikely that there would be a reply.

So now, all day I spend in the usual devotions; at night, I pray before the main Buddha. As there are only mountains around this monastery, even during the day, one need not worry about being seen by other people. Sitting with the blinds rolled up, I hear a late season warbler on a withered tree crying and crying, "*hito ku, hito ku,*" "people come, people come." It cries so urgently, I feel I should drop the blinds, so little am I in a sound state of mind.

Before long, as my period did arrive, I thought to leave the monastery, but as everyone in the city was talking about how I had become a nun, I thought I would feel very awkward going home, so I just removed to some lodgings apart from here.

From the city, my aunt came for a visit. I told her, "This is a strange place to live. I can't seem to settle down," and so on. Five or six days passed and the peak of the sixth month arrived.

Tree shadows in the moonlight are very moving. When I look into the darkness in the shadow of the hills, the fireflies seem to glow with a startling brilliance. Back at home in the old days when I was not so weighed down with sorrow, I used to get annoyed when I couldn't hear the "voice

"voice one will not hear twice" – Another phrase for which there is a poetic antecedent, this time a poem by Lady Ise in the *Gosenshū* anthology:

> You will not hear it twice
> the voice of the cuckoo bird
> the night deepens,
> I lie awake lest I
> miss its precious song. (Katagiri, *Gosen wakashū,* 55.)

waterrails – A kind of bird that makes a sound like knocking on a door.

thinking of him – Her son, Michitsuna.

pine needle diet – This is a hyperbole for a strict vegetarian diet.

shrine to the gods . . . priests intoning the sutras – Religion of the Heian period is known for being eclectic. In this case, it seems that Buddhist sutras were being chanted at a Shinto shrine.

My young one – Here is the last time she reverts to calling the young lord, her "young one," and it is notable that it occurs at a time when she is feeling the weight of responsibility for him.

not being in the world at all – That is, if she were to die.

such a move would probably be criticized – The impulse for and circumstances of becoming a nun greatly affected people's view of the act. When, as in the author's case, it could be interpreted as an antisocial act, not only an abandonment of her responsibilities as a parent but also a slap in the face to her husband, it would receive society's condemnation (see the introduction, pp. 24–25).

one will not hear twice." Here the cuckoo birds sing all over the place to their hearts' content. And the waterrails tap out their song; one would think they were right at the door. This is a dwelling where melancholy thoughts are all the more intense.

Since no one has forced me to do this, even if people do not come to visit and offer assistance, I would not dream of thinking ill of them and feel calm; yet, I brood on the fact that my decision to come to such a dwelling as this must be the result of past karma, and, along with that, what makes me really sad is thinking of him who has for many days been accompanying me on this fast. Even though he looks poorly, as there is no one else I can rely on, I am now refusing to let him poke his head out and having him exist on the same pine needle diet I have chosen for myself. Every time I watch him eating this food with difficulty, tears pour down all the more.

Living this way, my heart is calm, yet it is painful to be so easily moved to tears. The voices signaling the end of the day, the cries of the evening cicadas, the little bells in small monasteries around here calling "me too, me too" as though competing with each other, and, as there is a shrine to the gods on the hill in front of here, the voices of the priests intoning the sutras—listening to all this, I cannot help sinking deep into my thoughts. Since it is my period, I have nothing to do day and night, so I sit on the veranda, just gazing out and brooding. My young one says, "Get inside, get inside." And from his expression it looks to me as though he does not want me to dwell on my sorrows so much. "Why do you say that?" I ask him. "It's just bad, that's all. Besides, I want to sleep." "The only thing I want to do is disappear, but my concern for you obstructs me and thus I live on; what am I to do? I would become a nun as everyone is talking about. At least if I were to do that, it would be better than not being in the world at all. It would not be that worrisome to you; you would be able to visit me often enough; I would ask you to still care for your poor mother. Living like this seems right; that is how I feel about it for myself; it is just that, having only this poor food to offer you, it is terrible to watch you growing so painfully thin. If I were to become a nun, I am sure your father in the capital would still look after you. Yet making such a move would probably be criticized, I think of doing this, doing that . . ." When I say this, he says nothing in reply but just sobs aloud.

Then, as I was once more ritually clean in about five days, I went again up to the main hall. My aunt who had been visiting for a few days returned that day. As I stood lost in thought watching her carriage draw away, the more it went into the shadow of the trees, the more bereft I felt. While I was standing and staring, seeing her off, I became dizzy and felt

a priest who was in seclusion here – By the way she refers to him, it does not seem to be one of the resident monks but rather a visitor.

I had quite freely painted pictures of scenes like this – There are several places in the diary where she mentions painting pictures. Painting, along with calligraphy, was one of the many arts cultivated as a part of daily life by Heian aristocrats. It is particularly interesting, however, that she had chosen as a subject for illustration a woman withdrawn for solitary devotions to a mountain temple. At this point it should be mentioned that this passage is rather obscure in meaning and seems to have a number of places where the text is corrupt. The present translation is based on Shinozuka's gloss. Shinozuka notes that this passage reveals the author's predilection in her youth for romantic tales (*Kagerō nikki kokoro to hyōgen*, 409). Here we see the author wrestling with her attachment to the myth of romance. The picture is seductive: the heroine falls ill, in a lovely mountain setting, and services are said for her; to the chanting of the monk's voices, in a cloud of incense, she passes away just as her wayward lover reaches her side to tell her his life is meaningless without her. In real life it is not so romantic.

my sister from home – The sister who is living in the same house with her. Her aunt has just left. It seems as though the family is doing its best to keep in touch with her, perhaps to forestall her taking the step of becoming a nun.

Since no one had forced me to come here – This is the second time she asserts that her action of coming to the temple is by her own choice (see p. 239). In some sense, she seems to take responsibility for her action.

this person is probably from this place – That is, from her husband's place. It is as though she has been expecting this.

The messenger speaks her piece – Due to the absence of third person pronouns in classical Japanese, the gender of this messenger is not made clear, and commentators have discussed at length whether this messenger was a man or a woman. The final consensus is that it must be a woman, if only because relations between men and women were so circumscribed by protocol, it would be difficult for a man to speak so freely to her.

with you like this – That is, she has neither signaled the end to the relationship by actually becoming a nun nor in any other way made her real intentions known.

awful. As the sick feeling was particularly bad, I called a priest who was in seclusion here and had him perform rituals on my behalf.

In the evening, as I listened with such intensity to the intonement of the services, I thought about how, long ago, I would not have dreamed of something like this happening to me; I felt so forlorn and sad, yet I had quite freely painted pictures of scenes like this and, moved by an excess of feeling, had spoken of such things. Now realizing that my own situation was not one jot different from those weird visions I had had in the past, I felt as though something must have been informing me of what lay ahead by having me speak those things. Just when I was lying there thinking these thoughts, my sister from home, along with someone else, came to call. She crept close to me and first of all said, "Back home, I tried to imagine how you must be feeling here, but now actually having come up into the mountains, I feel it is so much more terrible than I had thought. What kind of place is this for you to live?" and she breaks into tears. Since no one had forced me to come here, I try my best to repress my tears, but I break down. Crying and laughing, we talked of a myriad things the whole night through. The next day, she says, "My companion has some urgent business to attend to, so I must return today, but I will come again sometime later. But really, how much longer can you go on like this?" Saying these things and saying them in such a forlorn way, she slips away.

Since I was feeling all right, I go out as usual to see her off, and as I am just standing there reflecting on things, a great din is raised with cries of, "Someone comes. Someone comes." And someone does arrive. Just as I think, *this person is probably from this place*, the scene grows very lively and feels just like back home in the capital; there are so many handsome servants, so many different costumes assembled and two carriages! Horses and riders are scattered all over the place; what a bustle of activity. Box lunches and the like are plentiful. Offerings for sutra readings, gifts of singlets and cloth are being distributed here and there to the rather impoverished-looking monks. The messenger speaks her piece, "This has all been arranged at the request of his lordship and thus I have come in his place. He had this to say, 'Although I went once myself, in the end, she would not come back. Even if I went again, surely it would be the same. Thinking it might be even worse if I went myself, I decided not to go. You go and pay my respects for me. What on earth do the monks think they are doing teaching her religion?' Really, what sort of person would carry on as you are. If, as everyone is saying, this is the end of your relationship, then I suppose there is really nothing further to say. But with you like this, without your husband saying anything, if you come down and go home, you will appear foolish. On the other hand, suppose he comes for you again sometime soon. Then if you still will not come back, you will

The people in the west of the capital – Who these people might be is unknown.

made me more aware of my misery – There has been a definite shift in mood in this passage. She goes from almost delight in the busy scene so reminiscent of life in the city to desolation after the tongue-lashing of the messenger.

My father – Apparently her father was serving as the governor of Tanba at this time.

by having the servant say such things – Perhaps she is hinting that he may come again to take her back.

strict fasting is observed – These were days in the temple when there was no eating at all after noon.

end up even more of a laughing stock." Thus she spoke with an air of self-importance, and just then, a message arrived, "The people in the west of the capital heard that you were here and said, 'Please, present these things to her.'" There was everything under the sun. My first thought was that for someone whose intention was to bury herself in the deep mountains, these things were somewhat inappropriate, so this actually made me more aware of my misery.

As evening was drawing on, she said, "We must be off. It is not that we can come every day to ask after you. What a worry. This is just awful. Come now, don't you have some idea of when you are going to come back?" To which I replied, "At this very moment, I simply cannot consider returning. If sometime soon it seems that I should return, then I will. After all, it is not as though I have a lot to do here." Having said that, I thought to myself, *whichever way I leave here now, I will look foolish; knowing that to be so, he has probably sent this person to say these things fully expecting me not to come back; at any rate, there is nothing particular for me to do at home*, "I might as well stay here like this for a while," was what I said. "So," she said, "you intend to stay here with no date fixed for return. More than anything else, I feel sorry for our young lord, who you have continuing this meaningless fast," then she breaks into tears again and again. When she goes to her carriage, some of my attendants go out to see her off, whereupon she says to them, "You are all being held responsible for this state of affairs by his lordship. Please, make her listen and have her come back quickly." Thus scattering such remarks around she goes back. This time, what was left behind was a desolation so different from before that everyone was on the verge of tears.

Thus, although one and then another tried to persuade me this way and that, my heart was somehow unmoved. My father, whose word about right or wrong I could not go against, was not in the capital, so I told him how things were in a letter, to which he replied, "Well, it seems all right. You could just stay there quietly for a bit longer and carry on your devotions." Seeing this I was greatly relieved.

I thought my husband might have been trying to cajole me by having the servant say such things, but since he had got so angry and come to see this place and returned, why had he not written to me? If something terrible were to happen to me, would he care, I wondered, and with such thoughts, I felt like withdrawing even deeper into the mountains.

Today is the fifteenth of the month when strict fasting is observed. Strongly urging my son, "Go and eat some fish," I sent him into the city this morning. As I brooded and watched, the sky grew dark, the sound of the wind in the pines rose, thunder cracked and rumbled. *It's going to rain again*, I thought, *how sad and unfortunate it will be if rain should catch*

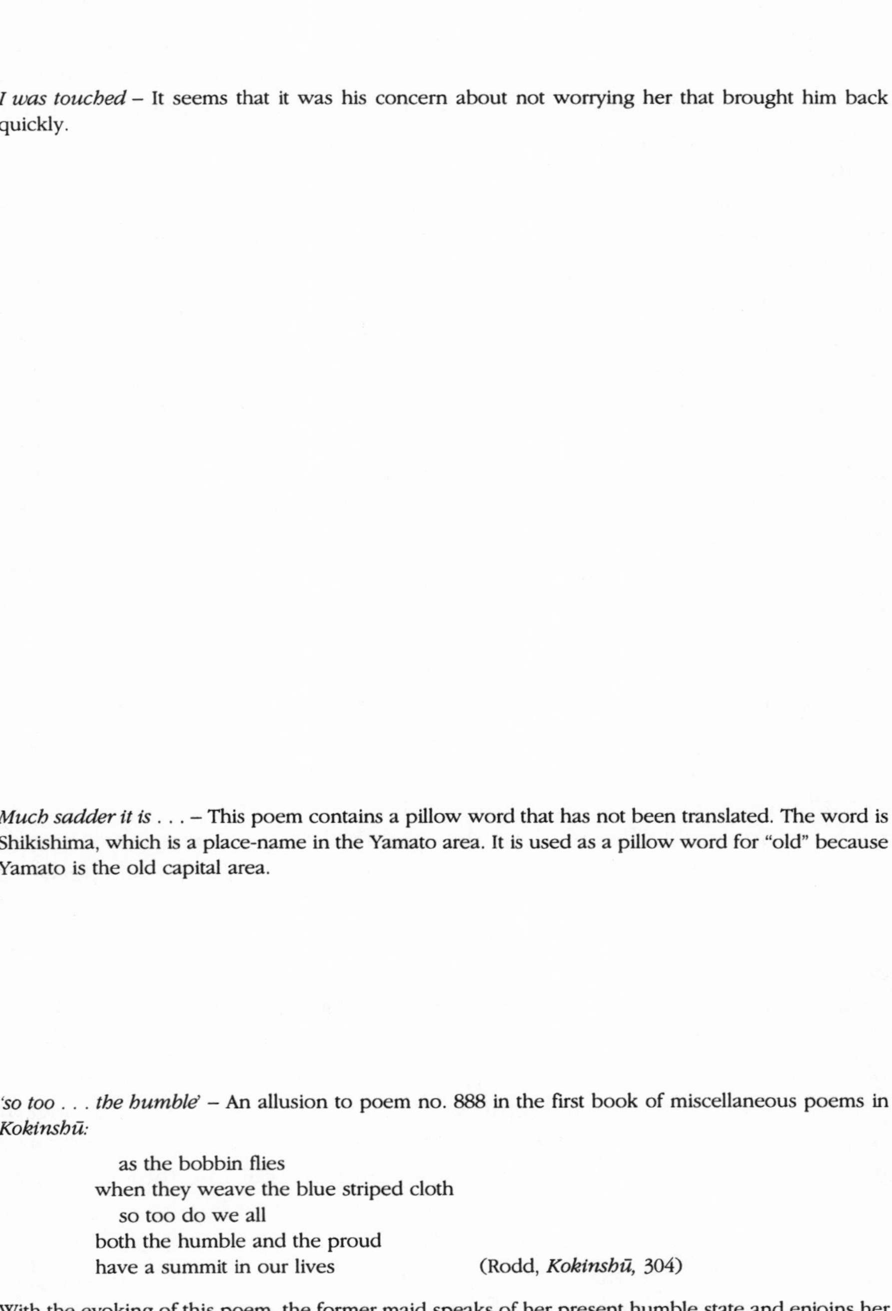

I was touched – It seems that it was his concern about not worrying her that brought him back quickly.

Much sadder it is . . . – This poem contains a pillow word that has not been translated. The word is Shikishima, which is a place-name in the Yamato area. It is used as a pillow word for "old" because Yamato is the old capital area.

'so too . . . the humble' – An allusion to poem no. 888 in the first book of miscellaneous poems in *Kokinshū:*

    as the bobbin flies
when they weave the blue striped cloth
    so too do we all
both the humble and the proud
have a summit in our lives (Rodd, *Kokinshū,* 304)

With the evoking of this poem, the former maid speaks of her present humble state and enjoins her former mistress and her attendants to accept their fate philosophically in the spirit of that poem.

him on the road and the thunder get worse, but—I wonder if it was because I prayed to the Buddha?—the sky cleared, and before long, he returned. "How was it?" I asked; he replied, "I thought it might really pour down, so at the first clap of thunder, I hurried back." Hearing him say this, I was touched. And this time, taking advantage of my son's visit, he had sent a letter. It said, "I returned so taken aback from my last visit, and I suspect that even if I came again and again, it would just be the same. You seem thoroughly disgusted with the world. If, by any chance, there will come a day when you will want to leave the mountains, do let me know. I will come to escort you. Since you seem to be in an alarming state of mind, I do not think it will be soon."

There were also letters from other people. One said, "Do you intend just to stay on there like that? As the days pass, I worry terribly about you," and so on. Various people sent notes of inquiry. The next day, to the one who had written, "Do you intend just to stay on there?" I reply, "I wasn't thinking of staying like this forever, but while I was lost in melancholy meditation, time passed fleetingly and days have piled up":

kakete dani	Not even in my dreams,
omohi ya ha seshi	did I expect to enter
yama fukaku	deep into these mountains
iriahi no kane ni	and accompany the voices of
ne wo sohemu to ha	vesper bells with cries of my own.

The next day, that person responded, "I am at a loss at what to write. That poem about the vesper bells broke my heart":

ifu yori mo	Much sadder it is
kiku zo kanashiki	to hear it than to say it,
shikishima no	as this friend grows old
yo ni furu sato no	awaiting you in your hometown,
hito ya nani nari.	what is there for me to do?

And while I was sunk in melancholy thoughts at the touching sadness of this, there came a letter for one of my attendants from a former maid who, among the many attendants, had usually served night duty. She wrote, "I always appreciated what a fine household we had. I want to let you know how sad I am that such an unexpected fate should have befallen our mistress since I left her service. I wonder how you all are. As it is said in the old poem, 'so too . . . the humble,' there is no way to convey all that I would say to you":

mi o sutete	Leaving the world behind,
uki o mo shiranu	even a traveler who has

'bobbin' – By calling her this, they let her know that they have caught the allusion in her letter.

I shall be scolded again – Michitsuna is in a difficult position in the middle of their quarrel.

our son seems loath to approach you again – She blatantly uses her son for an excuse to cover her own procrastination and to reproach her husband indirectly for ill humor.

what you wrote in the margin of your letter – Since the author has not mentioned what was written in the margin of his letter, this section is inscrutable.

Imperial Tombs – The area to the west of Ninnaji in the hills.

someone who would be considered a distant relative – Again we have no way of knowing who this might be. At any rate, the threat of her becoming a nun seems to have mobilized the whole extended family.

tabi dani mo	not known suffering
yamadji ni fukaku	will sink deeper into sorrow,
omohi koso ire	the deeper into the mountains he goes.

When they brought this out and read it to me, it touched me terribly. It was such a time that even the least little thing like this had a strong effect. I said, "Please give her a quick reply." I heard that they sent this: "And one would think that the 'bobbin' would not have known about this. Upon hearing your letter, even our mistress was so moved, she could not hold back the tears. For us seeing this, you must simply imagine our feelings":

omohi idzuru	When we recall
toki zo kanashiki	former times, we are so sad,
okuyama no	under the trees,
ko no shita tsuyu no	in the deep mountains the dew
itodo shigeki ni	lies all the more heavily.

The young lord said, "How about your answer to father's letter a day ago. If there's no answer, I shall be scolded again; I'll take it myself." "All right," I said and wrote a reply, "I intended to reply promptly to your letter, but for whatever reason, our son seems loath to approach you again. As for when I shall return, since I haven't really decided yet, there is no way I can tell you," and so on I wrote. Then for some reason or other, I added, "As for what you wrote in the margin of your letter, when I think of it, it makes me feel so bad, so I will speak no further of it. Yours." When I had sent him to deliver it, just like the other day, rain fell heavily, thunder crashed, and my chest contracted with worry. Around dark, when it had quieted down a little, he finally returned. How wretched I felt when he said, "It was really quite frightening around the area of the Imperial Tombs." I looked at his return letter, "You seem to be more weak spirited than the other night. I am wondering if you have fatigued yourself with your devotions. I feel sorry for you."

The day after that, someone who would be considered a distant relative came to visit. She brought a lot of prepared food with her. First, she says, "Why have you done this? What do you intend to do? If you don't have a really good reason, then this is a disagreeable thing to have done." To which I reply by telling her in bits and pieces just how I had been feeling and what had happened to me. She ends up saying that she quite understood and breaks into tears herself. Around twilight, with the evening cicada chattering away, saying the sad things one would say on such an occasion, she departs just as the vesper bells are over. Since she is a person of deep feeling, I imagined how truly sad she must have felt as she left. Then what should arrive from her the next day but a load of things that one needs for a long stay away from home. I was deeply moved and

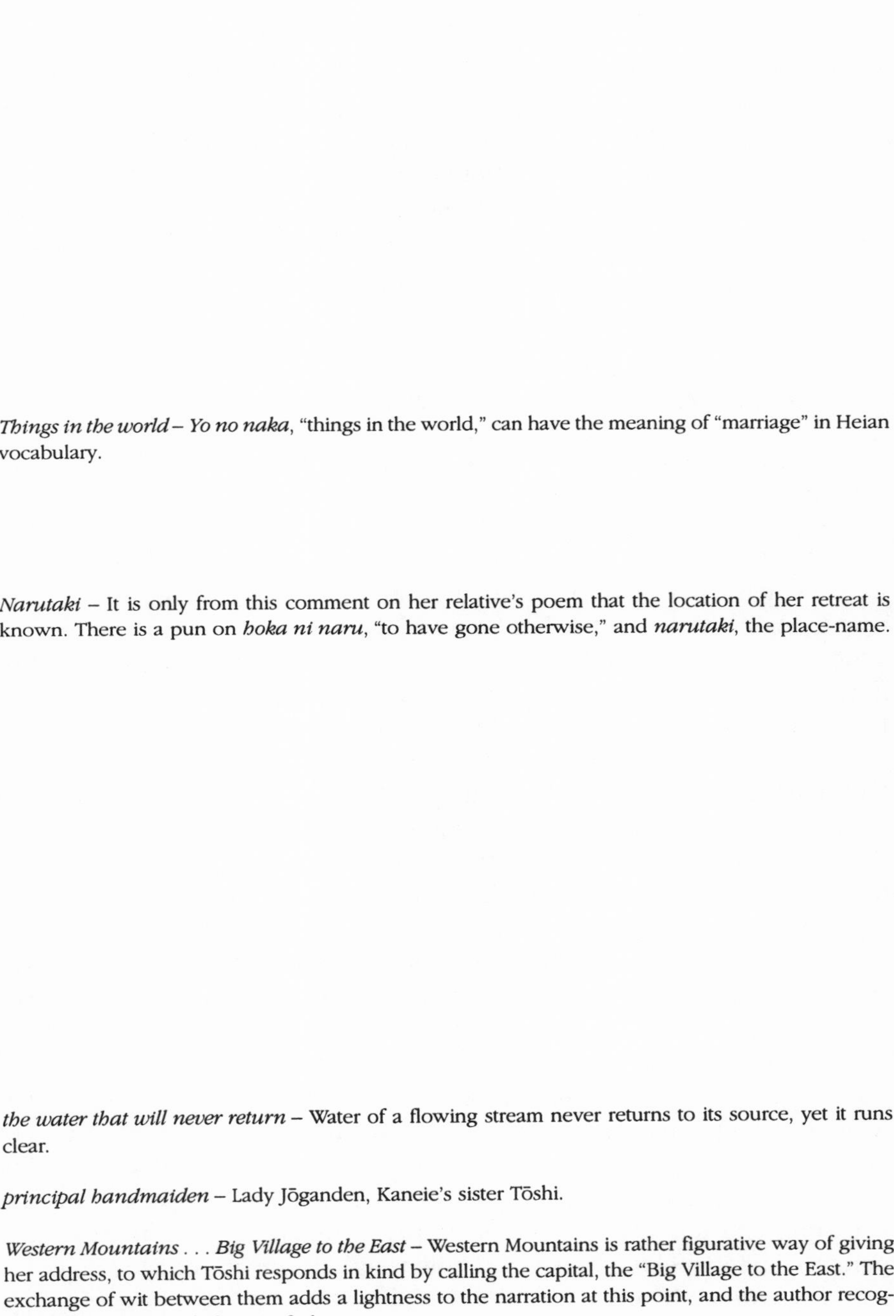

Things in the world – *Yo no naka*, "things in the world," can have the meaning of "marriage" in Heian vocabulary.

Narutaki – It is only from this comment on her relative's poem that the location of her retreat is known. There is a pun on *hoka ni naru*, "to have gone otherwise," and *narutaki*, the place-name.

the water that will never return – Water of a flowing stream never returns to its source, yet it runs clear.

principal handmaiden – Lady Jōganden, Kaneie's sister Tōshi.

Western Mountains . . . Big Village to the East – Western Mountains is rather figurative way of giving her address, to which Tōshi responds in kind by calling the capital, the "Big Village to the East." The exchange of wit between them adds a lightness to the narration at this point, and the author recognizes that it seems a little out of place.

at a loss for words to express it. She wrote many things, and among them this: "I barely noticed anything on the road home. I imagined you as you made your way through the tall trees of the mountain path; how very touching:

yo no naka no	If all things were right
yo no naka naraba	with you and yours in the world,
natsugusa no	I would not have come
shigeki yamabe mo	visiting you on that mountainside
tadzunezaramashi	grown rank with summer grass.

Having to leave you behind, thinking of you on the way home, I could barely see for tears and nearly lost my way. My dear one, you seem driven to distraction with the deep sorrow you bear:

yo no naka wa	Things in the world
omohi no hoka ni	have not gone as one would think,
narutaki no	and gone you have to
fukaki yamadji wo	Narutaki, who taught you
tare shirase kemu	the road through the deep mountains?"

She wrote down every little thing just as though she were talking to me in person. She mentions Narutaki because that is the name of the river that flows in front of here. In my reply as well, I told her all that was in my heart. "I have been thinking a lot about what you asked when you visited here, why am I doing this?

mono wo omohi	When you came to gauge
fukasa kurabe ni	the depth of my sorrowful thoughts,
kite mireba	you did surely see
natsu no shigeri mo	the rank growth of summer's green
mono naranaku ni	was nothing in comparison.

While I still have no idea when I shall return, and while I am troubled when I think about what you said:

mi hitotsu no	All by myself
kaku narutaki wo	thus having come to visit
tadzunureba	this Narutaki,
sara ni kaheranu	I see the water that will
midzu mo sumikeri	never return runs clear too.

Thus, I feel I have a good example to follow."

Then again, in reply to a letter from the principal handmaiden, I wrote and wrote about my worries. Having written on the envelope, "From the Western Mountains," I wondered what she might think about it. On

ascetic practitioner who was about to make a pilgrimage from Mitake to Kumano . . . – These were monks known also as *yamabushi*, "mountain monks," who practiced austerities to acquire spiritual powers. The pilgrimage along the mountain crest trail between Mitake and Kumano was one of their tests of endurance. It was and still is a rough trail requiring mountaineering skills to cross it safely. These mountain monks were a wild and free lot. It seems extraordinary that one of these monks would be moved to write a poem of sympathy to a melancholy aristocratic lady in retreat. If it has not been evident before, it certainly is apparent now that, ironically, her retreat to the mountains has actually resulted in her coming into contact with a wider range of people than she ever would in the capital.

Even in these hills . . . – The mountain monk's poem is full of double entendre. *Toyama* in the first line is a term referring to the mountains close to the capital, but can also mean the "far mountains" into which the monk departs. *Fukaki kokoro*, "deep heart," can mean her heart deep in sorrow or his heart deep in understanding. By "those who know and those who do not know," he is referring to those who know the details of the situation and those, presumably like himself, who do not.

the captain of the Guards – Michitaka, her husband's eldest son.

the captain has feelings toward her that are not ordinary – The plot thickens. Presumably this is the younger sister who just had a child, but now it seems as though Michitaka is a potential suitor for her as well.

"Do you remember meeting me so long ago?" – This was four years ago when Kaneie came to meet her on her way back from the pilgrimage to Hase Temple. He had brought Michitaka along as part of the guard.

you will not end up like this – That is, abandoned in a mountain temple.

the wrong impression – *Zenshū* commentators speculate that the author's meeting Michitaka has produced a complex emotional state, including wonder at the splendid vigor and youth of Michitaka, an awareness of her own aging, and the unfulfilled expectations regarding her relations with her husband (*Zenshū*, 281). However she interprets Michitaka's response to her emotion, it is evident that she does not feel that he understood her.

I would be happy to escort you right away – The real purpose for his visit is revealed.

her return letter, she wrote, "From the Big Village to the East." While I found it most delightful of her, I wondered what possessed us to joke thus.

Engaged with these things, the days passed and I sank even deeper into my own thoughts. An ascetic practitioner who was about to make a pilgrimage from Mitake to Kumano, crossing over the mountain crest trail, dropped this off:

toyama dani	Even in these hills,
kakarikeru wo to	it feels thus, those who know and
shira kumo no	those who do not know
fukaki kokoro ha	feel for your heart deep as the mountains
shiru mo shiranu mo	capped with white clouds where I go.

Thinking over such things as this, the time passed when one day around noon, in the direction of the main gate, there was the whinnying of horses and the sound of a lot of people. Looking out between the trees, here and there, I saw a number of servants, and they seemed to be coming this way. Just as I was thinking, *it looks like the captain of the Guards*, my young lord was called out and came back with this message, "Apologizing several times over for not having inquired of you before now, the captain has come to pay a visit." Reminded of the capital by watching him take his ease in the shade of the trees, I found it a charming scene. Around this time, my sister had come up again as she had said she would, and as it seems the captain has feelings toward her that are not ordinary, he was standing there painfully trying to look his best. I replied, "How happy I am to see you. Please come right up. I shall pray for all your sins to be cleansed." When this message was sent, he walked out of the shade, approached the balustrade, first washed his hands, and then came in.

In the course of talking about many different things, when I asked, "Do you remember meeting me so long ago?" he said, "Why, I remember it very well indeed, even though recently we have not had occasion to see each other." This brought so many things to mind, my speaking was constrained, and feeling my voice faltering, I stopped a moment to pull myself together; he was very moved as well and immediately stopped speaking. Then he said, "Your voice sounded as though you were about to cry, and I understand why, but I didn't want to make you feel even sadder. Certainly you will not end up like this." I thought he must have gotten the wrong impression to speak like that. He went on, "Father told me, 'If you are going to go up there, try and get her to listen to you.'" Whereupon, I said, "Why does he go on like that? Even without his saying that sort of thing, I am going to return soon anyway." He said, "If that's how it is and if it is all the same to you, why not return today? I would be happy to escort you right away. Right from the start I have felt how awful it has

a most regrettable thing for our young master – So much depends on the relationship between her and her husband, most notably her son's career, and though her father does not say it, his own.

"bobbing like a float on a fisherman's line" – She calls up a poem before the storm with this allusion to poem no. 509 in *Kokinshū:*

> Bobbing like a float
> on a fisherman's line in
> the sea of Ise,
> this heart of mine cannot
> settle on one thing alone.

been to see our young lord, when he has made his ever so rare visits into the capital, have to hurry back to this mountain temple as soon as the sun inclined a little." Thus he went on, but as I made no response, he waited a little while and then departed. Thus I agonize over leaving the mountain; deep in my heart I feel that since all the people who might be expected to call have been exhausted, now no one else will visit me.

As time passes in this way, there are letters from this and that person in the capital. I read them, they say, "Today, I hear his lordship is about to come for you. If you don't come down this time, everybody will think you frightful. And it would certainly be unlikely that he would come again. Then, if you were to come back later, how people would laugh." As they were all saying the same thing, it seemed very strange to me; what was I to do? Thinking that this time he will not take no for an answer, my mind was in an uproar when the one I rely on most, my father, having just come back to the capital from a tour of duty, came right away to see me. Telling me what was going on, he said, "I thought it would be all right for you to stay here for a while and continue your devotions, but it has been a most regrettable thing for our young master here. Return as quickly as possible to the capital. If today is as good a day as any, we could go back together. Today or tomorrow, I will escort you." To be spoken to thus in no uncertain terms, my strength left me as I agonized inwardly. He said, "Well then, tomorrow it is," and left.

Just "bobbing like a float on a fisherman's line," my thoughts were all awry; there was a commotion, someone arrived. *It must be him*, I thought, and felt suddenly lost and confused. This time with no reserve at all he marched directly in. Just as he entered, I drew a rather poor screen in front of me; while it hid a bit of me, it was really quite useless. Seeing me there, with a pile of incense alight, a rosary hanging from my hands, and a sutra laid out, he said, "How frightening. I had no idea it was like this. I feel that I can hardly approach you. I have come thinking that you might be ready to leave here, but now, it seems as though it would almost be a sin to move you. How about it, young lord: What do you think about just staying on like this?"

He replied, looking down, "I hate the idea but what's to be done about it?" "How sad," he exclaimed, "If that is how it is, one way or another, it is for you to decide. If she will leave, then let's have the carriage drawn up." Before he had finished saying this, my son leaped up and just began to gather all the things scattered around, wrapping them up, stuffing into bags the things that needed packing and stowing it all away in the carriage. Then he took down the curtains and folded up other things, roughly packing it all away. I sat there dazed, barely aware of who I was. While all this was happening, he looked on, exchanging glances with my

My sister, who had been with me – She has mentioned that her sister was there a few days earlier, but this is the first we are informed that she was at the scene of the forced removal.

since it was dark . . . – It would not be proper for the sister to be seen by Kaneie, but since it is dark, propriety is preserved.

"Would you listen to that . . ." – This is the first time she actually records the contents of Kaneie's jokes. He really is amusing here, and one senses his joke has a kernel of truth; the garden is one of her great attachments and the servants are held accountable for it.

I do not let even the merest hint of a smile show – It is almost as though the author is observing herself from the outside. Somehow through the experience of going on retreat to Narutaki, she has gained some distance from her mental suffering.

"What direction is forbidden to me right now?" – Looking for an escape from a difficult situation and perhaps even sensing that his wife needs a little time to herself, Kaneie consults the cosmological calendar and finds a convenient excuse.

I had never heard anything so absurd – He has never taken her away to a separate residence to observe directional taboos. Moreover, it is the middle of the night and she has just returned from something of an ordeal and a long carriage ride. At any rate, his suggestion here seems more for form's sake than to be taken seriously.

son, seeming very much amused. "Well, since things are done, it seems that you should come away now. Let the Buddha know your intentions. I believe that is the usual custom." Thus he turned the scene into a noisy farce. I was incapable of saying a word; though tears welled up, I held myself together. It seemed to take forever to bring the carriage up. Since he had arrived in the late afternoon, it was now almost time to light the lamps. As I sat there impassively, not moving, he finally said to my son, "All right, all right, I'm going. I leave it up to you." And when he had gone out, my son, on the verge of tears himself, said, "Come on now," and took me by the hand. I left feeling as though it was useless to say anything further; it was as though it was happening to somebody else.

As the carriage pulled out through the main gate, he got in. All the way back, he found all sorts of things to laugh at, whereas I sat wondering if this was a dream, unable to say anything at all. My sister, who had been with me, was riding in the same carriage with us—since it was dark, she thought it would be all right—she responded to his jokes from time to time. Since it was a long way, it was late at night when we arrived. Back in the capital, since someone had informed the household of his going to fetch me that day, they had had the good sense to clean the house and open the gate. Still not feeling quite myself, I got down from the carriage.

As I was not feeling well, I placed a screen of state between us and lay down in a place apart, at which point one of my household servants pops out and comes next to me. "I was going to gather the seeds from the maiden pinks, but they withered up; even the roots are gone. And that black bamboo, one clump fell over, but I had it put to right . . ." and so on. As I feel that this is not really the time for her to be talking about this sort of thing, I make no response, but he, who I had thought might be sleeping, had been listening very carefully to all this, and he calls over to my sister who was just on the other side of the partition. "Would you listen to that. It's quite something. There she is turning her back on the world, leaving her household behind, seeking enlightenment, but just now when you hear her servant talking to her, you'd think the maiden flowers were her own daughters, and the black bamboo's back on its feet, my, my, what worldly concerns." Hearing this, my sister bursts out laughing. I too think it is terribly funny, but I do not let even the merest hint of a smile show.

Thus it went, and it was already half way through the night when he said, "What direction is forbidden for me right now?" and counting the days, unfortunately, my direction just happened to be forbidden. "Well, what shall we do? What a bother. I suppose we could go together to some place near here." When he said this, I made no reply. This was hard to take; I had never heard anything so absurd, I thought as I lay there. Seeing

Please consider breaking your fast – He appears to be concerned that she may be stubbornly continuing her devotions.

six days of his period of abstinence – From his statement on the night that he brought her home from the mountain, it would appear that six days of abstinence normally follow an incident of directional taboo.

just like when a groom didn't show up on the third night – It will be remembered that Heian marriage custom required the groom to show up for three nights in a row in order to make the marriage official. If the groom did not show up for the third night, the marriage was void and the bride and her family lost face.

my mind taken away from my troubles a little – Before Narutaki, similar events to this had left her in despair only wanting to die, but now even the chance visit of a friend is diverting.

principal handmaiden –Kaneie's younger sister, Tōshi or Lady Jōganden, who has already appeared many times in the diary.

'grow ranker' – Allusion to poem no. 560 in *Kokinshū:*

> My love, it is like
> the grass growing hidden
> in the deep mountains,
> which grows ranker and ranker
> yet there is no one who knows.

there is one who 'will not be stopped' – Allusion to a poem from the *Shigeyuki Collection*:

> Tsukuba Mountain,
> Hayama Mountain, Shige Mountain
> many as they be
> my will to fulfill my
> intention will not be stopped. (*Zenshū*, 289)

Word association links this poem more closely with the poem alluded to immediately above than is apparent in the English translations. In the Shigeyuki poem, the name Shige Mountain and the word for "many," *shigekeredo*, echo the key word in the previous poem, *shigesama*, "plentiful, luxuriant," extended to mean "rank, overgrown" when said of plant life.

Tōshi's manner of expression here, "there is one who will not be stopped," is indirect perhaps because she is making an allusion. With the allusion is the attribution of strong intention to Michitsuna's Mother. This intention would be to have her marriage be a close relationship.

that it seemed I was not about to move, he said, "Even though it is troublesome, I'm afraid I will have to observe the custom. I think it would be better if I come when this direction is open for me. Of course, there will be the usual six-day period of abstinence." Looking pained as he said these things, he departed.

The next morning, a letter arrived. "I felt bad leaving so late at night. How are you? Please consider breaking your fast as soon as you can. Our young lord is looking so poorly." Well, he could write something like that even though his feelings were actually distant; thus I was plagued with doubts as the six days of his period of abstinence ended and the third day of the seventh month arrived.

Around noon, some attendants came from his place saying, "His lordship will be coming today. He told us to attend upon him here." My attendants flew into activity, clattering about, cleaning and arranging even rooms that for the last while had been let go. Looking on from the side, I spent the day in painful uneasiness. When the day came to an end, even his attendants who had come here began to say things like, "The carriage was all decked out and ready to go, why has it not arrived by now?" and little by little, the night grew late. Some people said, "This really is strange; we should send someone to go have a look." Someone was dispatched; he returned with this report. "It seems that now his lordship's carriage has been put away and his guard disbanded." So it had happened again as I feared; I felt so ashamed and sorrowful that thoughts were beyond expression. If I had stayed on the mountain, I would not have been subjected to this kind of crushing experience; it was just as I had foreseen, so I thought. This and that person in my household finding it so strange and terrible made a fuss talking it over. It was just like when a groom didn't show up on the third night. Just when I was driving myself to distraction thinking that if only I could ask why he hadn't come, I would be relieved, a guest arrived. While I felt in no mood for receiving guests, as we spoke of one thing and another, I found my mind taken away from my troubles a little.

Then, the next day, the young lord said, "I think I will just go and ask what happened yesterday," and so he paid a call. His report was, "It seems that he was ill last night. Father said, 'Suddenly, a great pain came on me so I wasn't able to come.'" Hearing that, I thought, so there had been no need to get so upset. Since it was an illness, if he had merely sent word, I would not have thought anything of it, and just as I was feeling irritated about that, a letter arrived from the principal handmaiden. It seems that she thought I was still in the mountains; she said some very touching things. "What is it I hear, that you are still making your dwelling where thoughts and foliage 'grow ranker.' Even so, I hear there is one who 'will

Man and Wife River . . . – *Imosegaha*, "Man and Wife River," is the name given to the stretch of the Yoshino River where it passes between Man and Wife Mountains. Actually the Yoshino River has three different names. In its upper reaches it is known as the Yoshino River; then as mentioned above it briefly becomes the Man and Wife River; and finally it becomes the Ki River at its lower reaches. This information is important for understanding the author's reply poem. The word *naka*, "middle," also means "relations," particularly those between husband and wife.

'when despair came again' – Allusion to a poem in the *Mitsune Collection*:

> Despairing of the world,
> a person enters the mountains,
> while in the mountains,
> when despair comes again,
> now where will she go? (*Zenshū*, 289)

just 'up in the sky' – Allusion to a poem from the *Tales of Ise*, section 21:

> Like a cloud just
> up in the sky, vanishing
> without a trace,
> such is this ephemeral
> self of mine. (Watanabe, *Ise monogatari*, 41)

Well, all right, so it goes . . . – The colloquial phrase beginning this poem, *yoshi ya*, "well, all right," is often found in poems involving the Yoshino River because of the similarity of sound. She is referring here to the change in name that the Yoshino River undergoes as it runs to the sea. Her relations with her husband have changed to the point where the term "marriage" is no longer appropriate. Moreover, there is one further allusion, this time to poem no. 828 in *Kokinshū:*

> Time and water flowing,
> Man and Wife Mountains
> are riven,
> well, all right, so it goes
> with relations in this world.

If the reader is thinking at this point that this correspondence between Tōshi and the author is even more recondite that usual, the reader is right. They make three allusions each to former poetry. The interweaving of sentiment and allusion in this communication is extraordinary. While the focus—concern for the author's marital situation—is the same as it has been for most of book two, there is an element of playfulness with respect to the author's treatment of it that is new.

It made no difference – What this phrase means depends on what her intention was. If she changed residences so that she could practice her devotions without disturbance, then it made no difference because she is disturbed. If she moved so that her devotions would not be a source of irritation to her husband, then it made no difference because, as we shall see, he gets very irritated.

he bursts in – That is, her husband, Kaneie. From his behavior, it appears that he is annoyed that she is taking to religion again. She must not have informed him of her plan to do the Hase pilgrimage with her father.

He spent the rest of the day here in pleasant leisure – A lot has been left out here; the description moves from Kaneie's wild actions to her casual notation of a pleasant visit. This leaves the reader to fill the scene in with imagination. We can speculate about what brought about the radical shift in his attitude. He was clearly alarmed that she might not have given up the idea of becoming a nun. However, when he arrived at her father's, he learns that she will be going on the pilgrimage with her father. Moreover, the Hase pilgrimage is so conventional a religious observance that it may not have seemed dangerous. Then, what about her? Why does she not take offense at his outrageous behavior? For one thing, she may have taken his outburst as a genuine expression of affection for her. For another, it must have given her some satisfaction to see her husband lose his sangfroid for once in a long while. He found himself in the position of getting upset over nothing; something she knew well from experience. Finally, he did stay the night, something that was always appreciated.

not be stopped,' yet you speak only of growing apart, so I worry about what is to become of you":

imose gaha	Man and Wife River,
mukashi nagara no	if it ran as in the old days
naka naraba	down its middle course,
hito no yukiki no	one would see the reflection
kage ha mitemashi	of him going to and fro.

For a reply, I sent this, "I intended to dwell in the mountains until I could see the autumn scenery, but 'when despair came again,' I hesitated, and now it seems I am just 'up in the sky.' I thought there was no one who knew the rankness of my thoughts. How did you hear? It is truly as you seem to have guessed":

yoshi ya mi no	Well, all right, so it goes,
asemu nageki ha	my sorrow for love gone shallow;
imosegaha	just as the water
naka yuku midzu no	that runs between Man and Wife
na mo kawarikeri	Mountains has changed its name.

Then that day, the fourth of the seventh month, was a free day for him; I heard the next day he was again observing abstinence. The day after that, my direction was forbidden; the next day, doggedly despite the disappointments of the past, I wondered if he would come; night drew on and I was graced with a visit. He spoke a lot about the circumstances of the night he hadn't come, making excuses, "At least tonight I thought I must spend it with you and rushed over here. The rest of my household, who are observing a directional taboo, had already gone off, and I was left on my own." Thus he spoke with no sense of fault on his part, quite unconcerned. There was no point in my saying anything. When dawn broke, he said, "I'm worried about my people who went off to a place I am not familiar with," and rushed off.

It was about seven or eight days after that. At my father, the provincial governor's place, there was a plan to make a pilgrimage to Hase Temple, and it was suggested that I go along, so I moved to my father's for preparatory rituals. It made no difference that I had changed dwellings. Around midday, there is a sudden commotion. Even my father is alarmed and shouts, "What's going on, who has opened that door over there?" Suddenly he bursts in, takes the incense burner and other usual implements for the day's observances and scatters them about, takes my rosary and throws it up on a high shelf, and otherwise behaves in a wild manner; it was astounding. He spent the rest of the day here in pleasant leisure and went back the next day.

With so many people going along – Her father would have quite an entourage.

the late grand counselor of Azechi – Her husband's uncle Morouji, who was kindly, hosted her and Kaneie on her return from Hase three years ago.

cormorant fishing boats – A form of fishing where live cormorants with rings around their necks are used to fish for *ayu*, "sweetfish." Flares on the bow of the boats draw the *ayu* to the surface close to the boat; the cormorant on leashes are sent out to scoop them up. The ring around their necks prevents them from swallowing the fish, which are then taken out of their mouths by the fishermen. This form of fishing is still practiced as a sightseeing attraction in several places around Japan.

boats with their load of sorrow – The *u* of *ubune* can mean both "cormorant" and "sorrow."

Nieno Pond and the Izumi River – She mentioned these places on her first trip to Hase (book one, p. 153).

Yotate Forest – Its location is no longer known.

Kasuga Shrine— The principal shrine in the old capital of Nara. The god of the shrine was a titular deity of the Fujiwara clan.

Well then, about seven or eight days later, we depart for Hase. We leave the house around midmorning. With so many people going along, it seems very ostentatious. Around midafternoon, we reached the Uji villa that had belonged to the late grand counselor of Azechi. Everyone bustled about, but I could barely enter into that feeling. As I looked around I felt some pangs; here was this place on which he had lavished so much care and affection; this very month they had performed the observances for the first anniversary of his passing, yet, even in such a short time, how the place had come to look untended. The people taking care of the place had prepared to receive us. The furnishings, everything one could see, had been chosen by the grand counselor. The rush blinds, woven bamboo screens, the curtain screens made with burnt umber dyed cloth hanging over frames of black persimmon wood—they were all so tasteful and appropriate, it was very moving. I was tired, and the wind was blowing so strongly it had even given me a headache, so a wind shelter was erected for me. Looking out from there, when it grew dark, I saw cormorant fishing boats with their flares all alight come out and fill the river. It was an endlessly fascinating sight. As it took my mind off my headache, I rolled up the blinds and looked out—*ah—it was at this very spot when I had made the pilgrimage to Hase on my own, after which, on the return, he had met me and we had gone back and forth to the villa. It was here that the Azechi counselor had come down and given us presents. How very sad and moving, in what world had such things been?* Thinking about this over and over again, I couldn't sleep and brooded on it well past the middle of the night, watching the cormorant boats going back and forth up and down the river:

uhe shita to	Burning up and down
kogaruru koto wo	the river, what is it?
tadzunureba	Besides these flames
mune no hoka ni ha	in my breast, it is cormorant
ubune narikeri	boats with their load of sorrow.

that was how I felt. When I looked again, toward dawn, they had changed their activity and were making fishing fires. This too was incomparably moving.

When it grew light, we departed immediately. When I saw that Nieno Pond and the Izumi River had not changed at all from the first time I had seen them, I could not help feeling touched.

There were many things I felt at the various sights, but we were moving along in such a bustle that my mind was quite distracted. We stopped the carriages at Yotate Forest and had our box lunches. Everyone seemed to enjoy eating. There was a suggestion to stop at Kasuga Shrine, so we stayed the night at some miserable temple lodgings.

"Three Umbrellas' Mountain" – Mt. Mikasa of Nara, which means "three umbrellas." The author makes a pun on the name.

Asuka Temple – This is assumed to be present-day Ganko Temple in Nara, which was famous for having a fresh, bubbling spring.

"One would love to stay" – A refrain from a Saibara folk song about the Asuka Spring.

Tsubaichi – The market town at which the final preparations for going up to the temple were made.

I think it must be – She is listening from inside the ox carriage.

the forest that is to be passed without making a sound – This, it is believed, was a superstition concerning the forest around the Hase Yamagushi Shrine, which was across the river valley from Hase Temple.

but since the women said – It is interesting that it is the women who opt for the most exciting way of going home.

Just as we left there, it began to rain and blow terribly. Though we went holding up "Three Umbrellas' Mountain," a great many people were drenched. Finally we arrived at the Kasuga Shrine, presented offerings and then set out toward Hase. We stopped at Asuka Temple to light votive candles; however, I didn't get out of the carriage but just had it pulled into the garden and the shafts placed on trestles. Looking around, I could see that it was a charming place with trees all around. The garden had a refreshing air; one wanted so much to drink the water from its pure spring that I could easily appreciate the refrain in the old folk song, "One would love to stay." But as the rain was falling even more heavily, there was nothing to do but move on.

At long last, we arrived at Tsubaichi, and just as we had completed the usual preparations and were about to start for the temple, night fell. The rain and the wind had still not let up, so even though we lit torches, they were blown out. Since it was terribly dark, it felt like traveling a road in a dream, so unsettling; I was quite lost in fears of what might happen. At long last we reach the Lustration Hall; I cannot tell if it is still raining or not, however the voice of the river water is so loud that, listening to it, I think it must be. As we go up to the main hall, I feel unwell. Even though I have so many pressing desires, I am feeling so sick that I cannot remember things clearly. I say nothing. Although they said that it was dawn, the rain poured down the same as before. Learning from the bitter experience of last night, we delayed our departure until noon.

In front of the forest that is to be passed without making a sound, our people, who normally go along raising a din, now are making hand gestures and shaking their heads; they look like fish out of water gasping for air, and I can't help finding it a funny sight. There seemed to be talk of our breaking our fast at Tsubaichi, but I still continue mine. From that point on, there so many places that wanted to host us, we could barely continue on our way. When we present our gifts, people seem to go to no end of trouble for us.

The Izumi River was very full. As we were wondering what to do, someone said, "A very skillful boatman has come up from Uji." The men were deciding "No, that's too much trouble, let's just cross the river and carry on by the usual route," but since the women said, "Let's go by boat instead," that was what we did, and all got on board. How skillful the boatman was taking us downstream such a long way. Starting with the oarsman himself, all sang loudly as we went along. At a place close to Uji, we got into carriages again. We were told, "Home is in a forbidden direction," so we stayed over at Uji.

As the preparations have been made ahead, there is an amazing number of cormorant fishing boats; the whole river is teeming with them.

not a pilgrimage of your own – Because she is part of her father's entourage.

"The return banquet for the sumo tournament . . ." – Upon the completion of the sumo tournament, it was the custom for the captains of the Right and Left Guards to host a return banquet. Kaneie's current post is captain of the Right Guard.

"Yet, after all" – Allusion to poem no. 713 in *Kokinshū:*

I know now your words
of love are false yet after all
is there anyone
whose promises I could trust
anyone who would be true (Rodd, *Kokinshū,* 254)

that kind of suffering – The suffering of waiting for word from someone you love.

'a cloud bank far away' – Allusion to a poem by Prince Motoyoshi as quoted in *Zoku Goshūishū,* poem no. 872:

Already now
the tree leaves have changed
color, so why
should a bank of clouds
far away start to pour? (*Zenshū,* 296–97)

She is likening herself to the bank of clouds that is far away, and the changing of the color of the leaves is his loss of love for her.

There was an immediate reply – As in the first days of their marriage, this always meant the communication had been effective.

We say, "We would like to see them from close up," so something is arranged right at the water's edge. The carriages are drawn up to trestles. When I get down, the cormorant boats are going back and forth right at my feet. As I have never seen live fish before, I stare in fascination. Even though I was tired from the journey, I watched so avidly that I didn't notice the night was growing late, whereupon this and that attendant said, "We had better go back now. There isn't really anything else to see." "All right, so be it," and we clambered up. Yet, I am not tired of watching. Just as before, the lamps of the fishing boats are lit the whole night. When I doze off for a little while, at the sound of things knocking on the sides of the boats I wake up, just as though those sounds were meant to rouse me on purpose. At dawn when I look out, I see that a lot of *ayu* had been caught. From there, they are preparing to distribute the fish to the various places they should. It is an activity that seems so fitting. Since we departed when the day was well on, it was dark by the time we arrived back at the capital. I had intended to leave immediately for my own residence, but as my people said they were tired, I stayed at my father's.

The next day, around noon, a letter arrives here from him. "I thought to go and meet you, but since it was not a pilgrimage of your own, I felt it might not be appropriate. Are you back home? I'll come over right away." Seeing this, my attendants urge me on, "Hurry, hurry," and no sooner had we arrived than he appeared. He seems to have remembered how it was in the old days and came on purpose because he knew I would be thinking about it. The next morning early, he left with this plausible excuse, "The return banquet for the sumo tournament is coming up." He always had a good excuse for the morning, recalling the old poem, "Yet, after all," I am sad.

And so it came to the time when the next month would be the eighth month. He had a usual period of abstinence for four days; that lifted and I saw him about two times. The return banquet was over; I heard he had gone to perform religious observances at a temple deep in the mountains. For three or four days I didn't hear a word from him, then, on a day when the rain fell miserably, this came. "Though having heard that in this forlorn mountain dwelling, people would ask after one, now there is one who suffers because that is not the case." For a reply, I sent, "While I would be the first to feel word should be sent, I thought to let you know that kind of suffering. Though I thought there was nothing left of the dew of my tears, 'a cloud bank far away' absurdly pours down." There was an immediate reply. Then about three days later, there was a message, "I'm coming back today," and that night he appeared. As always, since I could not really tell what he had in his heart, I hid my own feelings,

"surely now the hail is falling" – Allusion to *Kokinshū* poem no. 1077, one of five Shinto songs:

surely now the hail
is falling deep in the fair
mountains for on the
nearby slopes the creeping vines
are tinged with autumn's colors (Rodd, *Kokinshū,* 368)

the appeal to the Ishiyama Buddha – She is referring to her impulsive pilgrimage to Ishiyama last year; perhaps she is still waiting for the meaning of the strange dream she had there to be revealed.

I fall into old age – The venerable pun on *furi/furu*, "fall" (as of rain) and "to grow old."

only someone like me to rely on – The fate of her household members also depends on her relationship with her husband. There may have been relationships between Kaneie's attendants and her attendants, which resulted in some of the children of that morning. When her husband does not visit, it may have been difficult for their husbands to visit as well. I base this conjecture on evidence from fiction of the era. For example, in *The Tale of Genji*, when Genji begins to visit Yugao, his attendant makes it an opportunity to begin a liaison with one of Yugao's ladies as well. Moreover, in *Ochikubō monogatari*, there is a parallel love affair between the maid of Lady Ochikubō and her suitor's male attendant.

and he acted as though there was certainly no fault on his side. He barely visited every seven or eight days.

Late in the ninth month, the sky took on such a melancholy aspect. Then yesterday and today, the wind was very cold and an autumn drizzle fell from time to time. I felt a terrible sadness. Gazing out at the distant mountains, one would have thought they had been painted with indigo blue; it brought to mind the poem, "surely now the hail is falling." I remarked, "The landscape is so lovely, it makes one feel like going on a pilgrimage and combining it with sightseeing." Whereupon a close attendant said, "Indeed, what a wonderful idea. The next time we go to Hase, think about going just quietly on our own." I replied, "Well, last year, just for a try, we went in such wretched state to Ishiyama. Sometime next spring, after first seeing the results of the appeal to the Ishiyama Buddha, let's do as you suggest. Mind you, I am not sure I can go on living so miserably until then." Then murmuring forlornly:

sode hitsuru	I used to grieve
toki wo dani koso	when even my sleeves were
nageki shika	dampened with rain,
mi sahe shigure	now soaked to the skin, I fall
furi mo yuku kana	into old age with the autumn drizzle.

It was a time when I had lost my taste for life, and it seemed that all living and growing old in the world was meaningless. Going on in this way, dawn to dusk, the twentieth of the month arrived. When the dawn comes, I arise; when the sun sets, I go to bed; it feels so strange, but this morning, too, what am I to do about it. This morning when I looked out, the roofs were very white with frost. The children of the household still in their night clothes raise a din with, "We'd better not let the frost bite us." It is most touching. "Oh, it's so cold. This is a frost that puts snow to shame," others say covering their mouths with their sleeves. When I hear the mutterings of these people who have only someone like me to rely on, I hardly feel that I'm up to it. The tenth month passed, too, with me keenly regretting our separateness.

The eleventh month was just the same; when the twentieth arrived, he did visit, but after that he did not come for more than twenty days. He just sent letters twice. Matters being thus, although my heart was not at ease, as my emotions were spent and I was feeling weak, I was hardly aware of this or that, when this letter arrived, "I will be strictly observing a period of four days' abstinence. I was thinking of visiting right now today," and so on; I found it strange for him to be writing so minutely about his affairs. It was the sixteenth of the last month of the year.

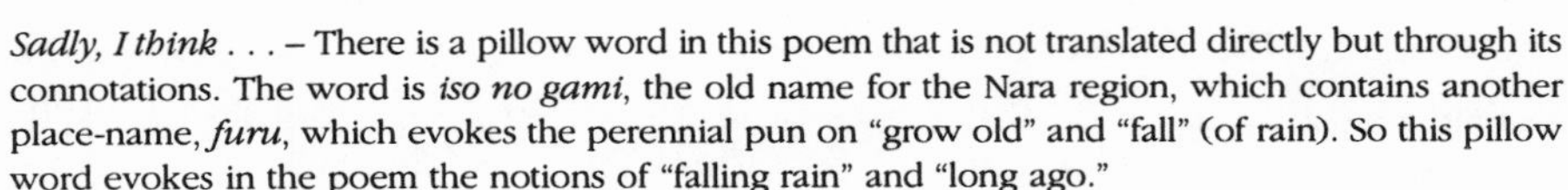

Sadly, I think . . . – There is a pillow word in this poem that is not translated directly but through its connotations. The word is *iso no gami*, the old name for the Nara region, which contains another place-name, *furu*, which evokes the perennial pun on "grow old" and "fall" (of rain). So this pillow word evokes in the poem the notions of "falling rain" and "long ago."

Since my direction was forbidden – By this point, it really begins to be suspicious that her direction is forbidden so often.

"rain frog" – The word in Japanese, *amagaheru*, is homophonous with "the nun returns," hence the joke.

a little sarcastically – I do not follow the *Zenshū* text for this translation. I follow Uemura and Shinozuka by keeping the text as *keshikute*, "sarcastically" (Uemura, *Taisei*, vol. 5, 873) rather than emending it to *monoshikute*, "gloomily."

"It seems no other direction is forbidden but mine" – The author appears to be indirectly accusing Kaneie of inventing directional taboos for his own convenience.

No help to the rain frog . . . – This poem takes its inspiration from the folk belief that if you put a dead frog on a plantain leaf, it would be brought back to life. The word for frog, *kaheru*, is worked into the last line in the meaning of "goes back on."

that place that was taboo to me – Presumably Ōmi's place. She is speaking figuratively when she says it is taboo to her.

In a little while the whole sky clouded up and it began to rain. This would be enough to stop anyone, I thought as I gazed out, and it looked as though dusk was falling. Since it was raining so hard, it only seemed reasonable that he wouldn't come, yet thinking of the past, tears welled up; I felt such a painful longing it was difficult to control. I sent someone to deliver this:

kanashiku mo	Sadly, I think,
omohitayuru ka	he has given up the thought
iso no gami	of me, even though
sawaranu mono to	long ago, he used to never
narahishi mono wo	let the falling rain stop him.

Just when I was thinking that the messenger must have arrived by now, I sensed there was someone outside the closed shutters of the south-facing bed chamber. My servants had not noticed; it was only I who felt something was strange. I pushed open the side door and in he walked. Because the terrible rain was just then at its peak, no one had heard a sound. But now everyone heard the loud voices, "Quickly get his lordship's carriage in out of the rain." He said, "You have held me at fault for many months and years, but I felt if I came tonight, you might forgive me." And "Tomorrow, this direction is forbidden, the day after that, it seems I must start a period of abstinence. . . ." He said many things cleverly. Thinking that he must have missed my messenger, I was much relieved. The rain let up during the evening, and he left saying, "Well then, until later tonight." Since my direction was forbidden, it was as I expected; I waited but he did not appear. There was a letter from him in the morning, "Last night, someone arrived and as it got late and I needed to begin the reading of the sutras, I canceled coming. As usual, I must have caused you a lot of worry."

After my coming back from the mountain retreat, he had nicknamed me "rain frog," so I sent this in reply. Among other things, I said a little sarcastically, "It seems no other direction is forbidden but mine":

ohoba kono	No help to the rain frog
kami no tasuke ya	is the god of the plaintain leaf,
nakarikemu	or so it seems—
chigirishi koto wo	even when he makes a promise,
omohi kaheru wa	he goes back on his intention.

And so it went and as usual; the days passed and the end of the month arrived.

Since there was someone informing me that he was going every night to that place that was taboo to me, I hardly passed the time with my heart at ease. Nevertheless, the days and the months passed, and here it

the last day of the year, the time to chase out devils – She gives us another account of this celebratory ritual at the latter part of book one (p. 147), when she and Tōshi are living in the same house.

was, the last day of the year, the time to chase out devils; I was terribly startled as both the adults and the children of the household rushed around shouting, "Devils out! Devils out!" I just listened and watched quietly. It seemed to me that this was the sort of thing that only households where everything was going well would want to perform. Someone said, "It is snowing heavily." As the year ended, it seemed that I had no attachments left to anything.

Book Three

Summary

Book three, which covers again three years, 972 to 974, is most like a conventional diary in that it has frequent entries that appear to have been written right on the heels of events. Moreover, the events are more miscellaneous, rather than being focused, as in book two, on the author's struggle with her feelings about her relationship. Indeed, in general the emotional intensity of the first two books is absent; a more objective point of view prevails as she brings into her narrative the stories of other people, notably the story of the mother of her adopted daughter, her son's courting of two women, and the pursuit of her adopted daughter by a rather determined older man. Yet, in this book too, a dual point of view is discernable. This is still her personal record, but as she tells the stories of herself and others objectively, the narration takes on some of the qualities of a fictional account. In the choice of details for description and even the choice of events themselves, there is evidence of the desire to make a good story. Accordingly, her mastery of prose narrative increases. It is as though we see the diarist turning into a novelist.

third year of Tenroku – Or 972. This is the first and only time that she mentions a specific year in the diary. The chronology of all the other entries has been established from this one.

ceremonial bow – This was a bow with dancelike movements performed in the four directions on New Year's Day.

sutra reading service – This was a customary way to start the new year. Since it would, as a religious rite, require abstinence during the days of the service, this indicates that she is not expecting Kaneie.

my period . . . inauspicious – The service would take a day or two, but if her period were to start, she would be ritually unclean and have to stop the observance. Since menstruation was considered a defilement, it seems like an inauspicious state in which to begin the new year.

emperor's Coming of Age Ceremony – Emperor Enyū, who had ascended the throne in 969. This year, he is fourteen by Asian count. Emperor Enyū was the fifth son of Emperor Murakami. He was mentioned in book one as the ultimate recipient of the string of goose eggs that Michitsuna's Mother had sent as a present to the junior consort, Fushi (p. 143).

Presentation of the White Horses Ceremony – On the seventh day of the first month, it was customary for the Horse Guard of the Right and Left to present twenty-one white horses for the emperor's inspection, after which the emperor hosted a banquet.

Shimotsuke, hey! – The ancient name for present-day Nikkō, which in turn was connected with two other place-names, Ooke, which is more or less homophonous with *oke*, "tub," and Futara, which is homophonous with *futa*, "lid." So Shimotsuke became a pillow word for anything to do with lids and tubs. Also floating in the background of this poem is the notion that if someone were thinking of you, their image would appear in water or a mirror.

Looking at the lid . . . – In their return poem, the attendants pun on *mi*, which can mean both "self" as in *mi o sutete*, "throwing away oneself," that is, "being earnest," and "fruit" or "snacks."

In this way, another new year dawns; it seems it is the third year of Tenroku. Feeling my gloom and pain have quite cleared away, I help dress our young lord and send him on his way to court. As I watch him run down into the garden and straightaway give a ceremonial bow, he looks so terribly splendid I want to cry. I think, *Shall I hold a sutra reading service tonight?* but then my period is likely to come. That is the sort of thing people usually consider inauspicious, and I wonder in my own heart once more how will things turn out for me. However, this year, having resolved firmly in my own mind that regardless of whether he might be the most annoying person in the world, I will not lament over things, my heart is very much at peace.

The third is the emperor's Coming of Age Ceremony; everyone is excited. Although it was the day of the Presentation of the White Horses Ceremony, I passed the seventh feeling rather uninterested in it all.

On the eighth day of the new year, he appeared saying, "This has been a time of an awful lot of festivities." In the morning, just as he was about to go back, one of his attendants who was waiting around wrote this and sent it in with a lid of a storage tub to my women attendants:

shimotsuke ya	Shimotsuke, hey!
woke no futara wo	This lid of a tub, we see
adjikinaku	unfortunately
kage mo uakabanu	is a mirror whereon
kagami to zo miru	your reflections do not float.

My attendants sent the lid back filled with sake and snacks. On an unglazed sake cup, one of them had written:

sashi idetaru	Looking at the lid
futara wo mireba	you sent out, we decided
mi wo sutete	that your earnestness
tanomu ha tama no	was not for apparitions
konu to sadametsu	to come but food and drink.

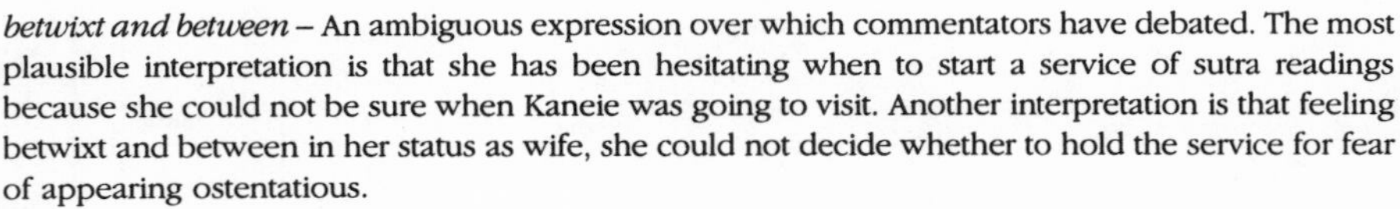

betwixt and between – An ambiguous expression over which commentators have debated. The most plausible interpretation is that she has been hesitating when to start a service of sutra readings because she could not be sure when Kaneie was going to visit. Another interpretation is that feeling betwixt and between in her status as wife, she could not decide whether to hold the service for fear of appearing ostentatious.

this my Chinese robe – "Robe" was also a conventional metaphor for spouse; an old, well-worn robe is the familiar wife. An undertone in this poem is his reference to her as his familiar wife.

the goods old – Refers to the used quality of the court robe, but is also a self-deprecating way of referring to herself.

Annual Promotions – The reassignment of duties and promotions for the new year.

first call of the warbler – The warbler has such a lovely, liquid song, and there is a special poignancy to the "first things" of the new year. Moreover, the backdrop to the scene is a rare snowfall. It was indeed a scene to evoke poetry.

senior counselor – This position was a vice minister position, something equivalent to becoming a member of cabinet in modern Japan (Uemura, *Taisei*, vol. 6, 69).

Thus feeling betwixt and between, the second week of the new year passed without my holding the services that most people were busy with at that time.

On the fourteenth, he sent over an old court jacket with this message, "Make this over." Although he said, "I need it by such and such a date," I didn't feel like rushing it. Then, a servant arrived the next morning with this message, "It is taking too long," and this:

hisashi to ha	Such a long time
obotsukanashi ya	really makes me worry,
karagoromo	this my Chinese robe,
uchi kite naramu	I would wear it forever,
sate okurase yo	so send it back as it is.

But going against his instructions, I rushed and got it done and sent it back without a letter, whereupon he sent this, "This seems quite good. What is bad is that you are never straight." Rather stung by this, I replied:

wabite mata	Put in a tight spot,
toku to sawagedo	I rushed and fussed to get it done,
kahi nakute	all to no avail,
hodo furu mono ha	that amount of time, the goods old,
kaku koso arikere	it would turn out like this.

After that, except for "Busy with the Annual Promotions," there is not a word from him.

Today, the twenty-third, before the shutters had been raised, someone rose early; she pushed open the door and just as she said, "What a lot of snow has fallen," I heard the first call of the warbler, but I feel as though I have aged terribly because even with such a scene as this, not a single word of poetry came to mind.

It is the Annual Promotions. On the twenty-fifth, although there is a great fuss made about his promotion to senior counselor, so far as I am concerned all this means is that he will have even less freedom to see me. It seems like a joke for people to come and express their congratulations; I'm not a bit happy. Only our young lord, although he cannot say anything, seems secretly very pleased. The very next day, he sends a note, "What's wrong with you? You don't even send a 'how very fortunate' sort of greeting. My happiness seems to be for nothing."

Then, on about the last day of the month, there was this. "What's wrong? It has been very busy over here. Why do I not hear even a single word from you. It hurts." Thus, in the end, it seems he had gotten upset back at me for not saying anything. That day too, I could not expect him to come here himself, so for a reply I sent only this, "Now that you will be

Since I am no longer uncertain – She alludes to a poem from *Kokin rokujō,* no. 1370:

> Uncertain whether
> you would come to me or I
> would go to you,
> not even locking the fine
> wood door, I fell asleep. (*Zenshū,* 204–5)

She turns this around by saying, "I am no longer uncertain about your coming, so I just leave the door locked."

"I wondered if it was locked because I bolted over here" – He makes a pun on the word, *sasu,* which means both to "do something directly" and "to lock a door."

in a soft court robe . . . – This is the first time in the diary that the author has given such a lovingly detailed description of Kaneie's appearance. Her particular attention to his clothes may be partly explained by the fact that she plays a major role in producing them.

"It seems they have done a rough job of burning the scrub in the front garden" – The burning of stubble and grassy areas in the winter was common practice in agriculture, but it appears it was also practiced in gardens. His surveying her grounds and making such a comment implies a sense of responsibility for her dwelling.

having seen him off, I looked out on the garden – She has accompanied him out onto the veranda to see him off. If the house has been closed up for a few days due to inclement weather, she will not have seen the garden for that period.

serving in the imperial presence, it is very unlikely you will have any leisure; I feel somewhat bereft."

Although our relations continued in this way, since I no longer fretted about things, I actually felt quite at peace. One night when, without a care, I had fallen into a deep sleep, I was quite surprised to be awoken by a knocking at the gate. Since the gate was opened immediately, I was very flustered to hear someone standing just outside the door saying, "Quickly open the door, hurry." My attendants had escaped and hid because they were all in various states of disarray. Feeling awkward, I crept to the door, and as I opened it, saying, "Since I am no longer uncertain about whether you will come or not, how stiff the lock has become." He replied, "I wondered if it was locked because I bolted over here." The next morning, the sound of the wind blowing in the pines was so loud. The many nights I have slept alone, the wind has never raised such a noise. Listening to it, I go so far as to think I must be under some divine protection to have had company on a night like this.

With the dawn, it seems it was already the second month. Rain was falling very gently. Even though the shutters were raised, I did not feel the usual fluster, perhaps because of the rain. However, I could not expect him to stay. In a while he asked, "Have my attendants arrived yet?" and getting up, going out of the room in a soft court robe, loosely belted, with one layer of his nicely full underrobe of lustrous red silk showing from under his hem, he sauntered out. My attendants warmly pressed him to take some breakfast, "Some gruel, your lordship," to which he replied good-humoredly, "Since I don't usually eat in the morning, I don't know why I would start now." And then, "Please fetch my sword quickly," whereupon our young lord brought it and waited for him on the veranda with the sword laid across his knee.

He walked leisurely out and looked around, "It seems they have done a rough job of burning the scrub in the front garden." Immediately, his carriage fitted with rain flaps was drawn up. While his attendants held it up as though it were ever so light, he got in. The lower blinds were firmly shut; the carriage was drawn out through the main gate, and even the voices of his outriders cheerfully clearing the way sounded hateful to me.

For some days now, the wind had been blowing quite strongly so we had not raised the shutters on the south side of the house. Now today, having seen him off, I looked out on the garden for awhile. The rain was falling gently; the garden looked quite neglected, but here and there, the grass was pushing up freshly green. I found it touching. Around noon, the wind shifted to blow from the other direction, and although the sky showed

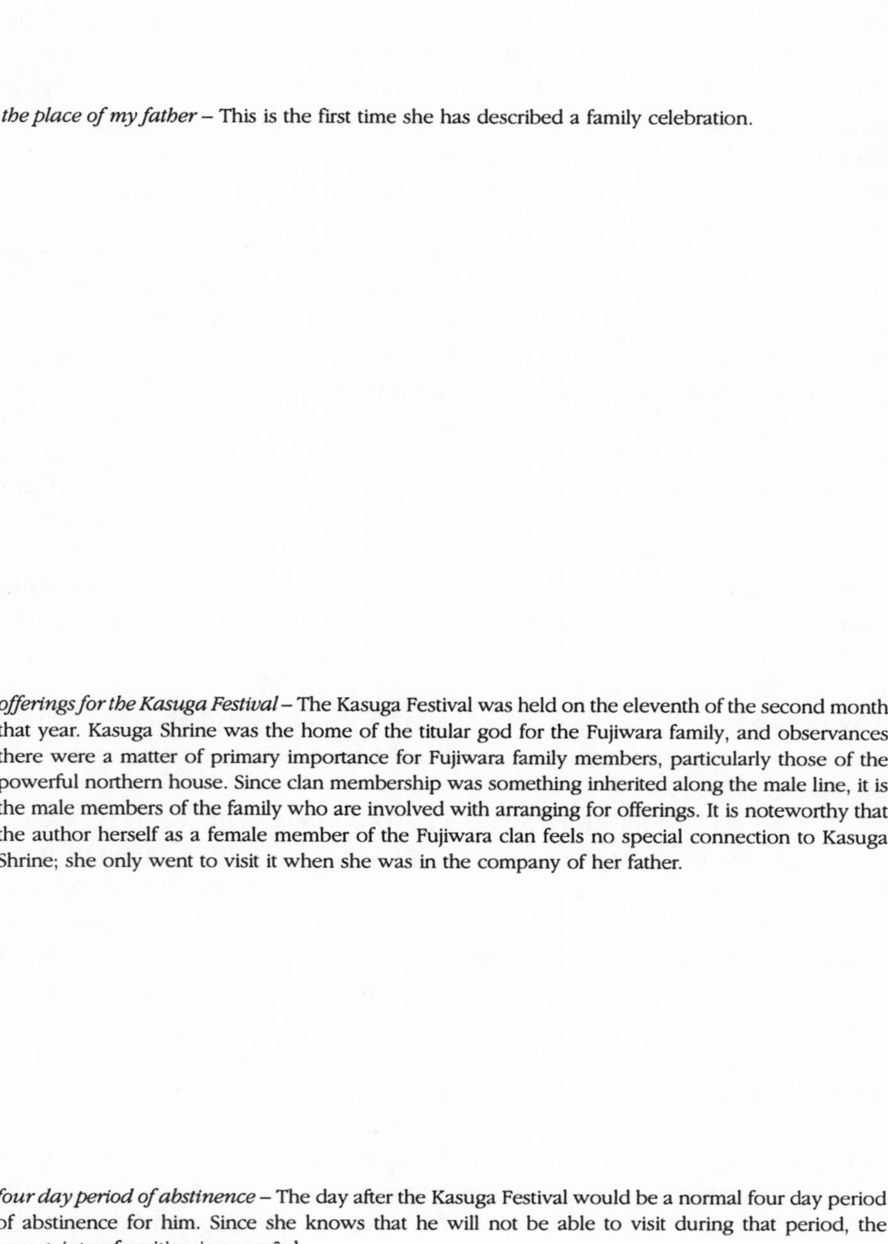

the place of my father – This is the first time she has described a family celebration.

offerings for the Kasuga Festival – The Kasuga Festival was held on the eleventh of the second month that year. Kasuga Shrine was the home of the titular god for the Fujiwara family, and observances there were a matter of primary importance for Fujiwara family members, particularly those of the powerful northern house. Since clan membership was something inherited along the male line, it is the male members of the family who are involved with arranging for offerings. It is noteworthy that the author herself as a female member of the Fujiwara clan feels no special connection to Kasuga Shrine; she only went to visit it when she was in the company of her father.

four day period of abstinence – The day after the Kasuga Festival would be a normal four day period of abstinence for him. Since she knows that he will not be able to visit during that period, the uncertainty of waiting is removed.

a clear face, I felt strangely unwell right up until sunset and spent the day in melancholy contemplation.

The third arrived and snow that had fallen during the night has piled up to about three or four inches. It is still snowing now. As I raise the blinds and gaze out, I hear voices here and there saying, "Oh, how cold." What's more the wind is keen. The whole world seems sad.

After that, for some days, the weather was fair, and on the eighth I went to visit the place of my father who has been away in the provinces. Many relatives were there; there seemed to be a lot of young people. Playing melodies that matched the season on koto and biwa, we spent the whole day in laughter. The next morning after we guests returned home, my heart felt peaceful.

Just upon returning home, there was a letter from him, "My time has been taken up with a long abstinence and the affairs of my new office, so I have been out of touch. I'm thinking of coming to see you today, quite soon." It was written very considerately. I sent a reply. Even though his letter seemed to indicate that he would come right away, *That will be the day*, I think as I pass the time musing on how I was gradually becoming someone he hardly knew. Then, just around midday, when everything is in a frightful state of disarray, there is a commotion, "His lordship arrives, his lordship arrives." He walks in just as we are all in a fluster. Hardly feeling like myself at all, seated across from him, I am quite absent. In a while trays of food are brought, and, after eating a little, about when it began to look as though the sun was setting, he says, "Tomorrow, as I have to see to sending off the offerings for the Kasuga Festival. . . ." Carefully arranging his costume, and gathering his many attendants together, with a very impressive clearing of the way, he leaves.

Immediately, my attendants all gather, "For him to come when things were in such a frightful mess, what must his lordship have thought?" and so on, one after another, they express their apologies. As for me, I felt even worse about all the unsightliness, but beyond that, I felt as though I had lost his favor.

For whatever reason, these days, it clears and then clouds up again; it seems like a year with a particularly cold spring. At night, the moon is bright. On the twelfth, snow blown by an east wind swirled and was scattered all around. From about midday, it turned into rain, and as it fell quietly the whole day, how melancholy the world felt. As for him whom I haven't heard from since that day, he has been acting as I had expected. Then when I remembered that from today he would likely be entering a four day period of abstinence, I felt a little more at ease.

It is the seventeenth. With rain falling gently, I recalled that my house was likely in a forbidden direction for him, and just as I was feeling

pilgrimage to Ishiyama – This was her impulsive pilgrimage to Ishiyama in the summer of 970 (pp. 206–15).

dharani – A sacred incantation, usually in Sanskrit.

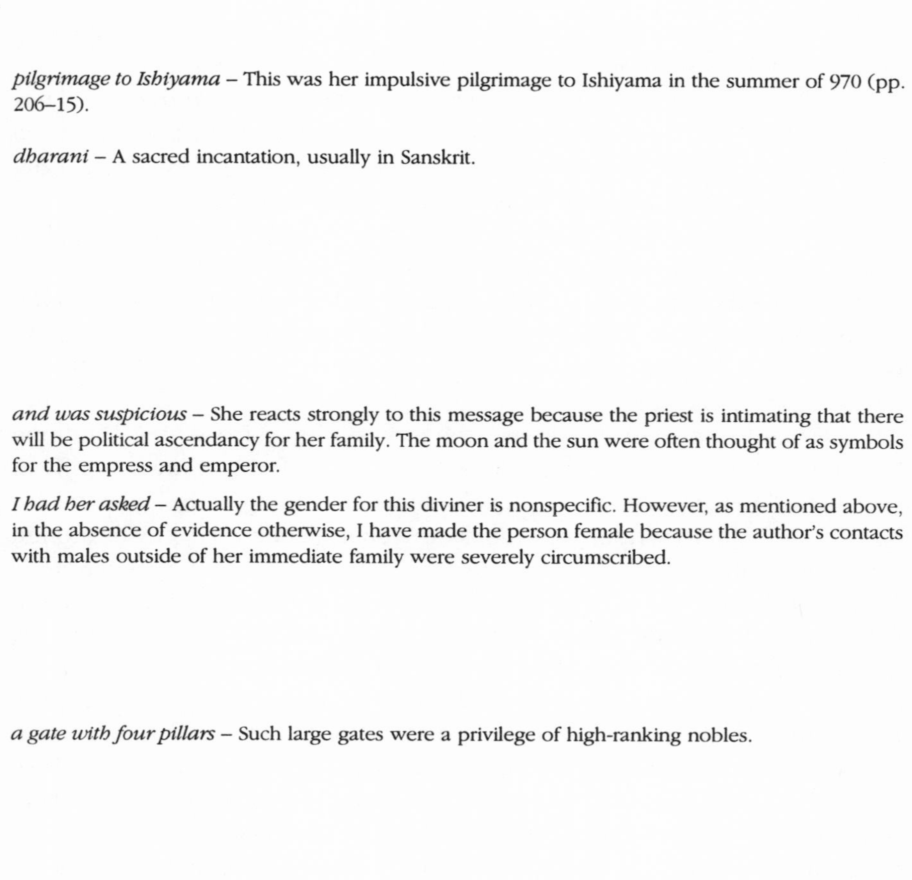

and was suspicious – She reacts strongly to this message because the priest is intimating that there will be political ascendancy for her family. The moon and the sun were often thought of as symbols for the empress and emperor.

I had her asked – Actually the gender for this diviner is nonspecific. However, as mentioned above, in the absence of evidence otherwise, I have made the person female because the author's contacts with males outside of her immediate family were severely circumscribed.

a gate with four pillars – Such large gates were a privilege of high-ranking nobles.

Since I had only one son – Having only one child put a woman of that period in a precarious position, and for women other than imperial consorts, if one were to have only one child it was better for it to be a daughter. The main Fujiwara clan was always in need of beautiful, talented daughters to marry into the imperial family. Moreover, just as daughters could marry into the imperial family, daughters could always marry "up" the social scale, whereas a son's future was much more tied to the combined statuses of his mother and father. Furthermore, in ironic reversal of the situation later in Japan, sons were to some extent lost to their families because they married "out," but daughters stayed with their mothers.

this one fervent prayer – Here she reveals what the main reason for her various pilgrimages over the years had been. It is evident that the gist of her prayers was for more children, and especially daughters.

I am reaching an age where it will be very difficult – She is approximately thirty-seven years old at this time and therefore reaching the end of her childbearing years.

forlorn about our relations, a message arrived from a monk whom I had met the year before last on my pilgrimage to Ishiyama. When I was passing night after night feeling so forlorn, there was a monk worshipping in the Sacred Image Hall who read the *dharani* in such a reverent tone. When I asked about him, I was told, "He has been on retreat here in the mountains since last year. He has been following an austere fast, taking no grains." I had said, "That being the case, please have him pray for me." The message from that monk was this, "On the night of the fifteenth last, I had a dream that your ladyship had received the sun and moon in your sleeves. The moon you stepped upon; the sun you clasped to your breast. This is what I seemed to see. Please have this dream divined." What an exaggeration, I thought, and was suspicious. As I felt somewhat foolish in this situation, I left it for awhile without having it divined. Then someone happened by who was able to divine dreams, and I had her asked to interpret this dream as though it had been someone else's dream. Just as I expected, she reacted with great surprise, "What kind of person had this dream? It means that person would like to control the throne and rule according to their own will." "So it is as I thought. The interpretation is not false; it is the monk who told me about it that I doubt. Let's say no more about it. It certainly doesn't fit my situation," and with that, I put an end to it.

But again, someone else said, "I had a dream where I saw that a gate with four pillars had been made for our residence, and I have been told, 'This dream means that a high-ranking minister will issue from this household.' One might think it was referring to your ladyship's husband who has recently become a grand minister, but it is not that. It speaks of the future of the young master."

Come to think of it, I myself had a dream the night before last where a man suddenly wrote the character "gate" on the sole of my foot and I drew my leg up to look at it. When I asked about this dream, I was told, "It has the same import." As this too seemed quite ridiculous, I thought it crazy, but then again, it wasn't as though such a thing were completely out of the question for a family like ours. Perhaps there might be an unexpectedly good fortune awaiting my only son; so I thought in my heart.

For all these good omens, with things as they were at the moment, I could only have uneasy feelings about the future. Since I had only one son, over the years I had made pilgrimages here and there making this one fervent prayer, but now I am reaching an age where it will be very difficult. For the last few months the thought has occurred to me, *How about taking in a girl from a good family, I could take care of her, she could be a good friend for my only son, and be there for me in my old age*; I have discussed the idea with this and that person. One person said, "I

Genji counselor Kanetada – This man was the descendant of Emperor Yōzei.

Shiga – Area on the shores of Lake Biwa.

That's right. There was something like that . . . – The following citation of her own speech is remarkable for its length and detail. She even quotes poems exchanged by her husband and another woman several years before, which would seem a prodigious feat of memory to do. One wonders if she did not consult notes she had kept from that time in order to create this narrative of the affair. In other words, perhaps this speech of hers was constructed rather than being a record of what she actually said. If so, this would be a place where her leaning toward "novelistic" writing is especially strong.

opportunity – A women left without protectors was vulnerable to casual advances.

returning with just a singlet of hers – The exchange of articles of clothing as love tokens was very common. There is some variation on the interpretation of this passage, some commentators think he gave the singlet to her.

The barrier crossed – The barrier is Ōsaka Barrier between the capital and Ōtsu on Lake Biwa, but because of its meaning, "meeting barrier," it was often used in love poetry to stand for the first meeting. Kaneie used this image in one of his first poems to the author. This poem was likely the first "morning after" poem in their relationship.

traveler's sleep – It is odd for her to say traveler's sleep of herself, because it is the man who "travels," not the woman.

I remember us laughing about that together – The author uses the phrase for "together," *morotomo ni*, very sparingly in the diary and only for moments of great intimacy with her husband. It is almost disconcerting to see that here the occasion for their intimacy is his sharing another love affair with her. It appears she was not jealous of all his affairs, only certain ones, and since this diary is essentially a record of emotion, it is the ones that occasioned the strongest feeling that get the most attention.

flames of longing – Her poem contains the perennial pun on *omo/hi*, *omohi*, "long for, love," and embedded in it, *hi*, "fire."

have heard that a very beautiful little girl was born to the late Genji counselor Kanetada's daughter, whom your husband used to visit in an amorous way. If it's all the same to you, why don't you make inquiries about her. I think the mother is now living at the foot of the mountains in Shiga, relying on her elder brother who is a monk." Upon hearing that person speak, it came back to me, "That's right. There was something like that. The family is descended from the late retired emperor Yōzei, is it not? When her father, the counselor, had died and she was still in mourning, since he was never one to pass up an opportunity like that, there was this and that exchange between them and it did end up in an affair. On his part, at first, it was just his usual sort of amusement; for her part, since her household was not a fashionable one and she was not very young, she probably didn't expect it to amount to anything. Nonetheless I believe that around the time she responded to his letters, he himself went to see her about two times. Now what was it? There was something about him returning with just a singlet of hers. There were quite a few incidents, but I've forgotten them. Now what was the poem he sent to her—

seki koete	The barrier crossed,
tabine naritsuru	having slept a traveler's sleep
kusa makura	on a pillow of grass,
karisome ni hata	yet, I do not think of it
omohoenu kana	as a transient affair.

was I believe what he sent; since it was such as it was, her reply was not terribly distinguished either:

obotsukana	In bewilderment,
ware nimo aranu	feeling that it was not me
kusa makura	on a pillow of grass,
mada koso shirane	never before had I known
kakaru tabine ha	such a traveler's sleep.

was what she wrote. 'It's a little strange that she used the phrase "traveler's sleep" too.' I remember us laughing about that together. After that, I didn't really hear very much about her, but I seem to remember she replied like this to some letter:

okisofuru	Dampened through and through
tsuyu ni yona yona	as night after night my tears
nurekoshi ha	fall with the dew,
omohi no naka ni	even in the flames of longing
kawaku sode kaha	how are these sleeves to dry?

And so on, like that, they grew further apart and it ended as a fleeting affair, but afterward I heard from his lordship, 'A girl was born at that

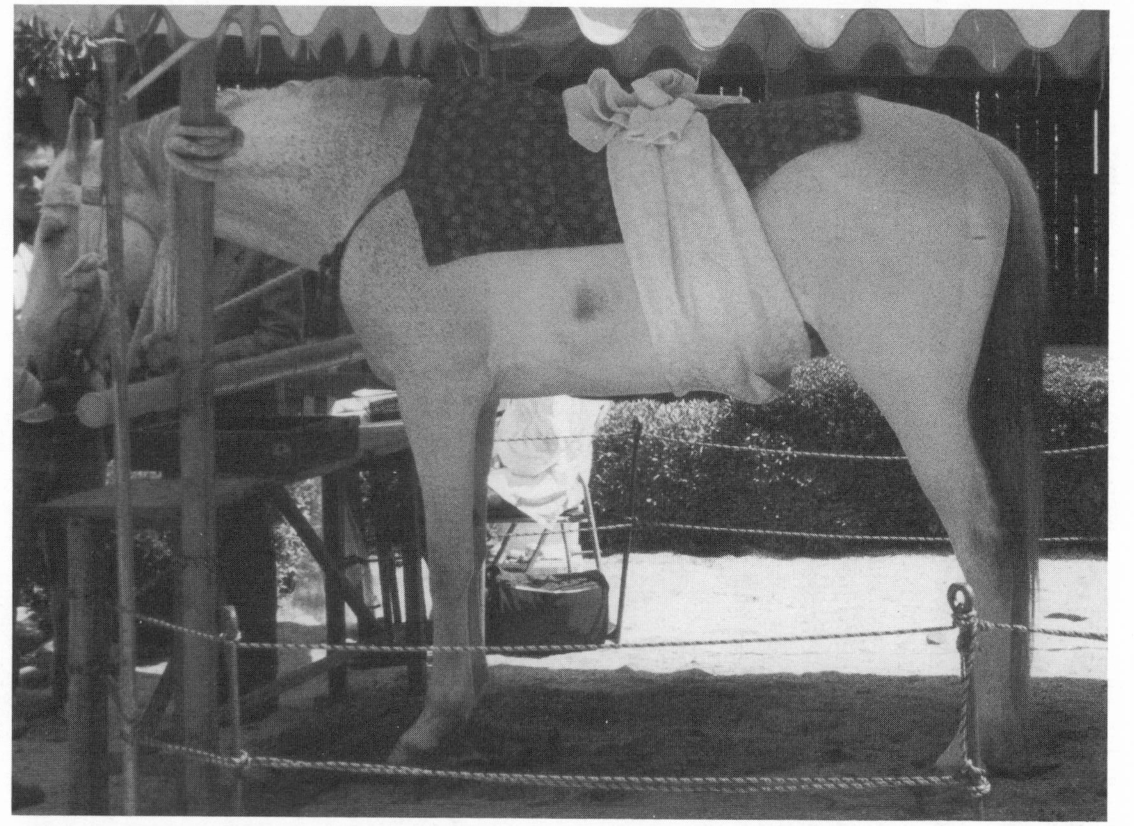

White horse presented as an offering to the Kamo Shrine on the occasion of the Aoi Festival. Traditionally, white horses were presented to the emperor as part of the New Year's festivities (see pp. 276–77, and 379).

Kiyomizu Temple. Michitsuna's Mother made a pilgrimage here in 972 (see pp. 300–301).

pinching myself to know another's pain – A proverbial expression for sympathizing with another's pain.

Naniwa – The ancient name for the Shiga area. As such, it is a name full of poetic connotations.

she must have feelings left in her heart, she must have words left to say – This is one of the places in book three where we see the author assuming something like a novelist's perspective. It is as though the author feels drawn to imagine and tell this woman's story.

half-brother – literally, "elder brother from another womb." The coolness between siblings of different mothers is also apparent in this passage.

had her go – Again there is no pronoun here in the original, but as has been my practice to this point, I assume the people she is speaking to are women unless specified otherwise.

his reverence – That is, her half-brother.

place I used to visit. She says it is mine. It may well be. Wouldn't it be good to bring the child here and place it with you?' It must be the same child. I shall do it," and thus, I came to decide. When I made inquiries through an intermediary, I heard that the young person unknown to her father was about twelve or thirteen years old. Apparently with only this daughter for a companion, the mother had come to live in the eastern foothills of Shiga; looking upon the lake in front and the Shiga Mountains behind, dawn to dusk, she was living an inexpressibly forlorn existence. When I heard this—as it is said, pinching myself to know another's pain—my first thought was, *there in Naniwa, living that way, she must have feelings left in her heart, she must have words left to say.*

Now her half-brother is a monk in the capital, and the person who brought up the idea in the first place is his acquaintance, so I had her go as an intermediary to bring him to discuss the idea. He said, "What could be the problem? At least in my opinion, it is a wonderful idea. Why, there she is trying to take care of her daughter, but the world has proven such an uncertain place for her, I understand she is even thinking of becoming a nun, and that is why she moved a few months ago to that lonely place." With that, the very next day, he crossed over the mountain and visited them. His sister apparently found it strange behavior on the part of a half-brother who had never seemed very concerned about her. When she asked, "What has brought you here?" he chatted with her about one thing and another for a while and then brought up the plan. At first, saying neither this nor that—one wonders what she really thought—she just cried and cried pitifully. Then she somehow finally pulled herself together to say, "I have felt this was the end for me, and although it has been very painful to have dragged such a child to such a place as this, what else was I to do? If some way or another, there might be something else for her, I beg you to do as you think best." So he returned the next day and reported what had happened. Amazingly it had gone as I hoped. Some karmic fate must have been at work. I was very moved. When he said, "Well then, would your ladyship please grace her with a letter?" I replied, "Of course," and composed this, "Since over the years I have heard about you but have never written to you before, I wonder how you could be anything other than bewildered and questioning who I am. Although you must find this very strange indeed, it seems that upon hearing from his reverence the hapless sorrow I relayed to him, you have deigned to make a favorable reply. I can only say that I am writing to you now with great joy. My request must seem very callous, but, since I heard that you are thinking of becoming a nun, I thought you might be willing to give up even such a beloved child." This was dispatched and there was a reply the next day. With such phrases

the thought that the father might now take care of his daughter – Though left unspoken between the two women, this must have been an important factor in both their decisions. By adopting a child of Kaneie's, the author could hope the child might strengthen the bond between her and her husband. For her part, the mother could hope Kaneie would take an interest in the daughter and look after her future. Out in the countryside and seemingly only with monks for uncles, the daughter would have been condemned to obscurity.

auspicious day – That is, according to the yin-yang diviner's astrological calendar.

rattan carriage – Used informally by the upper aristocracy and regularly by the middle aristocracy.

you've probably sought yourself out a young man – Ever since the return from Narutaki, the author's descriptions of her husband contain more examples of his wit and humor than before. One wonders if it is his personality that has changed or only her perception of him.

her hair was a little thin . . . – These details of her hair's appearance imply that she has led a life of hardship.

as, "I am happy," she gave her consent with good will. In this letter, she also wrote the gist of her conversations with his reverence. Yet, at the same time, imagining her feelings, I felt very sad indeed. She wrote on and on, a myriad things, and then at the end, "Enveloped in a mist of tears, I cannot tell what my brush writes; it feels strange." I felt that truly it must have been so for her.

After that, with the exchange of only about two letters, the matter was decided and his reverence went to bring the girl to the capital. It seems she was to travel all alone; thinking of that, I felt sad. It could not have been easy for the mother to let her go like that. She just must have in the back of her mind the thought that the father might now take care of his daughter. Even though one might hope for that, having her with me did not necessarily mean he would look after her as his own, and if it did not work out, then how very regrettable it would be. Although I felt worried by such thoughts, having made this promise, it was not as though I could change my mind now. "As the nineteenth of this month is an auspicious day . . . ," so it has been decided. I send a party out from here to greet her. Not wanting to attract a lot of attention, I just send a fresh-looking rattan carriage with four mounted attendants and a few extra servants. Our young lord gets in quickly, and I have the person who had first spoken of the girl to me ride in back.

Today, most unusually, there has been news from him. I instruct my son, "I fear he is on his way. It would not be good for you to run into each other. Go as quickly as you can. Keep her out of sight for awhile. We will just have to see how everything goes." This was to no avail, for my husband arrived ahead, and before anything could be done, just a few moments afterward, the welcoming party pulled in. When he asked, "Where has our young lord been?" I tried to put him off by saying one thing or another. However, since he seemed to suspect that something like this was going to happen today, I finally told him. "Since I am so forlorn, I have taken in a child that someone else seems to have abandoned." Whereupon he said, "Well, let's see it. Whose child is it? Since I've gotten old, you've probably sought yourself out a young man, and now you're going to dismiss me." This was most amusing; I ask him, "Well, shall I show her to you? Would you make her your own child?" "That would be fine. Please bring her out. Come on, come on." And as I was quite curious myself, I called her out.

She seemed very small for her age, in fact, she looked much like a child. Calling her closer, he said, "Stand up," and when she did we could see that she stood only about four feet high. It seemed that her hair was a little thin, tapering toward the ends and about four inches shorter than her height. She seemed quite charming; her hairline was lovely and her form

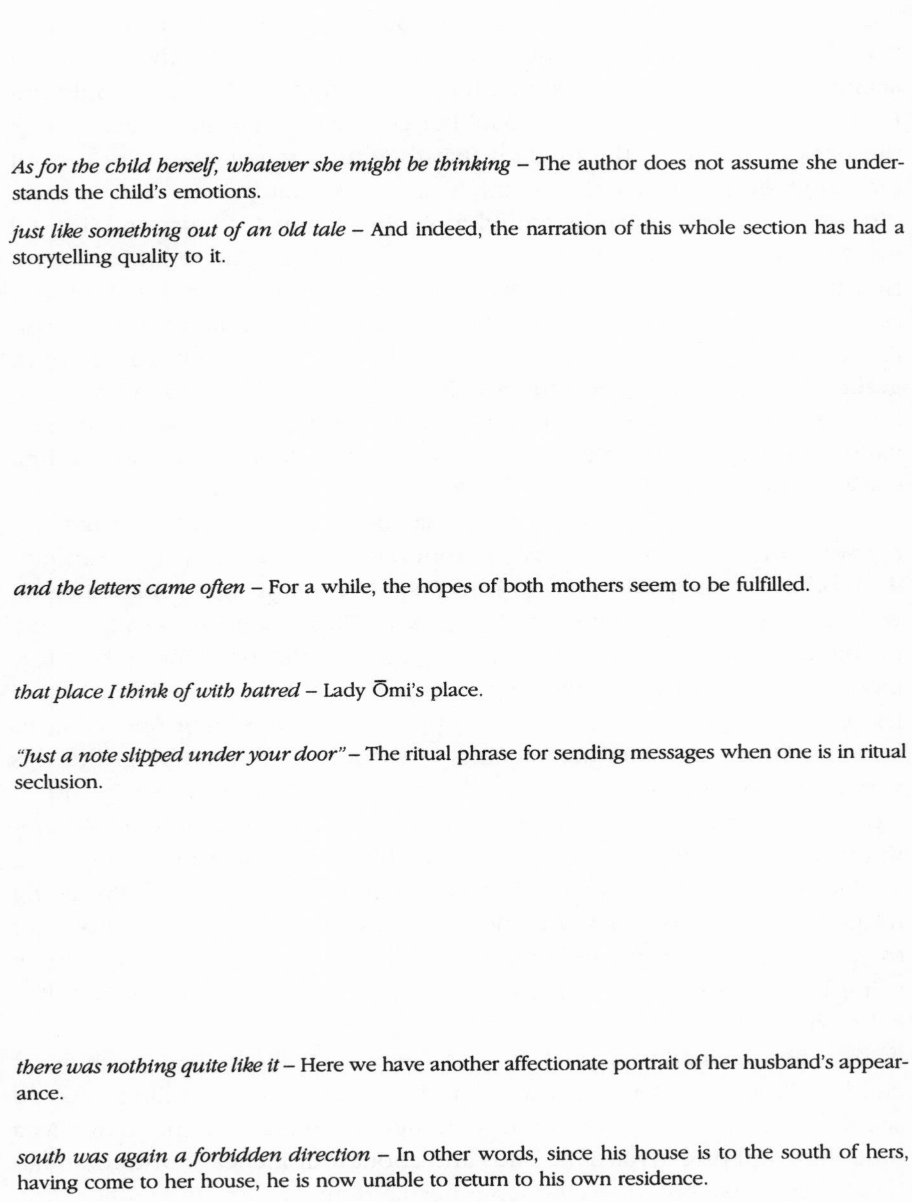

As for the child herself, whatever she might be thinking – The author does not assume she understands the child's emotions.

just like something out of an old tale – And indeed, the narration of this whole section has had a storytelling quality to it.

and the letters came often – For a while, the hopes of both mothers seem to be fulfilled.

that place I think of with hatred – Lady Ōmi's place.

"Just a note slipped under your door" – The ritual phrase for sending messages when one is in ritual seclusion.

there was nothing quite like it – Here we have another affectionate portrait of her husband's appearance.

south was again a forbidden direction – In other words, since his house is to the south of hers, having come to her house, he is now unable to return to his own residence.

elegant. Looking at her, he said, "Ah, how charming she is. Whose child is this? Come on, tell me." Thus pressed and thinking after all it was not likely to be an embarrassment, I may as well reveal it, I said, "Well then, do you really find her charming? Shall I tell you?" He pressed me even further. "What a fuss you make. Can't you tell, she is your very own child." He reacted with great surprise, "What? How? From where?" But since I didn't reply right away, he said, "I wonder, could she be the child I was told of at that place?" When I replied, "It would seem so," he went on, "How astonishing. I knew her mother must be living in some miserable state somewhere. But not to have seen the child until she was as old as this . . ." He broke into tears. As for the child herself, whatever she might be thinking, she too was looking down and crying. Those looking on found it so touching, just like something out of an old tale, and everyone cried. I couldn't help crying, bringing my sleeve to my eyes many times. He said, "Well, I never, out of the blue like this, just when I was thinking of not coming here anymore, now to have such a person here—I'll just have to take you home with me." So he joked, until quite late at night; we spent our time laughing and crying by turns, and then we all slept.

The next morning, when he was about to return, he called her out, looked at her, and seemed to find her so charming. "I'll take you with me right now. When the carriages come up, let's get in together." Then breaking out into laughter, he left. After that, when he wrote letters, he always asked, "How is the little one?" and the letters came often.

Then, on the night of the twenty-fifth, late in the evening, there is shouting. It is a fire. I heard them say, "It's quite close," and it turns out to be at that place I think of with hatred. While the twenty-fifth and twenty-sixth are a regular period of abstinence for him, still a letter comes addressed, "Just a note slipped under your door." It is most kind and concerned. These days, I find it strange when he writes that way. On the twenty-seventh, my direction is forbidden to him.

On the twenty-eighth, around midday, came the shouts of "His lordship arrives, his lordship arrives." The main gate was pushed open. I looked out and saw his carriage being drawn in. There were a lot of attendants holding on to the shafts; the outer blind was rolled up, the inner blinds pushed to the left and right. When the support for the shafts had been brought and placed, he leapt down. The red plums are just now in full bloom; he strolled a little under them; there was nothing quite like it. Lifting his voice and singing the refrain, "Ah, how charming it is . . . ," he climbed the stairs and came in. When he started thinking about the next day, he realized south was again a forbidden direction for him. "Why didn't you tell me," he asked. I replied, "If I had told you, what would you

teaching calligraphy, waka composition and the like to the little one – Now the education of her adopted daughter can serve as a diversion.

'Donning of the Train' ceremony – A ceremony for girls equivalent to the "Donning the Court Hat" ceremony for boys to signal the attainment of adulthood. That he speaks of holding the ceremony in concert with the ceremony for his second daughter by Tokihime, Senshi, is an indication that he is taking a serious interest in the girl's future.

I will go to the retired emperor's palace – The palace of former emperor Reizei. Presumably it is in a direction that will enable him to travel back to his own residence the next day without going in a southerly direction. His eldest daughter Chōshi is a consort of Emperor Reizei.

These days, the sky has mended its complexion . . . – This descriptive passage weaves together allusions to both Chinese and Japanese poetry. "A breeze that is neither warm nor cold" alludes to a couplet by the Chinese poet, Po Chü-i:

> Neither bright nor dark, the hazy moon,
> Neither warm nor cold, the gentle breeze.

"Wafts through the plums and invites the warbler" alludes to *Kokinshū* no. 13:

> I will send the scent
> of the plum blossoms along with
> the wind as messenger
> to invite the warbler
> and guide him here.

Finally, the last line gestures to another Po Chü-i couplet:

> At the roots of trees, snow disappears and reveals blooming flowers,
> At the edge of the pond, the ice melts releasing the grasses to grow.
> (*Zenshū*, 320–21)

This passage demonstrates the author's familiarity with Chinese poetry. Moreover, Shinozuka notes that Michitsuna's Mother's skillful combining of Chinese and Japanese poetic allusion with her own observation of the scene indicates her growing mastery of prose style (Shinozuka, *Kagerō nikki no kokoro to hyōgen*, 562–63).

intercalary second month – There is a second second month that year to adjust the calendar (see note for the intercalary fifth month in book two, p. 168).

Maybe I should just go back now that it's out – Kaneie is ever the tease.

what a cramped position I am in – Now as senior counselor, he cannot just travel about as he pleases.

have done?" "I would have prepared to avoid this direction." "Well, from now on, I must really try to divine what is really on your mind." And so it went; neither of us would let it be and ended up saying one thing and another. I turned to teaching calligraphy, *waka* composition and the like to the little one, thinking that with this at least, he could not find me at fault. Then, he said, "It would be bad not to do by her as expected. Sometime soon, let us hold a 'Donning of the Train' ceremony for her along with my daughter from the other place." Dusk fell. "As I mentioned before, I will go to the retired emperor's palace," he said, and with a loud clearing of the way, he departed.

These days, the sky has mended its complexion, and the air feels soft and gentle. A breeze that is neither warm nor cold wafts through the plums and invites the warbler. One hears the peaceful voices of the chickens in the garden. Gazing up to the roof, one sees the sparrows chirping as they go in and out from under the tiles, building their nests. The garden grasses raise faces released from the ice.

On the first day of the intercalary second month, rain falls gently. After that the sky clears. On the third, although my direction is clear for him, there is not a word. As night falls on the fourth day, thinking again and again to myself how strange this is, I go to bed only to be awoken in the middle of the night by the commotion of a fire somewhere. Although I can hear that it is close by, I feel a certain heaviness and do not get up. But one after another, people who might be expected to call come and ask how we are, including some people of such status that they would not normally come on foot. Well, I have to get up for them, so I come out and respond to their questions. When they hear, "The fire seems to have died down now," they go home. Just as I go back inside and lay down, I sense that outriders have stopped in front of our gate. As I listen, thinking it strange, "His lordship arrives," is called out. The lights have been extinguished, so it is very dark as he creeps into the room. "It's pitch black in here. I guess you thought you could make do with the light of the fire awhile ago. I came, you know, because it seemed the fire was close to here. Maybe I should just go back now that it's out," says he, as he slips into bed. "Actually, I had wanted to come earlier this evening, but since all my attendants were out, I couldn't leave. If it were the old days, I could have just come by myself on horseback, but now, what a cramped position I am in. Turning over in my mind just what would it take for me to be able make a visit at this time of night, I fell asleep, and then this big commotion happened. Why, how intriguingly convenient, I thought. It was really quite strange." He spoke with seeming concern for me. When dawn came, he said, "My carriage must be quite a sight," and returned quickly. I hear that the sixth and the seventh are a period of abstinence for

it sounds as though the moss on the rocks suffers – An unusual and powerful simile, conveying both the harshness of the rain and the sensitivity of her own state of consciousness.

Kamo – The Kamo Shrine in northeast Kyoto. This could be either the upper or lower shrine.

someone who said, "Let's go quietly together" – Of course, there is no way to know who the someone was, but it can be assumed it was a woman friend. "Quietly" means without ostentation.

I wonder if others would think them hard done by – The phrasing of this has occasioned speculation by commentators. It appears that she is drawing a contrast between what others might think and what she thinks. *Zenshū* commentators suggest that she regards the farmer's physical hard work as a manifestation of karmic retribution and writes this description to symbolically represent her own mental suffering (*Zenshū,* 322). Uemura posits that, faced with the sight of the laboring peasants, she is reflecting that "however physically hard their labor may be, they are probably spiritually happy. In contrast to that, she herself has a physically comfortable life, but her spiritual suffering is so deep she even feels envious of them. Of course, that is why the bright poem from the *Man'yōshū* . . . comes into her mind in the face of this scene" (Uemura, *Taisei*, vol. 6, 416).

Kitano – At that time, the general name for the north end of Kyoto.

old poem about picking watercress – Poem from *Man'yōshū,* book 10:

> For your sake
> plucking cress in the marsh
> of mountain fields,
> in the water from melted snow,
> the hem of my apron is drenched. (Aoki, *Man'yōshū,* vol. 3, 26)

Funaoka Hill – A hill in northwestern Kyoto.

that other place close to here – Ōmi's place. Since he has come so late at night without notice, she suspects that he had some kind of trouble at the other place, perhaps a quarrel.

I find this somewhat strange – It is strange that he came late in the evening when he knew he could not spend the night.

offerings for a special dispensation – If the taboo was broken, one could make amends to the gods with special offerings.

"But I shall not count this as one of the nights . . ." – This remark and the following section is interesting for the way it makes explicit the lover's account book they both kept in their minds.

the snipe flapping wings – Allusion to poem no. 761 in *Kokinshū*:

> one hundred times or
> more I hear the fluttering
> of the snipes' wings
> as I count the lonely hours
> till dawn when you have not come (Rodd, *Kokinshū*, 268)

him. On the eighth, it rains. At night, it sounds as though the moss on the rocks suffers.

On the tenth I made a pilgrimage to Kamo. Since there was someone who said, "Let's go quietly together," I thought, *why not*, and went with her. It is a place that always makes one feel fresh and new. Today, too, I felt my heart expanding. Even at the sight of farmers plowing the field, I wonder if others would think them hard done by. As in former times, we went by way of Kitano, and there we saw women and children picking something in the marsh. In a flash, the line from the old poem about picking watercress came to mind, and I imagined the hems of their aprons. Taking a tour around Funaoka Hill was also lovely. I returned home around dark and had just gotten to sleep when I heard urgent knocking at the door. Waking up with my heart pounding, I found just what I least expected, that it was he. The demon in my heart gave rise to the thought, I wonder if he has run into trouble at that other place close to here and has been sent home. While he looked perfectly nonchalant, I spent the night with doubts that did not melt away. The next morning, he returned when the sun had risen a little. Then, five or six days pass.

On the sixteenth, the pattering of the rain sounded so forlorn. As it gets light, I find that an affectionate letter has come from him while I was sleeping. It contains among other things the lines, "Today, it seems your place is in a forbidden direction for me. Though I won't be able to stay, what if I come anyway?" No sooner do I send off a reply than he arrives himself. Since it is getting on for dusk, one can imagine I find this somewhat strange. Night comes and he has the air of being undecided about leaving. "How about making some offerings for a special dispensation tonight?" he suggests. "That would not be the proper thing to do," I say, urging him to leave. Yet, as he moves to leave the room, in spite of myself, I murmur under my breath, "But I shall not count this as one of the nights that you actually visited." Hearing me, he says, "If that's the case, it did no good at all to come. I don't care about the other nights, but you must count tonight." Then, as might be expected after that, I didn't hear from him for awhile; the eighteenth or nineteenth arrived. Thinking about this, I could not get out of my mind that there had been something behind his saying, "You must count tonight." Although it was becoming a rare thing for me to do, I sent him a poem:

katatoki ni	Converting moments
kaheshi yo kazu wo	into whole nights, when you go
kazofureba	and count that way,
shigi no moro ha mo	along with the snipe flapping wings
tayushi to zo naku	so many times, I tire and cry.

the arrival of festival time – The Kamo Festival celebrated in the fourth month, in which flutes and *sakaki* leaves play an prominent part. The warm weather makes her think of the festival.

Since this was not unusual – That is, for him to send work without coming himself.

Yahata Festival – Festival held at Iwashimizu Yahata Shrine.

the young people who had been left in charge – Her son and adopted daughter.

Biro carriage – A lightweight carriage with woven lattice roof and sides, used only by people of high rank.

Reizei Palace gate – Apparently this was to the northeast of the present Nijōjō in Kyoto.

Kiyomizu – Temple in the eastern hills of Kyoto (see illustration on p. 289).

His reply:

ikanare ya shigi no hane gaki kazu shirazu omofu kahi naki kowe ni naku ramu	Well, what about it? As limitless as the snipe's flapping of wings, my love, but to no avail, it seems you still will cry.

Although it was a reply, it was enough to make me regret having sent a poem in the first place; I asked myself why did I do it. These days, in the garden, almost all the blossoms have fallen; it looks like a sea of petals.

Today, the twenty-seventh, rain fell from last night, and now the wind sweeps away the remaining blossoms.

The third month has arrived. The leaf buds on the trees are just big enough to hide the sparrows; sensing the arrival of festival time, one thinks fondly of *sakaki* leaves and flutes. Along with being moved by the season, since there has been no word from him for awhile, I still regret having sent that poem, and, more than during our usual periods of separation, I feel ill at ease. I wonder what's wrong with me.

The seventh day of this month arrived. Today I received this message: "Please sew this. I am afraid due to an abstinence that I cannot visit." Since this was not unusual, I simply sent back a nonchalant reply, "Missive received." From around noon, rain began to fall gently.

The tenth: there is a big fuss over the celebration of the Yahata Festival at court. Someone I knew was going, so I went along with that person, attracting as little attention as possible. When we got back around noon, since the young people who had been left in charge said, "We must see the sights. The procession hasn't passed by here yet." I sent them right out in the carriage we had just returned in.

The next day, people clamored to go and see the return procession. As I was feeling poorly and spending the day lying down, I certainly did not feel like sightseeing, but being pressed by this and that person, we finally did ride out in a Biro carriage in which only four could fit. We took up a place just north of the Reizei Palace gate. As we did not see many other people there, I began to feel more like myself. We had just been there for awhile when the procession went by. Two people I knew, one shrine musician and one dancer, were mixed in with the procession. These days, there is nothing special to speak of.

On the eighteenth, again I went unobtrusively along with someone making a pilgrimage to Kiyomizu. After the evening service was over and we had come back from the temple, it was around midnight. I returned to my companion's place, and we were just having something to eat when one of my attendants called out, "There appears to be a fire in

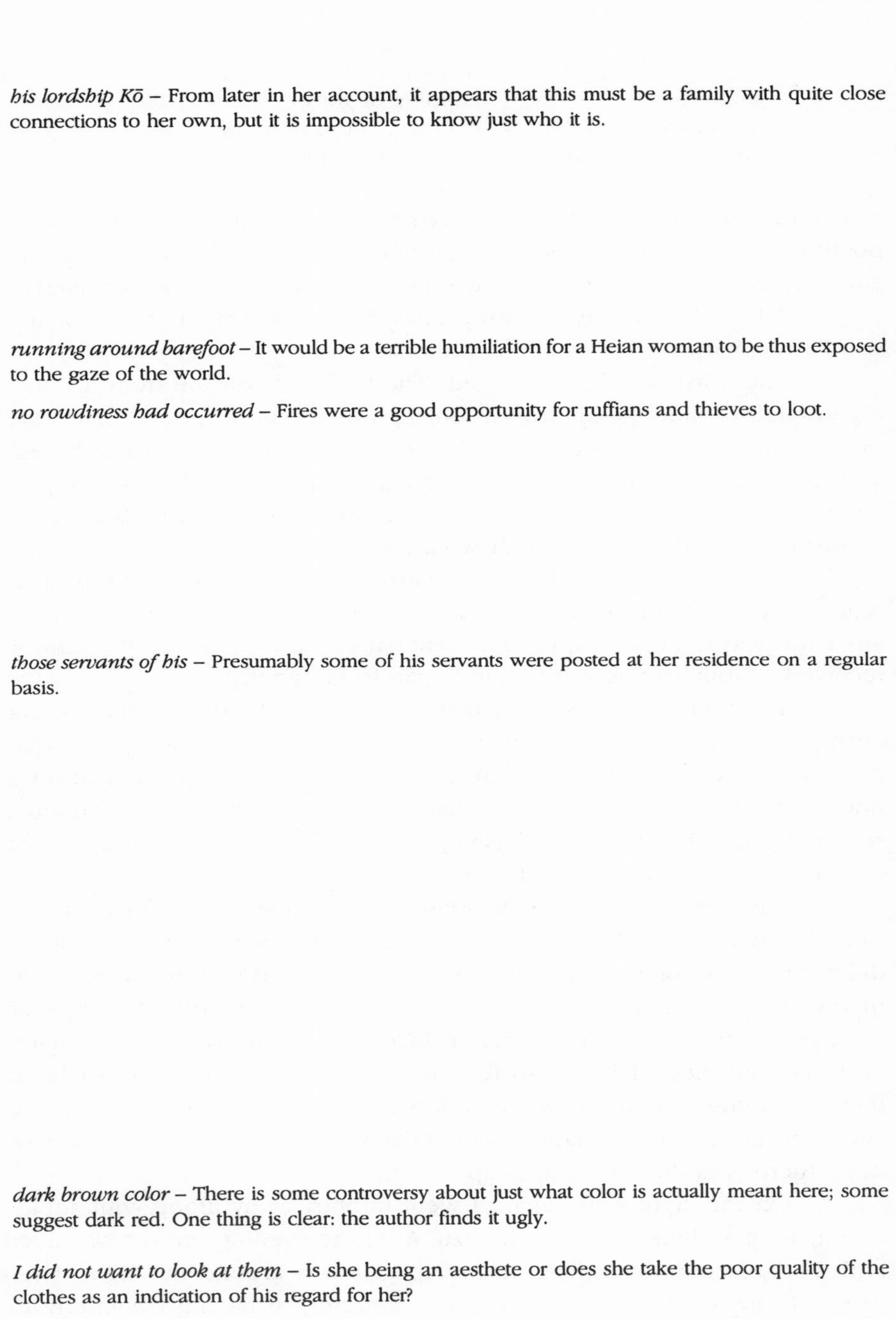

his lordship Kō – From later in her account, it appears that this must be a family with quite close connections to her own, but it is impossible to know just who it is.

running around barefoot – It would be a terrible humiliation for a Heian woman to be thus exposed to the gaze of the world.

no rowdiness had occurred – Fires were a good opportunity for ruffians and thieves to loot.

those servants of his – Presumably some of his servants were posted at her residence on a regular basis.

dark brown color – There is some controversy about just what color is actually meant here; some suggest dark red. One thing is clear: the author finds it ugly.

I did not want to look at them – Is she being an aesthete or does she take the poor quality of the clothes as an indication of his regard for her?

the northwest direction, let's go out and look." "It's still as far away as China," said another voice. Just as I was thinking to myself, *nevertheless, it is in a worrisome direction*, we heard from some people, "It is the residence of his lordship Kō." At this, my alarm was extreme. Since my house is only separated by a earthen wall from that residence, there was big commotion. I could only think how upsetting this must be for the young people, and, wanting to get back as quickly as possible, we left in confusion—it was hardly a time to worry about affixing the carriage blinds. By the time we had finally ridden back here, it was all over. Our house remained; our neighbors who had lost their house were gathered here. Thanks to the young lord being here, my daughter who I feared had been running around barefoot on the ground, was safely placed in a carriage, and the gate had been kept firmly shut during the confusion so no rowdiness had occurred. Seeing and hearing how well he had managed things as a man, I was choked with emotion. While the people who had come to stay here were lamenting, "We barely escaped with our lives," the fire died down. Although quite a while had passed, the one who ought to call had not come. Meanwhile from all over the place, even people whom we did not expect came inquiring after us. For so many years whenever he heard that there might be a fire in this neighborhood, he would rush over; how shocking to realize it had come to this. I had those servants of his who would be likely to tell him that something had happened here asked if he had been informed; when I heard that he had been told, it seemed stranger and stranger to me. Just at that point, there was a knocking at the door. A servant went to see who it was, and when I heard "His lordship has come," I felt my heart calm a little. Then, he said, "When my men who were here came and told me, I was so surprised. I regret alarming you by not coming sooner." Talking like this, the time passed until at last hearing again and again the crowing of the cocks, we went to bed. I must have slept very well because we slept right into the morning. Even now, as there is a commotion of people coming to ask after us, I rise to answer them. "It will probably only get busier," he said as he hurried off.

In a little while, there arrived from him a large quantity of men's clothing. "This is what I could put together. Please have the governor pick first, and then distribute the rest to the others gathered there," was the message. But as he had arranged this on the spur of the moment, the clothes were of a dark brown color. They were so wretched, I did not want to look at them. When I went to see how everyone was faring, three people had fallen ill and were complaining miserably.

And thus the sun set on the twentieth. I heard that from the twenty-first to the twenty-fourth he was in the usual ritual seclusion. Since for the people gathered here this year was one in which the southern direction

moved to my father's residence – One can surmise that the Kō family must have had a close relationship with the author's family.

the emblems of the next ritual seclusion – Taboo emblems were put up for a period of ritual seclusion to ward off evil influences and so that visitors would know not to call, and so on. If one really did not care about whether one lived or died, one would not bother to observe these rituals. Various commentators remark on the objectivity about her own situation that the author seems to have attained by book three. Here is a specific instance of it. She has just expressed how little desire she has to live, but then she takes a step back and observes her surroundings and makes an ironic comment on the attachment to life that the emblems represent.

festival – Here it is the Kamo Festival, which began with Lustration Ritual on the banks of the Kamo River.

Ichijō grand minister – Kaneie's elder brother, Koremasa, who in the previous year had just assumed the position of regent, the most powerful position in government.

hearing people say – In the original she also says *omofu hito mo kiku*, "I hear people thinking." How does one listen to people's thoughts? *Zenshū* commentators suggest she is speaking figuratively, of seeing people's admiration for Koremasa on their faces (*Zenshū,* 328).

Chisoku Temple – Apparently in the Murasakino district of northern Kyoto.

he apparently sent this – The verb ending for this phrase in the original, *meri*, indicates surmise on the speaker's part, based on some objective, often visual, evidence. However, it can also be used simply to soften statements. It is pertinent how she introduces this subject of her son's love poems, because the author will devote a lot of space to this poetry in the rest of book three. Some commentators suggest that she pays so much attention to her son's poems because she was actually their composer, or at least had a hand in them. In the poem collection at the end of the volume, a preface to a few of Michitsuna's courting poems plainly states that they were composed for him by his mother (p. 389). Others suggest that her recording of his poems reflects a mother's pride in son's first literary (and amatory?) efforts.

The other interesting issue involved with Michitsuna's love poems is that only poems from those suits that were ultimately unsuccessful are recorded. We know from other historical records that around this same time Michitsuna had formed a liaison with a woman who bore him a child a year later, but that affair is not mentioned at all in the diary.

Having begun to long . . . – His poem puns on *afuhi*, the name of the heartvine plant, which is the principal decoration for the Kamo Festival, and can also be construed as "meeting day."

was forbidden, they could not stay here long, so on the twentieth they all moved to my father's residence. While thinking it must be a relief for them, I only seemed to become more aware of my own misery. Since I am in such a wretched position, I feel as though I would hardly regret leaving this dreamlike life. Then, when I look around and see the emblems of the next ritual seclusion stuck on the pillars of the house, it seems that I am still very much attached to this life. We entered the period of ritual seclusion on the twenty-fifth. On the night it was to end, there was a knocking at the gate; when a servant said, "We are in seclusion, the gate is firmly shut," there was the sound of him leaving thwarted.

On the next day, even though he knew that my direction was forbidden to him, he appeared during the day, and left just about the time to light torches. After that, as per usual he sent messages with various excuses for not meeting.

Over here too, we had a lot of ritual seclusions; a little after the tenth of the month, the world began to buzz with excitement about the festival. Someone invited me to go along "on the quiet," so I saw everything starting with the Lustration Ritual on the banks of the Kamo. When I went to present my own offerings at the Kamo Shrine, I happened to be there at the same time as the Ichijō grand minister. If one spoke of an impressive commotion, that was it. Seeing his dignified bearing, I thought how much he resembled my husband, and it seemed to me that on public occasions my husband must not be inferior to him at all. But hearing people say, "Oh, how splendid, what a man," I was thrown back into my own melancholy thoughts.

Drawn along by someone who was not of the same cast of feelings, on another day I went to see the return procession around Chisoku Temple; the young lord followed behind in his own carriage. Just as the carriages were to return, he got attracted by a fine-looking woman's carriage and started to follow her. Although he chased her, doing his best not to be left behind—perhaps she did not want him to know where she lived—he soon lost her and then began to chase around making inquiries. On the next day, he apparently sent this:

omohi some	Having begun to long,
mono wo koso omohe	oh now, how I long for you.
kefu yori ha	From today
au hi haruka ni	the next Aoi Festival is far,
nariya shinuramu	must I wait so long to meet you?

This was what he sent, but it seems she only said, "I haven't the faintest idea what this is about." So, he wrote again:

my heart soars to the cedars – Michitsuna is indicating that he knows she is connected with the Yamato area around Nara by alluding to *Kokinshū* poem, no. 982:

  my hut stands at the
foot of Miwa Mountain so
  if you long to see
me once more come and visit
at the gate where cedars stand (Rodd, *Kokinshū*, 332)

The allusion also contains the invitation he hopes to receive.

There is also a pun in this poem on *sugitachi*, "cedars standing" and "have gone too far" (in terms of emotions).

Most inauspicious – She refers to a legend about a snake god of Miwa Mountain who visited a princess at night disguised as a man.

he was no more visible than the cuckoo in the unohana – She turns away from describing Michitsuna's courting to reflect on her relations with Kaneie. The *unohana* was the flower of the season. The cuckoo was traditionally thought to hide in the *unohana*. It will be remembered that in her first correspondence with her husband, she referred to him as a cuckoo.

longest iris roots – Part of the festivities of the Tango Festival on the fifth day of the fifth month was to gather iris roots and arrange them into festoons to decorate the eaves of the houses. Their fragrance was supposed to protect the household from illness during the coming heat of summer.

the one over there who is about the same age as our little one – Kaneie's second daughter by Tokihime, Senshi. Kaneie had spoken of holding the coming-of-age ceremonies for both girls at the same time.

In a hidden marsh . . . it began to grow – Obliquely referring to the author's adopted daughter.

The young lord also prepared another festoon for that place – Hereafter, when Michitsuna is sending a courting poem, "that place" or "the usual place" always refers to the Yamato woman's place.

These sleeves of mine – This translation makes the poem a little more explicit than it is in the original. The grammar of the original makes ambiguous what he wants to dry by laying them on someone else's sleeves; it could be the iris roots or it could be the sleeves. Either way, however, the poem is suggestive.

warinaku mo	I cannot help it,
sugitachi ni keru	my heart soars to the cedars
kokoro kana	at Miwa Mountain's foot,
miwa no yama moto	the first time I asked after you,
tadzune hajimete	I was already too far gone.

He said this because the person would seem to be from the Yamato area. I believe her reply was:

miwa no yama	Most inauspicious,
machi miru koto no	it would be to attend you
yuyushisa ni	at Miwa Mountain,
sugi tateri to mo	I surely would not tell you
e koso shirasene	even where the cedars stand.

Things going on in this way, even though it was getting on to the end of the month, he was no more visible than the cuckoo in the *unohana*, and the month ended without even a word from him.

Actually, on the twenty-eighth, it seems he had sent word on his way back from worshipping at the shrine, "I have not been feeling well. . . ."

The fifth month arrived. The young people here made quite a fuss over finding the longest iris roots, and since we didn't have much else to do, we gathered them up and strung them together into festoons. I said, "Let's send this to the one over there who is about the same age as our little one here." So I wrote this and attached it to the middle of the bundle:

kakure nu ni	In a hidden marsh,
ohisome ni keri	it was that it began to grow,
ayame gusa	this iris plant,
shiru hito nashi ni	without anyone knowing,
fukaki shita ne wo	it put down deep roots.

and sent it along with the young lord.

This was sent in reply:

ayame gusa	This iris plant root,
ne ni arawaruru	has been revealed to us
kefu koso ha	finally today
itsuka to machishi	waiting and wondering when,
kahi mo arikere	has met with good result.

The young lord also prepared another festoon for that place:

waga sode ha	These sleeves of mine
hiku to nurashitsu	in pulling up iris roots
ayame gusa	have gotten all damp,

sleeves with no design – The Yamato girl puns on *aya*, which means "design," as of a pattern on cloth, and also in the combination *aya naki*, which can mean "no design," "no plans," implying in this context, "I have no plans to fall in love with you."

some people have been swept away – Historical records for 972 do report extensive flooding in the capital that year.

monk I had met at Ishiyama Monastery – Whether this is the same monk who sent her the letter about the dream or not is not clear.

'If at least the wind blew not so cold . . .' – Allusion to a poem by Sone Yoshisada, a poet who was a contemporary of the author:

> On the night I wait
> if at least the wind blew
> not so cold
> I would not regret not seeing
> the one who does not come. (*Zenshū*, 333)

Since she quotes this poem in midsummer when the wind is anything but cold, it has a sarcastic ring to it. It is like saying, the wind isn't cold so I do not care whether I see you or not, but saying that would invite the misfortune of turning him away completely.

the aprons of those tending the fields – This looks like an allusion to an old poem, but no source poem has been definitely identified.

I have not even heard the voice of the cuckoo – Sensitivity to seasonal phenomena was highly cultivated by Heian society. The cuckoo only calls at night so one must sleep lightly to hear it.

hito no tamoto ni kakete kawakase	would that I could dry them by laying them over yours.

The reply:

hiki tsuramu tamoto ha shirazu ayame gusa aya naki sode ni kakezu mo aranamu	These sleeves that would draw themselves near with iris roots, I know them not at all, I would not have you lay them over sleeves with no design.

This is what she seems to have said.

From early in the morning on the sixth day, rain begins, and it falls for three or four days. The rivers overflow and they say some people have been swept away. That too has taken its place in my myriad melancholy thoughts, and even though my thoughts are quite beyond expression, since I am now used to it, I do not fret about what to do. In the midst of this train of thought, I receive this message from that monk I had met at Ishiyama Monastery, "I am praying for your ladyship," to which I reply, "Now, as I feel I am one who has reached the end, what could even the Buddha do for me. Only now, I would just have you pray for the young lord, that he might come into his own as a man." Yet, as I write this, I don't know why, my eyes cloud over and tears pour down.

The tenth arrived. Today, he sent a letter here with the young lord. "I have not been feeling well at all, and thus I have lost touch with you. How are you?" As for replying, I waited until the next day when the young lord was going for a visit and composed this: "Yesterday, I thought perhaps I ought to have sent back a reply right away, yet, it has gotten to the point where it feels awkward for me to send word to you unless our son is paying a visit. You deign to inquire, 'How are you?' I wonder, 'Well what is there to say?' It has become perfectly reasonable for things to be this way. Actually, not having seen you for months, my heart is very much at peace. Yet, were I to say, 'If at least the wind blew not so cold . . .' perhaps that would seem to invite misfortune." Dusk fell, the young lord reported, "He was away on a trip to the Kamo Springs, so I have returned without even delivering your reply." "Well, isn't that just fine," was what I said, although it is not what I felt.

These days, the appearance of the clouds is never calm, one never knows what the weather will do next, and I imagine how the aprons of those tending the fields are always drenched. I have not even heard the voice of the cuckoo. Although people who brood over love are not supposed to be able to sleep when they lie down, strangely enough, I seem to

had not yet nourished his ears – This phrase stands out in the original as a direct translation of a Chinese poetic expression.

'It's all right; it's all right' – Translates *yoi zo, yoi zo,* which is the old gardener's attempt to render what he hears as their message in an onomatopoeic way.

"That's so; that's so" – Translates *shika, shika,* which is the author's onomatopoeic rendering of the cicada's response. The voices of the cicada fill the summer air with a din that has an electric quality to it. In the buzz, many different sounds can be imagined.

how touching, and I was desolate – Her mention of desolation at the end of this delightful passage is unsettling. However, the association of beauty and sadness pervades classical Japanese discourse. Here, the elderly gardener suddenly being able to hear the cicadas, and thus freshly becoming aware of the season and its passing, evokes the poignancy of the passing of time and of old age. The author has reached the point where growing old is no longer a distant, inconceivable thing.

the usual place – The Yamato woman's place.

spindle tree – *Soba* tree, a variety of the *nishikigi* or "brocade tree," much admired for its autumn colors.

neglected, lamenting tree – Pun on *nageki,* "cast-off tree" and "to lament."

dipped in the vat of flattery – She turns the leaves of his natural image into "leaves of words" and then shifts to the imagery of an artificial process, the dyeing of cloth. The phrase "vat of flattery" is implicit in the original but made explicit in the translation.

be sleeping very well. But one or the other of my attendants will say, "Night before last, I heard its voice." "It was crying this morning at dawn too," and since others have heard it, I feel rather ashamed to say that I am one who hasn't yet, so not saying anything to others, just feeling this in my heart:

ware zo ke ni	Is it really so,
tokete nurameya	when I melt thus into sleep,
hototogisu	that my love longing
mono omohi masaru	becomes the voice of the cuckoo
kowe to naruramu	who then sings all the more sadly.

Thus, I spoke quietly to myself.

Like this, with time weighing heavily on my hands, I came into the sixth month. Since the heat from the morning sun on the east side of the house was unbearable, I moved over to rooms in the south gallery; just when I had moved there, I had the uncomfortable feeling that someone was close by, so quietly lying down behind something, I listened. The voices of the cicada were so exuberant, but there was an old man hard of hearing who had not yet nourished his ears with them. Broom in hand, he was about to sweep the garden; just as he was standing under a tree, suddenly the cicadas cried out so stridently, he was startled and looking up said something like this, "So you cicadas come to say, 'It's all right; it's all right.' Even you insects know your seasons." And in unison with his words, the cicadas filled the garden with cries of "That's so; that's so." The feeling arose, *how charming, how touching*, and I was desolate.

The young lord sends to the usual place this poem attached to a branch of the spindle tree, on which a few leaves had turned red:

natsu yama no	Since the dew is deep
ko no shita tsuyu no	under the trees of summer mountains,
fukakereba	so soon the color
katsu zo nageki no	can flame on branches of this
iro mo eni keru	neglected, lamenting tree.

She replied:

tsuyu ni nomi	Just touched with dew,
iro mo enureba	and they flame with such color?
koto no ha wo	I would like to know
iku shiho to ka ha	how many times your leaves of words
shiru bekaruramu	were dipped in the vat of flattery?

Around the time these words were being exchanged, I found myself staying up late into the night, and a rare, rather warmly written letter from him

I notice that he seems somewhat despondent – If one were to speculate on why Kaneie may have been feeling despondent around that time, one would consider the health of his eldest brother, the regent and chancellor, Koremasa. *Eiga monogatari* reports a lengthy illness for Koremasa that eventually lead to his resigning his duties in the tenth month and to his death in the eleventh month of this year (McCullough and McCullough, *A Tale of Flowering Fortunes*, 110. Note that McCullough gives the reading Koretada for Koremasa's name). It seems reasonable that members of the family would have been aware of his illness in the summer. Kaneie's recent good fortune had rested on his relationship with Koremasa. His relations with his second eldest brother, Kanemichi, were bad, so any danger to Koremasa's health must have made Kaneie nervous about his own political future, as well as making him poignantly aware of the uncertainty of life.

the house of my father . . . is torn down – Since she makes no mention of a disaster, we assume this was a demolition to make way for a new structure.

I wonder how it must look to the other people – In front of her relatives, she is embarrassed by his lack of attention.

worried over the offerings to be made for Obon – The annual observances for the dead in the eighth month. Arranging for offerings and so on seems to be one of the services that he has performed for her over the years, but she cannot be sure he will continue to do so. The uncertainty of knowing when the marriage relationship is over causes a variety of anxieties.

kutsukutsuboshi – An onomatopoeic name for a type of cicada.

"Only I saying nothing" – A line from a poem in *Utsubo monogatari*:

> So very noisy
> the voices of the insects
> perched in the greenery
> only I saying nothing
> grieve all the more.

(Kōno Tama, *Utsubo monogatari*, vol. 10 of *Nihon koten bungaku taikei* [Tokyo: Iwanami Shoten, 1959; reprint 1980], 212.)

I have been given a revelation – She may have had a dream or received the augury from a yin-yang diviner. This was possibly her thirty-seventh year, and according to traditional astrology, a women's thirty-third and thirty-seventh years were supposed to be particularly dangerous. In fact, the conjecture that the author was nineteen at the time of her marriage to Kaneie is based on calculating back from this year as her thirty-seventh year.

Even strike me or pinch me, why don't you? – It is as if Kaneie is trying to incite her old feelings of jealousy and chagrin. Perhaps he misses it.

arrived. The first word in over twenty days, how sporadic our communication has become. Since I have gotten used to this terrible state of affairs, there is really no use complaining, and I treat the letter as a matter of no great import, but then again I notice that he seems somewhat despondent and, feeling quite sorry for him, I reply with greater promptness than before.

Around that time, as the house of my father, away on duty in the provinces, is torn down, the whole household has moved here, and with so many relatives around, there is a bustle of activity from dawn to dusk, but there is not a word from him, to the point that I wonder how it must look to the other people.

After the tenth of the seventh month, when all the guests had returned home—you could hardly tell they had been here—again there was very little to do, I began to hear various sighs from my people as they worried over the offerings to be made for Obon; I felt very sad and anxious too. Then on the fourteenth, as per usual, the offerings were sent over with a note from his household office. I thought to myself, *I wonder for how long he will continue to do at least this.*

In this way, the eighth month arrived. On the first, rain falls all day. It is almost like autumn drizzle; around late afternoon, it clears up. Listening to the cries of the *kutsukutsuboshi* cicada, which are so noisy, I intone the old poem, "Only I saying nothing." For what reason I wonder, it is a day when I feel strangely forlorn and tears well up. I have been given a revelation that I might die next month; I wonder if it might even be this month. There is a great fuss being made over the return banquet for the sumo tournament, but I hear it as something outside my concern.

The eleventh arrived and a letter from him said, "I have had a very unexpected dream. One way or another, I need to talk to you," and so on, as per usual, he said many things I could hardly think were true,

[There is a break in the text here, a portion seems to be lost. Presumably, in the lost section, he arrives and they converse.]

As I could not say anything, he says, "Why don't you say something?" When I respond with "What is there for me to say?" I am assailed with, "Say, 'Why don't you come?' 'Why don't you ask after me?' Say, 'I hate you.' 'I'm miserable.' Even strike me or pinch me, why don't you?" "Since you have just said all that I would say, what is there left?" and so we stopped. The next morning, saying "Soon after this business of the return banquet is over, I will come and visit," he goes back. I heard that indeed the return banquet took place on the seventeenth.

As the end of the month arrives, although I notice that much time has passed since the business after which he promised to come was over,

the ill-omened month – The ninth month in which she is predicted to die.

she has never let him see anything in her own hand – She has never written anything in her own hand because it is a revelation that invites further intimacy. We will recall that the author did not send anything in her own hand to Kaneie for a long time, arousing just this same resentment (pp. 59–61).

In the evening . . . – The word for "wife," *tsuma*, is embedded in the word *tsumadzuma*, "corners." *Kakikeru* means "spin a web" but also can mean "to have written." The poem as a whole refers to the folk belief that if a spider spins a web near you, especially with a thread attached to your clothing, then you will be visited that night by your lover.

pricked into white paper – Apparently, she has pricked her poem with a sharp point into thick white paper, producing something like Braille. It is a very clever way of technically answering in her hand without actually revealing her hand (in more ways than one).

It is strange . . . – She picks up his pun on "to write" and "spin" and implies that if she writes in any serious fashion, he will be indiscreet with her letters.

Is this Tajima? – The poem alludes to a passage in *Nihon shoki*, "Chronicle of Japan," the eighth-century official history of Japan. The story tells how Prince Homutsuwaki, who apparently was unable to speak as a child, miraculously spoke his first words, "What is that?" when he saw a swan flying across the sky. His father was overjoyed and had a retainer follow the bird to capture it. The retainer eventually accomplished the task in the district of Tajima. Furthermore, Tajima, the place-name, was used as a pillow word for "white sand beach" in poetry, and "traces of a bird" became a figure for "writings of a brush."

too old fashioned for her – The allusions to a scholarly text in Chinese like the *Nihon shoki* may have appeared stuffy to the young woman.

I don't really feel anything about that now, but just pass the time feeling sad, pondering the ill-omened month that draws near.

The young lord sends a letter to the usual place. Since in all the various replies from before, she has never let him see anything in her own hand, he is feeling resentful:

yufu sare no	In the evening,
neya no tsumadzuma	as I gaze at the corners
nagamureba	of my bed chamber,
tedzukara nomi zo	I notice spider wives
kumo mo kakikeru	only spin by their own hand.

was what he sent. What did she think of it—she sent a reply that had been pricked into white paper:

kumo no kaku	It is strange about
ito zo ayashiki	the thread the spider spins;
kaze fukeba	when the wind blows,
sora ni midaruru	it is scattered in the sky,
mono to shiru shiru	this is something I know well.

To which he replied immediately:

tsuyu nite mo	With a life as
inochi kaketaru	fragile as dew depending
kumo no i ni	on the spider's web,
araki kaze wo ba	as for rough winds that blow,
tare ka fusekamu	who could ward them off but I?

They said, "It is already dark." There was no answering poem.

The next day, perhaps he was thinking of her poem on white paper from yesterday, he spoke thus:

tadjima no ya	Is this Tajima?
kuguhi no ato wo	Today I look for traces
kefu mireba	of that fine white swan,
yuki no shirahama	all I see is white on a
shirokute ha mishi	white sand beach covered with snow.

and sent it to her. But they said, "The mistress seems to be out," so there was no response. The next day, he went in person to beg for a word from her, "Has the lady returned? Is there a response?" But he was told, "Oh, yesterday's poem, the young mistress felt it was too old fashioned for her, so she didn't reply." The next day, he sent a note, "So my poem of the other day was too old fashioned. How very true":

How true it is . . . – He puns on *furu*, "time passing" and "to grow old," as well as being a place-name in the Yamato district, which links the poem to her personally.

I feel lost as though . . . – Again, he alludes to a story in the ancient chronicles, this time the legend of the sun goddess who, upset at her brother's outrageous behavior, locked herself in a cave in heaven, plunging the world into darkness. While Michitsuna spends sleepless nights longing for his love, it takes so long for dawn to come, that it is as though the sun goddess has locked herself away. He is also implying that the Yamato woman has locked herself away from him.

So that's how it is . . . – Kazuraki Mountain is in the Yamato area, so this place-name makes a connection with the Yamato woman. Another name for the god of that mountain is Hitogoto Nushinokami, the "One Word God."

Young people are prone to write like this – What is "like this"? We are clearly to get it from the context, but it is not so easily grasped at this point so distant in time and culture. On the one hand, Shinozuka suggests that she may be referring to her son's predilection in verse writing for references to ancient stories and mysterious legends. This in turn reminds her of her own youth and obsession with the romantic world of "the old tales" (Shinozuka, *Kagerō nikki no kokoro to hyōgen*, 614–15).

On the other hand, the author may be merely summarizing young love. Kakimoto glosses this passage as, "Young people pass their time exchanging love letters like this while I . . ." (*Zen chūshaku*, vol. 2, 103). This connects this passage by contrast with the description of her own activities that follow.

I paint pictures – This is the most explicit mention of her painting as a pastime.

waiting to die – It will be remembered that she had received some sort of augury that she was to die that month.

offended the earth god – In yin-yang cosmology, the earth god was thought to shift his residence with the seasons; in the spring, it was the hearth; the summer, the gate; autumn, the well; and winter, the garden. If one needed to repair any of those areas when the earth god was in residence, it was known as "offending the earth god." To escape retribution for this offense, one could move temporarily. Since this is autumn, they must have had to make some repairs on their well and hence the need for a temporary removal (Shinozuka, *Kagerō nikki no kokoro to hyōgen* 617).

kotowari ya	How true it is!
ihade nagekishi	During the months and years I have
toshi tsuki mo	lamented secretly for you,
furu no yashiro no	on the face of the god of Furu Shrine,
kami sabi ni kemu	moss has surely grown.

Even so, giving the excuse, "Today and tomorrow are periods of abstinence," there was no response. When it was still early on the morning of the day, he thought the abstinence would have been lifted, he sent this:

yume bakari	I feel lost as though
mite shi bakari ni	I have just been seeing
madohitsutsu	something like a dream,
akuru zo osoki	the dawn is slow to come
ama no tozashi ha	the door of heaven, slow to open.

This time too, they put him off with some excuse or another, so he wrote again:

samo koso ha	So that's how it is,
kadzuraki yama ni	you must be friends with the god
naretarame	of Kazuraki Mountain,
tada hito koto ya	you offer only one word
kagiri narikeru	and that is the end of it.

"Who taught you this?"

Young people are prone to writing like this.

As for me, usually on spring nights, or in the idleness of autumn, rather than spend my time in brooding thoughts, I paint pictures, thinking they may be looked upon as mementos by the people left behind. In the midst of this, I was living my life waiting to die, wondering, *Will it be now? Will it be today?* Nonetheless, as little by little the month drew to a close and the days went by, there it was, it appeared I was not going to die. While I reflected that it is the lives of people blessed with fortune that are short, as might be expected, the ninth month arrived with nothing untoward happening to me. Around the twenty-seventh or twenty-eighth, the household offended the earth god. Just at that time when I was spending a night elsewhere, most unusually there was a message from him delivered to my house. Even when my servant came to inform me of it, I didn't feel anything. Listlessly I did nothing.

It is the tenth month, and these days it seems to be drizzling more than usual. Sometime after the tenth of the month, persuaded by this and that attendant who suggests, "Let's go on a pilgrimage and view the maple

the usual mountain temple – Probably Narutaki, where she went for her retreat.

"The Ichijō grand minister has passed away" – Kaneie's eldest brother, Koremasa, whom the author had happened to see at the Kamo Festival the previous spring. He held the office of both regent and chancellor at his death. He was only forty-nine years old.

his increasing importance – The world was full of rumors about her husband's future, but the prognostications were not good. The death of Koremasa paved the way for the second brother, Kanemichi, to accede to the high offices of his elder brother. High on Kanemichi's priorities was to promote his own offspring and frustrate the aspirations of Kaneie and his children.

opening of the new year – It is the first year of the Ten'en era, 973.

it is a little strange how often he has appeared – The author seems unaware that Koremasa's death is a setback for her husband's political career. It has happened before that, when Kaneie had political troubles, he has sought out the author for company. The most noteworthy occasion was when he was given a post in the office of military affairs. While the author may have been a demanding partner in love, it seems that at least she was not interested in the relationship for the political benefits it might afford her family. In times of political adversity, this alone must have made her a comforting companion.

the color of these blossoms – The poem plays on the conceit that, in times of great suffering, people cried tears of blood.

leaves at the same time," I go to the usual mountain temple. Today, the drizzle falls and lets up by turns all day long; it is a time when this mountain is so beautiful. On the first of the eleventh month, the world goes into a turmoil with the news that, "The Ichijō grand minister has passed away." On the night we are commiserating, "How terrible a thing to happen," the first snow falls, leaving seven to eight inches on the ground. So sad, I imagine how it will be for his sons trudging in the funeral procession, but there was nothing I could do about it, and as I was thinking such thoughts, the world of affairs buzzes with the news of his increasing importance. Past the twentieth of the twelfth month, he did make an appearance here.

Then, when the year ended, as usual, there is a great bustle of activity with the opening of the new year, but although it is already the third or fourth day of the festivities, there is no feeling of renewal here. Only the warbler has been quick to sing; I listen to it deeply moved. He appeared during the day around the fifth and then on the tenth and again around the twentieth just as everyone was in dishabille on their way to bed. This month, it is a little strange how often he has appeared. Around this time, due to the New Year's Promotion activities, he seems to be extremely busy as usual.

The second month has arrived. The red plums are a deeper color this year than usual and are putting forth a splendid fragrance. It seems to be me alone who looks at them with deep emotion; there is no one else who sees them as anything special. However, the young lord breaks off a branch and sends it to the usual place:

kahi nakute	As fruitlessly I
toshi he ni keri to	have gazed at you from afar,
nagamureba	the years have gone by,
tamoto mo hana no	my sleeves have been steeped in
iro ni koso shime	the color of these blossoms.

Her reply:

toshi wo hete	As the years go by,
nado ka ayanaku	why do you without good sense
sora ni shimo	and to no avail,
hana no atari ni	stand around amid blossoms
tachi ha somekemu	to become stained by their hue?

"Well, isn't this just like her," he said as he looked at the awaited reply.

Then early in the month, on about the third, around midday, he appeared. Although it was very painful to feel the shame at having aged, what was there to do about it? After a bit, he rose to leave saying, "This

I do not say it because I dyed it, but the brocade pattern on his glowing cherry blossom damask . . . – Cherry blossom damask was apparently a fabric that was white on the surface with magenta threads showing from underneath. The actual appearance of these Heian textiles is difficult to reconstruct. There is something very touching about her recognition of the garments as her own creations. This is the second time she has described her husband in terms of his costume, and both times a feeling of fondness is woven through the description. The glowing quality of his appearance in the passage also serves to draw a contrast with her own feeling of shabbiness. Iwasa Miyoko has analyzed in detail the role of clothing description in the *Kagerō Diary*. In this passage, she underlines the quiet pride that suffuses this description of the author's textile creations, even despite the bleak contrast between these lustrous garments and the author's aged appearance (Iwasa Miyoko, "Waga sometaru to mo iwaji: Kagerō nikki fukushoku hyōgenkō" in *Ōchō nikki no shinkenkyū* [Tokyo: Kasama Shoin, 1995], 307–8).

I looked at my attire . . . – Here is another one of the places in book three where the author's "objectivity" with respect to her feelings and her situation is apparent. Gone, for example, is the litany of "I feel miserable, wretched, bereft." She just gives us the sensory data.

"How much more are the buds on this tree of sorrow made to swell" – This statement is a gesture toward a poem from *Kokin rokujō:*

> If the spring rains fall
> the flames of my thoughts
> will not even be extinguished
> how much more will the buds
> on this tree of sorrow be made to swell. (*Zenshū*, 342)

that hateful place – Ōmi's place, where there had been a fire the year before last.

small bow archery contest at the Reizei Palace – As we have seen in the past, archery contests were a customary event for the third month. It will be remembered that Kaneie is father-in-law to the retired emperor Reizei.

Yahata Festival – The festival held in the third month at Iwashimizu Hachiman Shrine. According to historical records, it was held on the twenty-seventh of the third month that year.

a letter from his lordship – This is the only place in the diary where the author refers to Kaneie with an honorific phrase in the narrative part of her prose. All other instances of the use of honorific forms with respect to her husband have been in quoted speech by others. *Zenshū* commentators explain this uncharacteristic usage by saying ". . . it becomes a style of writing where she puts distance between herself and Kaneie, treating him as an objective existence" (*Zenshū*, 343).

direction is forbidden for me." I do not say it because I dyed it, but the brocade pattern on his glowing cherry blossom damask was vivid, and the smooth pattern of his trousers was lustrous—as I listen to the cries of his outrunners fading into the distance, I think to myself, how painful to have been caught off guard in such a state; I looked at my attire, it is terribly shabby; I look in the mirror, my face seems so ugly. I can't stop thinking about how this time too, he must have ended up disgusted. Brooding endlessly over this sort of thing, since there had been a lot of rain from early in the month, all I could think of was, "How much more are the buds on this tree of sorrow made to swell." In the middle of the night on the fifth, I heard a great commotion in the vicinity. I found out that this time that hateful place, where there had been a fire before, had completely burned down. Around the tenth, once again he appears early in the mid-day. He even says, "It seems I must make a pilgrimage to the Kasuga Shrine; I'm concerned about you." Since this has become an unusual thing for him to say, it strikes me as strange.

Preparations for the small bow archery contest at the Reizei Palace have begun; there is a bustle of activity with the practicing. The teams are divided in the "before" and "after" and are costumed accordingly. I help with that for the young lord. The day of the contest arrives and afterward, his father tells me excitedly, "Many high-ranking nobles attended; there was no end to them this year. The lad had not been taking the small bow seriously enough and really concentrating on his practice, so I wondered what would happen, but on his first time up, both his arrows struck home. After that, one after another, so many hit the target, and then this arrow here struck home and the contest was won." Then, when even two or three days later he said, "Our young lord's two arrows striking the target moved me to tears," at that, I was moved to tears too.

In the world at large, as usual around this time, the Yahata Festival was being celebrated. Having nothing else to do, I parked my carriage inconspicuously to view the sights, when someone came along having their way cleared in a most ostentatious manner. When I looked, wondering who it was, I recognized some attendants among the advance guard. *So it's him*, I thought as I looked on, feeling all the more the wretchedness of my own position. The blinds were raised and inner curtains pulled aside so one could see quite clearly inside. Noticing my carriage, he quickly raised his fan to cover his face as he went by.

In the margin of a response to a letter from his lordship, I wrote, "My attendants have been saying, 'His lordship seemed to act shy as he passed by.' Why was that? You need not have and it seemed childish." His response went like this, "It was actually the embarrassment of old age. Anyone regarding it as the shyness of youth is just being spiteful."

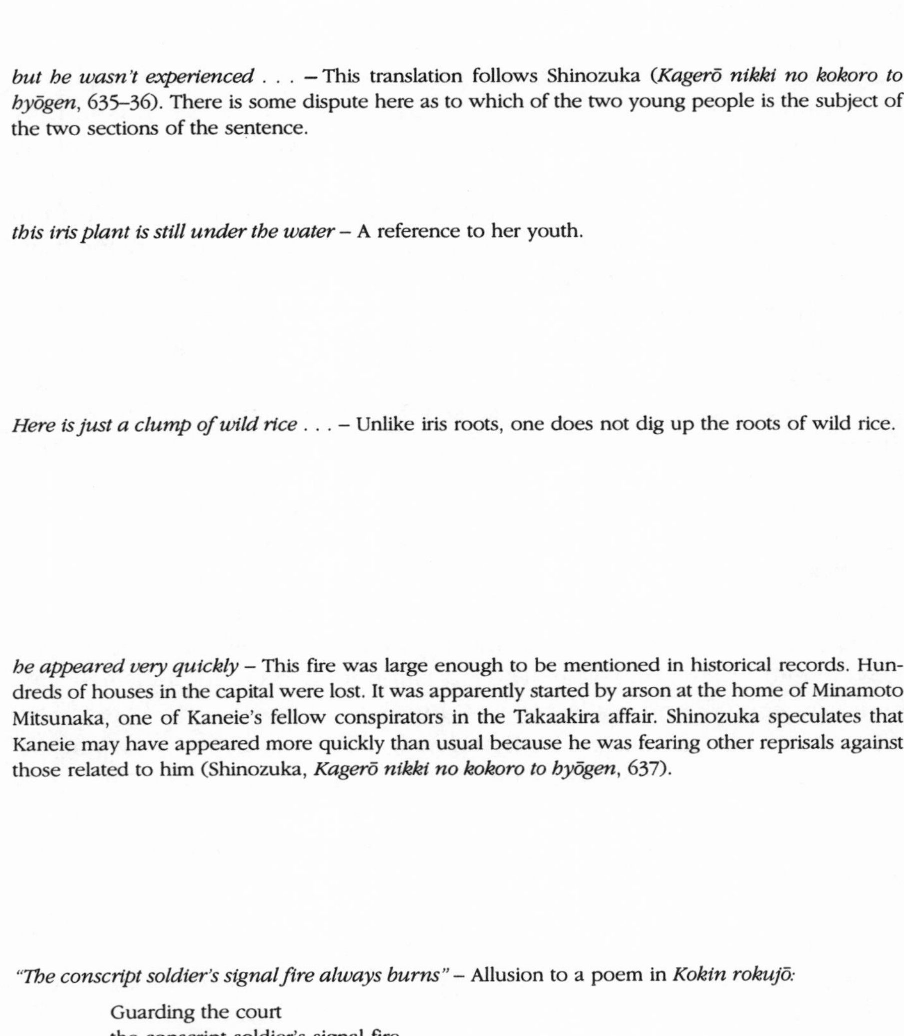

but he wasn't experienced . . . – This translation follows Shinozuka (*Kagerō nikki no kokoro to hyōgen*, 635–36). There is some dispute here as to which of the two young people is the subject of the two sections of the sentence.

this iris plant is still under the water – A reference to her youth.

Here is just a clump of wild rice . . . – Unlike iris roots, one does not dig up the roots of wild rice.

he appeared very quickly – This fire was large enough to be mentioned in historical records. Hundreds of houses in the capital were lost. It was apparently started by arson at the home of Minamoto Mitsunaka, one of Kaneie's fellow conspirators in the Takaakira affair. Shinozuka speculates that Kaneie may have appeared more quickly than usual because he was fearing other reprisals against those related to him (Shinozuka, *Kagerō nikki no kokoro to hyōgen*, 637).

"The conscript soldier's signal fire always burns" – Allusion to a poem in *Kokin rokujō:*

> Guarding the court
> the conscript soldier's signal fire
> burns at night
> in the day, it goes out
> but his longing is stronger than ever. (*Zenshū*, 345)

The cuckoo bird – Like the iris roots, the cuckoo bird is also an approved topic for the fifth month.

Then, for a while, communication ceased again, and the tenth of the month passed. As this seemed longer than the usual break in communication, I wondered again what was going to become of us. The young lord kept corresponding with the usual place, but he wasn't experienced and they kept talking about how much younger she is than he, and so he sent this:

mikagure no	Although it is said
hodo to ifu to mo	this iris plant is still
ayame gusa	under the water,
naho shita karuramu	yet, I would dig up its root,
omohi afu ya to	to see if our thoughts match or not.

The reply was rather ordinary:

shita karamu	Here is just a clump
hodo wo mo shirazu	of wild rice that knows nothing
makomo gusa	of dug up roots,
yo ni ohi sowaji	and to think of them taken
hito wa karu to mo	by someone not suitable?

Things going on in this way, he appeared again around the twentieth of the month. On the twenty-third or twenty-fourth, there was the commotion of a fire nearby. When the alarm went up, he appeared very quickly. It was windy. After a long time, the fire moved away and the cocks crowed. Saying, "It seems all right now," he went back. Listening to one of my attendants say, "Hearing the gateman talk about those people who heard that his lordship was here and came to pay their respects, how important it made one feel," I thought it probably looks that way to her when she contrasts it to the state our household has fallen into. Then, it was around the last day of the month. Coming into the room, he said, "On the night that the fire was close, it was really lively around this house, wasn't it?" To which I replied, "The conscript soldier's signal fire always burns."

When the first day of the fifth month arrived, the young lord carried on as usual:

uchitokete	The cuckoo bird
kefu dani kikamu	will have to let down her guard and
hototogisu	sing at least today,
shinobi mo ahenu	for the season now has come
toki ha ki ni keri	when she dare not hide away.

The reply:

hototogisu	This cuckoo bird,
kakurenaki ne wo	if she were to let you hear

unsheltered and abandoned – Both these meanings are present in the long *kakehanarenuru.*

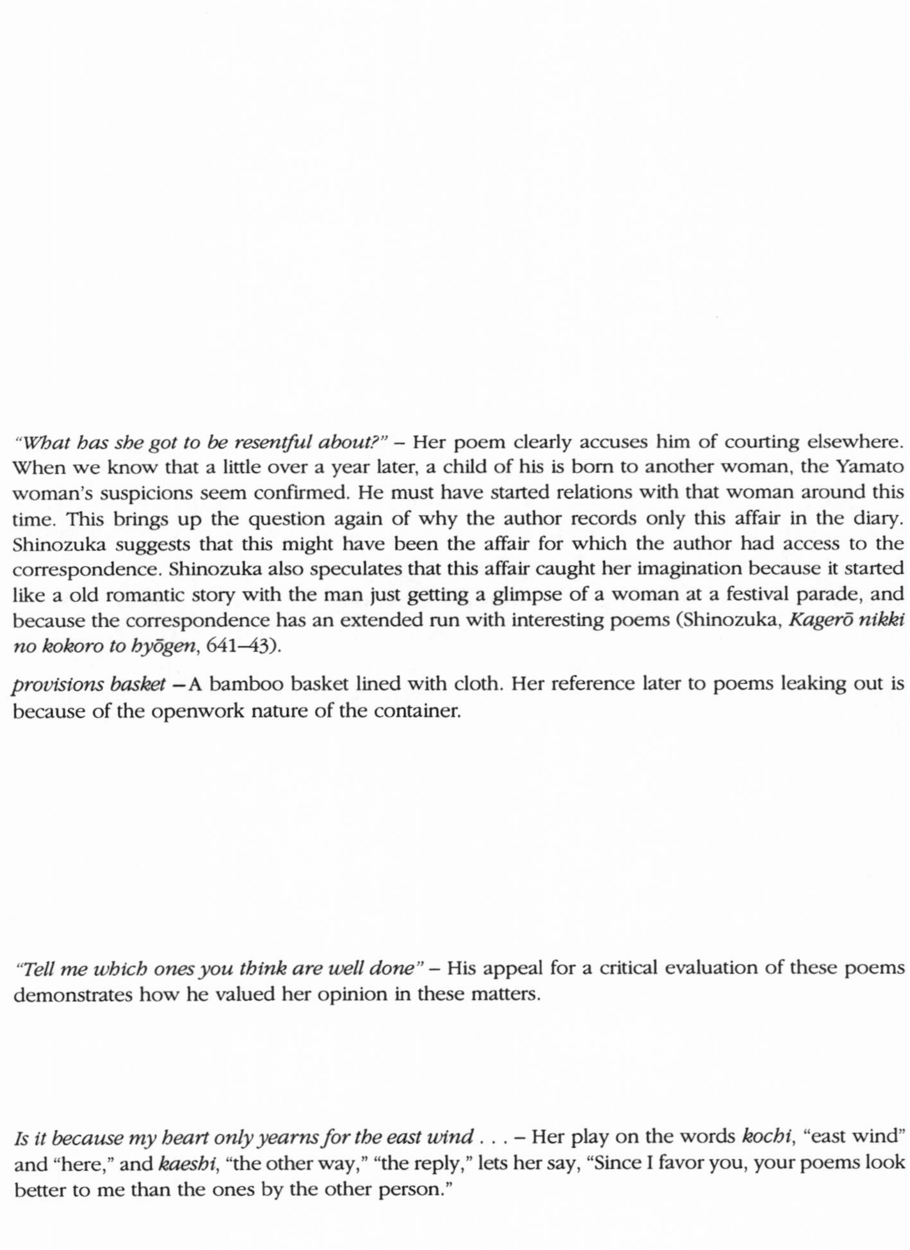

"What has she got to be resentful about?" – Her poem clearly accuses him of courting elsewhere. When we know that a little over a year later, a child of his is born to another woman, the Yamato woman's suspicions seem confirmed. He must have started relations with that woman around this time. This brings up the question again of why the author records only this affair in the diary. Shinozuka suggests that this might have been the affair for which the author had access to the correspondence. Shinozuka also speculates that this affair caught her imagination because it started like a old romantic story with the man just getting a glimpse of a woman at a festival parade, and because the correspondence has an extended run with interesting poems (Shinozuka, *Kagerō nikki no kokoro to hyōgen*, 641–43).

provisions basket – A bamboo basket lined with cloth. Her reference later to poems leaking out is because of the openwork nature of the container.

"Tell me which ones you think are well done" – His appeal for a critical evaluation of these poems demonstrates how he valued her opinion in these matters.

Is it because my heart only yearns for the east wind . . . – Her play on the words *kochi*, "east wind" and "here," and *kaeshi*, "the other way," "the reply," lets her say, "Since I favor you, your poems look better to me than the ones by the other person."

kikasete ha	her unhidden voice,
kakehanarenuru	she would become one
mi to ya naruramu	unsheltered and abandoned.

On the fifth, he sent:

mono omofu ni	Lost in love longing,
toshi he keri to mo	while the years have passed away,
ayame gusa	looking at irises,
kefu wo tabi tabi	today I realize how
sugushite zo shiru	many times I've seen them before.

The reply:

tsumori keru	I notice not
toshi no ayame mo	even the irises of the years
omohoezu	that have piled up,
kefu mo suginuru	since today I have seen that
kokoro miyureba	your heart has passed to another.

"What has she got to be resentful about?" he said, and seemed much puzzled.

Now, this month too, from time to time, I have brooded in the same way over the usual thing. Around the twentieth, there was this, "Please sew a cloth bag for this provisions basket that I want to give someone who is going far away." As I was sewing it, this came, "Have you finished it? Please fill it to the brim with poems. Over here, I haven't been feeling well at all and am not likely to compose any." How amusing, I thought to myself and sent back this, "The poems you ordered, I will compose as many as possible, but they might leak out of this bag and be lost. Hadn't you better send a different bag?" About two days later, this arrived, "Even though I was feeling so ill, it would have taken too long to send another bag, so I just gritted my teeth and filled the bag with poems myself. The poems I received in reply were as follows." He included the poems and added, "Tell me which ones you think are well done." Since this arrived while it was raining, there was something of an aura of refinement about it. I eagerly looked at the poems. I could see some that were excellent and some that were inferior, but it hardly felt appropriate for me to pronounce judgments with a knowing air, so I sent back this:

kochi to nomi	Is it because
kaze no kokoro wo	my heart only yearns for the
yosumereba	east wind to come here,
kaheshi ha fuku mo	that when the wind blows the other
otoruramu kashi	way, it does not seem as good.

the usual place – Presumably Ōmi's place.

Nakagawa at Hirohata – The Naka River is thought to be the present Kyōgoku River, or at least what is left of it, which runs west of and parallel to the Kamo River. The house was probably close to the present-day district of Teramachi in Kyoto. In the Heian period, this area was the northern extremity of the city, a sort of suburb. This decision to change residences is a signal that she has somehow accepted that the marriage, at least as a regular visiting arrangement, is over. There was no formal way to end a marriage in the Heian period. The husband simply stopped visiting, but the stopping itself was often sporadic. The phrase in the Heian period to describe this situation was *toko hanare*, "grown distant from the bed."

a fog had risen and rolled in . . . – A gesture toward a poem in *Kokin rokujō:*

> As river fog,
> has risen to enfold
> the foothills,
> now we see autumn mountains
> floating in the sky. (*Zenshū*, 349)

Time and the river flow in a bed – The verb "flow," *nagarete*, refers to both the passage of time and the current in a river. "Bed," *toko*, is both riverbed and marriage bed. Finally *waga naka*, "our marital relations," pivots into *nakagaha*, the Naka River.

This was all I sent.

The sixth and the seventh months passed by in much the same fashion. On the twenty-eighth at the end of the seventh month, he appeared saying, "The sumo tournament is going on. I was serving at court but I left early thinking to come and see you." But then, just like that, I do not see him again until past the twentieth of the eighth month. Asking around, I hear that his visits to the usual place are most generous. I realize how everything has changed. While I have been somewhat out of touch with reality, my dwelling place has fallen more and more into disrepair. As I don't really have enough people to keep it up, I am giving it up to someone else, and my father, whom I depend on, has decided that I should live in one of his houses. So today or the next day, I am to move to the area around Nakagawa at Hirohata. That such a thing might happen I have hinted to him before on several occasions, but now, since it is to be today, I thought I had better inform him. Although I sent the message, "I have something to tell you," the response was, "Due to an abstinence, his lordship is not to be disturbed." As he seems so little concerned, I thought, *why bother*, and moved without telling him.

It is close to the mountains, with one edge of the property a riverbank where water from the river is drawn in to use as we please. I feel it is a rather touching place to live. Two or three days passed and it seemed he still did not know that I had moved. About five or six days later, there was only this, "So you have moved without telling me." In response, I wrote in a rather final way, "I thought I would inform you that this move was about to happen, but I felt that it is hardly likely you would come to visit this inconvenient place. I had wanted to speak to you once more in the place where we used to meet." He responded, "So that is how it was, I understand. And as you say, you are now living in an inconvenient place. . . ." After that, I heard nothing from him.

The ninth month arrived, still very early in the morning, I raised the shutters and looked out; on the stream within the grounds and on the river outside, a fog had risen and rolled in. Gazing in the distance at the mountains, I couldn't see the foothills, such a sadness pervaded the scene:

nagarete no	Time and the river
toko to tanomite	flow in a bed I had come
ko shika domo	to rely on,
waga nakagaha ha	but between us the water
ase ni kerashimo	seems to have grown shallow.

This is what it brought to my lips. The rice in the fields in front of the east gate has been cut, bundled, and hung over the drying frames. When, rarely, there are visitors, we have the green blades of rice stalks cut to provide

I have thrown myself into such tasks . . . – This is the first time we see the author interested and involved in work other than clothing production. She would not have been involved with these agricultural activities before.

one who keeps small hawks – Michitsuna. We remember him at the age of fourteen letting all his hawks go as a gesture of determination to follow his mother into monastic life.

Like this, no one knots . . . – In the background of this poem are two folk beliefs. One is that the soul of a person desperately in love will leave his or her body at night in search of the beloved. The other is that if one sees a soul at night, one can exorcise it by chanting a spell three times and tying a knot in the hem of one's garment. This returns the wandering soul to its owner. Moreover, the expression "the cord of my soul" is related to the notion that the soul is connected to the body by an invisible cord. When the cord snaps, the person dies. Finally, the word for "skirt," *tsuma*, is homophonous with "wife."

The thick autumn dew – Of course, dew is also a metaphor for his tears.

I shall pass without recording it – This is an interesting editorial comment. It makes us wonder on what basis she chose to include and exclude poems.

I attended to the garments and sent them back without a letter – So the marriage in the sense of these duties does continue.

At the end of the month – This is the end of the tenth month. This would be a request for the preparation of winter clothes since the official date for changing into winter clothes was the first of the eleventh month.

a birth at the house of my father – Polygyny made it more possible for this kind of family situation to arise: a child is born to her father when the author is already thirty-eight years old, almost two generations older than her new half-sister. We know that the child is a girl from the reference to plum blossom in the poems. There is no information about the identity of the mother. There is some speculation that this half-sister grows up to become the mother of the author of the *Sarashina Diary*, which is the last of the major autobiographical diaries written by women in the Heian period.

fodder for the horses. I have thrown myself into such tasks as having grilled rice cakes made from the new grain. As there is one who keeps small hawks, several of the hawks rise and wheel in the sky right outside the gate. It seems he sent this to the usual place hoping to arouse her sympathy:

sa goromo no	Like this, no one knots
tsuma mo musubanu	their skirts for me night after night,
tama no wo no	the cord of my soul
taemi taezumi	is about to break, then it holds,
yo wo ya tsukusamu	I may not be long for this world.

There was no reply. So again after a while, he sent this:

tsuyu fukaki	The thick autumn dew
sode ni hietsutsu	chills my sleeve as I lie
akasu kana	awake until dawn,
tare nagaki yo no	meanwhile, these long cold nights,
kata ki naruramu	who have you lying by your side?

There was a response to this one, but I shall pass without recording it.

Even though it is already past the twentieth of this month, there has been no communication from him. Astonishingly, however, a pile of winter clothes has been brought with the instructions, "See to these." When the messenger said, "There was a letter but it got lost on the way," I was appalled by the stupidity of it all, saying, in that case, I would not send a return message. I gave up without finding out what it had been. I attended to the garments and sent them back without a letter.

After that, the path to him in my dreams was cut, and so the year grew old.

At the end of the month, work was delivered again. The instructions were "See to this," and once more there was not so much as a note. It was material for a underrobe. I hesitated over what to do, and I discussed it with one or two of my attendants. "Well, why don't you just do it this time and see how it turns out. Otherwise, it would seem ill-willed." And so it was decided. I kept it, did a not uncareful job on it, and, on the first of the month, sent it with the young lord, who reported back, "He said, 'How beautifully done,'" and that was the end of it. To say this was dumbfounding would be an understatement.

Then, this eleventh month, there has been a birth at the house of my father who has been away in the provinces, and it has passed without my being able to pay a visit. Now, the fiftieth day after the birth has come.

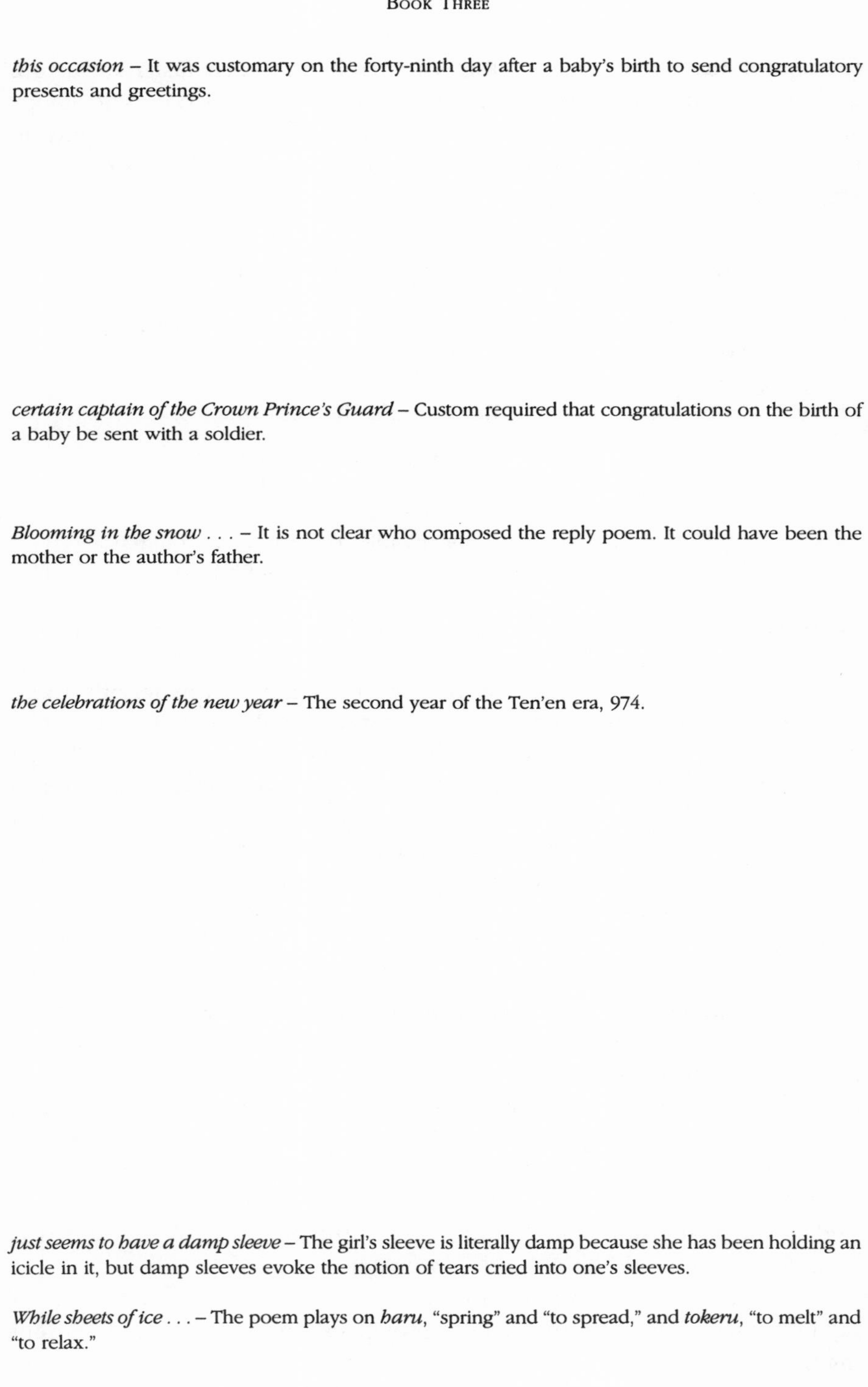

this occasion – It was customary on the forty-ninth day after a baby's birth to send congratulatory presents and greetings.

certain captain of the Crown Prince's Guard – Custom required that congratulations on the birth of a baby be sent with a soldier.

Blooming in the snow . . . – It is not clear who composed the reply poem. It could have been the mother or the author's father.

the celebrations of the new year – The second year of the Ten'en era, 974.

just seems to have a damp sleeve – The girl's sleeve is literally damp because she has been holding an icicle in it, but damp sleeves evoke the notion of tears cried into one's sleeves.

While sheets of ice . . . – The poem plays on *haru*, "spring" and "to spread," and *tokeru*, "to melt" and "to relax."

Although I thought that at least on this occasion, I would like to do something, I was not able to do anything elaborate. I just expressed my feeling of congratulations by sending words. This was according to custom. Taking a basket that had been painted white and placing a branch of plum blossom in it, I sent this poem:

fuyu gomori	Lost for what to do,
yuki ni madohishi	closed in by the snows of winter,
wori sugite	the occasion passed,
kefu zo kakine no	now today, I send my greetings
ume wo tadzuneru	to the plum blossoming in the hedge.

I sent this with a certain captain of the Crown Prince's Guard, having him arrive in the evening. The next morning, the messenger returned. He was bearing an overrobe of pale silk:

eda wakami	Blooming in the snow,
yuki ma ni sakeru	this first flower from a
hatsu hana ha	young branch of plum,
ika ni to tofu ni	upon receiving your greetings,
nihohi masu kana	grows even more radiant.

While these sorts of exchanges went on, the celebrations of the new year passed by too.

"How about going to some quiet out of the way place for a pilgrimage?" someone invited; "Why not?" I said and went along, but it turned out there were a lot of people making a pilgrimage to the same place. Even though it was unlikely there was anyone who would know me, I felt painfully self conscious. At the purification place, the icicles hung down indescribably. On the way back I kept looking at them thinking, "How lovely they are," and I noticed someone walking who, although she was an adult, was dressed in a child's costume with her hair done up nicely in plaits. Looking more closely, I could see she had one of the icicles wrapped up in the sleeve of her singlet and was eating it as she walked along. Just as I was thinking, there must be some reason for her behavior, my companion addressed her, whereupon, she responded with her mouth still full of ice, "Do you mean me, Ma'am?" Hearing her, we realized that she was of rather low status. Bowing low to us, she said, "Those who don't eat this ice don't get their wishes." I murmured to myself, "It hasn't brought her luck yet; the one who says it just seems to have a damp sleeve." Then I reflected:

waga sode no	While sheets of ice
kohori ha haru mo	spread on my sleeve know not
shiranaku ni	that spring has come,

Kamo Shrine – See book one, pp. 136–43.

Thus the twelfth month came and the eleventh month went – There is a time disjunction in the text here. Just a little while before she has mentioned the arrival of the new year, and the poem for her new half-sister and the poem immediately above both make reference to spring, but now the narrative returns to the eleventh and twelfth months, which she seems to have spent convalescing. This disjunction is likely the result of a copyist error. However, modern commentators have left the text as it has been transmitted.

the moon so lovely – Since the calendar is a lunar one, the fifteenth always coincides with the full moon.

"mountains of no thoughts" – An allusion again to the *Gosenshū* poem about wanting to escape the pain of seeing the cherry in full bloom (when one knows they must fall soon) by entering the "mountains of no thoughts" (see book two, p. 224).

Such were my feelings – In this passage, her emotions have moved from amusement and poignant appreciation of beauty to sadness and loneliness. While she seems to have accepted the inevitability of the end of her marriage, at moments of heightened perception the sorrow returns.

assistant director of the Right Stable – Most of the offices of the Heian court had "right" and "left" divisions. The Right Stable was in charge of administering the imperial stable of the right division, including managing pasturage in the various provinces for the provisioning of the horses. Since horses were prized possessions and played important roles in many court ceremonies, positions with the imperial stable carried more prestige than one might expect. There were two executive positions within the stable, the top position, *kami*, "director," and the second in command, *suke*, "assistant director" (as translated by McCullough and McCullough, *A Tale of Flowering Fortunes*, vol. 2, 816). The author from this point on will refer to her son only by his new title, and the director of his office will become a major figure in the narrative.

director of his new office, his paternal uncle – Tōnori, a younger half-brother to Kaneie by a different mother. Tōnori's age is not known, but judging from Kaneie's age and that of another younger brother, Tōnori is probably in his mid-thirties.

she was not old enough to be of any interest to him – Thus begins Tōnori's courting of the adopted daughter, which is the major story of the latter part of the diary. As mentioned immediately above, Tōnori was in his mid-thirties, and while such differences in age were not so exceptional during the Heian period, he is still rather old for a fourteen- or fifteen-year-old girl.

kokoro toketemo	others seem to walk about
hito no yuku kana	with hearts melted in good spirits.

About three days after coming back from there, I made a pilgrimage to the Kamo Shrine. The wind blew and snow fell, unspeakable weather and so dark. Not only was it a miserable trip, but I caught cold and languished in bed. Thus the twelfth month came and the eleventh month went.

The fifteenth of the first month, there is the burning of the New Year's decorations. When I hear our young lord's men servants raising a commotion, "Let's build the bonfire," one can tell they are getting too drunk. Then voices can be heard, "Hush, don't be so noisy." Amused by this, quietly I went out onto the veranda to take a look outside, and there was the moon so lovely. Gazing out toward the east, the mountains were veiled in mist, just barely visible—I feel desolate. Leaning against the pillar, the thought comes to mind, *there are no "mountains of no thoughts."* He hasn't communicated with me since the eighth month, and now, in vain has the new year already come; feeling this way, my tears well up in sobs and spill down. Then:

moro kowe ni	The one who should
naku beki mono wo	cry joining voices with mine,
uguhisu ha	the warbler,
mutsuki to mo mada	can it be he knows not
shirazu ya aruramu	the new year is already here.

Such were my feelings.

On the twenty-fifth, concerned about the promotion lists, the young lord busily makes observances at temples and shrines. Just as I was thinking, *why does he go to all this trouble*, the announcement of promotions arrived. In a rare letter from him, we were informed, "There has been a promotion to assistant director of the Right Stable." As our new assistant director went the rounds to express his appreciation, he also paid a visit to the director of his new office, his paternal uncle, who congratulated him warmly and in the course of another conversation asked, "The young lady in your household, what sort of a person is she? How old is she, how many years?"

When he returned and related to us that this had happened, I wondered how the director could have heard of her. The girl had no idea about that sort of thing yet and she was not old enough to be of any interest to him, so I put it out of my mind.

Around that time, there was excitement over the archery contest to be held at the Reizei Palace. The director and the assistant director were *lost portion of text* – Unfortunately, due to this lacunae, we never learn the content of her dream. However, there was likely some connection between her dream and the decision to go on a pilgrimage.

Not as deep in the mountains as all that – Phrase from a poem in *Tales of Yamato*, section 43, when a monk was asked where he had gone to practice austerities (*Yamato monogatari*, in *Nihon koten bungaku zenshū*, vol. 8, 297).

since the blossoms are strangely late – Allusions to two poems of the *Kokinshū* are woven into this passage, giving it a richness of texture. The first one is no. 10:

> has spring come early—
> or are the plum blossoms late—
> I would like to know
> but not even the song of
> the mountain thrush trills the answer (Rodd, *Kokinshū*, 52)

The second one is no. 535:

> would that my love could
> know my yearning deep as
> these lonely mountains
> where not even the songs of
> soaring wild birds can be heard (Rodd, *Kokinshū*, 202)

each bead of the rosary – There are 108 beads on a Buddhist rosary, so this is a relatively strenuous ritual.

Did I ever dream . . . – The word for "nun," *ama*, is embedded in both the word for "sky," *amatsu*, and "rain cloud," *amagumo*.

I seemed to feel – This is another place in book three where she seems to be speaking from a position of observing herself.

poor dear one who was right by my side – This is assumed to be a reference to her adopted daughter, which would indicate that this pilgrimage had been undertaken for her daughter's sake.

'Has his lordship said anything about this matter to you?' – From Tōnori's mode of speaking, it is evident that Tōnori's relationship with Kaneie is not close. It appears, for example, that he cannot expect to speak to his elder brother in person about this matter; he must use an intermediary like Michitsuna. In fact, Tōnori's interest in the stepdaughter may be primarily motivated by a desire to connect himself more closely with his more powerful brother.

on the same side, so they saw one another every day at practices at which the director would always talk about the same thing. "What must he have on his mind?" the assistant director asked as he related this to us. Then, on about the twentieth of the second month, I had a dream . . .

[Lost portion of text]

I decided to go secretly to a certain place. It is a place of which one might say, "Not as deep in the mountains as all that, but deep enough." It is around the time when the fields are burnt, but since the blossoms are strangely late this year, the path that one might have expected to be lovely is not yet so. Since it is very deep in the mountains where one does not hear the birds, even the warbler made not a sound. Only the water, in an unusually impressive way, gushed and gurgled as it flowed. So tired I was as I walked along, thinking over and over to myself, *there must be people who never have to do this, it just seems to be my miserable lot to go from one trouble to another.* We arrived just as the bell was being rung for the evening service. We lit votive offerings and performed our devotions, rising and sitting for each bead of the rosary, getting more and more tired. Just as we heard that dawn had come, it began to rain. Thinking how very unfortunate this was, we went along to the monastery living quarters, and as we were discussing what we should do, it became quite light. People bustle about with "Here are raincoats, here are rainhats." I stand quietly and gaze out—from the valley in front, clouds were softly rising, how strangely melancholy:

omohiki ya	Did I ever dream
amatsu sora naru	that I would come to tread this
amagumo wo	mountain like a nun,
sode shite wakuru	parting with my sleeves rain clouds
yama fumamu to ha	of the sky of heaven?

So I seemed to feel. Although the rain fell unspeakably hard, as we could not stay where we were, we simply made the best of it and departed. When I looked at my poor dear one who was right by my side, I felt so sadly moved I forgot my own tiredness.

We got back finally. The next day, the assistant director returning late at night from archery practice comes to where I am lying down and relates the following. "His lordship said, 'The director of your bureau has been going on a lot about this matter since last year. How is the girl over there doing? Has she grown? Does she have a woman's feelings?' Then when the director mentioned it again to me and asked, 'Has his lordship said anything about this matter to you?' I replied that he had. Then the

pay a courtesy call to the apartments of the waiting woman, Musashi – In the original, the use of honorifics in Tōnori's letter provide clues about his relationship to Musashi. He uses no honorifics with reference to Musashi, as though he were speaking of someone closely connected to himself, yet he appends an honorific to "apartments" since they belong to Michitsuna's Mother. This would indicate that Musashi may have been someone formerly in his employ. It was customary to use a servant in one's confidence to deliver love poems and to arrange meetings with the woman one was wooing. It is interesting how the arrangement of marital liaisons in aristocratic households still mimicked the conducting of a secret affair. In this case, Tōnori first approaches the father and then the stepmother of the girl to get their tacit permission; now he announces how he plans to send his billet-doux and arrange meetings with the girl. If the author were to agree to his courting, she would allow him at this point to proceed as he suggests.

old poem about 'Isonokami' – A poem from *Kokin rokujō:*

> At Isonokami
> even if the rain falls, how could
> I let it stop me
> since I have told my girl
> I would not fail to come. (*Zenshū,* 358)

deeper in color are these sleeves – He sends his message on scarlet paper with a branch of red plum. Colors deepen when wet. This all contributes to strengthening the conventional hyperbole about crying tears of blood when one suffers.

"My dear lord . . ." – The Isonokami foundation poem and the fact that he is waiting for a man has lead Tōnori to assume the persona of a woman in this poem and communication. He really abandons himself to the persona with the repeated entreaty of "My dear lord," but then seems to think better of it by crossing it out. His task at this juncture of the courting game is to convince the girl's guardian of the sincerity of his passion for the girl. Distress is part of the pose.

director said, 'The day after tomorrow will be an auspicious day, I'll send a letter of proposal then.'" Thinking over and over how bizarre this all was and that she was not yet ready for such attentions, I fell asleep.

Then, on that day, the letter arrives. Truly, it was the sort of letter one could not answer in an unguarded way. Among other things he said this, "For months, I have been thinking about her. When I had someone speak to his lordship about it, I was told, 'His lordship has listened to your request. Now, he says just go speak directly to her guardian.' Yet I refrained from speaking as I feared you might think ill of me as one having unsuitable intentions. Thus thinking that there just seemed to be no good chance, what should I find when I looked at the announcement of the new appointments but that your assistant director had been posted in the same bureau. So I thought, now no one could take it amiss if I were to come and visit." It was written as it should be, and in the margin, he wrote, "I should like to pay a courtesy call to the apartments of the waiting woman, Musashi." A reply had to be written, but first I wanted to ask her father about it. It was taken by the assistant director, but he came back with it saying, "I was told he was in ritual seclusion or something, that the timing was inconvenient, so I did not get to show it to him." By this time, it was the twenty-fifth or twenty-sixth.

The director seemed to feel very uneasy, for he called our assistant director to him with this message, "I have something urgent to speak to you about." The assistant director sent the servant back right away with the message, "Coming right away." Just at that point it began to rain, but saying it would be painful to have the director wait, he was just about to leave when he received another letter. Bringing it in, he looked at it. It was on thin scarlet paper to which a branch of red plum had been attached. It said, "You do, I believe, know the old poem about 'Isonokami'":

harusame ni	Even more than this
nuretaru hana no	branch of blossoms drenched in
eda yori mo	the spring rain, deeper
hito shirenu mi no	in color are these sleeves
sode zo warinaki	of one unknown, who suffers.

"My dear lord, my dear lord, you must come." It was written thus, but the "my dear lord" part had been crossed out. The assistant director said, "What shall I do about an answer?" "How very troublesome. You had better just leave and say you met the messenger on the way there," I said and sent him off. He returned and reported, "The director was awfully upset and complained, 'Couldn't a reply have been written to me even while you were waiting to hear news from his lordship?'"

might interpret his visits in a different way – That is, might think he was paying court to the author.

I am at a loss – She is in a difficult position to mount a diplomatic resistance. She does not want her adopted daughter to enter into marriage yet. She seems to have genuine concerns about the girl's youth. Moreover, she is likely hoping to do better for her. Tōnori is a little old and not on a distinguished career path. After all, one of Kaneie's daughters by Tokihime is already married to a retired emperor, and the other one is being groomed to become an imperial consort. The author must have hoped that Kaneie might do as well for this daughter. Yet, if such a brilliant future were not possible, then Tōnori, provided he proves reliable, might not be such a bad match. Thus she can neither risk encouraging him nor dare to alienate him.

'does not let people approach recklessly' – Allusion to a poem from *Gosenshū*:

> You say you want to
> see so very much the waterfall
> of Shirakawa
> but it is something that does not
> let people approach recklessly. (Katagiri, *Gosen wakashū,* 322)

With this cryptic note she lets him know he will not be welcomed into Musashi's apartments.

no auspicious days – As with so many other matters in Heian life, yin-yang cosmology determined days on which it was auspicious to marry.

I found this very strange that he should be so hastily choosing a date – The author is also in a difficult situation with Kaneie. She cannot refuse his choice if he decides that Tōnori is to marry her daughter; all she can do is stall as long as possible. For his part, Kaneie does not appear overly concerned with the girl's future. It seems that he neither wants to discourage Tōnori nor anger the author by rushing the match.

his usual handsome self –This remark seems a little odd because, so far as the diary has informed us, this is the first time she would have seen him. She could be speaking of his reputation for good looks or there is some slip in the time frame; as she writes remembering back, he was as handsome as she came to know was usual for him.

Now, two or three days later, the assistant director has reported, "I finally was able to show the letter to his lordship. He said, 'What is all the fuss about? I told him I would think about it and decide soon. As for a response, quickly write him a tactful letter. It is probably still not appropriate for him to visit. People do not generally know that there is a young girl there. They might interpret his visits in a different way.'" Hearing that, I thought, *How maddening, and just how did that person who might become the source of such rumors get to know that there was a young girl here?*

Well then, today I write the reply letter. "As I assumed we must owe the pleasure of your most unexpected letter to the recent reassignment of duties, I knew it should be responded to directly; however, your mention of having spoken 'to his lordship' was very puzzling and unsettling to me, and in the course of making inquiries, it took 'from here to China and back,' for which I express my apologies. Nevertheless, since I am not convinced about this, I am at a loss how to respond to you." In the margin, I added, "You mention visiting the apartment of the attendant Musashi, but I suspect she will tell you that she 'does not let people approach recklessly.'" In this fashion, he was answered. After that he sent the same kind of letter several times. As I did not respond to every letter, he restrained himself a good deal.

The third month arrived. It seems that the director has been using a lady attendant to press his affairs with his lordship, and he showed me one of the responses he had received from this intermediary. His letter went like this, "Since you seem to be so suspicious, I thought I would show you what his lordship has been saying." I looked at it. "'There are no auspicious days in this month. Let us consider next month.' This is the sort of thing, and if you would be so good as to look at a calendar, you will see that he is actually speaking about this month right now." I found this very strange that he should be so hastily choosing a date—what a thing to do—I did not consider it possible but rather suspected it to be the fabrication of the person who wrote the letter.

Around noon of the seventh or eighth day of the fourth month, someone calls out, "The director of the Right Stable has arrived." Just as I tell my attendants, "Quiet now. Tell him I am not here. I know he has something he wants to talk about but it is too soon and not appropriate," he enters the yard and stands waiting in front of a hedge where he is quite exposed. He is his usual handsome self in a well-filled glossy robe with a soft formal cloak over it and a sword slung from his waist. He does not look out of the ordinary, but as he stands there toying with a red-colored fan that is a little in disorder, and as the brisk wind blows up the ribbons of his court cap, it is just like a picture. "There's a handsome man here,"

their frightful sleeve openings – It is a kind of indecent exposure.

I want to sit here for the first time – The act of sitting on the veranda will make him feel as though he has actually had a first visit.

my frightful voice – Presumably a voice grown ugly with age.

invited into the gallery – In the Heian aristocratic residence, there was an outer veranda under the eaves that was otherwise exposed to the open air, an inner gallery that could be opened to the outside but was normally closed at night with lattice shutters, and inner chambers. She would be waiting for him in an inner chamber behind bamboo hanging blinds or a curtain. She places a light on the veranda so the two men can see one another dimly and then invites the director to sit on a cushion in the inner gallery space.

his clothes rustling in a pleasant way – The intentness of her listening is conveyed throughout this passage by the auditory detail in the description. It must be remembered that this is the first time in a long while that she has spoken to a man outside her immediate family circle.

say the serving women from the back of the house. Just at the moment when they come forward with their trains all in disarray to peek out at him, the wind blows the bamboo blinds in and then out. The women who are relying on the blinds for cover completely forget themselves in the commotion of pushing the blinds back out and then pulling them in. *My goodness*, I think, *he has seen everything right up to their frightful sleeve openings*; I could have died, it was so embarrassing. This happened while someone was going to rouse the assistant director, who had returned late from archery practice last night and was still sleeping. Finally, the assistant director gets up and gives the excuse that I am not in. Feeling uneasy about the wind, I had already had all the outer shutters of my room lowered earlier, so that what he said seemed perfectly reasonable. The director ventured to come up onto the veranda, "Today is an auspicious day. Lend me a straw cushion. I want to sit here for the first time." He went on talking for a while. Then he sighed, "What a waste it was to come today," and left.

About two days later, I dispatched a servant just to convey orally my regrets. "I understand you favored us with a visit while I was out, I am very sorry." After this came his perennial request, "I took my leave the other day with so many things uncertain in my mind, would you be so kind as to see me?" Because it was not suitable for him to come, I said, "I would be too embarrassed to have you hear my frightful voice," and thus did not allow an interview. Nonetheless, he arrived one night on the pretext, "There is something I want to tell the assistant director." What was I to do? I had only two bays of shutters raised, and a light placed on the veranda outside, then he was invited into the gallery room. The assistant director went to greet him. "Please come," he said, and the director came up onto the veranda. When the assistant director opened the gallery door and seemed to say, "Through here," the director made as to walk into the room but then drew back. In a quiet voice, he said, "I would have you first convey my respects to her ladyship." The assistant director came in to me and delivered the message. When I said, "He has my leave to come and speak in this place that he has been so interested in," the director chuckled a little and came into the room with his clothes rustling in a pleasant way.

He and the assistant director spoke so quietly together that all I could hear was the sound of his fan striking his baton of office from time to time. Within, I made not a sound. When quite some time had passed, the assistant director came to say, "He says to tell you, 'Since I took my leave that day without achieving anything, I have been fretting in suspense.'" The assistant director bade him speak to me directly. Although he did come closer, he didn't say anything right away. I was just as silent as

"This area has such an eerie atmosphere . . ." – This is an indirect way of hinting that he ought to leave; she is suggesting he may be reluctant to be on his way because it is such a unsettling place so far from the center of the capital.

At the thought that he might have been able to see at least my shadow – When the light on the veranda went out, she would have become visible by her faint light, because it would have been the only light.

One of his attendants replied, "It was nothing to us" – This passage is difficult to construe. It seems odd that she would have a direct conversation with one of the director's attendants when such elaborate procedure was necessary to bring her into direct conversation with the director himself.

the assistant director happened to see a dead dog . . . – Coming into contact with anything dead rendered him ritually polluted, so he could no longer participate in the rites.

ever. Thus we remained for awhile. I thought how uneasy he must be feeling and made a slight sound as though clearing my throat, which he seized upon as a chance to speak, beginning with "That day, I chose an inopportune occasion to wait on you. . . ." He went on at great length going right back to the first time he had taken an interest in the girl. From within, I replied in this fashion, "She is at an age when to consider such a thing is inauspicious. Your speaking like this is fantasy. Why, she is so little, she is hardly what the world calls a baby mouse. It is simply out of the question." When I heard him painfully trying to control his voice, it was very uncomfortable for me too. It was an evening when the rain fell with abandon and the voices of the frogs were very loud. As the night grew late, I ventured to say, "This area has such an eerie atmosphere, even we people who live here hardly feel at ease." To which he replied, "Not to worry. I am just thinking to take my leave shortly, and I am not afraid of anything." As he went on like this, the night got awfully late. He said, "The assistant director will soon be busy with getting ready for the Kamo Festival, and I expect I shall be calling on him to attend to various matters around that time. I shall report to his lordship what I have been told here, and receiving his reaction, I shall tell you what he has to say. I shall likely attend upon you tomorrow or the day after." Assuming he had left, I parted the curtains of the screen of state to look out, only to find that the light placed on the veranda had gone out sometime before. Because I had had a light placed behind something within, I had not been able to tell that the light out there had gone out. At the thought that he might have been able to see at least my shadow, I was appalled, and said, "That scoundrel, he didn't even tell me that the light had gone out." One of his attendants replied, "It was nothing to us," and then left.

Having come once, now he came often. Since he simply repeated the same thing, I responded with, "As for my position, when permission may be granted from the place it should come, then, even if we find it hard, we will just have to accept it, but until such time . . ." To this he would say, "I have the requisite permission," pressing his case most vigorously. Even though he pressured me with statements like, "His lordship has even said it is to be this very month. There is supposed to be an auspicious day after the twentieth," I could not possibly think of anything else while the assistant director was getting ready to serve as an attendant from his office for the Kamo Festival, and so the director was to wait until after that business was over. Then, on the day of the Lustration Ceremony, the assistant director happened to see a dead dog. There was nothing that could be done about it; he had to give up serving as an attendant.

Well, so far as I was concerned, I still felt that this talk of marriage was far too hasty, I couldn't really consider it, yet meanwhile, all we heard

Feeling much relieved – This gives her a reprieve of four months.

Whatever happened . . . – In his poem, he refers to himself as the cuckoo hidden in the *unohana* shrub.

Have a little patience . . . – The orange blossom is an emblem of the fifth month. The usual pun on *afuhi*, "heartvine" and "meeting day," indicates the present time, which is just after the Kamo Festival in the fourth month.

With this reply, the direct poetic correspondence between Tōnori and Michitsuna's Mother begins. Thus Tōnori's courtship of her daughter allows her by proxy to once again participate in the world of poetic romance. The author's mention of Tōnori's excellent hand in calligraphy is part of her evocation of that world.

from the director through the assistant director was, "Please press my case with your mother. Tell her I do have his lordship's permission." So I wrote to her father, "Why have you been speaking to the director in that fashion? As he has become most annoying, I must have something from you to show him. Please send a letter." He responded with this: "Although I actually had thought to let the marriage take place in the fourth month, what with all the business of the assistant director's attendance at the festival, it ended up getting postponed. If the director has no change of heart, let us think about having it take place around the eighth month." Feeling much relieved, I sent this to the director, "This would seem to be his lordship's intention. Indeed, this is why I kept saying that his hasty fixing of a date was not really certain." Without sending a response, in a little while he came in person. When he sent in the message, "I have come to say some very provoking things," I had someone say to him, "What is wrong? You appear to be in a most threatening mood. Such being the case, come in." He said, "Well, well, it seems my waiting in attendance like this day and night has actually delayed things." He did not come in but rather stayed outside talking with the assistant director. Getting up to leave, he asked for an inkstone and some paper. When these were sent out, he wrote something and, folding over both margins, sent it in to me. When I looked at it, this is what was written:

chigiri okishi	Whatever happened
udzuki ha ika ni	to the fourth month and our pledge?
hototogisu	This doleful cuckoo
waga mi no uki ni	must leave the shade of flowers
kake hanare tsutsu	becoming more and more estranged.

"What am I to do? I am so disheartened. 'Til this evening." The hand it was written in, too, would have put anyone to shame. I wrote this response and quickly sent it after him:

naho shinobe	Have a little patience.
hana tachibana no	Is there not a branch of
eda ya naki	orange blossom for you
afuhi suginuru	even though the fourth month and
udzuki naredomo	the heartvine's day of meeting is past.

Then, on the night of the twenty-second, which he had already chosen from before as the night of first meeting, he visited. This time, unlike other times, he was very serious, and the way he applied pressure was quite unbearable. He said, "His lordship's permission no longer opens the way. It seems so far off, please have some consideration for me; won't you let me see her?" "What must you be thinking of to talk in such a way?

I will at least do one or the other – That is, to see the daughter or the stepmother. Here, for the first time, there is a hint that Tōnori may have been paying court to the daughter with the thought in the back of his mind that an affair with the stepmother might be interesting. He must at least have been curious to see her, since later records credit her with having been one of the great beauties of the era.

How awfully late it seems to have become – Her sangfroid in the situation is impressive. She shows no alarm and so calms the situation.

Your calendar has been rolled up – That is, "you have no more time for me."

The cuckoo bird went . . . – The poem contains a pun on *tofu*, "to visit" and "to fly."

You speak of marriage as far off; her becoming a woman is also far off." To which he said, "No matter how young she is, she talks surely." "Such is not the case with her. Unfortunately, she is still so young she hates to meet strangers." Even though I spoke like this, he did not seem to understand and just looked miserable. "I am so wrought up, my heart is pounding in my chest. I'll leave only after I have had the satisfaction of waiting on you within your curtains. I will at least do one or the other. Please have some consideration for me." Saying this, he placed his hand on my curtain, and although it was most alarming, I pretended not to have heard him and said nonchalantly, "How awfully late it seems to have become. It is usually nighttime when one feels that way." He responded, "I really had no idea you could be as cold as this. I suppose I should be feeling awfully, terribly, endlessly happy that you allow me to visit at all. Your calendar has been rolled up. I have spoken badly to you and apologize for giving you offense," and so on. He looked so utterly depressed; with warm feeling for him, I said, "You see it was an unreasonable request. Just keep your mind off this sort of thing as you do during the day when you are serving at the palace or at court." He replied in such a miserable way, "Nothing could be more painful than to try and feel that way." There was really nothing I could say that had any effect. Since I was at a loss how to respond, in the end, I said nothing, whereupon he said, "How sorry I am. You seem to be out of temper. If that's how it is, unless you say something now, I will not speak further. I am so sorry." Snapping his fingers in irritation, he said nothing for awhile and then got up to leave. As he was departing, I sent someone to offer him a torch. When I heard, "He has already left without taking one," I felt very sorry for him, and the next morning early, I wrote this and sent it to him. "It is unfortunate that you seem to have gone back without even asking for a torch; I hope you returned home safely:

hototogisu	The cuckoo bird went
mata tofu beku mo	not even saying, "I will fly
katarahade	this way again—"
kaheru yamadji no	the road home through the mountains
ko kura kari kemu	among trees, black it must have been.

It pained me to think of you thus." The message was simply delivered without expecting a reply. However, just this came from him:

tofu kowe wa	Although it says not
itsu to nakeredo	when it will call again,
hototogisu	the cuckoo bird
akete kuyashiki	feels such remorse at dawn,
mono wo koso omohe	Oh, how he broods on things.

I know nothing of mountain peaks, but if you should want a guide for the valley – This seems to be an expression based on a tag of poetry, but no source poem has been positively identified. The consensus in interpretation is that losing oneself on a mountain peak is a euphemism for leaving the world, by either becoming a monk or dying, while going through the valley means staying in the world. She is offering to be his guide through the difficult time on his way to marriage, if he does not lose heart.

interestingly drawn women's pictures – These are pictures intended for women; that is, they are suitable pictures for illustrating romances. Drawing such pictures was a popular pastime among women.

What would I do if . . . – Lovely variation on the theme of poem no. 1093 in *Kokinshū*:

> if ever I should
> change my mind   and banish you
> from my heart   then would
> great ocean waves rise and cross
> Suenomatsu Mountain   (Rodd, *Kokinshū*, 372)

Suenomatsu means "pines of Sue." The author imagines that the woman in the picture is looking at the pines on the miniature island and considering the possibility of her lover's infidelity. The poem also makes the perennial pun on *matsu*, "to pine, to wait" and "pine tree."

"I am terribly sorry."

Even though he was sulking like that, he arrived at the gate the next day, calling out, "Assistant director, I have a round of visits to make today, and I came to see if you wanted to go into the office together." As before, he requested an inkstone and it was sent out with some paper. When I looked at what he sent back, it was written in a strange shaking hand, "What sins must I have committed in a former lifetime to become one so obstructed like this. Things just seem to get stranger, and to have what I want to have happen seems more difficult. But I would not speak of these things further. Soon I shall just lose myself on a mountain peak somewhere," and so on; he wrote profusely. I wrote this as a reply and sent it out, "How frightening. Why would you speak like this? The one to whom you should speak your resentment is not me. I know nothing of mountain peaks, but if you should want a guide for the valley . . ." Whereupon, he and the assistant director went off in the same carriage. The assistant director came back later riding on a beautiful horse that he had been given.

That evening, the director came again, "When I think of how the other night I said things for which I am sorry, I feel sorry all over again. Tonight, having turned over a new leaf, I have come intending to say, 'From now on, I shall simply abide by the term his lordship has decreed.' You said to me, 'Do not die,' but I feel that even were I blessed with a thousand years of longevity, the pain I'm feeling now would make me want to give it up. When I bend my fingers to count, three fingers mark the months that I shall somehow spend lying down and waking. When I think of the long distance ahead, all those days and months when I shall have nothing to do, I wonder if you wouldn't allow me just to be your night watchman and live on the veranda." Since he spoke like this so utterly at odds with my intentions, I replied accordingly, and tonight he returned quickly.

The assistant director is at the beck and call of the director, day or night; he is always over there. As there were some interestingly drawn women's pictures over there, he took them, put them in his pocket and brought them home. I looked at them and saw that one was the painting of a woman leaning on the balustrade of a building called a fishing pavilion, gazing at the pines on the little islands in the middle of the pond. I wrote this on a strip of paper and stuck it to the painting:

ika ni semu	What would I do if
ike no midzu nami	the waves of the pond water
sawagite ha	were all stirred up
kokoro no uchi no	and swept over the pines
matsu ni kakaraba	of pining within my heart.

Like the spider's thread . . . – We have seen the spider's thread used as a metaphor for love letters before in poems between Michitsuna and the Yamato woman. The spider thread image is introduced with the pillow world, *sasagani ni.* There is quite a network of puns in this poem, the *i* of *idzuko*, "where," means "thread"; *kakute* means "spinning hand," "writing hand," and "thus." With the meaning of "spinning hand" in mind, *amata*, "many," suggests the many legs of the spider.

The assistant director took this back to the director – Both poems above can be interpreted as hidden admonitions to the director. "My daughter fears you will be a fickle husband," and "You are probably the type of suitor who scatters your love letters everywhere." But as Shinozuka points out, the author takes such pleasure in this correspondence, it is not simply a case of wanting to discourage him (*Kagerō nikki no kokoro to hyōgen*, 721).

will he be entertained so lavishly over at your place all the while . . . – Kaneie displays something close to jealousy here. He seems to have intuited that Michitsuna's Mother is enjoying the communication with Tōnori.

"The cuckoos pass right through the house" – Apparently a proverb referring to the strident quality of the cuckoo's voice. Since she mentions worrying under a restless sky and such, people seem to have thought an excess of cuckoo's calls somehow ominous.

On another picture, where a bachelor leaves off writing letters and with his chin resting on his hands seems sunk in brooding thoughts, I wrote this:

sasagani ni	Like the spider's thread
idzuko to mo naku	cast upon the blowing wind,
fuku kaze ha	not sure where it will land,
kakute amata ni	thus he sits and writes so much,
nari zo sura shimo	wondering what will become of it.

The assistant director took this back to the director.

Thus the same kinds of things went on; as the director was always pressing me to plead his case with his lordship, I thought to get a response from him that I could display, so I wrote to him, "Since he just goes on like this, I am put in a difficult position to make an answer." He sent this. "The date has been set as we said; I wonder why he carries on like that? What the world seems to be gossiping about is, will he be entertained so lavishly over at your place all the while he waits for the eighth month? It just makes me want to sigh." For a while I just thought he was joking, but he made comments like that so often I found it odd and so sent this to him. "It is not I who am urging him on. I have found him most annoying and have told him, 'It is not just to me you should plead,' but he carries on all the more; it is really too much for me. And what do you mean by those insinuations?

ima sara ni	Now, more than ever,
ikanaru koma ka	what colt would think to draw near
natsuku beki	this abandoned grass,
susamenu kusa to	left to whither in the fields,
nogare ni shi mi wo	such a one am I.

How horrid of you."

The director kept demanding and pressing his suit while it was still the fourth month. These days more than in usual years, the cuckoos have been making a racket with their cries. As it is in the old saying, "The cuckoos pass right through the house." In the margin of a letter to the director, I wrote this, "As never before, the cuckoos make such a din with their visits, one worries under a restless sky." Since I wrote with a genuine sense of anxiety, the director did not respond with anything improper.

The assistant director was going to borrow a horse feeding trough from the director "for a while." In the margin of one of the usual letters from the director, he wrote, "Please tell the assistant director, 'If things don't go the way I want, there will be no trough either.'" In my response as well, I said, "As for the horse trough, since it seems to come full of

to lay the trough in the right place – There is just a touch of innuendo in the verb "to lay."

go on a pilgrimage to a certain place – She does not name it, but because she writes three poems, *Zenshū* commentators suggest it may be the Fushimi Inari Shrine again (*Zenshū*, 373).

I wonder if the goddess could divine what frame of mind I was in – *Zenshū* commentators, among others, remark here that she is again looking at herself objectively (*Zenshū*, 374). She has already basically accepted that her marriage as an intimate relationship with Kaneie is over, yet she writes these poems wistfully pleading for a renewal of their relationship. Perhaps she is wondering at the workings of her own heart as much as she is wondering about the perceptive powers of the goddess.

single-minded as this singlet – Pun on *hitohe*, "single-minded" and "singlet."

the fifth – The fifth day of the fifth month and therefore the Tango Festival, time to put up the iris decorations.

my brother – Again we assume this is Masayoshi.

obligations, perhaps it is more trouble than it is worth." He responded to this right away, "Certainly the obligation is mine; I shall come tomorrow or the next day to lay the trough in the right place."

Thus the fourth month ended. Perhaps he was discouraged now that the marriage was such a long way in the distance; the fifth month began with no word from him. On the fourth, just when it was raining heavily, this came addressed to the assistant director, "If the rain lets up, please drop by. There is something I have to tell you. Please tell your mother, 'Since you are well aware of the fate that has befallen me, I will say no more.'" Calling upon the assistant director just like that all the time wasn't for anything important, he just wanted to correspond for the fun of it.

Today, despite the rain, I intended to go on a pilgrimage to a certain place with someone from the household. As we were about to set out not letting the rain stop us, one of my attendants came up beside me and whispered, "For the goddess, they say it is good to make offerings of clothing one has sewn. Please do so." "Well, let's give it a try," I said and sewed three doll's outfits out of closely woven plain silk. On the under layer of each, I wrote these poems; I wonder if the goddess could divine what frame of mind I was in:

shirotahe no	This robe of pure white
koromo ha kami ni	like mulberry, to the goddess,
yudzuritemu	I offer it up,
hedatenu naka ni	may our relations return
kaeshi nasu beku	to the closeness of before.

And:

karagoromo	Chinese robe spouse,
nare ni shi tsuma wo	well-worn and familiar,
uchi kaheshi	now turned inside out,
waga shitagahi ni	oh, for a way to have things
nasu yoshi mogana	go again as I would have them.

And:

natsu goromo	This robe of summer
tatsu ya to zo miru	I cut looking for a sign,
chihayaburu	single-minded as
kami wo hitohe ni	this singlet, I place my trust
tanomu mi nareba	in the awe-inspiring gods.

We returned at dark.

The next day was the fifth. At dawn, my brother comes visiting. "Hey, why are you so late with your iris decorations today? You know it's

herb charms – It was traditional to weave herbs, ribbons, and flowers together into charms for good luck.

"Visiting mountain cuckoo . . ." – Reference to a poem in *Kokin rokujō*:

From foot wearying
far mountains, visiting cuckoo,
is it for today
the festival, that you trip among
the irises and sing. (*Zenshū*, 375)

Back and forth, no end . . . – There is a pun in this poem. *Waga naka* is "our relationship, friendship," which pivots into Nakagawa, the name of the river.

best to get them up by evening." When he says this, the servants awake, and when they could be heard thatching the irises, all the other attendants get up. As they are putting up the lattices, I say, "Leave them down for a while. Let's really think about how we are going to cover them. We can get a good look at them that way." But as everybody was already up and busy at it, they do the thatching in all sorts of different ways. The wind that swept away yesterday's clouds is still blowing, so the fragrance of the irises quickly fills the house, so lovely. The assistant director and I sit out on the veranda together, and have all kinds of herbs and plants gathered. "Let's make some really unusual herb charms," we say, and as we sit with our fingers busily occupied, there is a commotion about a flock of cuckoos on the outside roof. Cuckoos themselves are hardly worthy of note these days, and their voices are loud, yet, right now, hearing two or three voices together as they soar into the sky, the pleasure of it thrills me to the core and there is not a one of us who does not intone aloud the old poem, "Visiting mountain cuckoo, is it for today the festival?" The whole household seemed to enjoy making merry. When the sun is up a little, the director comes to say to the assistant director, "If I go to see the archery on horseback contest, will you come with me?" The assistant director says, "I will attend upon you." When someone came to urge them, "Hurry up, it's late," they left.

The next day early in the morning, the director does not come himself but sends this to the assistant director, "You were all having so much fun yesterday reciting poems, that I did not get a chance to say anything. As for the cold treatment your mother gives me, there is nothing I can say. Nonetheless, I would like to see my relations with your sister come to some fruition while I am alive. If I were to die, no matter how much I cared for her, what would it matter? All right, all right, these are just my private thoughts." Then about two days later, early in the morning, this arrives for the assistant director, "Would it be good for you to come here? Or shall I go there?" I say, "You go to him quickly. What is there for him to do here?" and send him off. He came back later saying as usual, "It was really nothing important." Now, about two days later, the director writes just this, "There is something I must tell you. Please come." It was still early in the morning. The assistant director sends the reply, "I will be there shortly." But then in a while, it began to rain heavily. It kept up right until evening, so he was unable to go. "What a shame," the assistant director said, "Well, I had better at least send him word." So he wrote this, "I am sorry to have been stopped by this terrible rain, as sorry as this"—

taezu yuku	Back and forth, no end
waga nakagaha no	to our friendship until the

speaking of your three fingers – Earlier he had spoken of bending fingers to count the three months he must wait before marrying.

"I suppose you'll get the autumn geese to cry as well" – Just flipping the calendar to the eighth month will not work, he will have to get the seasonal signals to cooperate too.

this letter – The letter from Kaneie where he suggests that people are gossiping about a flirtation between Tōnori and the author.

midzu masari	Nakagawa rose,
wochinaru hito zo	and I am left longing for
kohishikarikeru	you on the other side.

The reply:

awanu se wo	If we both languish
kohishi to omohaba	out of love, unable to meet,
omofu dochi	let us both languish
hemu nakagaha ni	together, let me live there
ware wo sumase yo	beside the Nakagawa.

While they were exchanging such messages, night arrived, the rain lifted, and the director came himself. He just goes on in the same vein about his anxieties, so I say, "Well, speaking of your three fingers, the time will pass just like that before you have time to bend even one." "Well, I wonder. Since there are things I cannot depend on, I get disheartened, and I may yet be made to bend my fingers for a further extension. The way I feel right now, I'd like somehow to get his lordship's calendar and cut out the middle section and then paste it together again." This struck us as a charming notion, so I respond with, "I suppose you'll get the autumn geese to cry as well," and we break into hearty laughter. Then I remember the remark about the lavish treatment the director has been getting here, "But seriously, this matter is not up to me alone, and I find it very difficult to press matters with his lordship," to which he replies, "What is going on here? Why is it difficult, tell me." As he pressed me again and again, I wanted somehow to let him know my situation, yet it was difficult for me to speak about it myself. So I said, "Even though I feel embarrassed to have you see this letter, it is just that seeing this, perhaps you will understand how difficult it is for me to speak to his lordship as you would wish." Tearing off the portion of the letter that I did not want him to see, I passed it out to him. He slipped out onto the veranda and putting it to the light of the hazy moon, looked at it for a long time and then brought it back in. "The writing got confused with the color of the paper; I could not make it out at all. I will come again during the day to have a look at it," he said and pushed it under my curtain. When I said, "I will tear it up now," he said, "No, please keep it for a while." There was not a trace in his facial expression that he had actually seen what was written there. He simply said, "Now, since the event over which I have fretted so much is getting close, that people would say I should refrain from coming here makes me utterly forlorn." From time to time, he was saying something I couldn't quite hear; he seemed to be chanting a poem. "Tomorrow morning, I have something I must attend to at the office. I will come directly here first to speak to the assistant director." With that, he left.

the part of the letter where I had written in response the poem, "What colt" – Presumably she had written out her response poem onto Kaneie's letter before drafting the clean copy. This was common practice when paper was so precious.

someone was under ritual prohibition here – She has suspected her husband of using ritual prohibitions of one sort or another to excuse delays or lack of communication, and here she is doing the same.

'what heart is hidden there' – Allusion to poem no. 720 in *Kokinshū:*

> Endlessly flowing
> the Asuka River, were
> it ever to stop
> what heart is hidden there is
> what people would wonder.

You may be thinking that the color of that letter might still be difficult to make out even in the light of day . . . – But come and see for yourself, is the invitation.

the cuckoo in his misery is wasting into a shadow in the unohana – Pun on *mi no u*, "one's misery" pivoting into *unohana*.

This seems indeed to be your response for yesterday – He has apologized for not responding promptly, but with this remark she assures him that he has made an appropriate reply for yesterday's poem.

The next day when I looked at the letter by my pillow that I showed him last night, I saw that I had torn off a different piece than I had thought, and not only that, but another piece had also been torn away. As I was thinking how very strange this was, I realized that he must have torn and taken away the part of the letter where I had written in response the poem, "What colt." Still early in the morning, a message arrived for the assistant director. "I seem to have caught a bad cold and am unable to come as I said I would. Please come here around midday." The assistant director, thinking that as usual it was not anything of real importance, had not yet gone there when this letter arrived from him for me. It said, "I intended to speak with you even sooner than usual but was unavoidably detained. The letter of last night was so terribly hard to read. It seems it has become very difficult for me to ask you specifically to speak to his lordship on my behalf, but I am begging you to do your best for me as the occasion arises. How sad it is that I have become this much of a pathetic figure." It was written with more restraint than usual and in a splendid hand.

As for a reply, thinking it wasn't necessary every time, I didn't send one. But then the next day, I felt sorry for him and also thought that perhaps I had been a little childish. I wrote this, "Yesterday, someone was under ritual prohibition here, and then it got dark, so I ended up not sending a letter. For you, it must have been as in the old poem, 'what heart is hidden there.' I am thinking what I could do for you as the occasion arises but, as you know, I have become one for whom such chances do not exist. You seemed so wretched at the end of your letter, truly I understand. You may be thinking that the color of that letter might still be difficult to make out even in the light of day." When this was delivered to his house, it so happened that it was just as a lot of monks arrived and there was quite a commotion; the messenger simply left the letter and came back. The next morning while it was still early, this came from him. "A number of men of the cloth came here yesterday and then it got late, so your messenger returned empty-handed:

nagekitsutsu	Sorrow, sorrowing,
akashi kuraseba	as he lives from dawn to dusk,
hototogisu	the cuckoo in his
mi no unohana no	misery is wasting into
kage ni naritsutsu	a shadow in the unohana.

What am I to do. Tonight, I fear I must send my regrets." My response was, "This seems indeed to be your response for yesterday. You seem so strange":

kage ni shimo	Wasting to a shadow,
nado ka naruramu	how should you ever come to that,
unohana no	when on the branch of

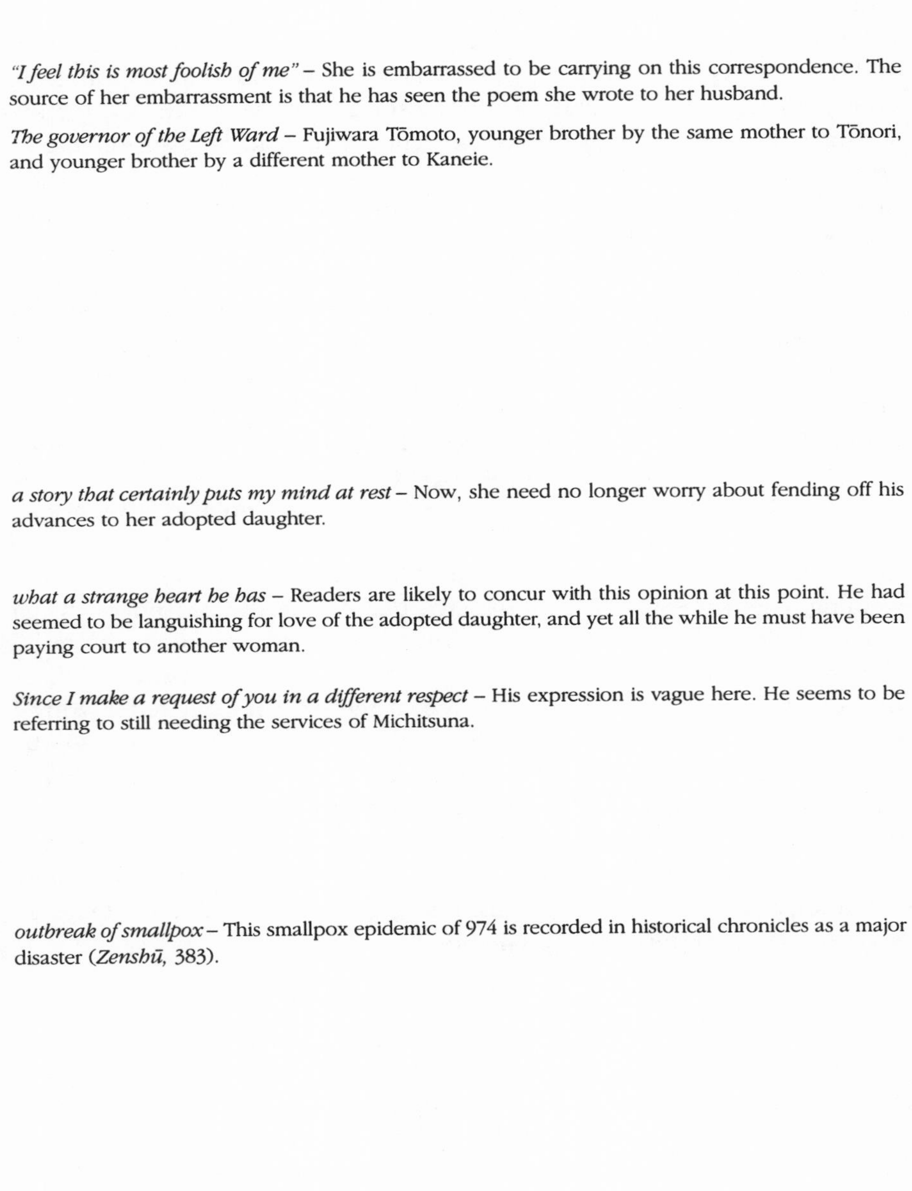

"I feel this is most foolish of me" – She is embarrassed to be carrying on this correspondence. The source of her embarrassment is that he has seen the poem she wrote to her husband.

The governor of the Left Ward – Fujiwara Tōmoto, younger brother by the same mother to Tōnori, and younger brother by a different mother to Kaneie.

a story that certainly puts my mind at rest – Now, she need no longer worry about fending off his advances to her adopted daughter.

what a strange heart he has – Readers are likely to concur with this opinion at this point. He had seemed to be languishing for love of the adopted daughter, and yet all the while he must have been paying court to another woman.

Since I make a request of you in a different respect – His expression is vague here. He seems to be referring to still needing the services of Michitsuna.

outbreak of smallpox – This smallpox epidemic of 974 is recorded in historical chronicles as a major disaster (*Zenshū,* 383).

Even the director, though he has lost face in the world – Of course, Michitsuna and Tōnori are still colleagues in the same office, so it is natural there would still be a connection. Nonetheless, it is noteworthy that his friendship with the author and her son survived his outrageous behavior.

eda ni shinobanu — unohana, you sing forth
kokoro to zo kiku — your heart for all to hear.

was what I wrote, but then I crossed the upper part out and wrote in the margin, "I feel this is most foolish of me."

In the meantime, he was informed that "The governor of the Left Ward has passed away." Consequently, he entered a period of strict mourning, retreating often to a mountain temple. From time to time he wrote, and so the sixth month passed.

The seventh month arrived. As I felt the eighth month growing nearer, the one that I was caring for still seemed so young, and I was lost in persistent thoughts of what was going to happen to her; all concerns I might have had for myself quite vanished. It was around the twentieth of the month. The director was being most aggressive and just at the time when I was very conscious of him depending on me, one of my attendants came up with this news, "It seems the director of the Right Stable has stolen another man's wife and hidden her away. It's incredible; everybody is talking about it." Hearing this, I thought to myself, *well now, this is a story that certainly puts my mind at rest. I had been worrying about what I was going to say to him at the end of the month. Yet, as I think about it, what a strange heart he has.* Then, a letter arrived from him. When I looked at it, it was as though he was responding to an inquiry from me. "Well, what a terrible thing. I must tell you of something I did not intend to happen; I won't be able to make my appointment in the eighth month. Since I make a request of you in a different respect, nevertheless . . ." In my reply, I said, "What did you mean by 'something you did not intend to happen'? However, to hear you say 'in a different respect' seems to indicate you have not forgotten entirely about us, which brings me some relief."

The eighth month arrived. The whole world is in a commotion about the outbreak of smallpox. Around the twentieth of the month, it reached our neighborhood. The assistant director has come down with an extremely severe case. There is no help for it. It is to the point that his father, with whom all communications have ceased, should be informed, but my feelings are in a whirl and I don't know what to do. *I simply have to tell him*, I think, but when I inform him by letter, his reply is very curt. And after that, he only had a servant inquire by word of mouth how the assistant director was. When I see that even people of whom it would not normally be expected are coming to pay him a visit, the feelings I have are accompanied by agitation. Even the director, though he has lost face in the world, comes often to visit. On the first of the ninth month, he recovered. Rain that began to fall around the twentieth of the eighth month has

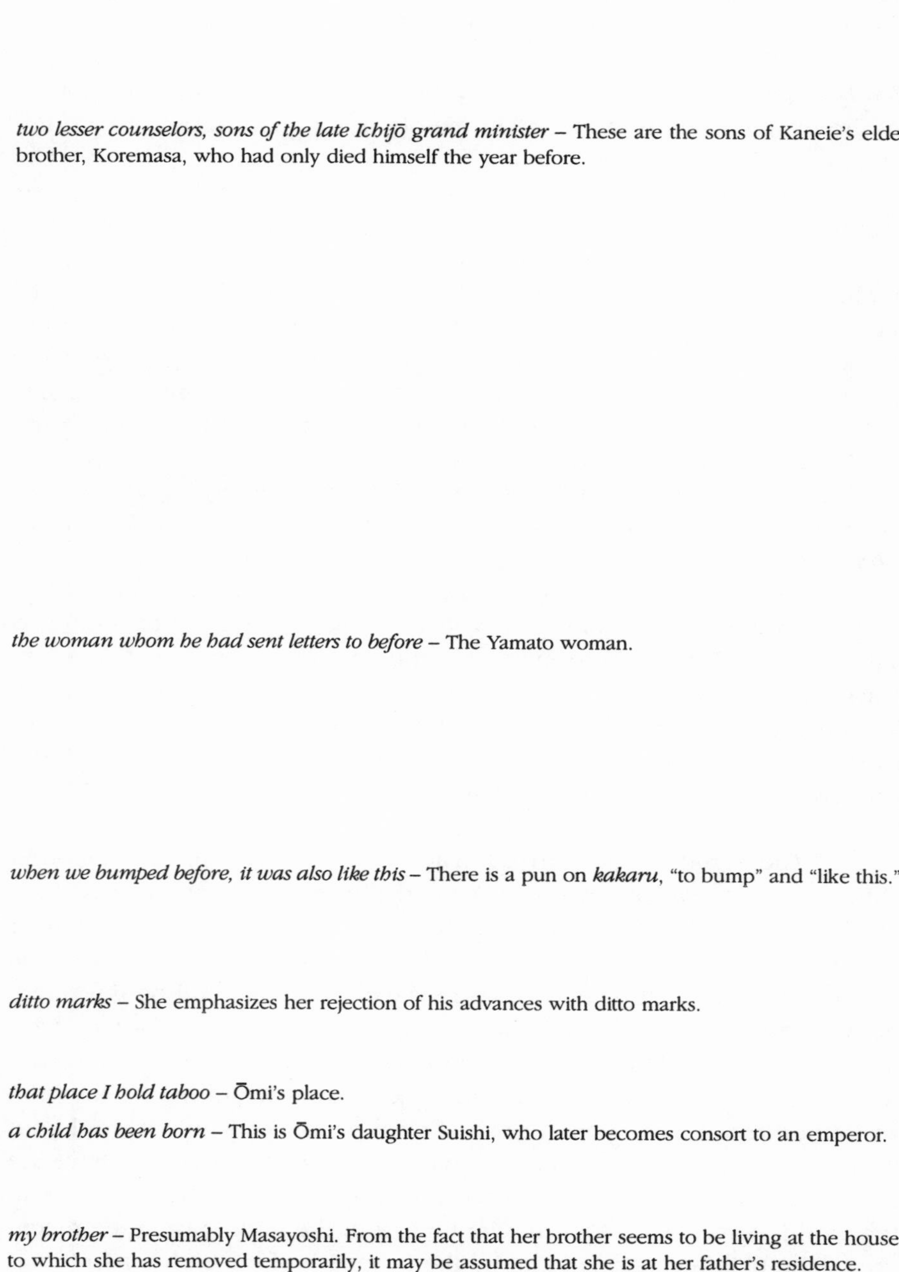

two lesser counselors, sons of the late Ichijō grand minister – These are the sons of Kaneie's elder brother, Koremasa, who had only died himself the year before.

the woman whom he had sent letters to before – The Yamato woman.

when we bumped before, it was also like this – There is a pun on *kakaru*, "to bump" and "like this."

ditto marks – She emphasizes her rejection of his advances with ditto marks.

that place I hold taboo – Ōmi's place.

a child has been born – This is Ōmi's daughter Suishi, who later becomes consort to an emperor.

my brother – Presumably Masayoshi. From the fact that her brother seems to be living at the house to which she has removed temporarily, it may be assumed that she is at her father's residence.

not let up this month either; it is dark with falling rain. Since it looks as though the Nakagawa and the Kamo River are about to flow together, I feel that at any moment even we might be swept away. The world has become a sad place indeed. We have not been able to gather in the harvest from the rice fields in front of the gate yet. In the rare breaks in the rainfall, to make a little bit of toasted rice, this is about all that has been done.

The smallpox spreads even further in the world; the two lesser counselors, sons of the late Ichijō grand minister, die on the same day, the sixteenth of this month; it is talked about everywhere. It is unbearable to imagine. Hearing about this, thinking of the one who has recovered, I feel awed. Even though the assistant director has recovered, because he has nothing in particular to do, he is not yet going out. Around the twentieth comes an ever-so-rare letter from him. "How is the assistant director? Everyone here has recovered and I was wondering why I had not seen him. I have been worried. Since you seem to feel a great dislike for me, even though I have not intended to estrange you, somehow the time has passed with our being at odds with each other. Although I have not forgotten you . . ." It was written with concern; I found it strange. In my reply, I wrote only about the one he had asked after, but then in the margin added, "Indeed, 'forgotten,' that is how it seems."

The first day that the assistant director went out, he met by chance on the road the carriage of the woman whom he had sent letters to before and somehow the axle hubs of their carriages knocked together and caused trouble. The next day, he sent this, "Yesterday evening, I did not know it was you. However—"

toshi tsuki no	The months and years
meguri kuruma no	have rolled round into the wheels
wa ni narite	of our carriages,
omoheba kakaru	I remember, when we bumped
wori mo arikeri	before, it was also like this.

So this was sent. She took it in, looked at it, adding in the margin of the letter in a very ordinary hand, "No it wasn't, not for me," with a lot of ditto marks, and it was returned that way; how very like that person.

Sometime after the twentieth, when I had moved temporarily to another residence due to a ritual transgression, I heard that at that place I hold taboo a child has been born. Although one would think I would feel hate upon hearing such a thing and not be able to let it be, I remained unconcerned. Then, in the evening, when the torches had been lit and I was just about to eat, my brother drew near and took out from his pocket a letter on thick white mulberry paper that had been tied into a knot and

those syllables from the poem I had regretted sending my husband – "What colt" is from her poem where she compared herself to withered grass. Clearly the person who has written this poem has seen her poem.

his lordship Horikawa – This is Kaneie's elder brother, Kanemichi. It is interesting that she guesses immediately who the poem is from. The relations between Kanemichi and Kaneie were antagonistic around this time, and Kanemichi was doing everything in his power to frustrate the career of Kaneie. This is recorded candidly in *Eiga monogatari*, a contemporary history (McCullough and McCullough, *A Tale of Flowering Fortunes*, 112–15). One is tempted to speculate why Kanemichi would send a flirtatious poem to the author at this time. Was he looking for a way to annoy his brother in a personal way by courting his former wife? Or was he genuinely interested in the author and feeling some sympathy for her neglect by Kaneie? Or was he simply desiring one of her poems for a literary memento?

my rather old-fashioned father – Her father has finished his last assignment as a provincial governor and is back living in the capital, looking for a new post. His appearance in this sequence suggests strongly that the author is staying at his residence.

Write a reply quickly, and it must be sent back with his lordship's servant – While her attitude toward this overture from Kanemichi is one of amusement, her father is very eager. He cannot afford to pass up, even through the proxy of his daughter, an opportunity for communication with the great and powerful.

a long time had passed without an answer, I found it most amusing – It is humorous to think of Kanemichi cudgeling his brains trying to frame a suitably witty response. Timing was everything with this kind of correspondence; once a certain amount of time had passed, he would no longer be able to send a response.

Special Secondary Kamo Festival – The official Kamo Festival was held in the fourth month. This was a special irregular festival held this year in the autumn, actually the twenty-third day of the eleventh month.

attached to a spray of withered pampas grass. When I say, "My, how odd. Whose is this?" he says, "Just have a look at it." I open it, and looking at it in the lamplight, see that it is in a hand resembling that of the person I am estranged from. This is what was written. "What ever happened to 'What colt'?"

shimokare no	Frost withered myself,
kusa no yukari zo	the bond I feel with the dry grass
aware naru	is sad and moving,
koma gaherite mo	becoming a colt again
natsukete shigana	I would want to draw near you.

"Ah, what a pity." Since it contained those syllables from the poem I had regretted sending to my husband, it was so strange. When I asked, "What is this?" and "Did it come from his lordship Horikawa?" I was told, "Yes, it is a letter from the grand minister. One of his attendants came with it and when told, 'Her ladyship is not in,' said, 'Please make sure she receives this,' and gave it to me." Although I thought and thought, it was so strange; I could not figure out how he could have heard of that poem. When I talked this over with others, my rather old-fashioned father, hearing of it, admonished me, "This is a very serious matter. Write a reply quickly, and it must be sent back with his lordship's servant." Well, I did not intend to write such a silly poem, but it was just tossed off:

sasa wakeba	Parting scrub bamboo,
are koso masame	you approach but the grass is
kusa kare no	more withered and distant,
koma natsuku beki	is it really beneath these trees
mori no shita ka ha	that a colt would want to draw near?

This is what I wrote and sent. I heard later from an attendant, "His lordship intended to write a reply to your poem, but after getting it half done, he said, 'I haven't quite got an ending yet,'" and since indeed a long time had passed without an answer, I found it most amusing.

The Special Secondary Kamo Festival is to be held day after tomorrow. At the last minute, the assistant director has been invited to be one of the dancers. This prompted his father to send a rare letter. "How are things going with your preparation?" it said, and along with it he sent all the things that would be needed for the performance. On the day of the rehearsal, this message came. "Since this is a period when I am on leave from my duties due to a defilement, I shall not be able to go to court for the rehearsal. I am thinking to come and get the assistant director ready to go from your place, but since you may not even let me in the door, I have been wondering what to do and feeling most uneasy." My

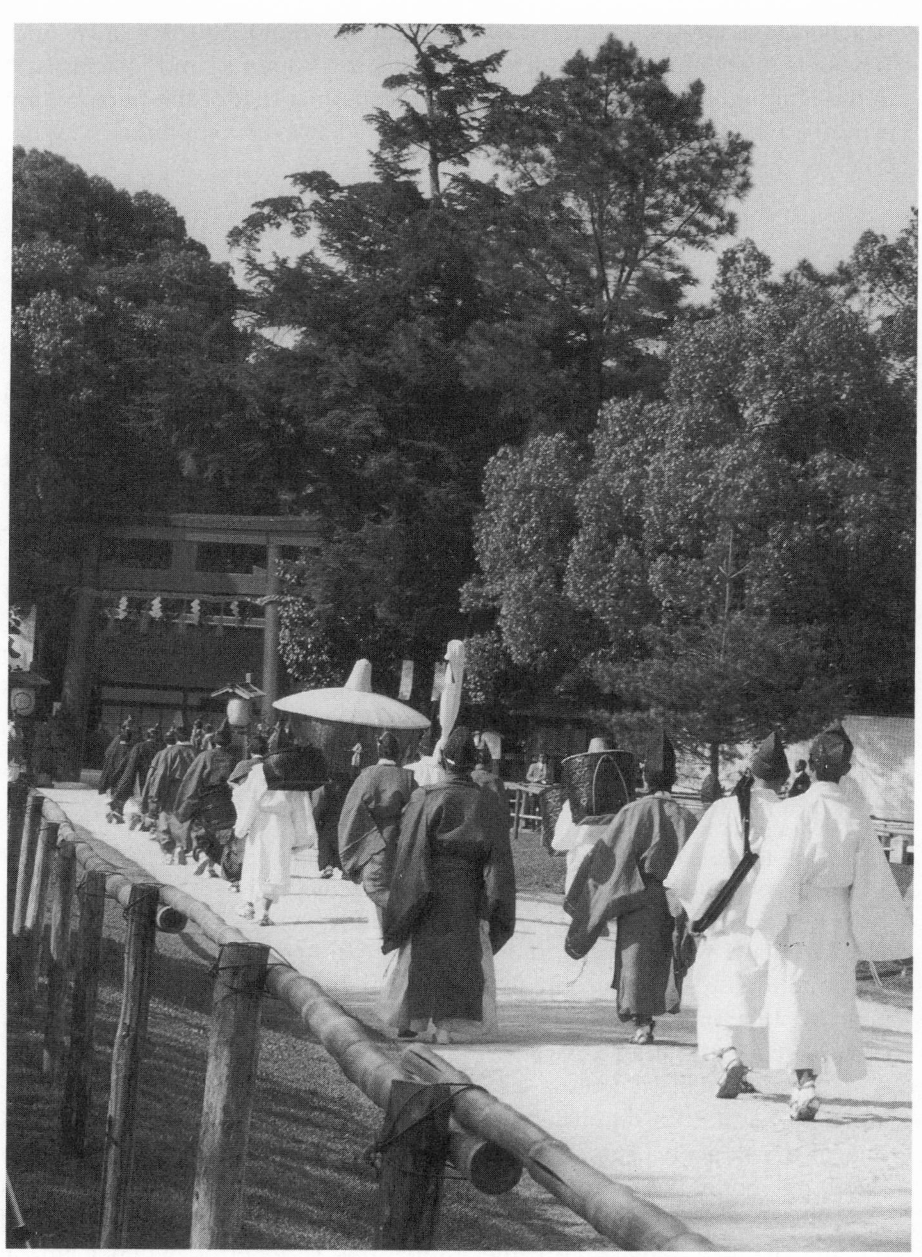

Procession entering Kamo Shrine. This photograph and the next three were taken during the Aoi (Kamo) Festival of April 1996. The contemporary festival is still celebrated in Heian-period costume. These images are presented to help readers visualize the scene of the Special Secondary Kamo Festival held in early winter of 974, which is described by Michitsuna's Mother on p. 371.

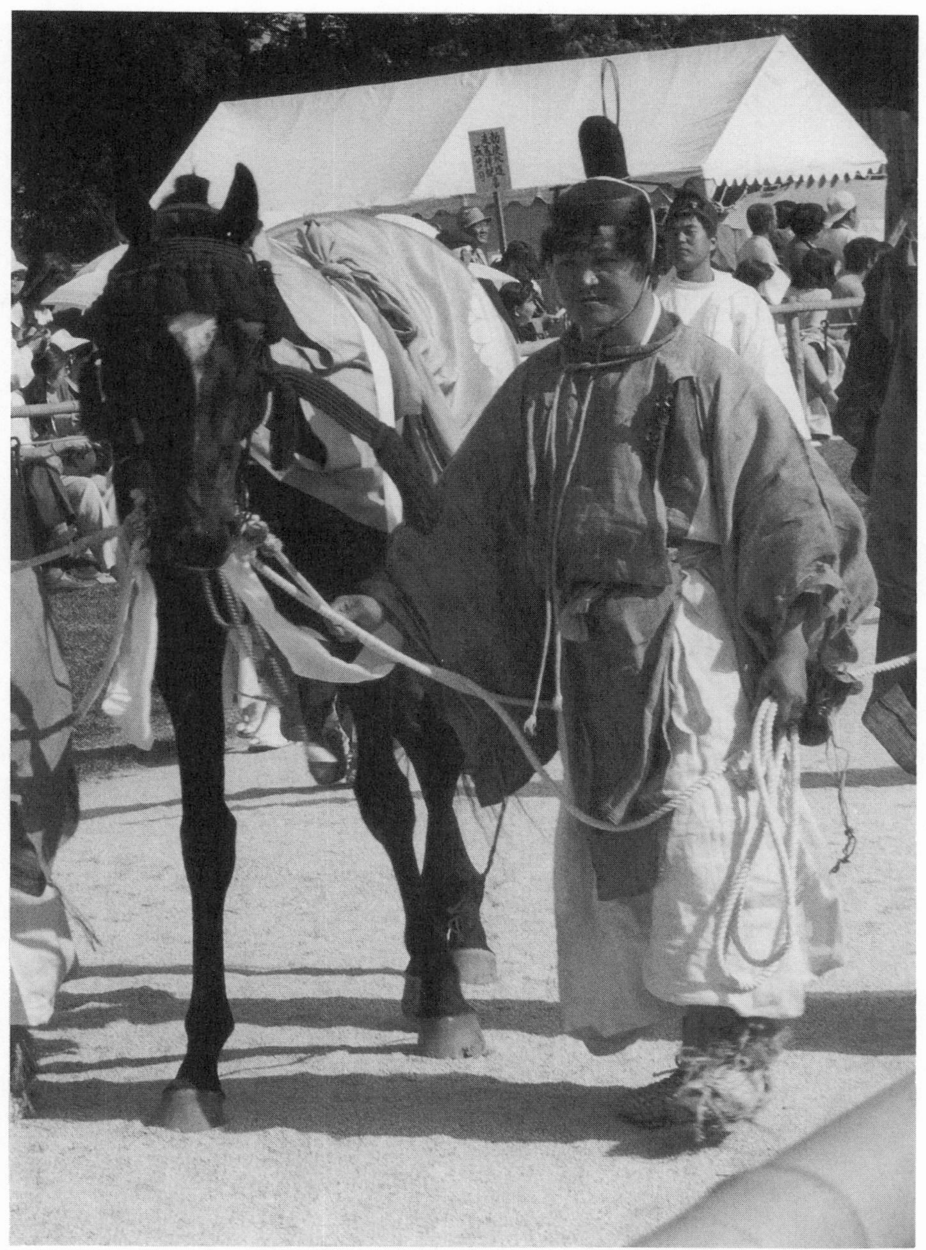

Man in Heian costume leading a horse in the Kamo Festival procession. The provision of horses for such ceremonial occasions as this would have been part of Michitsuna's responsibilities in his post as assistant director of the Right Stable (see pp. 332–33).

Kamo Festival musicians (see p. 371).

Kamo Festival musicians during a break in the proceedings. "My old-fashioned father, who was not permitted to be in the audience, was mingling among the musicians with blossom-festooned caps" (p. 371).

Sleeves of purple brocade layered over lustrous red silk spilled out – Women often let their sleeves trail out from under carriage blinds to attract notice.

a man of the sixth rank – The costumes of courtiers were coded to their rank. This man would have been wearing green, the color of the sixth rank.

men in costumes of red and black – Vermilion was the color of the fifth rank. The designation of color to rank changed several times during the Heian period, so it is difficult to know just which rank black represented at this time, but it is likely it was for courtiers above the fourth rank.

there are some men there we have seen before – This remark by one of her attendants makes it clear that it is Kaneie in the carriage.

Things had gotten underway a little earlier than usual – What she goes on to describe is not the parade proper but a rest stop for the participants.

the one I care deeply about – Her son, Michitsuna.

My old-fashioned father, who was not permitted to be in the audience, was mingling among the musicians – *Zenshū* commentators speculate that since her father was "out of office" at the time, he would not be permitted to view the event alongside the grand nobility. Mingling with the musicians gave him the opportunity to be a spectator (*Zenshū*, 359). He would not want to miss the chance to see his grandson in full regalia.

sought out in the crowd and offered a cup of sake – Presumably Kaneie has ordered that this special mark of respect be made to him.

just for that moment in time, I seemed to feel content – It is an unusual occasion in that the three most important men in her life are all gathered in one place around her. Kaneie is there with another woman, but she is no longer distressed by that. She basks in the reflected glory of her son. She appreciates the small mark of respect made to her father. *Zenshū* commentators remark that this scene can actually be regarded as the final scene in the diary (*Zenshū*, 389) because what follows is a sort of coda of love poems between Michitsuna and a new woman. This final scene provides the opportunity for the author to look with serenity on the men who have been important in her life.

The lady came from around the area of Yatsuhashi – Yatsuhashi, "Eight Bridges," is a place in Aichi Prefecture close to present-day Nagoya, made famous in the *Tales of Ise* by a poem on irises that Ariwara Narihira composed there on his way to the east. However, it was clearly too far away for the kind of correspondence that will be described, so it is assumed there was a place called Yatsuhashi within the Kyoto city limits, or, like the Yamato woman, the Yatsuhashi woman has some familial connection with Yatsuhashi.

Kazuraki God – The god that Michitsuna has invoked before in poetry who is famous for speaking only one word (see p. 317).

On the way back here . . . – At Yatsuhashi in Aichi Prefecture, the river fans out into many channels, evoking the image of a spider's web, hence the connection with spiders. There is a pun on *fumi*, "footsteps" and "letters."

heart felt crushed, now that things had come to such a pass, what could be done? Thoughts ran rampant. "Quickly change into your costume and go over there," I said and set about busily getting the assistant director ready to go, but the moment he was out the door, I burst into tears. His father practiced the dance with him and then sent him off to court.

On the day of the festival, no matter what, I had to go and have a look. As I set out, I noticed on the north side of the street an unremarkable palmwork carriage parked with its blinds, both in back and in front, pulled down. Sleeves of purple brocade layered over lustrous red silk spilled out from underneath the bamboo blind in front. Just as I was looking at this thinking it must be a woman's carriage, a man of the sixth rank with a sword at his waist approached from the gate of the house behind the carriage and with great dignity knelt with one knee on the ground to say something. With some surprise, when I looked more closely, I could see that beside the carriage that man had come out of, there were all sorts of men in costumes of red and black standing there all crammed together, so many I couldn't count them all. One of my attendants said, "If one looks carefully, there are some men there we have seen before." Things had got underway a little earlier than usual. The high nobility and their followers as well, all seemed to notice him; they stopped and parked their carriages in the same place with the fronts of their carriages facing his. As for the one I care deeply about, he and his attendants too looked magnificent even though they had had little time to prepare. When the high nobility offered him snacks with their own hands and spoke to him, I felt proud. My old-fashioned father, who was not permitted to be in the audience, was mingling among the musicians with blossom-festooned caps. When he was sought out in the crowd and offered a cup of sake brought forth from the other house, just for that moment in time, I seemed to feel content.

Now then, a person who liked to meddle in things said to the assistant director, "Are you going to stay a bachelor like this forever?" She had a woman for him to court. The lady came from around the area of Yatsuhashi. His first poem to her was:

kadzuraki ya	Kazuraki God,
kami yo no shirushi	if his tokens be still potent
fukakaraba	as in the Divine Age,
tada hito koto ni	then with this one word only
uchi mo tokenamu	would your heart melt and yield to me.

Apparently, there was no answer this time:

kaheru sa no	On the way back here,
kumo de ha idzuko	where did the spider's hand go?

even were your footsteps seen . . . – The pun on *fumi*, "footsteps" and "letters," is invoked again. The sense is, "Even if your letter were read, what could you possibly expect?"

Once setting foot has begun – Again through the pun on *fumi*, "letter," is understood, "Once we have started to exchange letters, I will depend on that to get us somewhere."

yatsuhashi no	At Yatsuhashi,
fumi mite kemu to	I depended on my footsteps
tanomu kahi naku.	being seen—to no avail.

There was a reply this time:

kayofu beki	Since Yatsuhashi
michi ni mo aranu	is not a road upon which
yatsuhashi wo	you will go to and fro,
fumi miteki to mo	even were your footsteps seen,
nani ni tanomuran	on what were you depending?

This had been written by an attendant with a fine hand. Again from here, he sent:

nani ka sono	What? Why should it be
kayohamu michi no	so difficult that path I
katakaramu	would take to and fro?
fumi hajimetaru	Once setting foot has begun,
ato wo tanomeba	I will depend on the track made.

Again, there was a response:

tadzunu tomo	Even if you look for me,
kahi ya nakaramu	it will be to no avail,
ohozora no	in the vast sky,
kumodji wa kayofu	traveling the path of clouds,
ato ha kamo araji	no track is ever left behind.

With a look of determination, not to be beaten, he replied:

ohozora mo	In the vast sky,
kumo no kakehashi	if there were no cloud ladders,
naku ha koso	in vain, it would be
kayofu hakanaki	to think of going to and fro,
nageki wo mo seme	then, indeed, would I lament.

Her reply:

fumi miredo	So you would try to
kumo no kakehashi	tread the ladder in the clouds,
aya fushi to	you don't even know
omohi shirazu mo	how fraught with danger it is,
tanomu naru kana	and thus you would depend on it.

And he wrote back:

naho woramu	Like this I shall stay
kokoro tanomoshi	with a heart ever hopeful,

Sleeves spread on one side alone – When people slept alone, they ranged their sleeves neatly on one side.

she sent back a branch of the soba tree with only, "I have seen it" – It is winter, so the branch of the soba tree will have no leaves and be only a branch, in Japanese, *miki*, which is homophonous with *miki*, "I have seen." In further complication, the verb *sobamu*, which can be conjugated in the past as *sobamiki*, means "to look askance" or "to look away." So her cryptic message could be construed, "I saw your letter and I am not interested."

are things so bad between us, we have to look away? – By recycling the vocabulary of her code, *soba*, "the soba tree," *sobamu*, "to look away," and *miki*, "branch" and "I have seen," he indicates that he understood her message.

Since I am a pine . . . – She incorporates another meaning of *soba*, "steep cliff," into her poem. While she is saying that her color is eternal green, it is also like saying, my feelings will never change toward you. Given that the feelings she has expressed this far have not been positive, she is not being encouraging.

seasonal juncture – This is *setsubun*, the day on which spring began in the solar calendar. Due to the slip between the solar and lunar calendars, this year spring is arriving before the year of the lunar calendar has ended.

the directional taboo – It was traditional to spend the night before the seasonal juncture in a house other than one's own. Of course, his invitation is rhetorical since virtually never did the woman visit the man's home.

that the longings in my heart would clear within the year, just as spring comes now – There is a pun on *haru*, "to clear" and "spring."

ashi tadzu no	do I not possess
kumodji orikuru	the wings with which the marsh cranes
tsubasa ya ha naki	fly the cloud paths and descend?

This time, with the excuse, "It's dark," she stopped writing.

The twelfth month arrived; he wrote again:

katashiki shi	Sleeves spread on one side
toshi ha furedomo	alone, thus have I slept as
sagoromo no	the years passed by,
namida ni shimuru	yet never have my night robes
toki ha nakariki	been so soaked with tears as now.

Her servants said, "She has gone out," so there was no answer. The next day, when he sent someone to ask for a response, she sent back a branch of the soba tree with only, "I have seen it." Right away, he wrote back:

waga naka ha	It makes me wonder,
soba minuru ka to	are things so bad between us,
omofu made	we have to look away?
miki to bakari mo	Is that what you meant to say
keshikibamu kana	with only, "I have seen it?"

Her reply:

amagumo no	Since I am a pine
yama no harukeki	growing on the far mountains
matsu nareba	where clouds meet the sky,
sobameru iro ha	my color on the high cliff
tokiha narikeri	is ever eternal green.

As the year drew to a close and the seasonal juncture arrived, he sent word to her, "You are welcome to observe the directional taboo by coming here":

ito semete	Somehow at least this,
omofu kokoro wo	that the longings in my heart
toshi no uchi ni	would clear within
haru kuru koto mo	the year, just as spring comes now,
shirase shigana	would that I could let you know.

There was no reply. It seems he tried again, "Really, if only for a little while, pass some time here":

kahi nakute	If it be so that
toshi kure hatsuru	the year has drawn to a close
mono naraba	all to no avail,

If you are pining . . . – Use of the perennial pun on *matsu*, "pine tree" and "to wait, pine," as well as an allusion to the old *Kokinshū* poem about the waves engulfing the pines of Sue if the lover was untrue.

occupied today with other business – This has been interpreted as meaning the household is preparing for the girl's marriage to someone else.

haru ni mo awanu	should we meet not in spring,
mi to mo koso nare	I shall not live to meet it alone.

Again this time there was no answer. Wondering what was happening, he heard, "There seem to be a lot of men addressing her in this way." So that was it:

ware naranu	If you are pining
hito matsu naraba	for someone other than me,
matsu to ihade	call not yourself "pine,"
itaku na koshi so	do not cause the white waves of
okitsu shiranami	the deep sea to engulf us.

Her reply:

koshi mo sezu	Neither beckoning
kosazu mo arazu	to be engulfed nor avoiding it,
nami yose no	this beach upon which
hama ha kaketsutsu	the waves approach and break
toshi wo koso fure	passes the year favoring none.

As the end of the year approached:

samo koso ha	So that's how it is,
nami no kokoro ha	the heart of these waves is cold,
tsurakarame	yet, there is a pine
toshi sahe koyuru	that would wait ever unchanging
matsu mo arikeri	for a whole year to pass.

Her reply:

chitose furu	For the pine tree that
matsu mo koso are	lives for a thousand years,
hodo mo naku	the going and coming
koete ha kaheru	of one year is hardly any
hodo ya tohokaru	time at all, you call it long?

This was what she wrote. It seemed strange; he wondered what was she talking about. At a time when the wind was blowing fiercely, he sent this:

fuku kaze ni	Stirred up with the
tsukete mo mono wo	blowing of the wind these
omofu kana	brooding, worrisome thoughts,
ohoumi no nami no	within the waves of a great sea,
shidzugokoro naku	my heart is not at ease.

To this was sent the response, "The person whom one would expect to reply is occupied today with other business." This was sent in a different

a branch with only one leaf – The presentation of this branch has been interpreted as meaning, this will be the last message. This long string of courting poems has provided a coda to the diary, and now it too has come to the end.

Although I regarded no one but you . . . – The phrase "one leaf," *hito ha*, is embedded in the line *hito hata soto ha*, "no one other." The "branch of sorrow," *nageki no eda*, can also be understood as "branch of a cast-off tree," since "cast-off tree" is an alternate meaning for *nageki.*

festival of the souls' return – The souls of those departed were thought to return on the last night of the year.

when the knocking comes to the door – On the last night of the year, it was traditional for guardsmen to go from house to house, banging on the door to chase away evil spirits. She has described this custom in book one when she and Lady Jōganden were staying in the same house and she had members of her household start the noisemaking even before it got dark (see book one, p. 147). It is somehow fitting that she ends the diary with a sound that betokens a beginning. There is never closure to life as we live it. It is also appropriate that she ends with a metaphor of being on the edge, both in terms of time, "at the edge of the year," and space, "at the edge of the capital." Her diary has largely been a record of being on an emotional edge.

hand, attached to a branch with only one leaf. He replied in turn, "How painful," and seems to have added this poem:

waga omofu	Although I regarded
hito hata soto ha	no one but you as the one
minasedomo	I was in love with,
nageki no eda ni	on this branch of sorrow, there
yasumaranu kana	is no peace for this one leaf.

This year the weather has not been particularly bad, we have only had snow that stayed in patches on the ground about two times. While I have been preparing the clothes for the assistant director's attendance at New Year's festivities and then at the Presentation of the White Horses, the end of the year has arrived. Having the clothes for tomorrow folded and rolled up, directing the work of the attendants, when I think of it, having lived on thus and arrived at this day, it seems somehow amazing. Even as I watch the festival of the souls' return, the year's edge has arrived with me deep in the usual endless thoughts. Since we are at the edge of the capital, it is very late at night indeed when the knocking comes to the door.

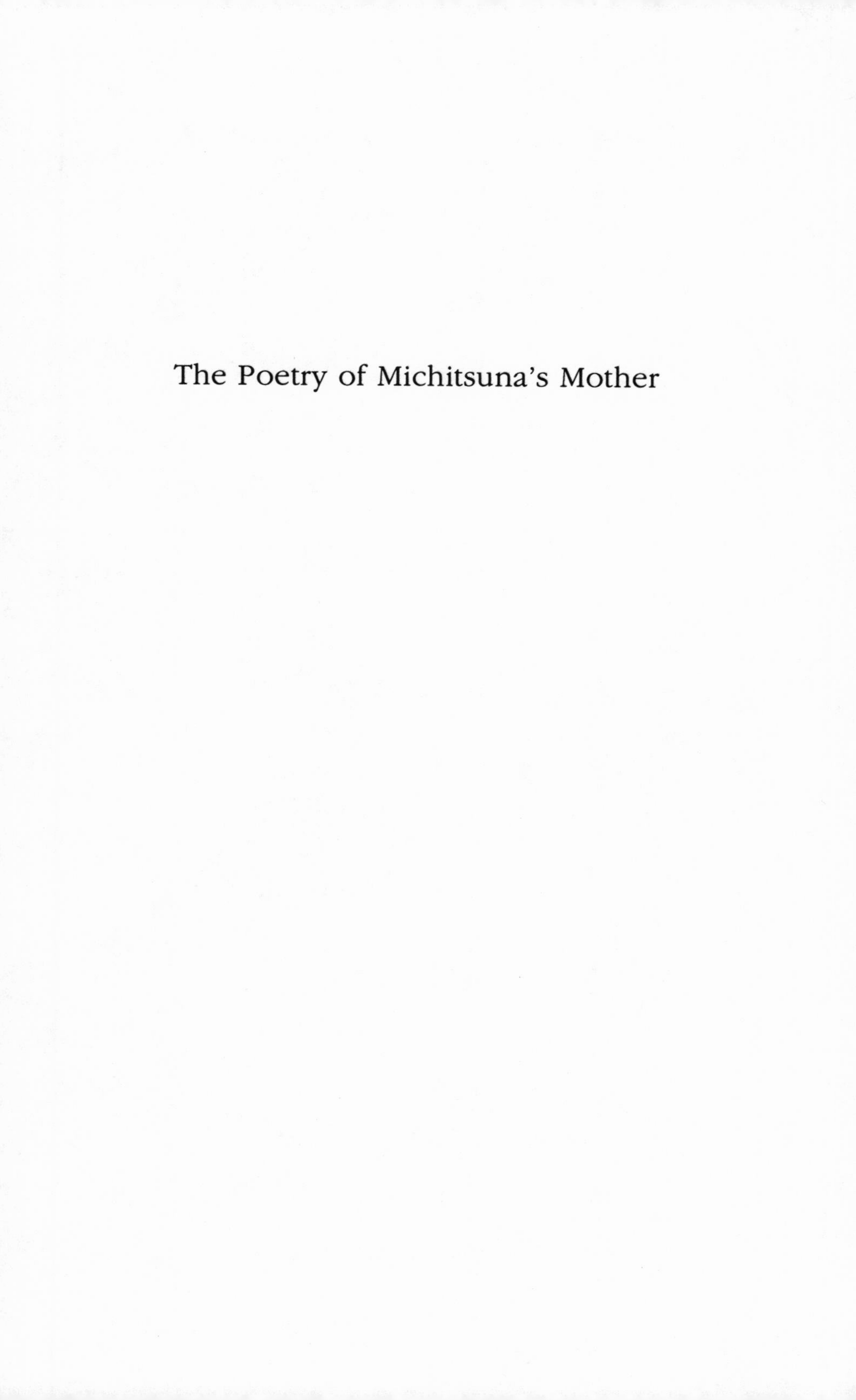

The Poetry of Michitsuna's Mother

Summary

All extant manuscripts of *Kagerō nikki* have this short collection of poetry appended to them. Since the narrative introductions to the poems use an honorific level of language in speaking about both Michitsuna's Mother and Michitsuna, it is clear that the collection was not assembled and annotated by either of them. When Michitsuna is mentioned, he is referred to by the title, imperial tutor, a post he assumed in 1007, which means the collection must have been compiled after that date. There is no indication who did the compiling.

The collection contains poems from various times in Michitsuna's Mother's life, but the majority of them are from the period after the diary ends. This is one of the things that makes the collection interesting, because in it we get brief glimpses of the author's life after 974. We see her sending poems to Kaneie's second daughter, Senshi, after she had become empress. There is further evidence of how often she was called upon to compose poems for others. One preface to a poem mentions specifically that she composed love poems for Michitsuna when he was just entering the courting game. There are quite a few of Michitsuna's courting poems in this collection, and one wonders if indeed we are to assume that all of them are compositions by his mother. Moreover, there are a number of poems composed expressly for poetry contests, in which we can get a sense of the author as "professional poet." If nothing else, this collection gives assurance that Michitsuna's Mother continued to be an active poet throughout her life.

Ceremony of Calling on the Buddha Names – Originally a ceremony held at court on the fifteenth of the twelfth month and lasting for three days, during which time the names of the various Buddhas were called upon to clear away the sins and defilements of the year. It later came to be practiced as a private ceremony having no fixed date or term in residences of the nobility.

Obon Ceremony – The summer observances for the dead. It will be remembered that arranging for the Obon services for her mother was something Kaneie did for Michitsuna's Mother over the years. There is no way to know which year this particular exchange took place. Once they had grown apart, she worried every year whether he would continue to do her this service.

she thinks as she waits for us – That is, the spirit of the author's mother.

Written in place of his lordship – Here is another place where it is clear she wrote poems for her husband.

festivities for the Day of the Rat – On the first Day of the Rat in the new year, the Day of the Rat being the first day of the Asian calendar's twelve-day cycle, it was traditional to hold a party to gather young herbs and pine shoots in the hills. This particular party was given in honor of the fourth prince, Emperor Murakami's fourth son, Tamehira, on the fifth day of the second month of 964 when Tamehira was twelve years old. It was a grand occasion, which a contemporary history, *Ōkagami*, characterizes as "the one time when it seemed Prince Tamehira had not lived in vain" (Helen McCullough, *Ōkagami*, 130–31). It will be remembered this is the same Prince Tamehira who married Minamoto Takaakira's daughter and was passed over in the succession to the throne due to the conspiracy of the Fujiwara.

the dowager empress – Murakami's consort, Tamehira's mother, Anshi, elder sister to Kaneie. She died on the twenty-ninth day of the fourth month of 964.

a spring of changed colors – In other words, a spring when the prince's sleeves and those of his attendants had changed to the colors of mourning.

The next morning after the Ceremony of Calling on the Buddha Names, when snow had fallen . . .

toshi no uchi ni	In this garden where
tsumi ketsu niwa ni	the sins of the year have melted away,
furu yuki ha	after such observances,
tsutomete nochi ha	I would have thought that next morning
tsumorazaramu	the fallen snow could not have stayed.

A long time had passed since his lordship had grown distant from her; then, on the fifteenth of the seventh month, the time for the Obon Ceremony, this was her reply to a letter from his lordship:

kakarikeru	Not knowing what state
kono yo mo shirazu	our relations have reached,
ima tote ya	"Now, they come,"
ahare hachisu no	she thinks as she waits for us
tsuyu wo matsuramu	to offer the lotus dew together.

Written in place of his lordship for the fourth prince on the occasion of festivities for the Day of the Rat:

mine no matsu	The pine on the peak,
ono ga yohahi no	how many thousand more
kazu yori mo	generations than
ima iku chiyo zo	one's own span of years does it live?
kimi ni hikarete	May it draw my lord along with it.

She had borrowed the journal of the festivities of the Day of the Rat from someone in the service of the prince. That year, the prince's mother, the dowager empress, passed away, and as the year came to an end, the new year and then spring, she returned the manuscript with the following written in the margin of the accompanying letter:

sode no iro	Not knowing this is
kahareru haru wo	a spring of changed colors
shirazu shite	for your sleeves,

principal handmaiden – Kaneie's sister Tōshi, otherwise known as Lady Jōganden, who has appeared in the diary many times before. Since she is referred to here by the name of the office she assumed in 969, it may be supposed that the poem was written sometime after that date.

to compose a poem on the theme, "The Angel's Feather Robe" – She is being asked to produce a poem as a performance rather than as an integral part of communication. "The Angel's Feather Robe" refers to a Japanese folktale in which a fisherman finds a feather robe left on a pine tree while an angel bathes in the sea. This feather robe is what enables the angel to fly to heaven. There are many different versions of the legend, some in which the fisherman forces the maiden to stay on earth and become his wife, and some in which he returns the robe and the angel returns to heaven.

To the damp robes of – The poem takes its point of departure from two puns, *nureginu*, which means both "damp robes" and "scandalous rumors," and *ama*, meaning both "heaven" and "fisherman." The author imagines a fisherman caught in rumors about a love affair. He uses the feather robe to soar away from his troubles, but since he left the fires of his salt kilns burning—which can also be interpreted as his smoldering feelings of love—the smoke from these unextinguished emotions spreads rumors that follow him to heaven. It is a playful poem of fantasy.

her father brought back . . . pictures he had painted of interesting places in Michinoku – Michinoku in northern Japan was her father's first post as provincial governor. His departure for Michinoku in 955 is recorded in the beginning of book one. Like many courtiers, her father was an amateur artist as well.

If I could but see . . . – Chika Island and Azalea Hill were famous places in Michinoku.

Kamo Festival – The big Kamo Shrine festival held annually in the fourth month.

happy as a heartvine – The *aoi* or heartvine was the emblematic flower for the Kamo Festival. *Aoi* in its ancient spelling *afuhi* is also homophonous with "meeting day." He makes use of the pun in his response.

she wrote this in place of the bride – Here is more evidence of her writing poems for others.

period of mourning for their father – Her father died in 977.

where grass grows deep –An image of neglect. She imagines the house falling into ruin now that the master is gone.

her brother-in-law, Tamemasa – This is the brother-in-law who married one of her sisters early in book one.

In all our hearts . . . – With associative language in the same vein, "deep grass," "fading away," "dew," "short rushes," he echoes her sentiments.

kozo ni naraheru	just learning from last year,
nobe no matsu kamo	the wild pines put forth green shoots.

When she was requested by the principal handmaiden to compose a poem on the theme, "The Angel's Feather Robe":

nure ginu ni	To the damp robes of
ama no hagoromo	scandalous rumors the fisher
musubikeri	tied the feather robe
katsu ha moshiho no	to soar away, but since he
hi wo shi ketaneba	left the fires of his salt kilns burning . . .

Written when her father brought back to the capital pictures he had painted of interesting places in Michinoku:

michinoku no	If I could but see
chika no shima nite	Michinoku's Chika Island
mimashikaba	from close up,
ikani tsutsuji no wo	how charming I would find
okashikaramashi	the slopes of Azalea Hill.

A certain person, on the day of the Kamo Festival, was thinking of taking in a son-in-law; the prospective groom sent word that he would be as "happy as a heartvine to make this the trysting day," and in response she wrote this in place of the bride:

tanomazu yo	On you, I rely not,
mikaki o sebami	just as the heartvine
afuhiba ha	find the sacred fence
shime no hoka ni mo	too narrow and stretch their leaves
ari to ifu nari	beyond, you have others too.

On the occasion of the period of mourning for their father, all the children gathered in one place; once the mourning period was fulfilled, the others returned to their own houses and she was the only one left:

fuka kusa no	Left behind to care
yado ni narinuru	for this house where grass grows deep,
yado moru to	feeling about as
tomareru tsuyu no	likely to live on as the dew
tanomoshige nasa	that stays on the grass blades.

A reply from her brother-in-law, Tamemasa:

fukakusa ha	In all our hearts,
tare mo kokoro ni	the deep grasses of sorrow
shigeritsutsu	have grown wild;
asadji ga hara no	we shall fade away like the
tsuyu to kenu beshi	dew on a field of short rushes.

Fiftieth Day Ceremony – The first big celebration for a newborn child was held on the fiftieth day after its birth.

birth of a prince – While there is some debate over whose birth this might be, the consensus is that it is most likely the birth of Senshi's first son, the future emperor Ichijō. That birth took place in 980. Senshi was Kaneie's daughter by Tokihime and was about the same age as the author's adopted daughter. It is suggested that the adopted daughter may have become an attendant to Senshi after she became empress (*Zenshū,* 92). If that is so, it would explain why the author maintained a correspondence with Senshi as evidenced by this poem and one other in the collection.

wild boar doll – Wild boars were famous for being very fertile and having large litters, and thus they came to be associated with the safe delivery of healthy children.

yamabuki – In English, the kerria rose, a small yellow flower that grows on a bushy shrub.

come in ten petals – The point of this poem, which escapes rendering in English, is that the word for "ten petals," *tohe*, is homophonous with "visit." She would rather he visited than send flowers. The cleverness of this pun had sufficient appeal for it to be included in the late Heian imperial anthology, *Shikashū,* completed in 1151 (*Zenshū*, 398). If nothing else, this fact demonstrates that the *Kagerō Diary* was circulating and read throughout the Heian period.

her brother was due to go down to Michinoku Province as governor – The entry does not specify which brother, and there is no outside corroboration for this because neither of her brothers is recorded in the court records as having taken up the post of governor in Michinoku.

Kahaku, "Dry God" – There was an Afu Kahaku Shrine in Michinoku Province. The characters with which the name is written mean "Chief of the River," but it is also roughly homophonous with *kawaku*, "dry," hence the pun that gives rise to the poem. Making this pun between *kahaku* and *kawaku* is possible evidence that the distinction in sound between *ha* and *wa* in middle syllables of words was collapsing at this time (*Zenshū*, 398).

Now truly I know . . . – The point of the poem is that since the god of the Kahaku Shrine appeared as the sun to dry up the rain, that god must be none other than the great sun goddess, Amaterasu no Ōmikami, the Heaven Shining Deity.

For the topic, "warbler on a willow branch" – This title indicates that this poem was written for a public occasion like a poetry contest, when poets were assigned set topics.

Though the threads . . . – The slender branches of the willow in early spring were conventionally thought to resemble long threads and therefore called up associative vocabulary for spinning and weaving, as in this poem, "threads," "fine," "spin out," and "endlessly," literally, "without being cut." This poem skillfully weaves that associative vocabulary together with the theme of the warbler's song, creating an effect of synesthesia. The poem was included in a personal poetry anthology by the later Heian poet, Nōin, and then was picked up for the late Kamakura imperial collection, the *Gyokuyōshū* (*Zenshū*, 399).

imperial tutor – This was a post that Michitsuna assumed in 1007 at the age of fifty-three. Although he only occupied the position for a year, since this was a high point of his official career, he was known for the rest of his life by this title. This reference suggests that this poetry collection at the end of the volume was compiled after 1007.

she wrote this in his place – Here is clear evidence that she did write a number of love poems for Michitsuna. This would support the interpretation that all the poems she records in the diary as Michitsuna's are in fact her own compositions. It is likely the case for all the poems that follow here.

On the occasion of the Fiftieth Day Ceremony after the birth of a prince, she sent this attached to a wild boar doll that she had made:

yorodzu yo wo	Celebrated for
yobafu yamabe no	a myriad generations,
wi no ko koso	may the mountain boar
kimi ga tsukafuru	roaming the hills ever
yohahi narubeshi	be at your beck and call.

Written when her lordship had sent her a present of some eight-petaled *yamabuki*:

tare ka kono	Who is it decided
kazu ha sadameshi	the number of their petals?
ware ha tada	Were it up to me,
tohe to zo omofu	I'd have them come in ten petals,
yamabuki no hana	these *yamabuki* blossoms.

It had been raining for a long time when her brother was due to go down to Michinoku Province as governor, but the day he was to leave, since it cleared up, he wrote this referring to the Kahaku, "Dry God," for that province:

waga kuni no	Has the god of my
kami no mori ya	province come to accompany me?
soherikemu	For a sign, look to
kawaku ke arishi	the wide blue sky where his
amatsu sora kana	dry spirit is evident.

Her reply:

ima zo shiru	Now truly I know
kawaku to kikeba	when I hear the name "Dry God"
kimi ga tame	for the sake of you,
amateru kami no	it is none other than the
na ni koso arikere	Heaven Shining Deity.

For the topic, "warbler on a willow branch":

waga yado no	Though the threads of
yanagi no ito ha	the willow at my lodging
hosokutomo	be ever so fine,
kuru uguhisu ha	would that the warbler spin out
taezu mo araramu	his song with them endlessly.

When the imperial tutor was first beginning to court women with letters, she wrote this in his place:

he made a likeness of a cuckoo – Again it could have been Michitsuna's Mother who made the likeness. Likeness could mean either a picture or a doll of some kind. The cuckoo is known for having other birds hatch its eggs and rear its young.

Flying back and forth – Since this poem accompanies the likeness of a cuckoo, it is understood as referring to that bird's flighty ways. There is a pun on *nageki*, meaning both "to lament" and "abandoned tree," and another pun on *kahesazaruramu*, "will not respond" and "will not hatch, nurture." The poem implies that the woman has been exchanging letters with other men but has not deigned to reply to Michitsuna.

What is to become . . . – This poem introduces the image of a spider's web with *sasagani no*, a pillow word for spider. Spiders in love poems are associated with the notion that if a spider attaches its web to you, you will be able to meet the beloved. However, here the spider's thread is a metaphor for the letters he has sent out to her. In the last line, *midaru* is a pun on "to be wild, disordered" and *mitaru*, "to have seen" (in this case, his letters). This translation is a little free in assigning agency to the wind playing havoc, by extension, with his meaning.

Relation cut off . . . – There is a pun on *e*, meaning "shore" and "karmic bond." Suminoe's shore refers to the shoreline of Sumiyoshi, where there was a famous shrine. Moreover, grasses with the power to make you forget the pain of love were thought to grow on Suminoe's shore as, for example, in *Kokinshū* no. 1111:

> if I knew the road,
> I would go there   to gather
> those grasses of love's
> forgetfulness they tell me
> grow on Suminoe's shores   (Rodd, *Kokinshū*, 378)

If she will not send him words, then he asks rhetorically for some medicine to help him forget.

Sumiyoshi – Sumiyoshi is a variation on the place-name Suminoe.

plans to marry her – We assume this is the same woman as in the previous exchange.

Sanekata, assistant captain of the Middle Palace Guards – Another member of the Fujiwara clan distantly related to Michitsuna. He is recorded to have held this office from 978 to 984.

he himself was still assistant lieutenant of the Left Palace Guards – "He himself" is Michitsuna, and he is recorded as holding this office from 983 to 984. The overlap in the tenure of the offices of these two men dates this exchange of poems to 983 or 984.

oak forest – A euphemistic expression for Sanekata's place of appointment, the Middle Palace Guards, hence standing for Sanekata.

Mikasa Mountain – A euphemistic expression for Michitsuna's place of appointment, the Left Palace Guards, hence standing for Michitsuna.

keeps loving to no avail – There is a pun in this last line that is not translated. *Kahi naki* can mean both "to no avail" and "there is no pass through the mountain."

kefu zo to ya	Thinking, "Surely today?"
tsuraku machi mimu	thus will I wait in misery,
waga kohi ha	this love of mine
hajime mo naki ga	would seem to have been here
konata naru beshi	from time immemorial.

Since time and again, there had been no response to his letters, he made a likeness of a cuckoo:

tobi chigafu	Flying back and forth,
tori no tsubasa wo	this flighty bird on the wing,
ika nareba	why did it come to this?
su tatsu nageki ni	It neither answers nor nurtures
kahesazaruramu	the one who cries to leave the nest.

And as still there was no response:

sasagani no	What is to become
ika ni naruramu	of me in this web of words?
kefu dani mo	At least today,
shirabaya kaze no	I want to know the wind's mien
midaru keshiki wo	as it plays havoc with my meaning.

and again:

taete naho	Relation cut off—
sumi no e ni naki	if there be no bond between us,
naka naraba	then I desire the
kishi ni ofunaru	forgetting grass that grows on
kusa mogana kimi	Suminoe's shore, this I beg you.

Her reply:

sumiyoshi no	That such a thing grows
kishi ni ofu to ha	on the shore of Sumiyoshi,
shiri ni keri	I have just found out,
tsumamu tsumaji ha	but to pluck it or pluck it not
kimi ga mani mani	is surely up to you, my lord.

He heard that there were plans to marry her to Sanekata, assistant captain of the Middle Palace Guards; this must have been while he himself was still assistant lieutenant of the Left Palace Guards:

kashihagi no	I hear that at least
mori dani shigeku	the oak forest grows lush
kiku mono wo	with leaves of words,
nado ka mikasa no	why is it that Mikasa Mountain
yama no kahi naki	keeps loving to no avail.

The oak forest and . . . – Speaking to Michitsuna, she is in effect saying, "both you and Sanekata are lush with greenery"—that is, send lots of billets-doux—"but I am not paying attention to either of you."

stalk of marsh sedge – This sets up the pun around which the poem is built. *Marokosuge*, "marsh sedge," contains both the word *maro*, a first-person pronoun, and *suge* of *sugenashi*, "nonchalant, casual." The entire word, *marokosuge*, can also be seen as a preface introducing *maro*, which is a very informal first-person pronoun. The poem is both playful and entreating. In essence, he asks her to judge his sincerity for herself.

Composed when he was ill – It is possible that this poem was written when he was ill with smallpox, which was in 974. However, if that is the case, then this poem is not in chronological order with the rest of the series, which, as mentioned above, can be dated to 983 or 984.

Three Fords River – Three Fords River is the river to the underworld after death.

Her reply – If one accepts the theory that the previous poem was written when Michitsuna was ill with smallpox, then the author of this poem would be different from that of the preceding series. The tone of the following poem is much more intimate than the other poems and seems to imply a prior relationship between the couple.

Written at a time when sometimes there was a reply from the woman and sometimes not – Again, depending on the interpretation of the previous poem, this could be a different woman or the same.

Seeing the spider's web suspended – The verb for "suspending" a spider's web is *kaku*, which is homophonous with the verb "to write." By this association, the spider's web becomes the woman's letters.

Tanabata, seventh day of the seventh month – A festival imported from China that celebrated the legend of the weavermaid and the herdsboy, who only get to meet for one night a year on the seventh day of the seventh month.

The thread I trail . . . – It was a custom on the night before Tanabata to hang colored streamers from a pole as tokens of the wishes one wanted fulfilled. In the morning one drew the streamers in. This poem puns on *tawamu*, which means both "to bend from the weight of moisture or snow" and "to yield."

Her reply:

kashihagi mo	The oak forest and
mikasa no yama mo	Mikasa Mountain, both are
natsu nareba	lush with greenery,
shigeredo aya na	because it is summer, yet
hito no shiranaku	no one is there to notice.

He heard that she was being prevented from answering by her parents or brothers, so he sent this attached to a stalk of marsh sedge:

uchi soba mi	Take a sidelong look,
kimi hitori miyo	just see for yourself alone,
marokosuge	these words on the sedge,
maro ha hito suge	while all the world accuses me
nashi to ifu nari	of being a trifler.

Composed when he was ill:

mitsuse gaha	I had always thought
asa no hodo mo	there was no way to know the depth
shirareji to	of Three Fords River,
omohi shiware ya	now it seems that I shall be
madzu watari namu	the first to cross and find out.

Her reply:

mitsuse gaha	At Three Fords River,
ware yori saki ni	if you are to cross over
watarinaba	ahead of me,
migiha ni waburu	shall I just be left alone
mi to ya narinamu	to mourn and weep on the bank?

Written at a time when sometimes there was a reply from the woman and sometimes not:

kakumeri to	Seeing the spider's
mireba taenuru	web suspended, then broken,
sasagani no	makes the wind
ito yuwe kaze no	seem more cruel than if the web
tsuraku mo aru kana	had never been there at all.

Tanabata, the seventh day of the seventh month:

tanabata ni	The thread I trail
kesa hiku ito no	this morning for Tanabata
tsuyu wo omomi	bends heavy with dew,
tawamu keshiki mo	will things end with my never
mide ya yaminamu	seeing you bend to me?

a "next morning" poem – That is, a poem written the morning after the consummation of a marriage. It will be remembered that Heian marriages began in a fashion that mimics a secret liaison, with the couple sleeping together for three nights in a row before the marriage is acknowledged by the family. If all the poems attributed to Michitsuna in this collection are assumed to be the compositions of his mother, it would mean that Michitsuna even received help from his mother in composing "next morning" poems.

Since parting from you . . . – The groom had to part from the bride before dawn on the first two nights. He would return home while dew was heavy on the garden foliage, hence his becoming drenched. The drenching of the dew is also a metaphor for the tears he sheds in the pain of parting.

Written on the part of Tamemasa's daughter . . . – Since Tamemasa was married to the author's elder sister, this daughter is the author's niece. The niece was married to Fujiwara Yoshichika, a cousin to Kaneie. Yoshichika took the tonsure upon the abdication of Emperor Kazan in 986, whereupon he became known as a lay priest. His relations with his wife would have ended with his becoming a priest.

sun-ray wig – This was a head piece, woven from thread, that was worn by Buddhist monks as a wig to cover their tonsured heads during attendance at Shinto ceremonies. It is speculated that the request of a wig here was for the Enthronement Rites of the next emperor after Emperor Kazan (*Zenshū*, 403).

weaving it together, us apart? – Pun on *musubu*, "to weave, tie" and "to join husband and wife."

Written when Senshi was still in the position of empress . . . – Senshi, Kaneie's second daughter by Tokihime, was made consort to Emperor Enyū and officially declared empress in 986. She took the tonsure in 991. The Eight Lectures on the Lotus Sutra was a special rite in which two lectures a day, one in the morning and one in the evening, were offered for four days. *Zenshū* commentators speculate that this particular service was held to mark the passing of Senshi's mother, Tokihime, in 990.

that sing in Mani Pond – Mani Pond is the lake in the Pure Land, a Buddhist heaven. The waves between the lotuses floating on the pond were thought to constantly sing hymns of praise.

imperial tutor – Michitsuna, this being the title by which he was generally known to posterity. Perhaps he sent the *tachibana* flowers as an offering for Senshi's service.

Have you called on us . . . – Her poem plays on three puns, *kabakari*, which can mean both "like this" and "fragrance alone," *e*, which means both "branch" and "bond," and *tobi*, which can mean both "to visit" or, with a slight sound change to *tobi*, "to fly." In the background of this poem is also the notion that the fragrance of the *tachibana* calls up the memory of someone in the past. In this case, Senshi may be implying that she is a person of the past for Michitsuna because he has not come to visit for a long while.

Even if the fruit is there . . . – Michitsuna makes his inferior status an excuse for not visiting more often. His poem echoes the associative language and the pun on "to visit" and "to fly" of Senshi's poem, and adds a pun on *mi*, which means both "fruit" and "status."

Ichijō captain – Fujiwara Naritoki, a cousin to Michitsuna. He held the position of captain over many years and died before Michitsuna was made imperial tutor, so the mention of ranks here does not help in dating the exchange.

Shirakawa – An area in the northeast corner of Kyoto where many aristocrats kept villas.

This was written as a "next morning" poem:

wakatsu yori ashita no sode zo nure ni keru nani wo hiruma no nagusame ni semu	Since parting from you, these sleeves of morning have been drenched with dew, what to do for consolation the long day while they dry.

Written on the part of Tamemasa's daughter when she was requested to weave a sun-ray wig for her former husband, the lay priest, some time after he had ceased to visit her:

kakete mishi suwe mo taenishi higage gusa nani ni yosohete kefu musuburamu	What I counted on seeing to the end has ended, this sun-ray piece to what should I compare it, today weaving it together, us apart?

Written when Senshi was still in the position of empress, on the occasion of her sponsoring Eight Lectures on the Lotus Sutra, to which she [Michitsuna's Mother] sent a rosary made of lotus seeds as an offering:

tonafunaru nami no kazu ni ha aranedomo hachisu no uhe no tsuyu ni kakaramu	Though its beads are not as numerous as the waves that sing in Mani Pond, let this be blessed with the dew on the lotus petals.

Around the same time, the imperial tutor presented some *tachibana* flowers to Senshi, and she sent back:

kabakari mo tohi ya ha shitsuru hototogisu hana tachibana no e ni koso arikere	Have you called on us before like this, yearning for the fragrance, cuckoo, your bond is with these branches of flowering *tachibana*.

His reply:

tachibana no nari mo noboranu mi wo shireba shidzue narade ha tohanu to zo kiku	Even if the fruit is there, as you know, I am not in a position to climb, I have always heard the cuckoo flies among the lower branches.

When the Ichijō captain was visiting Shirakawa, he sent word to the imperial tutor, "You must come to visit," but while he was waiting for him to come, it began to rain heavily, and the tutor was unable to go, so the

"heavy with rain" – An allusion to a poem from the *Kokin rokujō*:

I have been waiting
to hear the cuckoo but he
does not sing tonight,
perhaps he is avoiding
the path heavy with rain. (*Zenshū*, 404)

the Chūjō nun – This woman was a daughter of Minamoto Kiyotoki and is noted in contemporary court records as a poet.

The floating leaf of . . . – She imagines the lotus leaf in the Pure Land to be too narrow to make room for her as a dewdrop, just as the heart of the Chūjō nun was too small to provide her room in this world.

Her reply – That is, the reply of the Chūjō nun.

jewels of dew . . . our souls – There is a pun on *tama*, meaning "jewel" and "soul."

Awata – An area in the Higashiyama district of Kyoto.

Tamemasa – The author's brother-in-law. The exact date of his death is not known, but it is generally assumed to have happened prior to 1002.

Fumon Temple – This was a temple that once existed in the Iwakura district to the north of the capital.

Ono Villa – The Ono area is around present-day Ohara. Tamemasa's father apparently had a villa there.

Chopping firewood . . . – Chopping firewood is a metaphor for performing devotions to the *Lotus Sutra* that the author derives from a poem attributed to the early Heian holy man, Saint Gyōgi:

My understanding
of the *Lotus Sutra* rests in
chopping firewood,
plucking herbs, drawing water,
serving thus, I understand it. (*Zenshū,* 405)

The author also weaves into this poem a reference to a Chinese legend about a man who returned from working in the woods one day and came upon two old men playing chess. Absorbed with watching their game, he lost all track of time. What he did not realize was that the two men were immortals. When he woke up from his enchantment with their game, he had been there so long his axe handle had rotted. The word for "axe," *wono*, is also homophonous with the place-name Ono.

his lordship, the regent – Kaneie became regent in 986 with the accession of Emperor Ichijō, who was his grandson. However, the event related here most likely took place much earlier, when Kaneie was still captain of the Right Guards, a position that involved him with horse racing. Accordingly, the retired emperor here would be Reizei, to whom Kaneie's eldest daughter was married.

captain sent a retainer with the message, "heavy with rain" to inquire after him. The tutor's reply:

nuretsutsu mo	Even though it may
kohishiki michi ha	be soaked, the path of love is
yokanaku ni	not to be avoided,
mada kikoezu to	do not fret about not
omohazaramu	hearing from me yet.

She was going to borrow a house from the Chūjō nun. When it was not lent to her:

hachisu ba no	The floating leaf of
uki ha wo sebami	the lotus is so narrow,
kono yo ni mo	in this world as well,
yadoranu tsuyu to	there is no place for this dewlike
mi wo zo shirinuru	self to dwell as I now know.

Her reply:

hachisu ni mo	On the lotus there,
tama wi yo to koso	just as jewels of dew rest
musubi shika	here, our souls will find
tsuyu ha kokoro wo	a place, such is Buddha's bond,
okitagahekeri	your dewlike self has it wrong.

On her way back from seeing the fields of Awata:

hana susuki	The pampas grass plumes
maneki mo yamanu	never cease to beckon me—
yama sato ni	at that mountain village,
kokoro nogari to	it seems that I have left
tometsuru kana	behind my heart entirely.

She had attended a service held by the late Tamemasa for offering a thousand copies of the *Lotus Sutra* at Fumon Temple; on the way home the flowers of the Ono Villa were so enchanting that she had her carriage drawn into the yard, as she was about to return home:

takigi koru	Chopping firewood,
koto ha kinofu ni	we exhausted ourselves
tsuki nishi wo	all day yesterday,
iza wono no e ha	now here in Ono let us
koko ni kutasamu	let the axe handle rot away.

Since it became apparent that his lordship, the regent, had lost a horse race, at the loser-hosted banquet, he wanted to present a silver lunch box in the shape of a half melon to the retired emperor. So he came to her with

Lasting as a thousand . . . – This poem cleverly intertwines the two themes of melons and horse racing. The melon lasts a thousand generations because it is made of silver. Yamashiro no Koma, translated here as Colt's Field, is a famous place for the production of melons. Embedded in the place-name, as the translation here indicates, is *koma*, the word for "colt." *Koma ni kurabe* by itself can mean horse racing. However, another meaning for *kurabe* is "to enjoy oneself with friends." Thus, *kurabeshi uri* can mean "the melon enjoying itself." Finally, the phrase *suwe nari* means both "the fruit at the end of the vine" and "the result," which in this case is the winning of the race.

On a painting – Here is yet another example of poems done in response to art.

presented at the poetry contest held in the second year of the Kanna era – During this period it was still not common for women to participate in poetry contests in person. Michitsuna apparently took this composition of his mother's to the contest, which was held in 986.

On the great ocean . . . – This poem appears playfully irreverent. It puns on *ama*, which can mean both "fisherman" and "nun," as well as on *nori*, which means "to ride" and the Buddhist "law."

Written when his lordship had grown distant from her – This is the only poem from the diary that is repeated in the poetry collection. It will be remembered that she wrote this poem when Kaneie accused her of encouraging gossip by treating the adopted daughter's suitor, Tōnori, too warmly.

Presented at a poetry contest – This series of ten poems seems to have been prepared for a poetry contest held by the crown prince Iyasada on the fifth day of the fifth month in 994. The list of ten topics is identical with the topic list for that contest, and five of these poems, "Unohana," "Cuckoo," "Smudge Fire," "Cicadas," and "Love," are recorded in the proceedings of the contest as being the entries from the team of the right. How Michitsuna's Mother became involved with this contest is not known (*Zenshū*, 407).

unohana – The *unohana* puts forth a mass of white blooms at the beginning of summer.

the request, "I would like a poem to engrave on this." This is what she wrote:

chiyo mo heyo	Lasting as a thousand
tachikaheritsutsu	generations come and go,
yamashiro no	the merry melon
koma ni kurabeshi	at the end of the vine in
uri no suwe nari	Colt's Field honoring your win.

On a painting of a woman gazing out her window in a mountain village, just as the cuckoo calls:

miyako bito	People of the capital,
nete matsurameya	have you fallen asleep while waiting
hototogisu	for the cuckoo's call,
ima zo yamabe wo	which just now he sings forth
nakite sugunaru	as he passes through the hills.

This poem was presented at the poetry contest held in the second year of the Kanna era.

On the picture of a monk riding in a boat:

watatsuumi ha	On the great ocean,
ama no fune koso	boats of nuns are what there is,
ari to kike	thus have I heard,
noritagahetemo	perhaps the reverend monk has
kogi dekeru kana	rowed out in the wrong vessel.

Written when his lordship had grown distant from her and remarked to her, "There seems to be someone else visiting you":

ima sara ni	Now, more than ever,
ikanaru koma ka	what colt would think to draw near
natsuku beki	this abandoned grass,
susamenu kusa to	left to wither in the fields,
nogare ni shi mi wo	such a one am I.

Presented at a poetry contest:

Unohana

unohana no	The unohana
sakari naru beshi	must be coming into full bloom,
yama sato no	in mountain villages,
koro mo sahoseru	it will look as though summer
ori to miyuru ha	clothes have just been put out to dry.

Irises today . . . – On the fifth day of the fifth month, people searched for long iris roots. This poem puns on *ne*, which means both "root" and "voice." It rests on the conceit that the irises could hear the poet's voice.

Tokonatsu "Forever Summer" – Another name for the Japanese pink.

barley autumn – Barley is harvested in early summer, so it is a case where something associated with autumn—harvest—occurs in summer. Thus, one euphemism in Chinese for the fourth month (closer to May in the Western calendar) was "barley autumn." Moreover, some types of cicada start to sing in early summer, even though cicadas are traditionally thought in both China and Japan as "sending off" autumn, that is, singing it on its way. These two seasonal anomalies were joined in a single line in a Chinese poem by the T'ang poet Li Chia-yu as follows:

> The voices of the cicadas in the fifth month send off barley autumn.

The couplet containing this line was well known in Heian Japan even though the whole poem was lost very early. The couplet is anthologized in *Senzai kaku*, an anthology of Chinese couplets (ca. 947), and also in the later *Wakan rōeishū* (ca. 1018). Kawaguchi Hisao in his supplementary commentary to *Wakan rōeishū* identifies this poem of Michitsuna's Mother as a translation in *waka* form of the above line of poetry. If he is right, it is more evidence of Michitsuna's Mother's knowledge of Chinese poetry (Kawaguchi Hisao, *Wakan rōeishū*, 264).

Cuckoo

hototogisu
ima zo sa wataru
kowe sunaru
waga tsuge naku ni
hito ya kikikemu

Just now the cuckoo
flies by calling out as it passes,
even without
my telling my lover,
I wonder if he will hear it.

Irises

ayame gusa
kefu no migiha wo
tazunureba
ne wo shirite koso
katayori ni kere

Irises today
as I have come to seek them
by the water's edge,
knowing my voice as I know
their roots, they bend to me.

Fireflies

samidare ya
ko kuraki yado no
yufu sare ha
omo teru made mo
terasu hotaru ka

Fifth month rains,
these lodgings dark among the trees,
in the evening,
fireflies, is it you who shine
so bright that faces blush?

Tokonatsu "Forever Summer"

saki ni keru
eda nakariseba
tokonatsu mo
nodokeki na wo ya
nokosazaramashi

If there were no stems
that blossomed into flowers,
then surely we would
never have had such a
gentle name, "Forever summer."

Smudge Fire

aya nashi ya
yado no kayaribi
tsuke somete
katarafu mushi no
kowe wo saketsuru

A thoughtless thing to do—
since we first lit the smudge fire
at our lodging,
the voices of the insects we would
like to hear have moved away.

Cicadas

okuru to ifu
semi no hatsugowe
kiku yori zo
ima ka to mugi no
aki wo shirinuru

They send off the season,
so it is said, from hearing
the first cicadas,
I knew right at that moment—
so this is barley autumn.

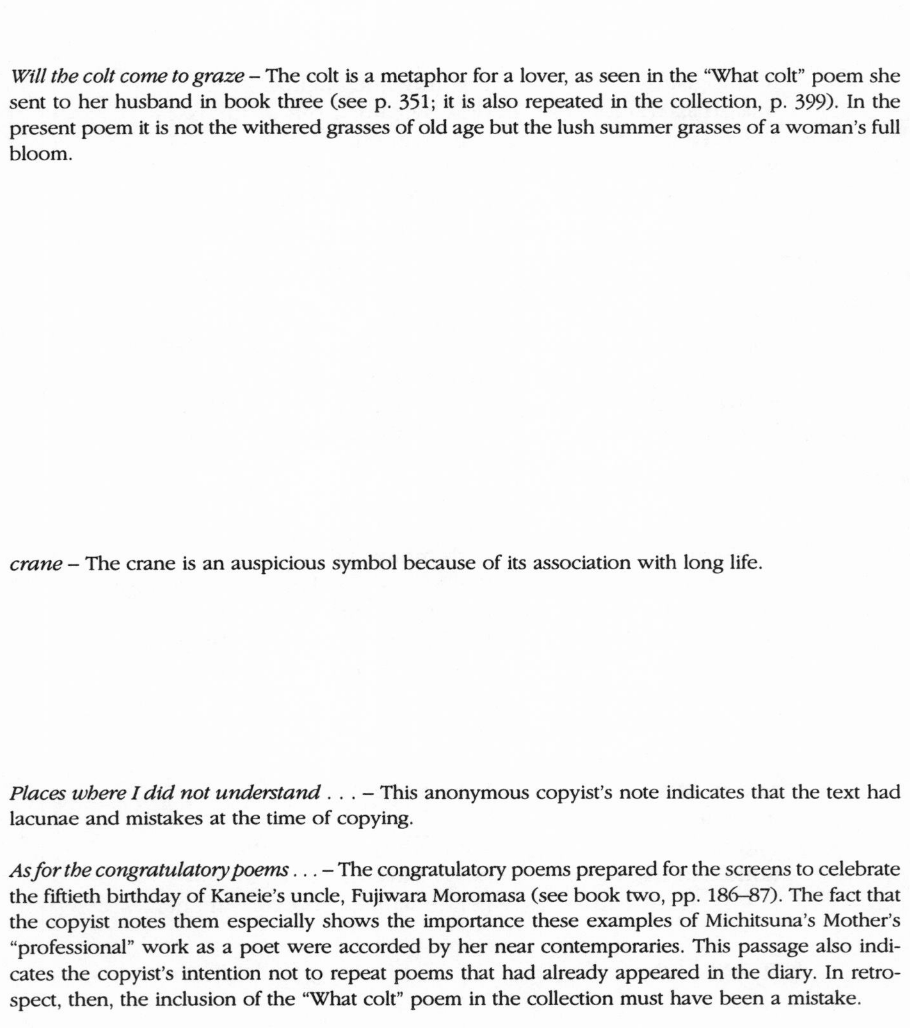

Will the colt come to graze – The colt is a metaphor for a lover, as seen in the "What colt" poem she sent to her husband in book three (see p. 351; it is also repeated in the collection, p. 399). In the present poem it is not the withered grasses of old age but the lush summer grasses of a woman's full bloom.

crane – The crane is an auspicious symbol because of its association with long life.

Places where I did not understand . . . – This anonymous copyist's note indicates that the text had lacunae and mistakes at the time of copying.

As for the congratulatory poems . . . – The congratulatory poems prepared for the screens to celebrate the fiftieth birthday of Kaneie's uncle, Fujiwara Moromasa (see book two, pp. 186–87). The fact that the copyist notes them especially shows the importance these examples of Michitsuna's Mother's "professional" work as a poet were accorded by her near contemporaries. This passage also indicates the copyist's intention not to repeat poems that had already appeared in the diary. In retrospect, then, the inclusion of the "What colt" poem in the collection must have been a mistake.

Summer Grass

koma ya kuru hito ya wakuru to matsu hodo ni shigeri nomi masu yado no natsugusa	Will the colt come to graze, will he come parting the grass? All the while I wait, it just grows more and more lush, the summer grass of my dwelling.

Love

omohitsutsu kohitsutsu ha neji afu to miru yume wo samete ha kuyashikarikeri	Thinking, thinking thus, loving thus, there is no sleep, I see him, we meet, to be woken from that dream that is suffering indeed.

Celebrating a Marriage

kazu shiranu masago ni tadzu no hodo yori ha chigiri somekemu chiyo zo sukunaki	Less than the countless grains of sand where the crane stands, less than his many years, the thousand years we have just pledged to each other are too few.

[Copyist's Note]

Places where I did not understand what was written, I just copied as it was in the text. As for the congratulatory poems, I did not write them here as they were included in the diary.

Bibliography

Akiyama Ken. *Ochō joryū bungaku no sekai.* Tokyo: Tōkyō Daigaku Shuppankai, 1972 (1984 reprint).

Aoki Takako et al. *Man'yōshū.* Tokyo: Shinchōsha, 1980.

Ariyoshi Tomotsu. *Hyakunin isshū zenyaku-chū.* Tokyo: Kōdansha, 1983.

Arntzen, Sonja. "Translating Difference: A New Translation for the Kagerō Diary." *Japan Foundation Newsletter* 21:3 (December 1993): 16–19.

Bowring, Richard. "The Female Hand in Heian Japan: A First Reading." In *The Female Autograph: Theory and Practice of Autobiography from the Tenth to the Twentieth Century,* 49–56. Donna C. Stanton, ed. Chicago: University of Chicago Press, 1987.

———, trans. *Murasaki Shikibu, Her Diary and Poetic Memoirs: A Translation and Study.* Princeton: Princeton University Press, 1982.

Brownstein, Rachel M. *Becoming a Heroine: Reading about Women in Novels.* Harmondsworth, England: Penguin Books, 1984.

Cranston, Edwin A., trans. *A Waka Anthology. Volume One: The Gem-Glistening Cup.* Stanford: Stanford University Press, 1993.

———, trans. *The Izumi Shikibu Diary: A Romance of the Heian Court.* [*Izumi shikibu nikki*] Cambridge, MA: Harvard University Press, 1969.

Eakin, Paul John. *Fictions in Autobiography: Studies in the Art of Self-Invention.* Princeton: Princeton University Press, 1985.

Fukuto Sanae. *Heian chō no haha to ko: kizoku to shomin no hazoku seikatsushi.* Tokyo: Chūō Kōronsha, 1991.

Fukuzawa Tōru, ed. *Kagerō nikki: kaisō to kaku koto.* Tokyo: Yuseidō, 1987.

Hasegawa Masaharu et al. *Tosa nikki. Kagerō nikki. Murasaki Shikibu nikki. Sarashina nikki.* Vol. 24 of *Shin Nihon koten bungaku taikei.* Tokyo: Iwanami Shoten, 1989.

Hérail, Francine. *La cour du Japon a l'époque de Heian.* Paris: Hachette Livre, 1995.

Hiroaki Sato, trans. *String of Beads: Complete Poems of Princess Shikishu.* Honolulu: University of Hawaii Press, 1993.

Iwasa Miyoko. "'Ware ga sometaru to mo ihaji'—Kagerō nikki fukushoku hyōgen kō." In *Ōchō nikki no shin kenkyū.* Tokyo: Kasama Shoin, 1995.

Jelinek, Estelle C. *The Tradition of Women's Autobiography from Antiquity to the Present.* Boston: Twayne, 1986.

Kakimoto Tsutomu. *Kagerō nikki zenchūshaku.* Tokyo: Kadokawa Shoten, 1966.

Katagiri Yōichi. *Gosen wakashū*. Vol. 6 of *Shin Nihon koten bungaku taikei*. Tokyo: Iwanami Shoten, 1990.

______, ed. *Taketori monogatari. Ise monogatari. Yamato monogatari. Heichū monogatari*. Vol. 8 of *Nihon koten bungaku zenshū*. Tokyo: Shōgakkan, 1972.

Kawaguchi Hisao, ed. *Wakan rōeishū. Ryōjin hishō*. Vol. 73 of *Nihon koten bungaku taikei*. Tokyo: Iwanami Shoten, 1965.

______, ed. *Tosa nikki. Kagerofu nikki. Izumi Shikibu nikki. Sarashina nikki*. Vol. 20 of *Nihon koten bungaku taikei*. Tokyo: Iwanami Shoten, 1963.

Keene, Donald. *Seeds in the Heart: Japanese Literature from Earliest Times to the Late Sixteenth Century*. Vol. 1 of *A History of Japanese Literature*. New York: Henry Holt, 1993.

______. *Dawn to the West: Japanese Literature of the Modern Era*. 2 vols. New York: Holt, Rinehart and Winston, 1984.

______, ed. *Anthology of Japanese Literature, from the Earliest Era to the Mid-Nineteenth Century*. New York: Grove, 1955.

______, trans. "The Tale of the Bamboo Cutter." In *Modern Japanese Fiction and Its Traditions*. Thomas J. Rimer, ed. Princeton: Princeton University Press, 1978.

Komachiya Teruhiko, *Shūi wakashū*. Vol. 7 of *Shin Nihon koten bungaku taikei*. Tokyo: Iwanami Shoten, 1990.

Kōno Tama. *Utsubo monogatari*. Vol. 10 of *Nihon koten bungaku taikei*. Tokyo: Iwanami Shoten, 1959 (1980 reprint).

Kunaichō Shoryōbu, ed. *Kokin waka rokujō*. In *Toshoryō sōkan*, 2 vols. Tokyo: Yōtokusha, 1967.

Kuroita Katsumi, ed. *Sonpi bunmyaku*. Vols. 58–60 in *Kokushi taikei*. Tokyo: Yoshikawa Kobunkan, 1924–64.

Marlatt, Daphne. *Ana Historic*. Toronto: Coach House Press, 1988.

Matsumura Sei'ichi, Kimura Masanori, and Imuta Tsunehisa, eds. *Tosa nikki. Kagerō nikki*. Vol. 9 of *Nihon koten bungaku zenshū*. Tokyo: Shōgakkan, 1973.

McCullough, Helen Craig, trans. *Classical Japanese Prose: An Anthology*. Stanford: Stanford University Press, 1990.

______, trans. *Kokin Wakashū: The First Imperial Anthology of Japanese Poetry*. Stanford: Stanford University Press, 1985.

______, trans. *Ōkagami, The Great Mirror: Fujiwara Michinaga (966–1027) and His Times*. Princeton: Princeton University Press, 1980. Reprinted Ann Arbor: Center for Japanese Studies, The University of Michigan, 1991.

______, trans. *The Tales of Ise: Lyrical Episodes from Tenth-Century Japan*. Stanford: Stanford University Press, 1968.

McCullough, William H. "Marriage Institutions in the Heian Period." *The Harvard Journal of Asiatic Studies* 27 (1967): 103–67.

______ and Helen Craig McCullough, trans. *A Tale of Flowering Fortunes: Annals of Japanese Aristocratic Life in the Heian Period* [*Eiga monogatari*]. 2 vols. Stanford: Stanford University Press, 1980.

Miller, Marilyn Jeanne. *The Poetics of Nikki Bungaku: A Comparison of the Traditions, Conventions, and Structure of Heian Japan's Literary Diaries with Western Autobiographical Writings*. New York: Garland, 1985.

Miner, Earl, trans. "Tosa Diary" and "The Diary of Izumi Shikibu." In *Japanese Poetic Diaries*, Earl Miner, ed. and trans. Berkeley: University of California Press, 1969.

———, Odagiri Hiroko, and Robert E. Morrell. *The Princeton Companion to Classical Japanese Literature*. Princeton: Princeton University Press, 1985.

Miyake, Lynn. "If 'I' Were 'She' and 'She' Were 'I': The Narration of the Kagerō Nikki." Unpublished conference paper for the Combined Western and Southwestern Conferences of the Association of Asian Studies, 1993.

———. "*Tōnomine shōshō monogatari*: A Translation and Critical Study." Ph.D. dissertation, University of California at Berkeley, 1985.

Morris, Ivan. *The World of the Shining Prince: Court Life in Ancient Japan*. Harmondsworth, England: Penguin Books, 1979.

———, trans. *As I Crossed a Bridge of Dreams: Recollections of a Woman in Eleventh-Century Japan* [*Sarashina nikki*]. Harmondsworth, England: Penguin Books, 1971.

———, trans. *The Pillow Book of Sei Shōnagon*. 2 vols. New York: Columbia University Press, 1967.

Mostow, Joshua. *Pictures of the Heart: The One Hundred Poets, One Poem Each Collection, Its Commentaries and Pictures*. Honolulu: University of Hawaii Press, 1996.

———. "Japanese *Nikki* as Political Memoirs." In *Political Memoir: Essays on the Politics of Memory*, 106–20. George Egerton, ed. London: Frank Cass, 1994.

———. "Self and Landscape in Kagerō Nikki." *Review of Japanese Culture and Society* (December 1993): 8–19.

———. "The Amorous Statesman and the Poetess: The Politics of Autobiography and the Kagerō Nikki." *Japan Forum* 4.2 (October 1992): 305–15.

Murai Jun. *Kagerofu nikki zenhyōkai*. 2 vols. Tokyo: Yūseidō, 1978.

Nickerson, Peter. "The Meaning of Matrilocality: Kinship, Property, and Politics in the Mid-Heian Period." *Monumenta Nipponica* 48.4 (1993): 429–67.

Oka Kazuo. *Michitsuna bo*. Rev. ed. Tokyo: Yūseidō, 1970 (1986 reprint).

Okada, H. Richard. *Figures of Resistance: Language, Poetry, and Narrating in the Tale of Genji and Other Mid-Heian Texts*. Durham: Duke University Press, 1991.

Okumura Tsuneya. *Kokin wakashū*. Tokyo: Shinchōsha, 1978.

Ono Susumu et al. *Iwanami kogo jiten*. Tokyo: Iwanami, 1974.

Rodd, Laurel Rasplica, trans. *Kokinshū: A Collection of Poems Ancient and Modern*. Princeton: Princeton University Press, 1984.

Sarra, Edith. *Fictions of Femininity: Literary Inventions of Gender in Japanese Court Women's Memoirs*. Stanford: Stanford University Press, 1996.

Seidensticker, Edward, trans. *The Tale of Genji*. New York: Knopf, 1976.

———, trans. *The Gossamer Years: The Diary of a Noblewoman of Heian Japan* [*Kagerō nikki*]. Rutland, VT: Charles E. Tuttle, 1964 (1985 reprint).

Shinozuka Sumiko. *Kagerō nikki no kokoro to hyōgen*. Tokyo: Benseisha, 1995.

———. "Kagerō nikki to afura bein no shokantai shōsetsu." In *Ōchō nikki no shinkenkyū*, 379–401. Ikeda Tsuyako, ed. Tokyo: Kasama Shoin, 1995.

———. "Women, Letters and Literature." Unpublished address at the Institute of Early Women's Writing, University of Alberta, September 1993.

———. "Shokan to bungaku: Richaadoson no shokantai shōsetsu to kagerō nikki o chūshin ni." *Kyōritsu: Kokusai bunka* 1.1 (March 1991): 135–45.

———. "Kagerō nikki no shudai o megutte." In *Joryū nikki bungaku kōza*, vol. 2, 97–117. Tokyo: Benseisha, 1990.

______. "Kagerō nikki nōto: atena no nai tegami." Nos. 1–87 in *Keisei* (March 1977–July 1991).

Tachibana Kenji. *Ōkagami / Ryōjin hishō*. Vol. 20 of *Nihon koten bungaku zenshū*. Tokyo: Shōgakkan, 1974.

Tahara, Mildred M. *Tales of Yamato: A Tenth Century Poem Tale* [*Yamato monogatari*]. Honolulu: University of Hawaii Press, 1980.

Uemura Etsuko. *Kagerō nikki kaishaku taisei*. 9 vols. Tokyo: Meiji Shoin, 1983–95.

Waley, Arthur, trans. *The Tale of Genji: A Novel in Six Parts by Lady Murasaki*. Boston: Houghton Mifflin, 1935.

Watanabe Minoru. "Style and Point of View in the Kagerō Nikki." Richard Bowring, trans. *Journal of Japanese Studies* 10.2 (1984): 365–84.

______. *Heianchō bunshōshi*. Tokyo: Tōkyō Daigaku Shuppankai, 1981.

______. "Tōjishateki hyōgen—Kagerō nikki." In *Heian bunshōshi*. Tokyo: Tōkyō Daigaku Shuppankai, 1981.

______. *Ise monogatari*. Tokyo: Shinchōsha, 1976.

Whitehead, Wilfred, and Eizo Yanagisawa. *The Tale of Lady Ochikubō*. Tokyo: Hokuseido, 1965.

Woolf, Virginia. *A Room of One's Own*. London: Grafton Books, 1977.

Index

ABOUT THE AUTHOR

Sonja Arntzen received her Ph.D. in Japanese Literature from the University of British Columbia and is currently an Associate Professor at the University of Alberta. In addition to numerous articles, she has published two books on the life and poetry of the Muromachi-period Zen monk, Ikkyū Sōjun: *The Crazy Cloud Anthology of Ikkyū Sōjun* (1986), and *Ikkyū Sōjun: A Zen Monk and His Poetry* (1973). She is actively involved in the promotion of Japanese art and theater in Canada.